T0262758

Data-Centric Artificial Intelligence for Multidisciplinary Applications

This book explores the need for a data-centric AI approach and its application in the multidisciplinary domain, compared to a model-centric approach. It examines the methodologies for data-centric approaches, the use of data-centric approaches in different domains, the need for edge AI and how it differs from cloud-based AI. It discusses the new category of AI technology, "data-centric AI" (DCAI), which focuses on comprehending, utilizing, and reaching conclusions from data. By adding machine learning and big data analytics tools, data-centric AI modifies this by enabling it to learn from data rather than depending on algorithms. It can therefore make wiser choices and deliver more precise outcomes. Additionally, it has the potential to be significantly more scalable than conventional AI methods.

- Includes a collection of case studies with experimentation results to adhere to the practical approaches
- Examines challenges in dataset generation, synthetic datasets, analysis, and prediction algorithms in stochastic ways
- Discusses methodologies to achieve accurate results by improving the quality of data
- Comprises cases in healthcare and agriculture with implementation and impact of quality data in building AI applications

Data-Centric Artificial Intelligence for Multidisciplinary Applications

Edited by
Parikshit N. Mahalle, Namrata N. Wasatkar, and
Gitanjali R. Shinde

CRC Press
Taylor & Francis Group
Boca Raton London New York

CRC Press is an imprint of the
Taylor & Francis Group, an **informa** business
A CHAPMAN & HALL BOOK

Designed cover image: ShutterStock

First edition published 2024
by CRC Press
2385 NW Executive Center Drive, Suite 320, Boca Raton FL 33431

and by CRC Press
4 Park Square, Milton Park, Abingdon, Oxon, OX14 4RN

CRC Press is an imprint of Taylor & Francis Group, LLC

ISBN: 9781032610061 (hbk)
ISBN: 9781032610078 (pbk)
ISBN: 9781003461500 (ebk)

DOI: 10.1201/9781003461500

Typeset in Times
by codeMantra

Contents

SECTION III   Building AI with Quality Data for Multidisciplinary Domains

Editors

Dr. Parikshit N. Mahalle is a senior member of the IEEE and is Professor and Head of Department of Artificial Intelligence and Data Science at Vishwakarma Institute of Information Technology, Pune, India. He completed his Ph.D. from Aalborg University, Denmark and continued as Post Doc Researcher at CMI, Copenhagen, Denmark. He has 23+ years of teaching and research experience. He is a member of the Board of Studies in Computer Engineering, Ex-Chairman Information Technology, SPPU and various Universities and autonomous colleges across India. He has 9 patents, 200+ research publications (Google Scholar citations-2250 plus, H index-22 and Scopus Citations are 1190 plus with H index -16), and authored/edited 42+ books with Springer, CRC Press, Cambridge University Press, etc. He is editor-in-chief for IGI Global – *International Journal of Rough Sets and Data Analysis*, Associate Editor for IGI Global – *International Journal of Synthetic Emotions, Inter-science International Journal of Grid and Utility Computing*, member of Editorial Review Board for IGI Global – *International Journal of Ambient Computing and Intelligence*. His research interests are machine learning, data science, algorithms, internet of things, identity management and security. He is a recognized Ph.D. guide of SSPU, Pune, guiding seven Ph.D. students in the area of IoT and machine learning. Recently, five students have successfully defended their Ph.D. He is also the recipient of the "Best Faculty Award" by Sinhgad Institutes and Cognizant Technologies Solutions. He has delivered 200 plus lectures at national and international levels. He is also the recipient of the best faculty award by Cognizant Technology Solutions.

Dr. Gitanjali R. Shinde is Head and Associate Professor in the Department of Computer Science & Engineering (AI &ML), Vishwakarma Institute of Information Technology, Pune, India. She completed her Ph.D. in Wireless Communication from CMI, Aalborg University, Copenhagen, Denmark on the Research Problem Statement "Cluster Framework for Internet of People, Things and Services" – Ph.D. awarded on 8 May 2018. She earned her M.E. in Computer Engineering from the University of Pune, Pune, in 2012 and B.E. in Computer Engineering degree from the University of Pune, Pune, in 2006. She received research funding for the project "Lightweight group authentication for IoT" by SPPU, Pune. She presented a research article in the World Wireless Research Forum (WWRF) meeting, Beijing, China. She received the best paper award at an international conference. She is also reviewer of various international journals Springer, IGI Global, IEEE Transaction and various conferences. She has published 50+ papers in National and International conferences and journals (Google Scholar citations-700 plus, H index-11). She is author of 10+ books with publishers Springer and CRC Press Taylor & Francis Group, and she is also editor of several books. Her book *Data Analytics for Pandemics A COVID 19 Case Study* was awarded outstanding Book of the year 2020.

Dr. Namrata N. Wasatkar is an Assistant Professor in the Department of Computer Engineering, Vishwakarma Institute of Information Technology, Pune, India. She did her Ph.D. in Computer Engineering from Savitribai Phule Pune University, Pune, India on the research problem statement "Rule based Machine translation of simple Marathi sentences to English sentences" – Ph.D. awarded on 17 November 2022. She earned an M.E. in Computer Engineering from the University of Pune, Pune, in 2014 and B.E. in Computer Engineering from the University of Pune, Pune, in 2012. She has received research funding for the project "SPPU online chatbot" by SPPU, Pune. She is also reviewer for various journals and conferences. She has published 15+ papers in National and International conferences and journals. She has authored a book titled *Data Centric Artificial Intelligence: A Beginner's Guide.*

Contributors

Jayashri Bagade
Department of Information Technology
Vishwakarma Institute of Information
    Technology
Pune, India

Anurag Bharde
Department of Information Technology
Walchand College of Engineering
Sangli, India

Paras Bhat
Vishwakarma Institute of Information
    Technology
Pune, India

Vedyant Bhat
Vishwakarma Institute of Information
    Technology
Pune, India

Komal M. Birare
Vishwakarma Institute of Information
    Technology
Pune, India

Pankaj Chandre
Department of Information Technology
MIT Art, Design and Technology
    University
Pune, India

Shylesha V. Channapattana
Department of Mechanical Engineering,
KLS Vishwanathrao Deshpande
    Institute of Technology
Haliyal, India

Shekhar Chaugule
Vishwakarma Institute of Information
    Technology
Pune, India

Pranali G. Chavhan
Vishwakarma Institute of Information
    Technology
Pune, India

Vilas Deotare
PCET's Nutan Maharashtra Institute of
    Engineering and Technology
Talegaon Dabhade, India

Ganesh Deshmukh
Department of Computer Science and
    Engineering
Vardhaman College of Engineering
Hyderabad, India

Jyoti Yogesh Deshmukh
Marathwada Mitramandal's Institute of
    Technology
Pune, India

Prashant Dhotre
Department of Information Technology
MIT Art, Design and Technology
    University
Pune, India

B. Sakthi Karthi Durai
School of Computing
Kalasalingam Academy of Research
    and Education
Srivilliputhur, India

Shreeyash Garde
PCET's Nutan Maharashtra Institute of
    Engineering and Technology
Talegaon Dabhade, India

Harshad Jagadale
Department of Information Technology
Walchand College of Engineering
Sangli, India

Swati Jaiswal
Department of Computer Engineering
Pimpri Chinchwad College of
    Engineering
Pune, India

Abhishek Kabade
Department of Information
    Technology
Walchand College of Engineering
Sangli, India

Renu Kachhoria
Department of AI and DS
Vishwakarma Institute of Information
    Technology
Pune, India

Sunil Kale
Department of AI and DS
Vishwakarma Institute of Information
    Technology
Pune, India

Rajeswari Kannan
Department of Computer Engineering
Pimpri Chinchwad College of
    Engineering
Pune, India

Manivannan Karunakaran
School of Computer Science and
    Engineering
JAIN (Deemed to be University)
Ramnagara, India

Pranav Khandagale
PCET's Nutan Maharashtra Institute of
    Engineering and Technology
Talegaon Dabhade, India

Chandrakant D. Kokane
PCET's Nutan Maharashtra Institute of
    Engineering and Technology
Talegaon Dabhade, India

Batri Krishnan
School of Computer Science and
    Engineering
JAIN (Deemed to be University)
Ramnagara, India

Pranali Kshirsagar
Vishwakarma Institute of Information
    Technology
Pune, India

Mehul Ligade
PCET's Nutan Maharashtra Institute of
    Engineering and Technology
Talegaon Dabhade, India

Rupali Atul Mahajan
Vishwakarma Institute of Information
    Technology
Pune, India

Parikshit N. Mahalle
Vishwakarma Institute of Information
    Technology
Pune, India

Manisha Mali
Vishwakarma Institute of Information
    Technology
Pune, India

Yogesh Kisan Mali
G H Raisoni College of Engineering
    and Management
Pune, India

Tanvi Mehta
Department of Computer Engineering
Pimpri Chinchwad College of
    Engineering
Pune, India

Riddhi Mirajkar
Vishwakarma Institute of Information
    Technology
Pune, India

Prasad Raghunath Mutkule
Sanjivani College of Engineering
Kopargaon, India

M. Neelakantappa
Department of Information Technology
Vasavi College of Engineering
Hyderabad, India

Bhakti Palkar
K.J. Somaiya College of Engineering
Pune, India

Rajkumar Patil
Department of Information
    Technology
MIT Art, Design and Technology
    University
Pune, India

Sujal Dilip Patil
Vishwakarma Institute of Information
    Technology
Pune, India

Swati Patil
Vishwakarma Institute of Information
    Technology
Pune, India

Ghongade Prashant
Department of Electrical and
    Electronics Engineering
Guru Nanak Dev Engineering College
Bidar, India

J. Benadict Raja
Department of Computer Science and
    Engineering
PSNA College of Engineering and
    Technology
Dindigul, India

Snehal Rathi
Vishwakarma Institute of Information
    Technology
Pune, India

Vijay U. Rathod
G H Raisoni College of Engineering
    and Management
Pune, India

Nilesh Popat Sable
Department of Computer Science &
    Engineering (Artificial Intelligence)
Vishwakarma Institute of Information
    Technology
Pune, India

Rachna Sable
G H Raisoni College of Engineering
    and Management
Pune, India

Nitin Sakhare
Vishwakarma Institute of Information
    Technology,
Pune, India

D. Shanthi
Department of Computer Science and
    Engineering
PSNA College of Engineering and
    Technology
Dindigul, India

Chaitali Shewale
Vishwakarma Institute of Information
    Technology
Pune, India

Gitanjali R. Shinde
Vishwakarma Institute of Information
    Technology
Pune, India

Shivam Singh
PCET's Nutan Maharashtra Institute of
   Engineering and Technology
Talegaon Dabhade, India

S. P. Sonavane
Department of Information Technology
Walchand College of Engineering
Sangli, India

Sneha Kiran Thombre
Information Technology Department
MKSSS'S Cummins College of
   Engineering for Women
Pune, India

Mukesh Kumar Tripathi
Department of Computer Science and
   Engineering
Vardhaman College of Engineering
Hyderabad, India

Sarthak Turki
Vishwakarma Institute of Information
   Technology
Pune, India

Makarand Ramesh Velankar
Information Technology Department
MKSSS'S Cummins College of
   Engineering for Women
Pune, India

Harshad Suryakant Wadkar
Information Technology Department
MKSSS'S Cummins College of
   Engineering for Women
Pune, India

Namrata N. Wasatkar
Vishwakarma Institute of Information
   Technology
Pune, India

Tushar Waykole
PCET's Nutan Maharashtra Institute of
   Engineering and Technology
Talegaon Dabhade, India

Section I

Recent Developments in Data-Centric AI

1 Advancements in Data-Centric AI Foundations, Ethics, and Emerging Technology

Sujal Dilip Patil, Rupali Atul Mahajan, and Nitin Sakhare

1.1 INTRODUCTION

Data-centric artificial intelligence (AI) denotes an approach within AI and machine learning (ML) that places significant emphasis on the pivotal role of meticulously curated, high-quality data in the development and implementation of AI models and systems [1]. Under this paradigm, data assumes the bedrock upon which AI algorithms are constructed and honed, and its effective handling, pre-processing, and analysis stand as pivotal factors for achieving precise and dependable AI outcomes [2]. The essence of data-centric AI springs from the recognition that the performance of AI models is intricately linked to the calibre and quantity of data employed for training, validation, and testing. This methodology underscores the understanding that even the most advanced AI algorithms might grapple to yield meaningful outcomes if the input data is incomplete, biased, laden with noise, or inadequately structured [3]. The overall chapter consists of key aspects of data-centric AI described in Section 1.1.1, Applications of Data-Centric AI, Various techniques – Machine Learning, Deep Learning used in AI, etc. are explained in Section 1.2. The various technologies that are part of data-centric AI are mentioned in Sections 1.3, 1.4, 1.5, and 1.6. The ethical implications of AI technologies are described in Section 1.7. This chapter also covers various AI Governance and Regulation Strategies for Responsible AI Implementation and Oversight.

Key aspects of Data-Centric AI include:

- **Data Collection and Preparation:** Careful and meticulous collection of relevant and representative data is essential. Data needs to be cleaned, pre-processed, and transformed to ensure its suitability for training and testing AI models. This process may involve dealing with missing values, removing outliers, and addressing data imbalance.

DOI: 10.1201/9781003461500-2

- **Data Quality:** Ensuring data quality involves maintaining accuracy, consistency, and reliability throughout the data lifecycle. Quality control measures should be in place to detect and correct errors that could impact AI model performance.
- **Data Bias and Fairness:** Data-centric AI acknowledges the potential for bias in training data and strives to identify and mitigate biases that could lead to unfair or discriminatory AI outcomes. Addressing bias requires diverse and representative data as well as techniques for bias detection and reduction.
- **Data Augmentation:** To enhance model generalization and robustness, data augmentation techniques can be employed. These involve creating new training examples by applying various transformations to existing data, which helps models perform better on unseen data.
- **Active Learning:** Active learning strategies involve selecting the most informative samples for annotation, reducing the amount of labelled data needed to achieve a desired level of model performance [4]. This approach optimizes the learning process and minimizes the labelling cost.
- **Data Privacy and Security:** Protecting sensitive and private data is paramount. Data-centric AI incorporates privacy-preserving techniques to prevent unauthorized access, sharing, or misuse of sensitive information.
- **Continuous Monitoring and Maintenance**: The data-centric approach extends beyond model deployment. Continuous monitoring of model performance in real-world scenarios helps identify potential issues or drift and allows for timely model updates and retraining.
- **Data Labelling and Annotation:** Labelled data is often required for supervised learning, where inputs are associated with corresponding desired outputs. Data-centric AI emphasizes the need for accurate and consistent labelling, as errors in labelling can propagate through the training process and affect model performance.
- **Domain Expertise:** Effective data-centric AI requires collaboration between AI practitioners and domain experts [5]. Domain experts provide valuable insights into the nuances of the data and help guide the preprocessing, feature engineering, and model selection processes.
- **Feature Engineering:** Feature engineering involves selecting, transforming, or creating relevant features from the raw data to improve model performance. This process requires an understanding of the data's characteristics and the problem at hand.
- **Data Versioning and Lineage:** Maintaining a record of data versioning and lineage is crucial for transparency and reproducibility. It enables tracking changes to the data over time, which is essential for debugging and ensuring consistent model behaviour [6].
- **Data Governance:** Establishing clear data governance policies ensures that data is managed in a compliant and ethical manner. This includes defining roles and responsibilities, access controls, and policies for data sharing and usage.

- **Data Pipelines:** Building efficient data pipelines for data preprocessing, augmentation, and model training streamlines the data-centric AI workflow [7]. Well-organized pipelines contribute to consistent and reproducible results.
- **Scalability and Efficiency:** As datasets grow in size and complexity, data-centric AI also focuses on scalable solutions that can handle large volumes of data efficiently. This might involve distributed computing, parallel processing, and optimized storage [8].
- **Feedback Loops:** Integrating feedback loops into the AI process allows models to continuously learn and adapt from real-world usage. This iterative approach helps models stay relevant and effective over time.
- **Data Visualization and Interpretability:** Visualizing data and model outcomes aids in understanding patterns and insights. Additionally, interpretability techniques provide insights into how models arrive at their decisions, enhancing trust and transparency.
- **Transfer Learning and Pretrained Models:** Leveraging pretrained models and transfer learning techniques can accelerate the training process and improve model performance, particularly when labelled data is limited.
- **Data-Centric AI Ethics:** Ethical considerations are paramount in data-centric AI. This involves ensuring that the data used respects user privacy, consent, and confidentiality and that the AI systems deployed adhere to ethical guidelines [9].
- **Data Federations:** In situations where data cannot be centralized due to privacy or security concerns, data federations allow AI models to be trained across decentralized datasets while maintaining data ownership and privacy.
- **Quantifying Data Value:** Data-centric AI acknowledges that not all data is equally valuable. Some data might have a greater impact on model performance than others. Techniques to quantify data value help allocate resources efficiently during data collection and labelling.

Data-centric AI represents a paradigm shift from focusing solely on algorithmic advancements to recognizing the pivotal role of data in AI success. By addressing the challenges and opportunities within the data lifecycle, this approach strives to create AI models that are accurate, fair, transparent, and adaptable to real-world scenarios. These real-world scenarios and use cases are described in Section 1.2.

1.2 APPLICATIONS OF DATA-CENTRIC AI IN VARIOUS DOMAINS

Data-centric AI has a wide range of applications across various domains, where the emphasis on high-quality data and effective data management significantly enhances the performance and impact of AI models. Here are some examples of how data-centric AI is applied in different fields:

1.2.1 HEALTHCARE

Data-centric AI improves the accuracy of medical image analysis, aiding in diagnosing diseases like cancer, detecting anomalies, and predicting patient outcomes [10]. AI-driven analysis of molecular data accelerates drug discovery by predicting drug interactions, identifying potential drug candidates, and optimizing drug designs [11]. By analysing patient data, including genetic, clinical, and lifestyle factors, AI helps tailor treatment plans and predicts patient responses to therapies [12].

1.2.2 FINANCE

Data-centric AI enhances credit risk assessment, fraud detection, and anti-money laundering efforts by analysing transactional and behavioural data for patterns. AI models analyse market data to make high-frequency trading decisions, optimizing trading strategies, and portfolio management. AI-driven analytics of customer data improve marketing strategies, customer segmentation, and churn prediction [13].

1.2.3 RETAIL AND E-COMMERCE

Data-centric AI predicts product demand, optimizing inventory management and supply chain operations. AI-powered recommendation engines analyse customer behaviour to provide personalized product recommendations, enhancing user experience and sales. AI models analyse pricing data and market trends to optimize pricing strategies and increase competitiveness.

1.2.4 MANUFACTURING

Data-centric AI monitors and analyses sensor data from manufacturing processes to identify defects, reduce waste, and ensure product quality. AI models analyse equipment sensor data to predict maintenance needs, minimizing downtime and optimizing maintenance schedules. AI-driven analysis of supply chain data improves inventory management, demand forecasting, and logistics planning.

1.2.5 ENERGY AND UTILITIES

Data-centric AI optimizes energy distribution by analysing consumption patterns, predicting demand, and identifying areas for efficiency improvements. AI models analyse weather and energy production data to optimize the integration and output of renewable energy sources like solar and wind [14].

1.2.6 TRANSPORTATION

Data-centric AI powers self-driving cars by analysing sensor data to make real-time driving decisions and ensure passenger safety [15]. AI-driven analysis of traffic data improves traffic flow, reduces congestion, and enhances urban mobility.

1.2.7 AGRICULTURE

Data-centric AI analyses data from sensors, drones, and satellites to optimize crop management, irrigation, and fertilization for increased yield and resource efficiency. AI models analyse images of plants to detect diseases early, enabling targeted interventions and reducing crop loss.

1.2.8 NATURAL LANGUAGE PROCESSING (NLP)

Data-centric AI analyses text data from social media and reviews to gauge public sentiment about products, services, or events. AI-powered translation models analyse large volumes of text to provide accurate and context-aware translations between languages. These examples highlight how data-centric AI is revolutionizing various industries by leveraging high-quality data to develop more accurate, efficient, and insightful AI applications. The approach is adaptable to a wide range of domains, each benefiting from improved decision-making, enhanced customer experiences, and increased operational efficiency.

The various technologies that are part of data-centric AI are discussed below:

1.3 MACHINE LEARNING

ML is a branch of AI and computer science which focuses on the use of data and algorithms to imitate the way that humans learn, gradually improving its accuracy.

1.3.1 SUPERVISED LEARNING

Supervised learning stands as a type of ML wherein the algorithm gains insights from labelled training data. In this context, the dataset is composed of pairs denoting inputs and their associated outputs. The algorithm's objective revolves around mastering the mapping between inputs and the anticipated outputs. The ultimate aim is for the algorithm to extrapolate from the training dataset and generate precise predictions or classifications for fresh, previously unseen data.

In supervised learning, the algorithm is furnished with datasets comprising labelled pairs of inputs and their corresponding outputs. The primary goal of supervised learning is for the algorithm to discern and internalize a mapping function. This function should enable the algorithm to make precise predictions or classifications for new, previously unseen instances. Supervised learning encompasses diverse tasks, with classification and regression standing out. Classification entails assigning labels to inputs, while regression involves predicting continuous values. A range of algorithms are utilized in supervised learning, including decision trees, support vector machines, neural networks, and linear regression. These algorithms are tailored to address various types of data and tasks.

1.3.2 Unsupervised Learning

Unsupervised learning entails training an ML model using unlabelled data, where explicit output labels are absent [16]. The algorithm's objective is to uncover patterns, structures, or relationships inherent within the data. This is frequently accomplished by clustering similar instances together or reducing the data's dimensionality. Unlabelled data is provided, and the algorithm seeks to identify underlying patterns or groupings. The goal is to explore the inherent structure of the data, uncover hidden patterns, or reduce its complexity. Unsupervised learning encompasses tasks such as clustering, where similar data points are grouped together, and dimensionality reduction, which involves condensing the number of features while preserving vital information [17]. A variety of algorithms are employed in unsupervised learning, including k-means clustering, hierarchical clustering, principal component analysis, and t-distributed Stochastic Neighbor Embedding. These algorithms cater to different aspects of data exploration and pattern recognition.

1.3.3 Reinforcement Learning

Reinforcement learning (RL) stands as an ML category in which an agent learns to formulate decisions through interactions with an environment. This agent garners feedback in the shape of rewards or penalties contingent on its actions, striving to acquire a policy that maximizes the cumulative reward across a span of time. RL frequently finds application in tasks involving sequential decision-making.

- **Training Data:** The agent learns through trial and error by interacting with an environment.
- **Objective:** The agent aims to learn a policy that maximizes the expected cumulative reward over a sequence of actions.
- **Examples:** Game playing, robotic control, and autonomous driving are typical applications of RL.
- **Algorithms:** Q-learning, Deep Q-Networks, and policy gradient methods are common RL algorithms.

These three fundamental learning algorithms constitute the bedrock of ML, serving as pivotal components for constructing a diverse array of AI applications. Depending on the nature of the challenge and the accessibility of labelled data, each learning algorithm category possesses its own merits and constraints. The selection of an algorithm hinges upon the particular task at hand and the distinct attributes of the data involved.

1.4 DEEP LEARNING FUNDAMENTALS: NEURAL NETWORK ARCHITECTURE AND DESIGN

Deep learning constitutes a subset of ML, focusing on the creation and training of neural networks to acquire knowledge and formulate predictions from data. Neural networks, inspired by the human brain's structure and operation, serve as computational models. These networks are comprised of interconnected nodes (neurons) organized into layers, capable of grasping intricate patterns and representations from data through a process termed training.

1. Architecture of Neural Networks:
   a. **Input Layer:** The initial layer accepts raw data, with each neuron corresponding to a data attribute or feature.
   b. **Hidden Layers:** Found between input and output layers, these intermediary layers house neurons that process input data through weighted connections and activation functions [18].
   c. **Output Layer:** The final prediction or output of the network emerges from this layer. Neuron count in the output layer depends on the task, like classification (number of classes) or regression (single output).
2. Neuron (Node) Function in Neural Networks:
   i. A neuron within a neural network executes these steps:
      a. **Weighted Sum:** Neuron inputs are multiplied by weights, and the cumulative weighted inputs are computed.
      b. **Activation Function:** The weighted sum undergoes an activation function, introducing non-linearity. ReLU, Sigmoid, and Tanh are common activation functions.
3. Design Considerations:
   a. **Activation Functions:** Choice of activation functions influences learning and complex relationship modelling. ReLU is prevalent in hidden layers due to its ability to address vanishing gradient issues.
   b. **Loss Function:** Evaluating discrepancies between predictions and actual targets, this function guides optimization in training. Distinct tasks (classification and regression) necessitate distinct loss functions (e.g., cross-entropy and mean squared error) [19].
   c. **Optimization Algorithm:** Optimization algorithms (e.g., Gradient Descent and Adam) adapt network weights based on loss gradients. They aim to minimize loss for enhanced model performance.
   d. **Regularization:** Techniques like dropout, L1/L2 regularization, and batch normalization counter overfitting by controlling network complexity and enhancing generalization.
   e. **Architecture Decisions:** Determining layer count, neurons per layer, and overall structure mandates experimentation, considering factors like dataset size, complexity, and available resources [20].
4. Training and Backpropagation:
   i. Training a neural network encompasses these steps:
      a. **Forward Pass:** Input data traverses the network for predictions. Comparing predicted and actual outcomes using the loss function ensues [21].
      b. **Backpropagation:** Utilizing the chain rule, gradients of loss concerning weights are computed. Updating weights in the opposite gradient direction minimizes loss.

c. **Iterative Optimization:** Forward pass and backpropagation repeat over multiple iterations (epochs) with data batches. The goal is to identify weight configurations minimizing loss.
d. **Validation and Testing:** Model evaluation transpires on validation and test datasets, gauging generalization performance.

Deep learning and neural networks have propelled advancements in diverse domains, such as computer vision, NLP, and RL. Effective deep learning model development, enabling precise predictions and discovery of intricate data patterns, demands prudent architecture design and rigorous training [22].

1.5   CONVOLUTIONAL NEURAL NETWORKS IN IMAGE ANALYSIS

Convolutional Neural Networks (CNNs) represent a specialized variant of neural network architecture meticulously crafted for the examination and interpretation of grid-like data, encompassing images, video frames, and various structured data formats. Renowned for their prowess in computer vision pursuits, CNNs excel in tasks like image classification, object detection, image segmentation, and beyond. The blueprint of CNNs takes inspiration from the visual processing mechanisms inherent within the human brain. In convolutional layers, a collection of adaptable filters (termed kernels) is applied to the input image. These filters discern a multitude of features, encompassing edges, textures, or intricate patterns [23]. The convolution operation entails sliding the filter across the input image. Element-wise multiplications and subsequent summation yield feature maps. Common activation functions implemented in CNNs comprise ReLU (Rectified Linear Unit). ReLU introduces non-linearity to the network, thereby facilitating the modelling of intricate relationships. Pooling layers execute the down-sampling of feature map spatial dimensions. This action curtails computational intricacy while constructing a tiered portrayal of features. Max pooling and average pooling are typical pooling methodologies, wherein the maximum or average value within a pooling window is preserved. Fully connected layers are used in the later stages of a CNN to make predictions or decisions based on the extracted features. These layers connect every neuron to every neuron in the previous and subsequent layers, like traditional neural networks. Images are usually pre-processed before feeding them into CNNs. This includes resizing images to a consistent size, normalizing pixel values (scaling to a certain range), and data augmentation (applying random transformations to increase dataset diversity). A typical CNN architecture consists of alternating convolutional and pooling layers. Multiple convolutional layers with increasing complexity can capture different levels of features.

After the convolutional layers, the feature maps are flattened into a vector and passed through fully connected layers to perform classification or other tasks. The output layer depends on the specific task. For image classification, it often has soft-max activation for multi-class classification, providing probabilities for each class. Transfer learning is a powerful technique in CNNs where pre-trained models (such as Visual Geometry Group ResNet, and Inception) are used as starting points for a specific task. The lower layers of these networks capture general features, and fine-tuning can be performed on higher layers to adapt the model to the specific dataset.

1.5.1 APPLICATIONS OF CNNs

CNNs have demonstrated remarkable performance in various image analysis tasks:

- **Image Classification:** Assigning a label to an input image from a set of predefined classes.
- **Object Detection:** Locating and classifying objects within an image.
- **Image Segmentation:** Assigning a label to each pixel in an image, distinguishing different object regions.
- **Facial Recognition:** Identifying individuals from facial features.
- **Medical Image Analysis:** Diagnosing diseases from medical images (X-rays, MRIs, etc.).
- **Autonomous Vehicles:** Detecting pedestrians, vehicles, and obstacles in real time.
- CNNs have revolutionized computer vision and image analysis, enabling machines to understand and interpret visual information with increasing accuracy and efficiency.

1.6 RECURRENT NEURAL NETWORKS FOR SEQUENTIAL DATA

Recurrent Neural Networks (RNNs) denote a subset of neural networks tailored to manage sequential data, wherein the arrangement of elements holds significance. Their proficiency notably shines in domains like NLP, speech recognition, time series analysis, and any context-entailing sequences. RNNs boast a capacity for internal memory retention, thus rendering them adept at apprehending temporal dependencies and patterns. RNNs process input data step by step, where each step corresponds to a time step in the sequence. They maintain hidden states that capture information from previous time steps [24]. RNNs have recurrent connections that allow information to flow from one time step to the next. This enables the network to maintain context and capture sequential dependencies [25]. The hidden state of an RNN at each time step stores information from the current input and the previous hidden state. It serves as the network's memory. RNNs can suffer from vanishing gradient problems, where gradients become extremely small as they are propagated back in time during training. This can hinder long-range dependencies.

1.6.1 TYPES OF RNNs

1. **Simple RNN:** The basic RNN architecture processes sequences step by step, but it suffers from the vanishing gradient problem, making it difficult to capture long-term dependencies.
2. **Long Short-Term Memory (LSTM):** LSTM networks address the vanishing gradient problem by incorporating specialized memory cells that can store and access information over long sequences.

3. **Gated Recurrent Unit (GRU):** Similar to LSTM, GRU also mitigates the vanishing gradient problem using gating mechanisms. It has a simplified structure with fewer parameters.

1.6.2 Applications of RNNs

RNNs are widely used in various applications involving sequential data:

- **NLP:** Language modelling, machine translation, sentiment analysis, and text generation.
- **Speech Recognition:** Converting spoken language into text.
- **Time Series Analysis:** Predicting future values in financial markets, weather forecasting, and stock prices.
- **Music Generation:** Creating new music sequences.
- **Video Analysis:** Action recognition and video captioning.

While RNNs are powerful for handling sequential data, they also have limitations, such as difficulty in capturing very long-range dependencies. More advanced architectures like Transformers have emerged to address some of these limitations and have gained popularity in various applications as well [26].

The above-discussed AI technologies have some ethical and legal implications in modern day-to-day life decision-making processes. These implications are discussed below.

1.7 UNDERSTANDING THE ETHICAL IMPLICATIONS OF AI TECHNOLOGIES

Understanding the ethical implications of AI technologies is crucial as AI systems become increasingly integrated into our lives and decision-making processes [27]. AI technologies have the potential to bring about transformative benefits, but they also raise ethical concerns that need to be carefully considered and addressed. AI systems are susceptible to inheriting biases embedded within their training data, culminating in outcomes that are unjust or discriminatory. This is particularly evident in domains such as recruitment, lending, and criminal justice. Ensuring fairness and reducing bias require careful data collection, unbiased model design, and ongoing monitoring. Many AI models, especially deep learning models, can be difficult to interpret and explain. This lack of transparency can lead to distrust and hinder accountability. Efforts are being made to develop methods for explaining AI decisions, providing transparency, and making models more interpretable [28]. AI systems frequently engage in the processing of extensive personal data, giving rise to apprehensions about potential breaches of privacy and unauthorized data access. Privacy-preserving techniques and strict data-handling practices are necessary to protect individuals' sensitive information. The automation of certain tasks by AI could lead to job displacement in certain industries, potentially affecting workers and local economies. Addressing the economic and social impact of automation may require upskilling and reskilling programmes. Determining responsibility when AI systems make errors or harmful decisions can be challenging. There may be questions about whether the responsibility lies with the developers, users, or the technology itself [29]. Also, clear guidelines for accountability and liability are essential, especially in safety-critical applications. AI systems become more autonomous, questions arise about who has control over their decisions and actions. Ensuring human oversight, intervention mechanisms, and fail-safes are crucial to prevent unintended consequences. AI systems can be vulnerable to adversarial attacks, where malicious actors manipulate inputs to deceive the system. Robustness testing and security measures are necessary to safeguard AI systems from such attacks. Complex AI systems can exhibit behaviour that was not explicitly programmed, leading to unexpected outcomes. Comprehensive testing and validation procedures are essential to identify and mitigate unintended consequences. AI technologies have the potential to reshape society in profound ways, impacting economies, job markets, and social norms. Long-term ethical considerations and societal implications should guide the development and deployment of AI technologies [30]. Ensuring that AI technologies benefit all of humanity, regardless of geographic location or socioeconomic status, is a significant ethical concern. Efforts should be made to bridge the digital divide and prevent exacerbating existing inequalities. Addressing these ethical implications requires collaboration between policymakers, researchers, industry stakeholders, and society as a whole. Ethical frameworks, regulations, and guidelines are being developed to ensure that AI technologies are developed and deployed in ways that prioritize human well-being, fairness, and accountability.

1.8   PRIVACY AND DATA PROTECTION IN AI-DRIVEN SYSTEMS

Ensuring privacy and safeguarding data are pivotal considerations in the design and implementation of AI-driven systems. With the increasing prevalence and advancement of AI technologies, substantial data access is often imperative for optimal functionality. However, this access must be coupled with robust mechanisms that ensure the confidentiality and security of individuals' sensitive information. The following key aspects merit attention:

- **Prudent Data Collection:** Gather only the essential data required for the intended purpose of the AI system. Restricting data acquisition mitigates the potential for privacy breaches and unauthorized utilization [31].
- **Knowledgeable Consent:** Prior to collecting and utilizing personal data, secure informed and explicit consent from individuals. Individuals should have a comprehensive understanding of data usage and the opportunity to opt out [32].
- **Anonymization and De-identification:** Modify or eliminate personally identifiable information from data to avert direct individual identification. Notably, it's vital to acknowledge that anonymization might not always guarantee privacy, considering potential re-identification attacks.
- **Robust Data Security:** Enforce stringent security measures to shield amassed data from unauthorized access, breaches, and cyber threats. Encryption, secure storage, and access controls assume paramount importance.

- **Purpose Constraint:** Confine the utilization of collected data to the specific purposes for which consent was granted. Utilizing data for unrelated objectives should be avoided unless supplementary consent is obtained.
- **User Oversight and Transparency:** Furnish users with lucid, easily accessible details regarding data application. Empower users to manage their data and extend choices for data erasure.
- **Data Retention Guidelines:** Define and abide by data retention durations that align with the rationale behind data collection. Protracted data retention beyond necessity should be averted.
- **Cross-Border Data Transfer:** Be mindful of regulations and laws regarding the transfer of data across borders. Different jurisdictions may have varying requirements for data protection.
- **Third-Party Data Sharing:** If sharing data with third parties (such as cloud providers), ensure they adhere to strict data protection and privacy standards. Contracts should outline data handling practices.
- **Bias and Fairness:** Be vigilant about potential biases in AI models and data. Biased models could lead to discriminatory outcomes, impacting privacy and fairness.
- **Regulatory Compliance:** Take the initiative to acquaint yourself with pertinent data protection regulations, such as Europe's General Data Protection Regulation (GDPR) or the United States' California Consumer Privacy Act (CCPA). It is crucial to uphold compliance with these regulations to ensure responsible and ethical data handling practices.
- **Ethical Data Use:** Develop ethical guidelines and policies that govern the use of data in AI systems. Ensure that data usage aligns with ethical principles and societal norms.
- **Regular Audits and Assessments:** Periodically assess data privacy practices, conduct privacy impact assessments, and perform audits to ensure ongoing compliance and identify areas for improvement.

   Balancing the benefits of AI-driven systems with the protection of individuals' privacy is a complex but essential task [33]. Striving for transparency, accountability, and ethical use of data is fundamental to building trust and ensuring that AI technologies are developed and deployed responsibly.

The roles and responsibilities of data-centric AI in various applications are given in the following section.

1.9 DATA-CENTRIC AI IN FINANCE

Data-centric AI refers to an approach that places data at the core of AI applications, focusing on the collection, processing, analysis, and interpretation of data to derive valuable insights and make informed decisions.

   Financial institutions gather data from various sources, including customer transactions, market data, social media, and economic indicators. Data-centric AI involves integrating and aggregating this diverse data efficiently to create a comprehensive and unified dataset. Since financial data can be noisy and incomplete, preprocessing and cleaning are essential steps in data-centric AI [34]. Advanced algorithms are used to clean and transform data, ensuring its quality and consistency. Data-centric AI in finance heavily relies on ML and AI algorithms to analyse the data, discover patterns, and make predictions. Algorithms such as regression, classification, clustering, and deep learning models are commonly used. Financial institutions utilize data-centric AI to assess and manage risks associated with investments, loans, and other financial products. By analysing historical data and market trends, AI models can identify potential risks and provide insights to improve risk management strategies. Data-centric AI enables financial institutions to offer personalized services and recommendations to their customers. By analysing customer behaviour and preferences, AI models can suggest tailored financial products and services that meet individual needs. AI-powered fraud detection systems are increasingly used in finance to identify suspicious activities and transactions [35]. These systems can detect anomalies in real-time and prevent fraudulent activities, protecting both customers and financial institutions. Data-centric AI plays a crucial role in ensuring regulatory compliance for financial institutions. AI models can analyse vast amounts of data to identify any non-compliance issues and assist in meeting reporting requirements. Data-centric AI can analyse market trends, news, and other economic factors to inform trading decisions. This approach is commonly used in algorithmic trading and quantitative finance [36].

1.10 AI FOR FRAUD DETECTION

AI-powered fraud detection systems use ML algorithms to analyse large volumes of data and identify patterns that may indicate fraudulent activities [37]. These systems can detect both known and unknown fraud patterns, providing real-time alerts to prevent potential financial losses. Key features of AI for fraud detection include:

- **Anomaly Detection:** AI algorithms can identify unusual behaviour or transactions that deviate from normal patterns, helping to detect fraudulent activities.
- **Behavioural Analysis:** By analysing historical customer behaviour, AI can recognize changes or deviations in behaviour that might indicate fraud [38].
- **Network Analysis:** AI can assess relationships between various entities, such as customers, merchants, and accounts, to identify potential fraud networks.
- ML **Models:** Supervised and unsupervised learning techniques are commonly used to train models for fraud detection. These models continuously learn from new data to improve accuracy.
- **AI for Risk Assessment:** AI finds application in financial risk assessment, enhancing comprehension and management of diverse risk categories such as credit, market, operational, and liquidity risks. Employing AI techniques empowers financial entities to make judicious choices and allocate resources adeptly. Notable applications encompass:
- **Credit Risk Evaluation:** AI models analyse a borrower's credit history, financial data, and other relevant factors to assess the risk associated with extending credit.

- **Market Risk Prediction:** AI algorithms analyse market data and historical trends to predict potential fluctuations and market movements.
- **Operational Risk Management:** AI can be employed to identify potential operational risks and provide insights into improving internal processes.
- **Stress Testing:** AI-powered stress testing models assess how financial institutions' portfolios and balance sheets would perform under adverse scenarios.
- **AI for Algorithmic Trading:** Algorithmic trading involves using pre-defined rules and AI-powered algorithms to execute trades at high speeds and frequencies. AI helps traders make data-driven decisions, identify patterns in market data, and execute trades more efficiently. Key aspects of AI in algorithmic trading include:
- **Market Analysis:** AI models analyse large volumes of historical and real-time market data to identify trading opportunities and patterns.
- **NLP:** AI can process and understand news articles and other textual data to assess their impact on the financial markets.
- **RL:** AI agents can use RL techniques to learn and adapt trading strategies based on feedback from the market [39].
- **Risk Management:** AI models can dynamically adjust trading strategies to manage risk exposure and avoid large losses.

1.11   ENSURING FAIRNESS AND TRANSPARENCY IN FINANCIAL AI APPLICATIONS

Ensuring fairness and transparency in financial AI applications is crucial to building trust, preventing bias, and maintaining ethical standards in the financial industry. Here are some key considerations to achieve fairness and transparency:

1. Data Quality and Bias Mitigation
   - Start with high-quality and diverse data to avoid bias in AI models. Ensure that the data used for training is representative of the entire population and includes samples from different demographics.
   - Use techniques such as data preprocessing, augmentation, and balancing to mitigate bias and address data imbalances [40].
2. Algorithmic Fairness
   - Choose AI algorithms that are known for their fairness and interpretability. Certain algorithms may inherently introduce biases, so it's essential to evaluate their impacts on different groups.
   - Implement fairness-aware ML techniques that explicitly consider fairness constraints during model training and decision-making processes.
3. Interpretability
   - Utilize AI models that can provide explanations for their decisions. Explainable AI helps users understand the factors that influenced a specific outcome, making it easier to detect and address potential biases.

- Choose interpretable models, such as decision trees or linear regression, whenever possible, as they offer clearer insights into how decisions are made.
4. Regulatory Compliance
   - Maintain awareness regarding pertinent financial regulations and data protection legislation. Adherence to laws such as GDPR or CCPA is of paramount importance when dealing with sensitive financial information [41].
   - Ensure that AI applications meet the necessary legal and regulatory requirements, including anti-discrimination laws.
5. Model Validation and Testing
   - Thoroughly evaluate AI models for fairness before deployment. Use fairness metrics to assess the impact on different groups and demographics [42].
   - Conduct rigorous testing, including stress testing, to identify potential biases and weaknesses in the AI system.
6. Human Oversight
   - Involve human experts in the development and monitoring of AI applications. Humans can provide insights into potential biases that AI might not detect.
   - Establish a governance framework that includes ethical committees or review boards to oversee AI usage and decision-making.
7. Continuous Monitoring and Feedback
   - Sustain a perpetual vigil over the performance of AI models in live operation to identify potential drift or bias that may emerge over time.
   - Instigate a culture of eliciting feedback from end-users and stakeholders, a process that unveils and rectifies fairness or transparency concerns.
8. Transparency in Decision-Making
   - Communicate openly about the use of AI in financial applications with customers and stakeholders.
   - Be transparent about the factors that AI models consider in decision-making processes.

There may have been significant developments in AI. Key emerging technologies and trends in AI up to the point are discussed in Section 1.12.

1.12   EMERGING TECHNOLOGIES IN AI

Edge AI and Internet of Things (IoT) applications are two intertwined emerging technologies that bear considerable potential for shaping the trajectory of AI in the future. Edge AI signifies the integration of AI algorithms onto edge devices, encompassing smartphones, sensors, cameras, and various IoT devices, in contrast to relying on centralized cloud servers for computation [43]. This approach, processing data directly on the device, imparts a range of benefits:

1.12.1 EDGE AI AND INTERNET OF THINGS APPLICATIONS

- **Real-time Processing:** Edge AI enables faster decision-making as data is processed on the device without the need for round-trips to cloud servers, reducing latency.
- **Privacy and Security:** Since data remains on the device and is not transmitted to external servers, Edge AI can enhance data privacy and security.
- **Bandwidth Efficiency:** Edge AI diminishes the volume of data necessitating transmission to cloud servers, thereby optimizing network bandwidth and curbing expenses associated with data transfers [44].
- **Offline Functionality:** Edge AI allows devices to perform AI tasks even when they are disconnected from the internet, making them more resilient in remote or low-connectivity environments.
- **Scalability:** Distributing AI computation across edge devices can scale effectively without overburdening centralized cloud infrastructure.
- **IoT Applications:** The IoT constitutes a network encompassing interconnected devices, imbued with sensors, software, and other technological components that empower them to gather and share data via the internet. The amalgamation of AI with IoT devices ushers in a myriad of prospects for a wide array of applications.
- **Smart Home Automation:** AI-powered IoT devices can learn and adapt to users' preferences, optimizing energy consumption and enhancing home security.
- **Industrial IoT:** The amalgamation of AI and IoT within industrial environments facilitates predictive maintenance, process enhancement, and automation. This synergy translates to heightened efficiency and minimized downtime.
- **Healthcare IoT:** IoT devices with AI capabilities can monitor patients' health conditions remotely, facilitate early disease detection, and improve healthcare outcomes [45].
- **Smart Cities:** AI-driven IoT infrastructure can improve urban planning, traffic management, waste management, and public safety.
- **Environmental Monitoring:** IoT sensors with AI analytics can track environmental parameters, such as air quality and water quality, for better environmental management.
- **Agriculture:** AI-powered IoT devices assist in precision agriculture by optimizing irrigation, monitoring crop health, and predicting weather patterns.
- **Wearable Devices:** Wearable IoT devices with AI functionalities can monitor fitness, health metrics, and provide personalized insights.

Both Edge AI and IoT applications are evolving rapidly, and their combined potential has significant implications for various industries, ranging from consumer electronics to healthcare, manufacturing, transportation, and beyond. The integration of AI capabilities at the edge with IoT devices is expected to drive further innovation and enhance the efficiency, intelligence, and capabilities of connected devices and systems.

Quantum computing has the potential to revolutionize AI by significantly speeding up complex computations, enabling researchers to tackle more intricate AI problems.

1.13   QUANTUM COMPUTING AND ITS POTENTIAL IMPACT ON AI

Quantum computing possesses the potential to usher in a revolutionary transformation within the realm of AI, offering unparalleled computational prowess and resolving intricate problems that currently remain beyond the reach of classical computers. Rooted in the principles of quantum mechanics, quantum computing harnesses quantum bits (qubits) that can exist in a multitude of states concurrently. This attribute facilitates parallel processing and exponential scalability, thereby presenting new horizons for computational capabilities. Quantum computing's ability to perform complex calculations exponentially faster than classical computers could significantly speed up AI algorithms. Tasks like optimization, search, and pattern recognition could be accelerated, leading to more efficient AI systems [46]. Quantum computing can enhance ML algorithms by enabling the exploration of larger feature spaces and optimizing models with higher-dimensional data. Quantum ML algorithms may outperform classical counterparts in certain scenarios. Quantum computing can efficiently analyse vast amounts of data, making it valuable for processing and extracting insights from big data, which is essential for AI applications. Quantum computing's parallel processing capabilities make it ideal for solving complex optimization problems. AI applications that rely on optimization, such as portfolio optimization in finance or resource allocation in logistics, could benefit from quantum-enhanced algorithms. Researchers are exploring the concept of quantum neural networks, which leverage quantum entanglement and superposition to process information. Quantum neural networks may be more adept at processing complex data and making predictions in specific scenarios [47]. Quantum computing could improve NLP tasks like language translation, sentiment analysis, and document summarization by processing large amounts of text data more efficiently. Quantum computers could simulate complex quantum systems, which would be invaluable for quantum-inspired AI research, quantum chemistry, and drug discovery. Despite these promising prospects, it's important to note that practical quantum computing is still in its early stages. Building reliable, error-corrected quantum computers remains a considerable challenge due to quantum decoherence and noise. Currently, most quantum processors are noisy and limited in qubit count, making them unsuitable for many large-scale AI applications. As quantum computing technology advances and matures, it is expected to have a transformative impact on AI [48]. Researchers are actively exploring quantum algorithms, hybrid quantum-classical approaches, and the integration of quantum computing with classical AI techniques to harness the full potential of quantum computing for AI applications.

1.14 AI GOVERNANCE AND REGULATION

AI governance and regulation refer to the policies, rules, and frameworks established by governments, organizations, and international bodies to guide the responsible development, deployment, and use of AI technologies. Given the potential societal impact of AI, it is essential to ensure that these technologies are developed and used in an ethical, transparent, and accountable manner [49]. Many AI governance initiatives are based on ethical principles that promote fairness, transparency, accountability, privacy, and human rights. These principles serve as guiding values to ensure that AI systems benefit society while minimizing potential risks and harm. Regulations may require AI developers to ensure transparency in how their systems operate and provide explanations for the decisions made by AI algorithms, especially in critical domains like healthcare and finance. Regulations often address data protection concerns related to AI applications, ensuring that personal and sensitive data are handled securely and with user consent. Governance frameworks strive to mitigate algorithmic bias and ensure that AI systems do not discriminate against individuals or groups based on attributes like race, gender, or religion. Clear guidelines on accountability and liability are crucial to determine responsibility when AI systems cause harm or make erroneous decisions [50]. Some regulations focus on high-risk AI applications, such as critical infrastructure, healthcare, and autonomous vehicles, requiring additional scrutiny, testing, and certification. In an interconnected world, international cooperation is necessary to address cross-border data flows, privacy concerns, and regulatory harmonization. Effective governance involves engaging with the public, AI developers, researchers, and other stakeholders to understand concerns, assess risks, and foster trust. Regulations might address the impact of AI on the workforce, promoting responsible workforce management, and addressing potential job displacement. Governments may invest in AI research, promote collaboration between academia and industry, and encourage responsible AI innovation. Developing AI standards and certification processes can help ensure compliance with regulations and foster a culture of responsible AI development. In light of the worldwide reach of AI technologies, fostering international collaboration among governments and organizations is imperative to establish uniform and effective governance principles. The landscape of AI governance and regulation is dynamically evolving, with diverse countries and organizations adopting varied strategies to tackle the ethical, legal, and societal quandaries posed by AI [51]. As AI technologies advance, maintaining an equilibrium between fostering innovation and ensuring responsible AI development and utilization for the greater good of humanity remains pivotal.

1.15 STRATEGIES FOR RESPONSIBLE AI IMPLEMENTATION AND OVERSIGHT

Enforcing responsible AI implementation and vigilant oversight is vital to ensure that AI systems are conceived, rolled out, and employed in a manner that aligns with ethical tenets, legal requisites, and societal values. Following are some strategies:

- Incorporate ethical considerations into the inception of AI systems' design and development.
- Engage multidisciplinary teams encompassing ethicists, data scientists, and domain experts to pinpoint potential biases, equity concerns, and ethical ramifications [52].
- Affirm transparency and comprehensibility in AI systems, furnishing insights into their decision-making processes.
- Leverage interpretable AI methodologies to expound AI predictions and actions, especially in critical domains like healthcare and finance.
- Assign primacy to top-tier, diverse data to preclude bias in AI models. Employ data preprocessing techniques to curb bias and tackle data imbalances.
- Undertake periodic audits and surveillance of data to detect potential biases [53].
- Incorporate human oversight and intervention mechanisms in AI systems.
- Establish feedback loops where users can report issues and provide feedback to improve system performance and mitigate biases.
- Thoroughly test AI algorithms before deployment to identify and address potential biases and shortcomings, and conduct robust validation processes including evaluating AI performance on diverse datasets and simulated scenarios.
- Continuously monitor AI systems in real-world settings to detect any unintended consequences or changes in behaviour. Implement auditing mechanisms to assess AI performance regularly.
- Establish review boards or ethics committees to assess and evaluate AI projects, especially in sensitive domains like healthcare and criminal justice.
- Undertake comprehensive assessments to comprehend the potential ramifications of introducing AI systems in diverse contexts, taking into account social, ethical, and legal ramifications.
- Craft and adhere to lucid guidelines and policies governing the ethical deployment of AI within organizational frameworks. These directives should encompass aspects such as data privacy, security, impartiality, and ethical considerations. Stay attuned to pertinent AI regulations and ensure alignment with regulations on data protection and privacy.
- Acquire a deep understanding of the regulatory milieu in regions where AI systems will be implemented.
- Foster awareness among end-users regarding the capabilities and limitations of AI systems, furnishing unambiguous details about data usage.
- Secure informed consent before collecting and processing personal data. Implement robust risk management strategies to address potential AI-related risks, including financial, reputational, and operational risks.
- Establish mechanisms to report AI-related incidents or concerns, and be transparent with stakeholders about actions taken to address such issues.

1.16 COLLABORATION AND KNOWLEDGE SHARING

Engage in knowledge sharing and collaboration with other organizations and stakeholders to learn from best practices and collectively address challenges related to responsible AI deployment. By following these strategies, organizations can deploy

AI systems responsibly and ensure that AI technologies contribute positively to society while minimizing potential risks and negative impacts. Effective monitoring will allow for continuous improvement and ensure that AI systems remain aligned with ethical and societal standards over time.

1.17   FUTURE OF DATA-CENTRIC AI

The future of data-centric AI is expected to be shaped by several trends and developments in AI technologies while simultaneously facing ethical challenges that need to be addressed responsibly.

1.17.1   TRENDS AND FUTURE DEVELOPMENTS IN AI TECHNOLOGIES

Deep learning will continue to evolve, enabling more complex and sophisticated AI applications. Researchers may explore novel architectures and optimization techniques to improve the performance of deep neural networks. Transfer learning and few-shot learning approaches will become more prevalent, allowing AI models to learn from one task and apply that knowledge to new tasks with limited data. AI systems will integrate information from multiple sources, such as text, images, speech, and sensor data, to create more comprehensive and context-aware models. XAI will gain prominence to address the black-box nature of some AI models, making AI systems more transparent and interpretable, especially in critical applications like healthcare and finance. As quantum computing advances, quantum-inspired AI algorithms will emerge, leveraging quantum principles to accelerate AI computations. Edge AI is poised to maintain its increasing significance, facilitating AI computations on edge devices such as IoT devices. This trend brings about reduced latency, heightened privacy, and enhanced efficiency. Generative AI models will evolve to create more realistic and creative outputs, impacting domains like art, design, and content generation. AI will play a vital role in drug discovery, personalized medicine, and disease prediction, contributing to advancements in biotechnology and healthcare. AI will continue to be integrated into autonomous vehicles, drones, and robots, enabling safer and more intelligent automation.

1.18   ETHICAL CHALLENGES IN EVOLVING AI LANDSCAPES

1. **Addressing Bias and Ensuring Fairness:** AI systems have the potential to adopt and magnify biases ingrained in the data, resulting in inequitable results. The imperative to maintain fairness and counteract bias will persist as central concerns in AI advancement
2. **Safeguarding Privacy and Data:** Given AI's dependence on extensive data, safeguarding user privacy and confidential information assumes paramount significance, mandating the implementation of robust data protection protocols.
3. **AI in Employment:** The impact of AI on the workforce raises ethical considerations about job displacement and the need for reskilling and up-skilling programs.

4. **Autonomous Systems and Safety:** As AI powers autonomous systems, ensuring their safety and accountability becomes essential to prevent potential harm.

5. **Weaponization of AI:** The misuse of AI technologies for malicious purposes, such as in cyber-attacks or autonomous weapons, poses significant ethical challenges.

6. **Transparency and Explainability:** AI systems' lack of transparency and explainability can lead to a loss of trust, making it essential to address these issues for critical applications.

7. **Social Impact:** AI's influence on society, from misinformation to echo chambers in social media, requires ethical considerations and responsible design.

8. **Regulatory and Legal Challenges:** Developing and enforcing AI regulations that strike the right balance between innovation and accountability remains a challenge for policymakers. Tackling these ethical dilemmas demands a collective endeavour involving researchers, policymakers, enterprises, and the general public. Nurturing responsible AI advancement, continuous vigilance, and unwavering commitment to ethical directives will stand as paramount. This approach is pivotal to guarantee that AI technologies serve humanity's welfare while upholding ethical benchmarks and societal principles.

REFERENCES

1. Abdi, H., and Williams, L. J. Principal component analysis. *Wiley Interdisciplinary Reviews: Computational Statistics* 2, 4 (2010), 433–459.
2. Ahsan, M. M., Mahmud, M. P., Saha, P. K., Gupta, K. D., and Siddiqe, Z. Effect of data scaling methods on machine learning algorithms and model performance. *Technologies* 9, 3 (2021), 52
3. Agarwal, A., Dahleh, M., & Sarkar, T. A marketplace for data: An algorithmic solution. In Proceedings of the 2019 ACM Conference on Economics and Computation (2019) (pp. 701–726).
4. Ali, P. J. M., Faraj, R. H., Koya, E., Ali, P. J. M., and Faraj, R. H. Data normalization and standardization: a technical report. *Machine Learning Technical Reports* 1, 1 (2014), 1–6.
5. Armbrust, M., Ghodsi, A., Xin, R., & Zaharia, M. (2021, January). Lakehouse: a new generation of open platforms that unify data warehousing and advanced analytics. In Proceedings of CIDR (Vol. 8).6. Arocena, P. C., Glavic, B., Mecca, G., Miller, R. J., Papotti, P., and Santoro, D. Benchmarking data curation systems. *IEEE Data Engineering Bulletin* 39, 2 (2016), 47–62.
7. Aroyo, L., Lease, M., Paritosh, P., & Schaekermann, M. (2022). Data excellence for AI: why should you care?. Interactions, 29, 2, 66–69.
8. Azhagusundari, B., Thanamani, A. S. et al. Feature selection based on information gain. *International Journal of Innovative Technology and Exploring Engineering (IJITEE)* 2, 2 (2013), 18–21.
9. Azizzadenesheli, K., Liu, A., Yang, F., & Anandkumar, A. (2019). Regularized learning for domain adaptation under label shifts. arXiv preprint arXiv:1903.09734.10. Anand, D., and Kumar, A. IoT-based automated healthcare system. In*: 5th International Conference on Computing Methodologies and Communication (ICCMC)*, Erode, India (2021).

11. Pao, L. Y., and Frei, C. W. A comparison of parallel and sequential implementations of a multisensor multitarget tracking algorithm. In: *Proceedings of the American Control Conference*, vol. 3, Seattle, WA, June (1995), pp. 1683–1687.

12. D'Mello, S., and Graesser, A. (2012). Dynamics of affective states during complex learning. *Learning and Instruction* 22(2), 145–157

13. Baik, C., Jagadish, H. V., & Li, Y. (2019, April). Bridging the semantic gap with SQL query logs in natural language interfaces to databases. In 2019 IEEE 35th International Conference on Data Engineering (ICDE) (pp. 374–385). IEEE.

14. Barandas, M., Folgado, D., Fernandes, L., Santos, S., Abreu, M., Bota, P., Liu, H., Schultz, T. and Gamboa, H., 2020. TSFEL: Time series feature extraction library. SoftwareX, 11, p.100456.

15. Basu, A., & Blanning, R. W. (1995, January). Discovering implicit integrity constraints in rule bases using metagraphs. In Proceedings of the Twenty-Eighth Annual Hawaii International Conference on System Sciences (Vol. 3, pp. 321–329). IEEE.

16. Batini, C., Cappiello, C., Francalanci, C., and Maurino, A. Methodologies for data quality assessment and improvement. *ACM Computing Surveys (CSUR)* 41, 3 (2009), 1–52.

17. Baylor, D., Breck, E., Cheng, H. T., Fiedel, N., Foo, C. Y., Haque, Z., ... & Zinkevich, M. (2017, August). Tfx: A tensorflow-based production-scale machine learning platform. In: Proceedings of the 23rd ACM SIGKDD International Conference on Knowledge Discovery and Data Mining (pp. 1387–1395)

18. Bertini, E., & Lalanne, D. (2009, June). Surveying the complementary role of automatic data analysis and visualization in knowledge discovery. In: Proceedings of the ACM SIGKDD Workshop on Visual Analytics and Knowledge Discovery: Integrating Automated Analysis with Interactive Exploration (pp. 12–20).

19. Yin, L., Lin, S., Sun, Z., Wang, S., Li, R., & He, Y. (2024). PriMonitor: An adaptive tuning privacy-preserving approach for multimodal emotion detection. *World Wide Web* 27(2), 1–28.

20. D'Mello, S., Kory, J., and Dieterle, E. Affective computing: Challenges, techniques, and evaluation. In: S. D'Mello, R. A. Calvo, and J. Gratch (Eds.), *Handbook of Affective Computing*, Oxford University Press (2015), pp. 401–414.

21. Li, Y., Chen, Z., Zha, D., Zhou, K., Jin, H., Chen, H., and Hu, X. Automated anomaly detection via curiosity-guided search and self-imitation learning. *IEEE Transactions on Neural Networks and Learning Systems* 33, 6 (2021), 2365–2377.

22. Li, Y., Chen, Z., Zha, D., Zhou, K., Jin, H., Chen, H., & Hu, X. (2021, April). Autood: Neural architecture search for outlier detection. In: 2021 IEEE 37th International Conference on Data Engineering (ICDE) (pp. 2117–2122). IEEE.

23. Liu, P., Yuan, W., Fu, J., Jiang, Z., Hayashi, H., and Neubig, G. Pre-train, prompt, and predict: a systematic survey of prompting methods in natural language processing. *ACM Computing Surveys* 55, 9 (2023), 1–35.

24. Li, Y., Zha, D., Venugopal, P., Zou, N., and Hu, X. PyODDS: An end-to-end outlier detection system with automated machine learning. In: *Companion Proceedings of the Web Conference 2020* (2020).

25. Liu, Z., Chen, S., Zhou, K., Zha, D., Huang, X., and Hu, X. RSC: Accelerating graph neural networks training via randomized sparse computations. In: Proceedings of the 40th International Conference on Machine Learning, PMLR 202:21951-21968, 2023.

26. Liu, Z., Wei, P., Jiang, J., Cao, W., Bian, J., and Chang, Y. MESA: boost ensemble imbalanced learning with meta-sampler. In: *Advances in Neural Information Processing Systems 33 (NeurIPS 2020)* (2020).

27. Lucic, Ana, Harrie Oosterhuis, Hinda Haned and M. de Rijke. FOCUS: Flexible Optimizable Counterfactual Explanations for Tree Ensembles. AAAI Conference on Artificial Intelligence (2019).

28. Luo, Y., Qin, X., Tang, N., and Li, G. DeepEye: Towards automatic data visualization. In: *2018 IEEE 34th International Conference on Data Engineering (ICDE)*, IEEE (2018), pp. 101–112.

29. Madry, A., Makelov, A., Schmidt, L., Tsipras, D., and Vladu, A. Towards deep learning models resistant to adversarial attacks. In: *6th International Conference on Learning Representations, ICLR 2018 - Conference Track Proceedings*. (2018)8.

30. Marcus, Ryan, Andreas Kipf, Alexander van Renen, Mihail Stoian, Sanchit Misra, Alfons Kemper, Thomas Neumann and Tim Kraska. Benchmarking learned indexes. In: Proceedings of the VLDB Endowment 14 (2020): 1–13.

31. M. Feurer, A. Klein, K. Eggensperger, J. Springenberg, M. Blum, and F. Hutter. Ecient and robust automated machine learning. Advances in neural information processing systems, 28, 2015.

32. Moosavi-Dezfooli, S., Fawzi, A., & Frossard, P. DeepFool: A Simple and Accurate Method to Fool Deep Neural Networks. 2016 IEEE Conference on Computer Vision and Pattern Recognition (CVPR), 2574–2582. (2016).

33. Mazumder, M., Banbury, C.R., Yao, X., Karlavs, B., Rojas, W.G., Diamos, S., Diamos, G.F., He, L., Kiela, D., Jurado, D., Kanter, D., Mosquera, R., Ciro, J., Aroyo, L., Acun, B., Eyuboglu, S., Ghorbani, A., Goodman, E.D., Kane, T., Kirkpatrick, C.R., Kuo, T., Mueller, J.W., Thrush, T., Vanschoren, J., Warren, M.J., Williams, A., Yeung, S., Ardalani, N., Paritosh, P.K., Zhang, C., Zou, J.Y., Wu, C., Coleman, C., Ng, A.Y., Mattson, P., & Reddi, V.J. DataPerf: Benchmarks for Data-Centric AI Development. ArXiv, abs/2207.10062. (2022).

34. Meduri, V., Popa, L., Sen, P., & Sarwat, M. (2020). A Comprehensive Benchmark Framework for Active Learning Methods in Entity Matching. Proceedings of the 2020 ACM SIGMOD International Conference on Management of Data. (2020).

35. Mehrabi, N., Morstatter, F., Saxena, N.A., Lerman, K., & Galstyan, A.G. A Survey on Bias and Fairness in Machine Learning. ACM Computing Surveys (CSUR), 54, pp. 1– 35. (2019)

36. Meng, C., Trinh, L., Xu, N., Enouen, J., & Liu, Y. Interpretability and fairness evaluation of deep learning models on MIMIC-IV dataset. Scientific Reports, 12. (2022).

37. Milutinovic, M., Schoenfeld, B., Martinez-Garcia, D., Ray, S., Shah, S., and Yan, D. On evaluation of autoML systems In: *Computer Science* (2020).

38. Mintz, M.D., Bills, S., Snow, R., & Jurafsky, D. Distant supervision for relation extraction without labeled data. Annual Meeting of the Association for Computational Linguistics. (2009).

39. Miotto, R., Wang, F., Wang, S., Jiang, X., and Dudley, J. T. Deep learning for healthcare: review, opportunities and challenges. *Briefings in Bioinformatics* 19, 6 (2018).

40. Miranda, L. J. Towards data-centric machine learning: a short review. *Communications of the ACM*, 66, 8, pp. 84–92 10.1145/3571724 (2023)

41. Mirdita, M., Von Den Driesch, L., Galiez, C., Martin, M. J., Söding, J., and Steinegger, M. Uniclust databases of clustered and deeply annotated protein sequences and alignments. *Nucleic Acids Research* 45, D1 (2017), D170–D176.

42. Mnih, V., Kavukcuoglu, K., Silver, D., Graves, A., Antonoglou, I., Wierstra, D. & Riedmiller, M. Playing atari with deep reinforcement learning. arXiv preprint arXiv:1312.5602. (2013).

43. Nanni, L., Paci, M., Brahnam, S., and Lumini, A. Comparison of different image data augmentation approaches. *Journal of Imaging* 7, 12 (2021).

44. Nargesian, F., Zhu, E., Pu, K. Q., and Miller, R. J. Table union search on open data. In: *Proceedings of the VLDB Endowment* 11, 7 813–825 (2018). https://doi.org/10.14778/3192965.3192973

45. Kim, J. S., Jin, H. et al., Location-based social network data generation based on patterns of life. In: *2020 21st IEEE International Conference on Mobile Data Management (MDM)*, IEEE (2020), pp. 158–167.

46. Kumar, A., Dabas, V., and Hooda, P., 2020. Collaboration Big Data. Internet of data: a SWOT analysis. *International Journal of Information Technology* 12 (2020) 1159–1169.

47. Van Aken, D., Pavlo, A., Gordon, G. J., and Zhang, B. Automatic database management system tuning through large-scale machine learning. In *SIGMOD '17: Proceedings of the 2017 ACM International Conference on Management of Data* May (2017) 1009–1024 https://doi.org/10.1145/3035918.3064029 (2017).

48. Venkatasubramanian, S., and Alfano, M., 2020. The philosophical basis of algorithmic recourse. *In Proceedings of the 2020 conference on fairness, accountability, and transparency*, pp. 284–293.

49. Zha, D., Lai, K.-H., Tan, Q., Ding, S., Zou, N., and Hu, X. B. Towards automated imbalanced learning with deep hierarchical reinforcement learning. In Proceedings of the 31st ACM International Conference on Information & Knowledge Management. 2476–2485. (2022).

50. Pedrozo, W. G., Nievola, J. C., and Ribeiro, D. C. An adaptive approach for index tuning with learning classifier systems on hybrid storage environments, In: *Hybrid Artificial Intelligent Systems: 13th International Conference, HAIS 2018, Proceedings*, vol. 13, Oviedo, Spain, June 20–22, 2018, Springer (2018), pp. 716–729.

51. Bodenheimer, T., Sinsky, C., and Froman, R. *Improving Primary Care Access and Continuity: A Framework and Quality Improvement Toolkit for Achieving the Institute for Healthcare Improvement's Triple Aim.* Agency for Healthcare Research and Quality (US) (2018).

52. Woolf, B. P. *Building Intelligent Interactive Tutors: Student-Centered Strategies for Revolutionizing E-Learning.* Morgan Kaufmann (2010).

53. Lee, Y., Im, D., and Shim, J., 2019. Data labeling research for deep learning based fire detection system. In: *2019 International Conference on Systems of Collaboration Big Data. Internet of Things and Security (SysCoBIoTS),* IEEE (2021), pp. 1–4.

2 Emerging Development and Challenges in Data-Centric AI

Chaitali Shewale

2.1 INTRODUCTION

Data are crucial for training models, assessing performance, and generating predictions in artificial intelligence (AI). The concept that the quality and quantity of data have a direct impact on the efficacy of AI models is at the heart of data-centric AI (DCAI). This chapter aims to shed light on how the AI community is developing to adapt to the changing landscape of data by examining the new trends and difficulties in DCAI. In this fast-growing world, AI has rapidly transformed much of our human work into a machine world with one click. The main core of this transformation lies in the paradigm shift toward DCAI, where the huge and unprecedented growth along with the availability of data has become a challenge and also an advantage for us. With this huge amount of data, there is a need for a mechanism to separate and distribute data to make it used more efficiently and in a much better way. The concept of DCAI will have a direct effect on data arrangement and data distribution [1]. We will delve into the techniques and strategies employed in data preprocessing, augmentation, and feature engineering that contribute to the enhancement of data quality and subsequent efficacy of models.

Applications for DCAI are prevalent across a range of industries, highlighting the critical role that data plays in forming and improving AI models. The use of large medical imaging data by AI models for the accurate detection of diseases like cancer and the analysis of electronic health records to identify patterns and provide individualized therapies are two notable examples. By anticipating maintenance requirements and minimizing downtime, predictive maintenance, based on sensor data analysis, optimizes operations. Image processing and data analysis help quality control find defects in manufactured goods and guarantee excellent quality. AI models analyze transaction history to find anomalous tendencies suggestive of probable fraud in financial transactions. Energy consumption optimization increases the effectiveness of energy distribution and lowers costs, whereas traffic management enhances the efficiency of transportation networks and traffic flow through data analysis. Through the use of multilingual text data, AI models are trained to improve the accuracy of language translation systems. Sentiment analysis uses a massive amount of text data from reviews, surveys, and social media to

DOI: 10.1201/9781003461500-3

evaluate public opinion on a variety of topics. Analyzing historical soil, crop, and meteorological data helps predict crop yields, increasing farm production. Real-time decision-making and obstacle identification are made possible for autonomous cars through image and sensor processing. By making recommendations for goods or services based on user preferences, recommender systems increase consumer happiness and revenue. In order to keep the right amount of inventory on hand, inventory optimization analyzes sales data and demand forecasts. In finance, risk assessment is evaluating and predicting investment risks by examining market and economic data. These fields have undergone a revolution, thanks to DCAI, which emphasizes how crucial it is to have high-quality, diversified data for AI applications. These illustrations highlight how DCAI applications use a wealth of data to build models, forecast the future, and streamline processes in a variety of industries, ultimately enhancing productivity, accuracy, and judgment.

2.2   DATA-CENTRIC AI (DCAI)

The development of AI models using machine learning (ML) generally assumes that the dataset is reasonably clean and well-curated (for example, pictures of dogs and cats), and the task is to create the best model for this dataset. The ML study covers a variety of models such as neural networks, decision trees, etc., training methods such as regularization, optimization algorithms, loss functions, etc., and model/hyperparameter selection methods including model ensembling [2]. This theory is known

In real-world applications, the data are not fixed like it is assumed when developing AI model. Many times we are allowed to alter the dataset to improve modeling accuracy or even add more data when your budget permits. Experienced data scientists are aware that examining and improving the data is a better investment than fiddling with models, but this process can be time-consuming for huge datasets. The majority of data improvement has been done manually under the direction of human intuition or knowledge. Alternatively, we can methodically design data to create superior AI systems. This approach is referred to as DCAI [3]. DCAI uses AI technologies to more systematically identify and address problems that frequently afflict real-world datasets, whereas manual exploratory data analysis is an important initial step in understanding and enhancing any dataset. AI that is data-centric can take one of two shapes:

1. AI algorithms that comprehend data and enhance models with that knowledge. This is seen in curriculum learning, where ML models are initially trained on "easy data".
2. Data-modifying AI algorithms that enhance AI models. This is exemplified by confident learning, in which ML models are trained on a filtered dataset with incorrectly identified data eliminated [4].

Both of the aforementioned examples use algorithms to analyze the outputs of trained ML models to automatically estimate which data is simple or incorrectly categorized.

The foundation of DCAI is the collection of diverse, high-quality data [5]. The popularity of methods like active learning and federated learning has made it possible to collect data from many sources effectively [6]. Additionally, data labeling and annotation are essential to supervised learning. The process of annotating data is being revolutionized by improvements in methodologies like weak supervision and semi-supervised learning, which make the procedure more effective and scalable. Cleaning, standardization, and feature scaling are examples of preprocessing techniques used to get data ready for AI models. By broadening the dataset, data augmentation methods including rotation, translation, and generative approaches improve model performance. In order for the AI model to extract reliable and generalized patterns from the data, preprocessing and augmentation are necessary. The privacy of user data is a major concern in DCAI. Data privacy must be protected throughout the AI lifecycle due to rising data breaches and privacy laws. Emerging technologies like differential privacy, federated learning and homomorphic encryption enable AI progress while protecting individual privacy. As a result of its use in modifying AI models for certain applications, domain-specific data is becoming more and more important. A potent method to use domain-specific data is transfer learning, a technique where models learned on one task are adapted for another related one. Pre-trained models can be fine-tuned to drastically cut down on training time and data requirements, opening up AI to more specialized sectors. Biases found in training data can make AI models continue to be unfair and discriminatory. A persistent problem in DCAI is addressing biases in the data and assuring fairness. To reduce biases and encourage justice in AI applications, strategies like adversarial debiasing and fairness restrictions are being investigated. Despite improvements, there are still problems in the field of DCAI. Managing biases and ensuring privacy, along with the rising demand for large-scale, high-quality data, provide significant hurdles. To meet the changing demands of DCAI, future initiatives include establishing standardized

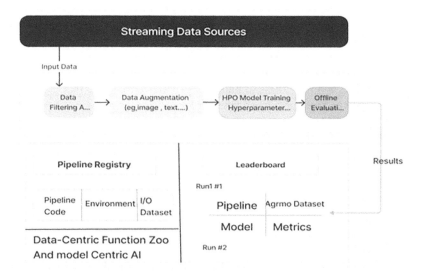

FIGURE 2.1 AI development life cycle.

tools for data management, producing synthetic data for improved generalization, and encouraging interdisciplinary collaboration.

DCAI is the discipline of systematically engineering data used to build an AI system [7]. Many researchers have defined DCAI in many different ways, some of them as "the discipline of systematically engineering the data used to build an AI system". As shown in Figure 2.1, the prime approach in DCAI is to take data to center stage or move the data to a centralized unit to make data accessible in the entire AI development lifecycle. Here, we can access data taken at all the stages of the AI lifecycle.

DCAI is based on the objective of providing the best dataset to feed a given ML model, while model-centric AI is based on the goal of producing the best model for a given dataset [8]. One should do both in order to implement the best-supervised learning systems in practice. A DCAI includes the following activities:

1. Investigate the data, correct any major problems, and then change it so that it is ML-appropriate.
2. Utilizing the correctly prepared dataset, train a foundational ML model.
3. Make use of this model to help you enhance the dataset using the methods covered in this class.
4. To obtain the optimal model, experiment with various modeling strategies on the improved dataset

The greatest way to boost performance in real-world ML applications is frequently through the study of techniques to enhance datasets, which is what DCAI is studying. While competent data scientists have long used trial-and-error and intuition to improve data, DCAI views data improvement as a structured engineering discipline.

2.2.1   Key Components of DCAI

1. Image Data Augmentation

Data augmentation in simple words means increasing the size and diversity of a dataset by creating a new set of data by applying transformations to existing data. The main goal of data augmentation is to improve the separation quality, and robustness of data in a generalized form so that it can be easily used and available in a particular form.

Key features of data augmentation are as follows:
- Rotation is the rotation by a certain angle to simulate different orientations.
- Flipping of images horizontally or vertically to create mirror images.
- Color jittering light and color of the image be adjusted and simulated.
- Data augmentation provides befts like reduced overfitting by preventing memorizing, effectively increase the amount of training dataset and many more.

2. Data Acquisition and Collection

The main and core point in DCAI is the acquisition of relevant and diverse datasets.

Here, identifying and collecting high-quality data is the main challenge for us. These are again divided into structured data, unstructured data, and semi-structured data.

3. Data Preprocessing and Cleaning

Data preprocessing plays a crucial role in DCAI applications, as the quality and suitability of the data used for training models directly impact their performance and reliability. One of the most challenging and tedious tasks is cleaning the data because the data does not only have a set of data but also data with biased data which need to be sorted and separated for further implementation. Data preprocessing involves cleaning, transforming, and standardizing the data to make it suitable for model training as we know that AI models learn for meaningful patterns from the data. Its emphasis is placed on the quality, diversity, and effective processing of data.

4. Model Training and Tuning

In DCAI, models are trained using large volumes of high-quality data. The iterative process of model training and hyperparameter tuning aims to optimize the model's performance by learning from the patterns.

5. Training data

i. Training data is a collection of data instances used to teach ML models. Constructing high-quality training data is critical to achieving DCAI. It is again subdivided into five parts – Data collection (Gathering of raw data)

ii. Data labeling (Adding an extra bit of information to data samples)

iii. Data preparation (Transforming raw data to suitable form)

iv. Data reduction (Reducing data size and making it simple and understandable)

v. Data augmentation (Increasing data diversity by creating modified samples without collecting extra data)

6. Data Preprocessing and cleaning

DCAI approach expects the removal or correction of inaccuracies, inconsistencies, and errors in the dataset to enhance data quality and convert data into a standardized format for better model performance and reducing biases as shown in Figure 2.2.

Nearly, every industry experiences problems with data quality, and handling them manually is incredibly time-consuming. It becomes impossible to guarantee the quality of datasets as they get bigger without the use of

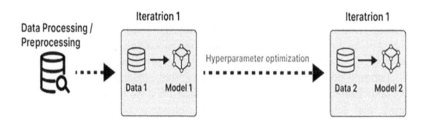

FIGURE 2.2 Data preprocessing.

algorithms [9]. In an effort to address problems brought on by low-quality training data, recent ML systems trained on large datasets like ChatGPT have depended heavily on labor (human feedback); nonetheless, such efforts have not been completely successful [10]. To guarantee that ML models are being trained with clean data, we require automated procedures and methodical engineering principles more than before. It is crucial that these systems are trained in a trustworthy manner as ML becomes more and more integrated into our daily lives in the areas of healthcare, finance, and transportation. Recent studies have shown how useful DCAI is for a variety of applications. A recent benchmark investigated various techniques to train models under increasing noise rates in the renowned Cifar-10 dataset [11] for image classification with noisy labeled data. The results showed that simple methods that adaptively alter the dataset can provide models that are significantly more accurate than methods that attempt to account for noise through complex modeling techniques.

2.3   EVALUATION OF DATA

The assessment of data within a DCAI framework is a vital step to ensure that the data utilized for training and operating AI models is of high quality and relevance. This involves a methodical evaluation of the data's appropriateness for the intended AI application. Key considerations encompass verifying data accuracy, distribution, bias, and label reliability. Additionally, it involves analyzing diversity, temporal dynamics, and potential for data augmentations. Ensuring ethical compliance and implementing validation techniques further enhance the data's reliability and its impact on model performance. Through this comprehensive evaluation, organizations can identify potential issues, ensuring the data's integrity and the effectiveness of AI models in real-world scenarios.

Assessing and understanding the model quality is crucial before deployment. Hence, there is a need to validate the data. In DCAI, two techniques are used, namely

- In-distribution evaluation data (evaluation data refers to testing samples that follow the same distribution as the training data.)
- Out-distribution evaluation data (evaluation data means the testing samples follow a distribution that differs from the training data)

2.4   DATA MAINTENANCE

Data management in DCAI involves maintaining the quality and relevance of data used for training models. This encompasses continuous data collection, monitoring, and cleaning. It also requires accurate labeling, data augmentation, and adapting data to changing domains. Feedback between model performance and data quality is important. Ethical considerations and privacy must be upheld. Documentation, versioning, and data governance are crucial. Long-term planning and automation enhance sustainability. Effective data maintenance ensures AI systems provide accurate insights over time. In production scenarios, data is not created once but rather continuously updated. Data maintenance is a significant challenge that DCAI has to consider to ensure data reliability in a dynamic environment.

2.5 MODEL-CENTRIC AI

In AI, a "model" is something that is referred to as a mathematical or computational representation that understands behavior within data by capturing various patterns and relationships. Models are the core of many AI techniques such as ML and deep learning [12].

In model-centric AI, the main or brute force approach is developing experimental research to improve the ML model performance. This involves selecting the best model architecture that will be favorable to that dataset and training process from a wide range of possibilities as follows:

- Model Design and Architecture
- Model Interpretability
- Model transfer and adaptation
- Model optimization and training techniques
- Model ethical and responsible AI
- Model Lifecycle Management

Currently, many AI applications are based on model-centric AI. In this, we focus on the improvement of code or model architecture to make the use of data in a much more efficient way. As we know, here, data is now stored in proper structure and the proper format it makes it easy for us to get and set data which again makes it more convenient and efficient for us to use that data. The distinction between model-centric AI and data-centric AI is summarized in Table 2.1

TABLE 2.1
Comparison between Model-Centric and Data-Centric AI

Category	Model-Centric AI	Data-Centric AI
System Development Process	Progressive upgrade of algorithm and code having constant volume and fixed type of data	Enhancing the data quality consistently while keeping the model hyperparameters constant
Performance	Excels primarily while dealing with substantial or extensive datasets	Shows optimal performance while working with a modest or compact dataset
Robustness	Susceptible to adversarial samples	Higher adversarial robustness
Applicability	In model-centric AI, selecting the right hyperparameters is critical for achieving optimal model performance	Data-centric AI often involves using a variety of ML algorithms and models to extract insights from data
Generalization	Balanced complexity of the model is essential overlay complex model may fit the data perfectly but fails the generalization to new data	Generalization starts with the collection of drivers and representative data from real world

2.6   TRANSFORMING FROM MODEL-CENTRIC AI TO DCAI

In previous years, ML research primarily concentrated on enhancing the design of models to achieve better performance. This involved comparing different model architectures using established datasets, both in practical competitions and academic studies. This approach, centered around improving models, led to significant advancements in model architectures over time.

However, this strategy of solely refining model architectures has reached a point of diminishing returns in terms of substantial performance improvements on well-known datasets. Likewise, focusing on refining complex model architectures does not always lead to significant performance gains when dealing with real-world datasets. Additionally, practitioners often aim to apply ML to models. Because of this, the attention of both researchers and practitioners is gradually shifting toward the importance of data – the somewhat overlooked component in the development of AI systems.

Particularly, there's a growing realization that systematic work with data is crucial for enhancing the data used to train ML models. Data plays a pivotal role in enabling an ML model to derive insights. Therefore, the quantity of data (such as the number of instances) and its quality (including relevance and accuracy of labels) have a substantial impact on the performance of AI systems. The concepts of DCAI embody the shift in perspective. It emphasizes the significance of data as a focal point for improving AI systems, acknowledging that the quality and quantity of data fundamentally influence how well these systems perform.

DCAI and model-centric AI differ in their core focus, the role of domain knowledge, and the understanding of data quality:

1. **Focus**:

    In DCAI, the primary emphasis is on keeping the model architecture constant while striving to enhance performance by improving the quality and quantity of the data used for training.

    On the other hand, model-centric revolves around refining the model's design and structure to achieve better performance, with the dataset being relatively fixed.

2. **Data Work and Domain Knowledge**:

    DCAI demands a deep understanding of both the specific model architecture being employed and the domain of the problem at hand. This includes a comprehensive grasp of the underlying data. The process involves domain-specific data manipulation and analysis. Moreover, the development of techniques and tools that partially automate tasks contributes to the creation of effective AI systems.

    Model-centric AI may not require as detailed a domain understanding, as the primary efforts are directed toward optimizing the model's structure.

3. **Data Quality Understanding**:

    Modifying the foundation data raises the performance enhancements in DCAI. Consequently, shifts in metrics used to measure the effectiveness of ML models also reflect the impact of data adjustments. This offers a fresh perspective on gauging data quality, approximated by changes in ML metrics.

In model-centric AI, changes in performance metrics are more directly attributed to adjustments in the model architecture.

2.7 CHALLENGES IN DCAI

Although very advantageous, adopting a data-centric strategy in AI poses a number of difficulties that businesses and practitioners must successfully overcome to fully realize the potential of their AI models. These are the main issues with DCAI – Modeling and Design of Data. To address these issues and lay the groundwork for DCAI, a multidisciplinary strategy is needed that incorporates technological breakthroughs, effective data management techniques, ethical considerations, and regulatory compliance.

- Data Corruption
- Data Imbalance
- Continuous data collection and updating
- Data Fusion and Integration
- Data privacy and security
- Data bias and fairness

2.7.1 MODELING AND DESIGN OF DATA

One of the basic and most important things is structuring the data in the correct form as when data we are getting in bulk form and dealing with such a huge amount of is not so easy, and if we do not arrange it in the specific order or the correct manner, then it will have the huge time complexity and it will be also unsecured.

Effective data modeling and design are essential for building AI systems that deliver valuable insights and predictions. The process is iterative and may involve experimentation with different modeling techniques and data representations to achieve the best results for your specific problem.

Collaboration between data scientists, domain experts, and IT professionals is often necessary to ensure a successful DCAI project.

- Data Exploration and Understanding
- Data Preprocessing
- Data Collection
- Data Splitting
- Model Selecting
- Model Training

2.7.2 DATA CORRUPTION

As we know if our data is not correct or is corrupted, then it will produce the wrong output and lead disform of our system. So, data correctness is the most important part, and to correct this, data on a huge scale is a big challenge because the sources from which we are getting the data are not reliable, so need a strong method to make it more successful work. Data corruption can occur at various stages of the AI life-cycle and can have several.

Data is a fundamental component of AI systems, and its quality directly impacts the performance and reliability of these models. Data corruption can occur at various stages of the AI lifecycle and can stem from several causes.

- Data collection Errors
- Data Storage and Transfer Issues
- Data Preprocessing Mistakes
- Data Labeling Errors
- Data Integration Challenges
- Data Augmentation Issues

2.7.3 DATA IMBALANCE

In real-world scenarios, data may be unevenly distributed across classes or catego-ries. It is a situation where the distribution of classes or categories in a dataset is sig-nificantly skewed, with some classes having much fewer instances than others. This can lead to models that are biased toward the majority class and perform poorly on minority classes. This imbalance can pose challenges when training and evaluating ML models, as the models may become biased toward the majority class and perform poorly on minority classes.

2.7.4 CONTINUOUS DATA COLLECTION AND UPDATING

The updating of data gives a user correct information about the current situation and continuously updates with new data to adapt to changing conditions. Also, maintain-ing the model's performance as new data becomes available can be complex. To ensure that AI models remain effective, it's essential to establish processes for ongo-ing data collection, updating, and integration.

Continuous data collection and updating are integral to the success of DCAI sys-tems, as they help ensure that models are adaptive, accurate, and capable of providing valuable insights in dynamic environments. Also, there is a need for reviewing and optimizing data collection processes, which is an ongoing effort that is essential for staying competitive and relevant in AI-driven applications.

2.7.5 DATA FUSION AND INTEGRATION

In data fusion, we combine data from multiple sources, especially when dealing with heterogeneous data and can be challenging due to differences in formats, scales, and quality.

Also, we have seen an imbalance in that her data is heterogeneous, which may lead to incorrect structure formation and will directly hurt the whole data format.

The main goal is to extract meaningful insights or knowledge by combining diverse sources of information so that it is easily available.

- **Sensor Data Fusion**: Here, we have combined data from multiple sensors to improve the accuracy and reliability of measurements. This is sometimes often used in fields like robotics, autonomous vehicles, and military applications.
- **Feature-Level Fusion**: Here, we combine different features or attributes of data from various sources. For example, combining different text data with image data in natural language processing and computer vision applications.
- **Decision-Level Fusion**– Combining the decisions or outputs of multiple algorithms or models to make a final decision. This is common in ensemble learning where multiple models are combined to improve.

2.7.6 DATA PRIVACY AND SECURITY

Working with sensitive data we need to ensure that data is safe and secure. Anonymization, encryption, and access control techniques like this should be implemented to protect sensitive data. In this interconnected world, the security and protection of data is one of the most important and tedious tasks, along with data management. This involves safeguarding sensitive information from unauthorized access, breaches, and misuse while respecting individual's rights to control their data.

- **Key Principles**
  - **Consent**: Individuals should have informed consent for the collection and use of their data.
  - **Data Minimization**: Collect data which need and avoid additional access to data used on the current user login.
  - **Transparency**: One of the main and important policies that should be specified to the user is transparency; it should be all clear to the user and nothing should be hidden.

2.7.7 DATA BIAS AND FAIRNESS

We know that AI is created on some data, if the data is biased that can lead to a biased AI model. Developing techniques and metrics to measure and reduce bias in AI models is one of the important challenges. The bias can lead to inaccurate and improper predictions or reinforce existing system enforcement.

- **Fairness**: Fairness in ML refers to the goal of ensuring that models and algorithms treat all individuals and do not discriminate against any particular demographic or social group. Achieving fairness is essential to prevent the reinforcement of existing biases and to promote ethical and equitable outcomes.
  - **Individual Fairness**: This principle aims to treat similar individuals similarly. In other words, if any two things and these two things have similarities in them, then the model preparation should be similar.
  - **Group fairness**: It focuses on ensuring that predictions are fair at a group level, particularly concerning sensitive attributes like race, gender, or ethnicity.

This involves avoiding disparate impact, where certain groups are disproportionately affected by a model's predictions.

Data bias and fairness are ongoing concerns in the field of ML, and addressing these issues is crucial for building trustworthy and ethical AI systems that benefit society as a whole.

Design scalable and enhanced data architecture which is the need for your AI. Use proper database systems and data storage solutions to manage and fetch data easily and efficiently. We can create data pipelines that self-operate the process of cleaning, transforming, and integrating data [5], which check data accuracy before setting data into AI. We can implement a self-operating data validation process that identifies the inconsistencies in the incoming data. Create data recovery systems like backups and versioning to restore clean data if it gets corrupted. Apply techniques like the Synthetic Minority Oversampling Technique (SMOTE) to balance class distribution in training data. Real-time data ingestion pipelines collect real-time data and process it, which ensures that AI has updated data. If we can Store the data in the blockchain and provide access to data can resolve the problem of security, as we have seen that data is getting imbalance, we will divide the data in form of small, distributed, and structured chunks so that the data is now in structured and distributed format; this chunks will be the single block of this blockchain and will be accessed by the authenticated user only.

2.8   CONCLUSION

This chapter describes that model-centric AI and DCAI have highlighted important factors that have a big impact on the efficiency and dependability of AI models. When developing and implementing AI systems, the problems outlined in the data-centric approach must be taken into account. The distinctions between model-centric AI and DCAI were emphasized, highlighting the significance of creating a scalable and improved data architecture for successful AI implementation. Important tactics include using appropriate database systems, applying data validation procedures, and using methods like SMOTE for data balance. In addition, utilizing blockchain for distributed, secure data storage is a viable answer to the problems with data security and imbalance. To design AI systems that are dependable, precise, and unbiased and eventually contribute to a more robust and fairer AI-driven future, it is crucial to acknowledge and effectively address these problems in DCAI.

REFERENCES

1. Zha, Daochen, Bhat, Zaid Pervaiz, Lai, Kwei-Herng, Hu, Xia et al. (2023). Data-centric AI: Perspectives and challenges. doi:10.48550/arXiv.2301.04819.
2. Mingyang, Wan, Zha, Daochen, Liu, Ninghao, and Zou, Na. (2023). In-processing modeling techniques for machine learning fairness: A survey. *ACM Transactions on Knowledge Discovery from Data* 17, 3, 1–27
3. Press, G. (2021). Andrew Ng launches a campaign for data-centric AI. *Forbes*.
4. Northcutt, C., Jiang, L., and Chuang, I. L. (2021) Confident learning: Estimating uncertainty in dataset labels. *Journal of Artificial Intelligence Research*, 70, 1373–1411

5. Patel, Hima, Guttula, Shanmukha, Gupta, Nitin, Hans, Sandeep, Mittal, Ruhi, and Lokesh, N. (2023). A data centric AI framework for automating exploratory data analysis and data quality tasks. *Journal of Data and Information Quality*. doi:10.1145/3603709.

6. Zhang, Huaizheng, Huang, Yizheng, and Li, Yuanming. (2023). DataCI: A platform for data-centric AI on streaming data.

7. Verdecchia, Roberto, Cruz, Luís, Sallou, June, Lin, Michelle, Wickenden, James, and Hotellier, Estelle. (2022). Data-centric green AI: An exploratory empirical study. doi:10.1109/ICT4S55073.2022.00015.

8. Khang P.H, Alex, Gujrati, Rashmi, Rani, Sita, Uygun, Hayri, and Gupta, Dr-Shashi. (2023). Designing workforce management systems for industry 4.0: Data-centric and AI-enabled approaches. doi:10.1201/9781003357070.

9. Chiang, T. (2023). ChatGPT is a blurry JPEG of the Web, February, 2023, https://www.newyorker.com

10. Lee, Youngjune, Kwon, Oh Joon, Lee, Haeju, Kim, Joonyoung, Lee, Kangwook and Kim, Kee-Eung. (2021). Augment, valuate: A data enhancement pipeline for data-Centric AI. In: *NeurIPS Data-Centric AI Workshop*. arXiv preprint arXiv:2112.03837.

11. Redman, T. (2016). Bad data costs the U.S. \$3 trillion per year. *Harvard Business Review*, 22, 11–18.

12. Jarrahi, Mohammad, Memariani, Ali, and Guha, Shion. (2022). The principles of data-centric AI (DCAI). doi:10.48550/arXiv.2211.14611.

3 Unleashing the Power of Industry 4.0

A Harmonious Blend of Data-Centric and Model-Centric AI

Manivannan Karunakaran, Batri Krishnan,
D. Shanthi, J. Benadict Raja,
and B. Sakthi Karthi Durai

3.1 INTRODUCTION

Industry 4.0, often referred to as the fourth industrial revolution, has ignited a transformative wave of automation, leading to the emergence of novel industrial applications that have the potential to reshape how humans interact with machines [1]. In response to this revolution, businesses are progressively moving away from conventional automation approaches, which heavily depend on the expertise of human developers and the use of application programming interfaces for service platforms [2]. The fourth industrial revolution, also known as Industry 4.0, has brought about a transformation in engineering systems, seamlessly integrating sensing capabilities, computational power, control, and networking into cyber-physical objects. These objects are interconnected through the Internet of Things (IoTs) [3].

Industry 4.0 is distinguished by its reliance on data, which plays a prominent role across various technologies [4]. Cloud computing facilitates the effective storage, analysis, and processing of vast amounts of data in the cloud [5]. Edge computing, on the other hand, minimizes latency in real-time production operations by efficiently analyzing data near the sensors [6]. Digital twins play a crucial role in simulating various systems' processes in virtual environments, utilizing data from IoT sensors and interconnected objects [7]. Artificial intelligence (AI) and machine learning (ML) are crucial components in handling the vast data volumes of Industry 4.0 [8]. AI systems, mainly algorithms (code), learn prototypical features from extensive data to solve problems across different formats like text, audio, image, and video. ML, a subset of AI, enables AI systems to detect imperceptible patterns using general-purpose procedures, solving problems without explicit programming [9].

Data preparation involves human experts labeling and curating data for context and interpretation, known as "data annotation." In the context of AI and ML,

DOI: 10.1201/9781003461500-4

data-centric AI and model-centric AI represent two distinct approaches to improving AI system performance [10]. Model-centric AI focuses on iterative upgrades to the algorithm while keeping data volumes and types constant. In contrast, data-centric AI emphasizes continuous improvement of data quality to achieve optimal performance, irrespective of the model [11]. Rather than advocating for either approach exclusively, this chapter advocates a balanced "both/and" perspective, reconciling data-centric AI with model-centric AI. It highlights the limitations of model-centric AI and underscores the importance of integrating data-centric AI to overcome these limitations [12]. Within the ML community, there are two contrasting perspectives when it comes to enhancing AI system performance: model-centric AI and data-centric AI. Model-centric AI involves continuous iterations to improve the algorithm while keeping the data volume and type constant. Conversely, data-centric AI emphasizes the continual enhancement of data quality to achieve superior performance in managing data noise (Figure 3.1). Both model-centric AI and data-centric AI involve continuous, iterative processes, often referred to as model-cycle and data-cycle approaches [13]. For the past three decades, model-centric AI has been the prevailing approach in both research and industry, representing over 90% of published AI research projects [14]. However, in recent times, there has been a notable shift in favor of data-centric AI. This change in perspective is driven by several factors, such as the limited availability of large datasets and the growing demand for customized solutions [15]. Andrew Ng, the founder of "DeepLearning.AI" and Adjunct Professor at Stanford University, introduced the concept of data-centric AI. This approach demonstrated remarkable superiority over the model-centric approach in terms of accuracy and learning speed for detecting steel defects. Furthermore, the data-centric approach exhibited excellent performance in other tasks, including solar defect detection and surface inspection [16]. Interestingly, when the audience was asked whether to enhance the model's accuracy by improving the code or the data, the majority of voters in the live stream opted to improve the data, highlighting the

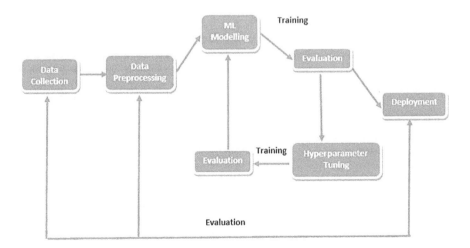

FIGURE 3.1   Data-centric AI.

growing recognition of the importance of data-centric AI [17]. Rather than advocating for a rigid "either/or" perspective, this work promotes a more inclusive "both/and" approach. While illustrating the relative effectiveness of data-centric AI would require rigorous experimental procedures comparing it to model-centric AI, conducting such a comprehensive study exceeds the current research scope. Nevertheless, there is a discernible shift in the AI/ML community, with more researchers endorsing the transition from model-centric to data-centric approaches. While showcasing the capabilities of data-centric AI is crucial, it is essential to acknowledge that isolated success stories from experimental research cannot conclusively establish its superiority over other alternatives, including model-centric AI. To truly demonstrate the superiority of data-centric AI, experimental results should be provided across various applications, acknowledging the challenges inherent in research studies [18].

3.1.1 CONTRIBUTION

This chapter significantly extends prior research [19]. We employ a comparative analysis methodology to contrast data-centric AI and model-centric AI (Table 3.1). The analysis draws from Andrew Ng's live stream presentation on 24 March 2021 [20]. This chapter also considers the growing number of researchers who support the transition from model-centric AI to data-centric AI. The main thesis of this chapter is that while model-centric AI may have its limitations in terms of performance, embracing a collaborative approach that combines both data-centric and model-centric methodologies would lead to more substantial advancements in current AI technology compared to focusing solely on improving datasets, despite the critical importance of dataset enhancement. The key contributions of this chapter can be summarized as follows:

In Section 3.2, we present a succinct review and comprehensive discussion of the deep learning (DL) technique and its pivotal role in propelling current AI advancements. Sections 3.4 and 3.5 establish crucial connections between current AI, cyber security, and natural language inference (NLI). We emphasize the drawbacks of model-centric AI, particularly regarding its algorithmic stability and robustness. We specifically point out examples like adversarial samples and hypothesis-only biases to illustrate the difficulties faced in this approach. In Section 3.6, we delve into the motivation for adopting the data-centric AI approach, particularly emphasizing the significant impact of the IoTs' continuous expansion, supported by the latest relevant data. Finally, in Section 3.7, we reconcile the data-centric AI perspective with model-centric AI, presenting additional arguments in favor of the "both/and" approach over the less optimal "either/or" stance. By exploring the benefits of combining both methodologies, we shed light on the synergistic potential of this collaborative approach.

3.2 RELATED WORK

3.2.1 THE CRUCIAL ROLE OF DL IN CONTEMPORARY AI

In history, it was John McCarthy (1927–2011) who first coined the term "Artificial Intelligence" in 1956. He provided a definition, describing AI as the "science and

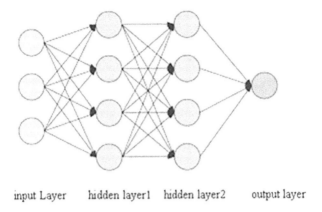

input Layer   hidden layer1   hidden layer2   output layer

FIGURE 3.2 Artificial neural network with hidden layer.

engineering of creating intelligent machines, particularly intelligent computer programs" [21]. In modern times, much of the excitement in the field of AI is centered
around DL [22], an advanced form of artificial neural network (ANN) (Figure 3.2).
In the rapid advancement of AI/ML capabilities, DL has consistently demonstrated
human-level performance in various applications. DL has demonstrated remarkable
capabilities in various domains. It excels in tasks like object classification, outper-
forming human performance, and defeating world-class players in complex games
like Go and Poker. Additionally, DL has showcased its potential in medical applications, accurately identifying cancer from X-ray scans [23]. Furthermore, it has
proven to be effective in natural language processing tasks, facilitating text translation across different languages. Curiously, although the theoretical groundwork
for DL was established as early as the 1940s, it wasn't until 2012 that researchers
from the AI/ML community and related domains recognized its resemblance to the
mechanisms of the human brain. This revelation solidified DL as the technique that
most closely resembles the complex neural processes underlying human intelligence.
Their DL algorithm demonstrated significantly higher performance and accuracy
compared to previous state-of-the-art algorithms, solidifying DL's position as a
groundbreaking technique in the field of AI. This victory in the ImageNet contest
highlighted the transformative potential of DL and its ability to outperform traditional approaches in complex tasks, further fueling the excitement surrounding this
powerful AI methodology.

In a typical ANN, learning takes place by adjusting the "weights," represented as
w, that amplify or attenuate signals denoted by x, which are transmitted through connections between nodes in the ANN. The ANN contains several hidden layers, resembling processing centers akin to those in the human brain and employs backpropagation
of gradients. In each layer of ANNs, the total input z is calculated as the weighted
sum of the outputs from the previous layer. Subsequently, a nonlinear function $f(.)$ is
applied to z, generating the output of the unit. Commonly used nonlinear functions in
ANNs include the rectified linear unit (ReLU) $f(z) = \max(0, z)$, as well as traditional
sigmoids such as the hyperbolic tangent $f(z) = (\exp(z) - \exp(-z))/(\exp(z) + \exp(-z))$

and the logistic function $f(z) = 1/(1 + \exp(-z))$ [3]. These activation functions introduce nonlinearity to the neural network, enabling it to model complex relationships and learn from data more effectively.

In contrast to traditional ANNs, DL networks acquire data representations at various levels of abstraction. The achievement of modeling complex relationships in neural networks is made possible by employing a significantly higher number of layers. These layers consist of simple, nonlinear modules known as neurons, which play a pivotal role in transforming the internal representation of specific input data aspects from one layer to a higher-level internal representation. As data passes through multiple layers, the neural network learns to abstract and represent increasingly complex features, allowing it to capture intricate patterns and relationships in the data. This hierarchical approach to representation learning enables deep neural networks to tackle challenging tasks and achieve remarkable performance in various applications. The backpropagation algorithm fine-tunes the neural network's weights by working back down through the layers, adjusting each weight proportionally based on its contribution to the overall error. DL networks are characterized by their significant depth, typically ranging from 5 to 20 layers, which is what earned them the name "deep" networks. However, in modern commercial applications, neural network models frequently employ over 100 layers, emphasizing their ability to scale too much larger depths. This substantial depth enables DL models to learn hierarchical representations and abstract complex features from raw input data, allowing them to handle intricate tasks effectively. In contrast to classical ML techniques, which rely on human experts to carefully engineer features and extract relevant aspects of input data, DL models possess the ability to autonomously learn these representations directly from the data. This process, known as feature learning or representation learning, allows DL models to operate without explicit human intervention in the feature extraction step. This characteristic is particularly advantageous as it reduces the burden of manual feature engineering and enables DL models to adapt to a wide range of tasks and datasets, making them highly flexible and powerful tools in various applications. DL algorithms implicitly learn features from data using general-purpose procedures. The exceptional capability of DL has drawn comparisons to the problem-solving approach of the human brain. Additionally, a significant finding in the field is that ANNs, with a non-polynomial activation function, possess the ability to approximate any continuous function with arbitrary accuracy. This finding, known as the universal approximation theorem, mathematically establishes the equivalence of ANNs to universal computers. In essence, this theorem confirms that DL models can represent and approximate a wide range of complex functions, making them highly versatile and powerful tools for solving diverse problems. This unique combination of human brain-like problem-solving and mathematical prowess has contributed to the widespread success and adoption of DL in numerous domains and applications.

The evolution of DL into its current state and the fulfillment of many early aspirations of AI researchers can be attributed to several significant factors. A critical aspect is DL's ability to excel when presented with abundant and diverse data from various sources in the Global Data sphere. This extensive data sphere encompasses textual, visual, and acoustic data and comprises a wide range of sources, including

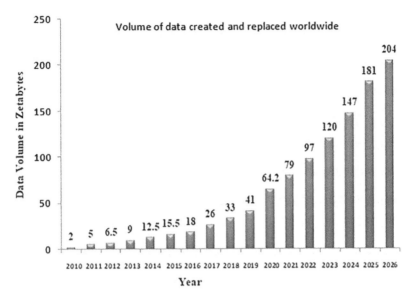

FIGURE 3.3   Projected annual data creation, consumption, and storage according to IDC.

cloud data centers, enterprise infrastructure, endpoints such as PCs, smartphones, sensors, social media platforms, wearable devices, and many more. The availability of such large volumes of data from diverse origins has been instrumental in fueling the advancement and success of DL, enabling it to achieve exceptional performance across a multitude of applications and domains. DL algorithms require data to train models capable of identifying statistical similarities between current and previously observed instances to uncover hidden patterns through unsupervised learning and make future predictions for unseen instances through supervised learning. The performance and accuracy of the underlying algorithm increase with more granular, voluminous, and diverse data. As per the International Data Corporation (IDC), a renowned market intelligence company, the Global Data sphere is anticipated to experience an almost exponential growth (Figure 3.3). Notably, the volume of data created and replicated in 2010 was relatively modest, not surpassing 1 zettabyte (ZB). However, by the year 2020, this volume had expanded significantly, reaching 64.2 ZB, and it is projected to exceed 180 ZB by 2025 (1 ZB = 10^12 gigabytes). These staggering figures indicate the rapid expansion of data generation and replication on a global scale, highlighting the substantial growth potential and the immense data-driven opportunities that lie ahead for DL and other AI techniques.

3.3   GAP ANALYSIS

The book chapter "Driving Compact and Robust Industry 4.0 Solutions: The Synergy between Data-Centric and Model-Centric AI" delves into the integration of data-centric and model-centric approaches in developing Industry 4.0 solutions. The chapter emphasizes the significance of both methodologies and proposes a complementary interplay to optimize AI-driven solutions within the context of Industry 4.0. While the chapter provides valuable insights, several gaps in its content could be addressed to enhance its comprehensiveness and practicality. First, the chapter could benefit from more in-depth case studies that illustrate the successful application of data-centric and model-centric AI in real-world Industry 4.0 scenarios. These case studies would provide practical examples of how these approaches have been deployed, the challenges faced, and the solutions derived from their integration. Additionally, a comprehensive comparative analysis of the strengths and limitations of data-centric and model-centric AI would offer valuable insights into their individual contributions and the potential benefits of combining them. Another area that requires further exploration is the consideration of ethical aspects and data biases in AI applications. While the chapter briefly mentions the importance of addressing data biases, a more extensive discussion on techniques to mitigate biases and ensure fairness in AI models would be beneficial. Moreover, the challenges of real-time data processing in Industry 4.0 environments are crucial to address, as agile decision-making relies on timely feedback. Understanding the computational and architectural requirements for real-time data processing in both data-centric and model-centric AI models is essential for their practical implementation. The book chapter highlights the importance of integrating data-centric and model-centric AI approaches for robust Industry 4.0 solutions. However, addressing the identified gaps, such as the need for in-depth case studies, a comparative analysis, ethical considerations, and real-time data processing challenges would enhance the chapter's insights. By bridging these gaps, the chapter can offer valuable guidance to researchers, practitioners, and industry leaders seeking to harness the full potential of AI in Industry 4.0.

3.4   CHALLENGES FACED BY MODEL-CENTRIC AI

Model-centric AI primarily focuses on optimizing model architectures (algorithm/code) and their hyperparameters, while keeping the collected data fixed throughout the AI system's development. However, this approach faces significant limitations, including Model-centric AI performs well in businesses and industries with generalized solutions, where a single AI system can satisfy the majority of users, leaving outliers as negligible. Companies like Google and Facebook with vast standardized data in the advertising industry benefit from such solutions. However, industries like manufacturing, agriculture, and healthcare require tailored solutions, which cannot be provided by standardized models. Customized approaches, encompassing comprehensive and consistently labeled data, are essential for these sectors. Model-centric AI, especially DL networks, is susceptible to adversarial samples – instances with small, deliberate perturbations that cause false predictions. This phenomenon raises concerns about the stability and robustness of DL networks, potentially leading to security issues in various applications. For instance, in autonomous cars, adversaries can manipulate DL models, leading to dangerous situations. Healthcare applications relying on DL systems may also be compromised, affecting patient outcomes and costs. Model-centric AI algorithms may achieve high performance by exploiting annotation artifacts – context-free associations created during the dataset annotation process. In NLI, human annotators introduce cognitive heuristics, resulting in datasets with biases. While the model performs well on such datasets, it lacks generalization to new data without similar biases, demonstrating its low generalization capacity.

Prior to the widespread recognition of "data-centric AI," AI researchers and ML practitioners devoted significant efforts to curating datasets for training ML models. While some data instances were discovered to be invalid due to mislabeling, ambiguity, or irrelevance, their influence on model performance was often deemed insignificant. However, businesses and industries have now come to realize the crucial significance of prioritizing high-quality datasets throughout the entire development process of AI systems.

The foremost challenge lies in the scarcity of sufficiently large and diverse datasets. Unlike internet companies, manufacturing industries often have limited data, with training datasets containing only thousands of relevant data points. Consequently, ML models built on such limited data struggle to perform effectively when compared to models trained on massive datasets. In industries like manufacturing, where a variety of products are produced, a one-size-fits-all AI system for fault detection may not be sufficient. Each product demands its own uniquely trained ML system to ensure effective performance and accurate fault detection.

3.5   CHARACTERISTICS OF DATA-CENTRIC AI

Data-centric AI involves continuous evaluation of the AI model along with data updates (Table 3.1). Unlike model-centric AI, where the model is trained on a dataset only once during production, data-centric AI assumes successive improvements in data. This is especially beneficial for businesses and industries with limited data points, such as manufacturing, agriculture, and healthcare. The data-centric approach allows the model to encounter novel data instances during its lifespan, leading to more frequent model assessments and the ability to recognize and adapt to distributional data drifts. According to Statista and Transforma Insights, the number of IoT-connected devices worldwide is anticipated to undergo significant growth, with projections showing a tripling from 9.7 billion in 2020 to over 29 billion in 2030 and an increase from 7.6 billion in 2019 to 24.1 billion in 2030, respectively. This substantial growth is attributed to the escalating impact of digital transformation, further amplified by the effects of the COVID-19 pandemic. The increasing adoption of IoT technologies is driving this exponential growth, transforming industries across the globe and shaping the future of AI and data-centric AI applications.

The implementation of a data-centric approach involves a series of interconnected steps. It demands the integration of diverse expertise from different disciplines to empower AI systems and achieve optimal performance. In the following sections, we delineate several practical rules and criteria that play a pivotal role in successfully embracing a data-centric approach, ultimately leading to the development of more effective and efficient AI systems. One essential aspect of achieving a data-centric approach is curating datasets to ensure both the sufficiency and representativeness of data inputs. To achieve this, the devised model should access a wide range of task-relevant data inputs, including relevant information and noise present in real-life situations. Similar to the human brain's selective attention, the model should focus on goal-relevant aspects while filtering out distracting and noisy information. The success of AI models heavily relies on the quality of the data used for their training. In the data-centric AI paradigm, the focus shifts from merely fine-tuning the model's architecture and hyperparameters to prioritizing the acquisition of sufficient and representative data inputs. This chapter aims to explore the significance of adequate and representative data inputs for data-centric AI and how they contribute to achieving peak performance and robustness in AI systems. Data is the lifeblood of AI systems, serving as the foundation upon which models learn to make decisions and predictions. In data-centric AI, the emphasis is on obtaining datasets that not only contain a large volume of data but also encompass a diverse range of examples that reflect real-world scenarios. Adequate data inputs are crucial to ensure that AI models have enough information to learn complex patterns and relationships within the data, making them capable of solving the specific task at hand. The sufficiency of data inputs plays a pivotal role in the effectiveness of data-centric AI. Insufficient data can lead to underfitting, where the model fails to capture the underlying patterns in the data, resulting in poor performance. To ensure data sufficiency, researchers and practitioners need to carefully curate datasets that encompass a broad spectrum of instances relevant to the task. This includes not only positive examples but also negative and ambiguous instances, providing the model with a comprehensive understanding of the problem space. In addition to sufficiency, the data inputs must also be representative of the real-world scenarios that the AI system will encounter. A dataset that is biased or lacks diversity can lead to a model that performs well on the training data but fails to generalize to unseen data from different distributions. To address this, researchers must be vigilant in avoiding bias during data collection and ensure that the dataset accurately reflects the target population.

Curating datasets with adequate and representative data inputs can be challenging, especially in domains where data is scarce or subject to privacy constraints. However, there are several strategies to overcome these challenges. Collaborating with domain experts and stakeholders can help in identifying critical data attributes and real-world use cases. Data augmentation techniques can also be employed to increase the diversity of the dataset, enabling the model to learn from a wider range of instances. Adequate and representative data inputs are fundamental to the success of data-centric AI. By prioritizing the quality of data during the AI model development process, researchers and practitioners can create more robust and effective AI systems capable of generalizing to real-world scenarios. As the AI field continues to advance, the importance of data-centric AI will only grow, making it imperative for data scientists and AI engineers to focus on obtaining high-quality data inputs for their models.

Another key step in implementing a data-centric approach is ensuring high-quality data during data preparation. Research teams must be cautious of potential biases introduced during data labeling. To address this, textual descriptions can be incorporated as an intermediate step between data inputs and label assignments. These descriptions, consisting of 3–10-word sentences, provide contextual information reflecting human perspectives. Although this approach may extend data creation time, it proves beneficial for AI engineers as it ensures the collected data vividly captures the essential concepts required for effective learning by AI systems. Consequently,

AI systems can efficiently learn from smaller datasets, a common scenario in various industries. The third step entails the continuous engagement of both AI- and business-domain experts. Domain experts should take charge of data engineering as they possess in-depth knowledge of specific business use cases, enabling them to provide domain-specific representations of the real world. Their involvement in the evaluation process can enhance it significantly by designing domain-sensitive tests for the AI model, making AI more applicable and accessible across various industries. The fourth step involves the implementation of MLOps (Machine Learning Operations) platforms. By leveraging these platforms, research teams can reduce the time and effort spent on software development, leading to a decrease in the maintenance cost of AI applications. MLOps platforms offer essential software scaffolding for the production of AI systems, considerably reducing the time from proof of concept to production, transforming the timeline from years to mere weeks. These platforms encompass a range of MLOp tools that cater to both data-centric and model-centric AI, including data labeling, data cleaning, model storage, continuous integration, training, and deployment tools. Their adoption streamlines the development and deployment process, fostering efficient and scalable AI applications.

3.7   RECONCILING DATA-CENTRIC AI WITH MODEL-CENTRIC AI

At first glance, the instinct may be to concentrate on refining the model (algorithm/code), rather than enhancing the data to improve the performance and robustness of an AI system. Nevertheless, taking into account the constraints of model-centric AI and the challenges encountered by DL-based models, as discussed in Section 3.5 (or summarized in Table 3.1), the significance of data-centric approaches becomes

---

TABLE 3.1
Distinguishing Traits of Model-Centric AI and Data-Centric AI

Category	Model-Centric AI	Data-Centric AI
• System development lifecycle	• The iterative enhancement of a model (algorithm/code) using a fixed volume and type of data	• Consistent enhancement in the data quality with unchanging model hyperparameters
• Performance	• Demonstrates high performance primarily with extensive datasets	• Demonstrates strong performance even with smaller datasets
• Robustness	• Vulnerable to adversarial samples	• Exhibits higher resilience against adversarial samples
• Applicability	• Suitable for evaluating algorithmic solutions in applications with specific and limited tasks	• Especially well-suited for real-world scenarios and applications
• Generalization	• Limited ability to generalize across datasets due to a lack of contextual understanding	• Likely to achieve good generalization across various datasets beyond the ones used for testing

apparent. We advocate for a balanced approach, recognizing that both model-centric and data-centric methods are interconnected aspects that influence each other. Embracing this interconnectedness allows for a more comprehensive and effective AI development strategy, fostering advancements in performance and robustness while capitalizing on the strengths of both approaches.

While the idea of transitioning to data-centric AI due to model-centric limitations is appealing, creating new datasets can be costly and may not guarantee freedom from new artifacts or biases. Human annotators might still introduce subtle cognitive strategies, affecting the model's generalization capability. Therefore, a better approach is to simultaneously improve both the model and data, recognizing their interdependence and treating them as complementary aspects. Effective problem-solving in AI systems necessitates a holistic consideration of both the "how-to" (model) and the "what-is" (data) aspects. Just as our natural problem-solving approach involves both action and understanding properties, AI development also requires a balanced focus on algorithm design and hyperparameter optimization to devise effective models. Simultaneously, the utilization of a consistent dataset is essential for accurate model comparison and comprehensive performance evaluation. By integrating these components, AI developers can create robust and high-performing AI systems, leveraging the interplay between algorithms and datasets to achieve optimal problem-solving capabilities.

Conversely, adopting a model-centric approach offers valuable opportunities to accumulate experience in real-world problem-solving and computational solutions. By taking action and gaining insights, developers can develop a deeper understanding of the environment, analogous to how intelligent agents learn through reinforcement learning, a celebrated ML technique [6,8]. This process of iterative learning and continuous improvement allows AI systems to refine their problem-solving capabilities over time, adapting to complex and dynamic environments effectively. The model-centric approach serves as a stepping stone for honing AI systems' performance and enabling them to achieve increasingly sophisticated problem-solving skills. Indeed, the limitations of models do not necessarily equate to the limitation of modeling itself. Aristotle's first-principles thinking underscores the importance of understanding fundamental aspects to discover effective solutions. In the context of the NLI task, models might learn from annotation artifacts, resulting in high performance on biased datasets but faltering on unbiased ones. This observation highlights the significance of being mindful of the underlying biases and limitations of the data when designing AI models. It also emphasizes the need for more comprehensive and unbiased datasets to foster the development of robust and unbiased AI systems capable of generalizing effectively to diverse real-world scenarios.

Absolutely, acknowledging the limitations of models does not imply that the model-centric approach is inherently restricted, especially in the context of NLI. A deeper understanding of how artifacts emerge from disregarding premise-hypothesis relationships can inform the design of models to mitigate such learning issues. For instance, Belinkov et al. proposed an innovative approach by inputting both the hypothesis and the entailment label to predict the premise. This diverges from the conventional NLI models that predict an entailment label based on a premise-hypothesis pair. By adopting novel strategies that capture and exploit crucial relationships, model-centric AI can overcome certain limitations, leading to more accurate and robust performance in NLI tasks and other applications. This showcases the dynamic nature of the model-centric approach, which can evolve and adapt to address specific challenges and achieve improved results in various AI tasks. To enhance the robustness of DL/ML models and foster a harmonious interplay between data-centric and model-centric AI, aligning algorithms with nature's intuitive and powerful mechanisms, such as the learning and problem-solving mechanisms observed in the human brain, is essential. One such mechanism is common sense, which pertains to the ability of humans (and animals) to acquire world models by accumulating vast contextual knowledge about the functioning of the world and the causal relationships that govern events. This knowledge is then employed to predict future outcomes.

By incorporating common-sense reasoning into AI models, we can infuse them with a more human-like understanding of the world, allowing them to adapt to various situations with greater accuracy and robustness. This interdisciplinary approach, drawing inspiration from the complexities of the human brain, holds great potential for advancing AI systems and bridging the gap between data-centric and model-centric methodologies. Emulating the intuitive mechanisms found in nature can lead to more sophisticated and comprehensive AI systems capable of achieving greater problem-solving capabilities and generalizing effectively across diverse scenarios. Indeed, current AI and ML systems often lack the innate ability of common-sense reasoning that humans possess. For instance, while a human driver can intuitively predict the negative outcome of driving too fast based on their understanding of physics and prior experiences, an AI system in an autonomous vehicle would require thousands of reinforcement learning trials to acquire similar knowledge. This discrepancy highlights the disparity between human intelligence, which relies on accumulated knowledge and affordances provided by the brain during problem-solving, and AI systems, which typically require extensive data and learning iterations to reach comparable conclusions. Humans can adapt and navigate new situations by leveraging their interactions with the environment and their inherent cognitive abilities. In contrast, AI systems often require vast amounts of labeled data and complex learning algorithms to handle even seemingly simple scenarios. Bridging this gap between human intelligence and AI remains a significant challenge in the field of AI research. Integrating common-sense reasoning and leveraging human-like cognitive affordances could potentially lead to the development of more robust and versatile AI systems capable of handling new and unforeseen situations with greater efficiency and accuracy.

The use of adversarial samples in cyber attacks, where data can be freely submitted into a running DL/ML algorithm, underscores the need for a complementary approach involving both data-centric and model-centric AI. Initially, false predictions in DL networks with perturbed dataset samples were attributed to extreme nonlinearity, insufficient model averaging, and inadequate regularization in purely supervised learning. This highlights the importance of incorporating both data-centric and model-centric methodologies to address vulnerabilities and enhance AI system robustness. Subsequently, a deeper understanding revealed that adversarial samples actually arise from the inherent linear characteristics of neural networks in general. Adversarial samples are not random artifacts arising from typical variability during propagation learning runs, nor are they caused by overfitting or incomplete model training. Instead, they demonstrate resilience to random noise and can transfer between neural network models, even when these models differ in the number of layers, hyperparameters, and training data. This remarkable characteristic emphasizes the robustness challenges faced by AI systems and underscores the importance of considering both data-centric and model-centric approaches to enhance their performance and security. This suggests that the robustness of a deep neural network model based on backpropagation is not solely determined by the datasets used for training. Instead, it is influenced by the structural connection between the network and the data distribution. Therefore, a combination of both data-centric and model-centric approaches is essential when striving to enhance the network's robustness. By addressing both aspects, AI researchers and practitioners can create more resilient and secure neural network models.

3.8   CONCLUSIONS

The AI/ML community is witnessing a surge of interest in data-centric AI, potentially heralding a paradigm shift in AI/ML model development. Our thorough analysis explored the advantages and disadvantages of both data-centric and model-centric approaches, culminating in a balanced perspective that harmonizes the two approaches. While we concur with fellow researchers on the importance of data-centric AI, we firmly assert that this shift should not diminish the significance of model-centric AI. Embracing the data-centric approach is a crucial advancement in AI capabilities, as it places a strong emphasis on high-quality datasets, enabling models to better comprehend and predict real-world scenarios.

However, it is equally vital not to overlook the significance of model-centric AI, which concentrates on refining and optimizing the algorithms and hyperparameters that form the backbone of AI models. This approach has proven highly valuable in achieving superior performance and efficiency across various applications. Achieving a balance and recognizing the complementary nature of both data-centric and model-centric AI is the key. By amalgamating the strengths of both approaches, we can forge more resilient and potent AI systems that excel in diverse situations. The context of Industry 4.0, promising revolutionary automation and IoT-driven interaction among cyber-physical objects, accentuates the critical interplay between data-centric and model-centric AI. The triumph of Industry 4.0 technologies hinges on effective data utilization and sophisticated AI models. Merging both approaches empowers us to fully leverage AI's potential in Industry 4.0 applications, leading to heightened efficiency and innovation across multiple domains.

In conclusion, embracing the data-centric AI approach represents significant progress, but it must not overshadow the importance of model-centric AI. Instead, recognizing the value of both approaches and synergistically incorporating them can usher in groundbreaking AI technologies, particularly in the context of Industry 4.0's ambitious goals. By striking a harmonious balance, we pave the way for a new era of AI development, where data-centric and model-centric AI unite to reshape the frontiers of AI, transcending limitations and unlocking untapped potential.

3.9 FUTURE WORK

In the realm of data-centric AI and model-centric AI, future endeavors should focus on maximizing the potential of AI technologies through various avenues. First, advancements in data-centric AI demand refinement of data preparation techniques to ensure datasets are sufficient and representative, along with strategies to identify and mitigate biases. Exploring unsupervised and self-supervised learning methods can further enrich AI systems with common-sense knowledge. Second, integrating human domain expertise into data engineering and model development will lead to tailored and effective AI solutions.

In the realm of model-centric AI, continuous improvement of DL architectures, optimization algorithms, and regularization techniques will enhance model performance, robustness, and interpretability. MLOps and deployment platforms can significantly streamline the development and deployment of AI applications, making them more efficient and agile. Exploring hybrid approaches that combine data-driven and model-driven optimization can lead to more robust and versatile AI systems. Additionally, addressing ethical and social implications, such as developing guidelines for responsible AI deployment, fairness, transparency, and privacy protection, is paramount. Establishing standardized benchmarks and metrics for fair AI model comparisons, as well as real-world deployment and validation in collaboration with industries, will provide valuable insights for further improvements in AI technologies. By embracing these directions, the AI community can unlock the full potential of data-centric and model-centric AI paradigms and drive innovation in the field.

REFERENCES

[1] Bender, E.M.; Gebru, T.; McMillan-Major, A.; Shmitchell, S. On the dangers of stochastic parrots: Can language models be too big? In: *Proceedings of the 2021 ACM Conference on Fairness, Accountability, and Transparency*, Toronto, ON, Canada, 3–10 March 2021

[2] Bhatt, S. The Big Fight: RPA Versus Traditional Automation. 2018. https://www.botreetechnologies.com/blog/the-big-fight-robotic-process-automation-vs-traditional-automation (accessed on 3 January 2023).

[3] Boubin, J.; Banerjee, A.; Yun, J.; Qi, H.; Fang, Y.; Chang, S.; Srinivasan, K.; Ramnath, R.; Arora, A. *PROWESS: An Open Testbed for Programmable Wireless Edge Systems*. Association for Computing Machinery, New York, NY, USA, 2022

[4] Chen, T.; Moreau, T.; Jiang, Z.; Zheng, L.; Yan, E.; Shen, H.; Cowan, M.; Wang, L.; Hu, Y.; Ceze, L. et al. {TVM}: An automated {End-to-End} optimizing compiler for deep learning. In: *Proceedings of the 13th USENIX Symposium on Operating Systems Design and Implementation (OSDI 18)*, Carlsbad, CA, USA, 8–10 October 2018, pp. 578–594.

[5] Fujita, H. AI-based computer-aided diagnosis (AI-CAD): The latest review to read first. *Radiological Physics and Technology* 2020, 13, 6–19.

[6] Hack, U. What Is the Real Story Behind the Explosive Growth of Data? 2021. https://www.red-gate.com/blog/database-development/whats-the-real-story-behind-the-explosive-growth-of-data (accessed on 3 January 2023).

[7] Hamid, O.H.; Braun, J. Reinforcement learning and attractor neural network models of associative learning. In: *Computational Intelligence: Proceedings of the 9th International Joint Conference, IJCCI 2017*, Funchal–Madeira, Portugal, 1–3 November 2017, Revised Selected Papers, Springer, New York, NY, USA, 2019, pp. 327–349.

[8] Hamid, O.H. From model-centric to data-centric AI: A paradigm shift or rather a complementary approach? In: *Proceedings of the 2022 8th International Conference on Information Technology Trends (ITT)*, Dubai, United Arab Emirates, 25–26 May 2022, IEEE, Piscataway, NJ, USA, 2022, pp. 196–199

[9] Tian, Q.; Yang, Y.; Lin, C.; Li, Q.; Shen, C. Improving Adversarial Robustness with Data-Centric Learning. 2022. https://alisec-competition.oss-cn-shanghai.aliyuncs.com/competition_papers/20211201/rank5.pdf

[10] Jiang, Y.; Zhu, Y.; Lan, C.; Yi, B.; Cui, Y.; Guo, C. A unified architecture for accelerating distributed {DNN} training in heterogeneous {GPU/CPU} clusters. In: *Proceedings of the 14th USENIX Symposium on Operating Systems Design and Implementation (OSDI 20)*, 4–6 November 2020, pp. 463–479.

[11] Kotsiopoulos, T.; Sarigiannidis, P.; Ioannidis, D.; Tzovaras, D. Machine learning and deep learning in smart manufacturing: The smart grid paradigm. *Computer Science Review* 2021, 40, 100341.

[12] Krishnan, S.; Wang, J.; Wu, E.; Franklin, M.J.; Goldberg, K. Activeclean: Interactive data cleaning for statistical modeling. *Proceedings of the VLDB Endowment* 2016, 9, 948–959.

[13] Mazumder, M.; Banbury, C.; Yao, X.; Karlaš, B.; Rojas, W.G.; Diamos, S.; Diamos, G.; He, L.; Kiela, D.; Jurado, D. et al. DataPerf: Benchmarks for data-centric AI development. 2022. Dataperf: Benchmarks for data-centric ai development. *arXiv preprint arXiv:2207.10062*.

[14] Miranda, L.J. Towards Data-Centric Machine Learning: A Short Review. https://ljvmiranda921.github.io/notebook/2021/07/30/data-centric-ml

[15] Molnar, C. Interpretable Machine Learning. 2022. https://christophm.github.io/interpretable-ml-book (accessed on 3 January 2023).

[16] Pareek, P.; Shankar, P.; Pathak, M.P.; Sakariya, M.N. Predicting music popularity using machine learning algorithm and music metrics available in Spotify. *Center for Development Economics Studies* 2022, 9, 10–19.

[17] Reinsel, D.; Rydning, J.; Gantz, J.F. Worldwide Global Datasphere Forecast, 2021–2025: The World Keeps Creating More Data-Now, What Do We Do With it All? 2021. https://www.marketresearch.com/IDC-v2477/Worldwide-Global-DataSphere-Forecast-Keeps-14315439/

[18] Renggli, C.; Karlaš, B.; Ding, B.; Liu, F.; Schawinski, K.; Wu, W.; Zhang, C. Continuous integration of machine learning models with ease. ml/ci: Towards a rigorous yet practical treatment. *Proceedings of Machine Learning and Systems* 2019, 1, 322–333.

[19] Russell, B.C.; Torralba, A.; Murphy, K.P.; Freeman, W.T. LabelMe: A database and web-based tool for image annotation. *International Journal of Computer Vision* 2008, 77, 157–173.

[20] Schlegl, T.; Stino, H.; Niederleithner, M.; Pollreisz, A.; Schmidt-Erfurth, U.; Drexler, W.; Leitgeb, R.A.; Schmoll, T. Data-centric AI approach to improve optic nerve head segmentation and localization in OCT en face images. *arXiv preprint arXiv:2208.03868*.

[21] van Moorselaar, D.; Slagter, H.A. Inhibition in selective attention. *Annals of the New York Academy of Sciences* 2020, 1464, 204–221.

[22] Vartak, M.; Subramanyam, H.; Lee, W.E.; Viswanathan, S.; Husnoo, S.; Madden, S.; Zaharia, M. ModelDB: A system for machine learning model management. In: *Proceedings of the Workshop on Human-In-the-Loop Data Analytics*, San Francisco, CA, USA, 26 June–1 July 2016, pp. 1–3.

[23] Zhang, H.; Li, Y.; Huang, Y.; Wen, Y.; Yin, J.; Guan, K. MLmodelCI: An automatic cloud platform for efficient MLaaS. In: *Proceedings of the 28th ACM International Conference on Multimedia*, Seattle, WA, USA, 12–16 October 2020, pp. 4453–4456.

4 Data-Centric AI Approaches for Machine Translation

Chandrakant D. Kokane, Pranav Khandagale,
Mehul Ligade, Shreeyash Garde, and Vilas Deotare

4.1 INTRODUCTION

Machine translation, a fundamental component of interlingual communication in our increasingly globalized world, has witnessed significant advancements in recent years.[1] As the demand for accurate and efficient translation grows, the integration of machine learning techniques has emerged as a transformative force in enhancing the quality and efficacy of machine translation systems.

The automated translation of text or speech from one language into another is referred to as machine translation. It makes cross-cultural communication easier in a number of different professions, such as business, diplomacy, and academia. Historically, rule-based and statistical approaches have been utilized to address the challenges of translation. These approaches could not adequately handle the intrinsic language complexity, resulting in fewer accurate translations and poor translation quality.

With the advent of machine learning, a revolutionary approach that focuses on the development of algorithms capable of learning and improving from data, a paradigm shift has occurred in the field of machine translation. Machine learning algorithms, powered by neural networks, have demonstrated exceptional capabilities in capturing the complex patterns and linguistic nuances present in diverse language pairs.

By leveraging large-scale parallel corpora and sophisticated neural network architectures, machine learning techniques enable machine translation systems to comprehend and generate translations that exhibit higher fidelity to the original meaning and context. This paradigm shift toward data-driven, machine learning-based translation systems, commonly known as neural machine translation, has led to remarkable advancements and a significant improvement in translation quality.

The incorporation of machine learning in machine translation not only addresses the limitations of traditional approaches but also opens up new avenues for exploration and innovation.[1] The ability of machine learning models to learn from vast amounts of training data and adapt to different language pairs has fueled the progress in achieving state-of-the-art translation performance.

The key contributions of the book chapter aim to explore the pivotal role of machine learning techniques in advancing machine translation. By delving into

DOI: 10.1201/9781003461500-5

the fundamental concepts and cutting-edge developments in the field, we will examine the transformative impact of machine learning algorithms on translation accuracy, fluency, and efficiency. Furthermore, we will discuss the challenges and future directions in machine translation, paving the way for a deeper understanding and broader adoption of machine learning techniques in this multidisciplinary domain.

Through this exploration, we strive to contribute to the growing body of knowledge surrounding machine translation and to inspire further research and innovation in this crucial area of language technology.

4.2 MACHINE TRANSLATION SYSTEMS OVERVIEW

Over time, machine translation systems have developed, moving from statistical and rule-based methods to the more modern paradigm of neural machine translation.[2] This section gives a general overview of these many kinds of machine translation systems, emphasizing their unique qualities and the necessity of using machine learning methods and the overview of the machine translation systems given in Figure 4.1.

Rule-based machine translation (RBMT) systems translate texts based on a preset set of linguistic rules and patterns.[2] These systems use multilingual dictionaries and lexicons together with manual encoding of grammatical and syntactic rules. Despite its early popularity, RBMT systems have limitations since developing rules is labor intensive and it is difficult to account for all linguistic differences and exceptions. Consequently, rule-based systems' precision and adaptability may be limited.

In place of rule-based methods, statistical machine translation (SMT) systems have been developed. SMT uses statistical models that gather information from big parallel corpora to learn translation patterns. SMT systems calculate the most likely translations by looking at the frequency and co-occurrence of words and phrases in these corpora. SMT still has issues, while being a major improvement over rule-based approaches. SMT struggles to handle word sense disambiguation and uncommon or unseen terms, is susceptible to the quality of the input data, and lacks contextual comprehension.

The development of machine learning techniques, notably neural networks, revolutionized the area of machine translation by overcoming the drawbacks of rule-based and statistical approaches. Deep learning architectures are used by neural machine translation (NMT) systems to recognize complex correlations and relationships in language input.[5] By directly learning from huge parallel corpora, certain architectures, such as recurrent neural networks (RNNs) and transformer models, make end-to-end translation possible. By utilizing their capacity to record context, manage long-range dependencies, and generalize across several language pairs, NMT systems have demonstrated significant improvement in delivering more accurate and fluent translations.

Machine translation research and application have undergone considerable change as a result of the introduction of machine learning techniques, notably neural machine translation. Machine learning has paved the way for more reliable and context-aware translation systems by eschewing rigid rule-based systems and statistical models constrained by data scarcity.[5] As a result, machine translation has advanced in terms

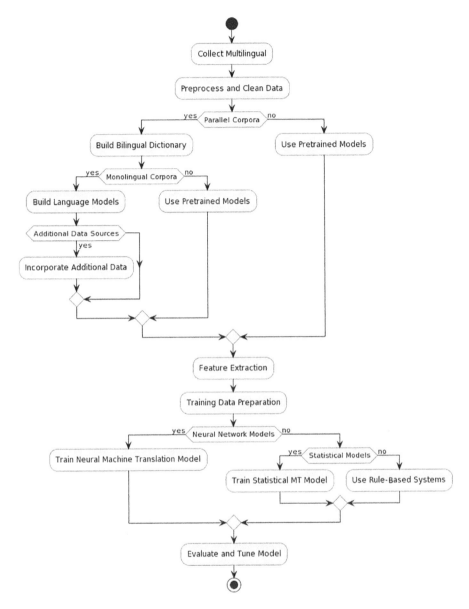

FIGURE 4.1 Overview of machine translation systems.

of accuracy, idiomatic expression handling, and ability to adapt to various domains and language combinations.

The limits of rule-based and statistical approaches are the driving force for the use of machine learning techniques in machine translation, which is highlighted in this overview. In the parts that follow, we'll go into greater detail on how machine learning techniques, particularly neural networks, are used and how they affect machine translation quality and performance.

4.3   MACHINE LEARNING TECHNIQUES

With new opportunities for enhancing translation accuracy and quality, machine learning techniques have revolutionized machine translation. The core ideas and algorithms used in machine learning for machine translation are explained in this section, along with their advantages over earlier rule-based methods. RNNs and transformer models, two well-known machine learning models used in machine translation, are also examined.

Machine learning for machine translation is based on neural networks, computational models inspired by the structure and function of the human brain. Artificial neurons that are interconnected and arranged in layers make up neural networks. Deep learning, a subset of machine learning, is the process of learning and extracting complicated patterns from data using deep neural networks, which include numerous layers.

Machine learning techniques, in contrast to conventional rule-based methods, learn patterns and correlations directly from data. The models may capture the fundamental structure of language using this data-driven methodology and generate predictions based on observed patterns. Machine learning algorithms can find patterns in language structures, word associations, and semantic linkages by using massive parallel corpora.

Machine learning techniques provide numerous benefits over conventional rule-based approaches in machine translation. In order to produce more accurate and natural translations, machine learning models can capture the subtleties and intricacies of language, such as idiomatic phrases and word sense disambiguation. Additionally, machine learning approaches are more adaptable since they can pick up new vocabulary from different language pairs and data from different domains.

A common class of machine learning models used in machine translation are RNNs. By integrating feedback connections, RNNs are created to process sequential data and keep track of prior inputs. This memory component enables RNNs to take into account word dependencies and context, resulting in more accurate and contextually appropriate translations.

Transformer models, yet another important machine learning architecture, have become more well-known in recent years due to their outstanding translation capabilities. Transformer models use self-attention techniques to identify long-range relationships in sentences, which enables the models to successfully align the information in the source and target languages during translation. This attention technique enables improved word reordering management, increased fluency, and improved translation quality.

In conclusion, machine learning methods have transformed machine translation by enabling data-driven learning and capturing the complexity of language, particularly neural networks like RNNs and transformer models. These approaches have a number of advantages over traditional rule-based approaches, including improved accuracy, adaptability, and the ability to handle linguistic peculiarities.

4.4   PREPROCESSING AND FEATURE ENGINEERING

Preprocessing procedures and feature engineering methods are essential in the field of machine translation for improving translation quality. In addition to concentrating on the necessary preprocessing stages, such as tokenization, sentence alignment, and language model training, this section also explores feature engineering strategies that help to improve translation results.

The segmentation of text into discrete tokens or words, or tokenization, is a crucial preparatory step in machine translation.[2] Machine translation systems obtain a detailed grasp of the input by breaking sentences down into tokens, which enables better handling of linguistic structures and syntactic variations. Depending on the language and particular needs of the translation process, different tokenization strategies may be used.

Another crucial preprocessing step called sentence alignment lines up related sentences in parallel corpora to achieve exact correspondences between source and target languages.[2] As a foundation for understanding translation patterns and aligning parallel sentences during the translation process, this alignment is essential for training machine translation models. Sentence alignment uses a variety of techniques, including the Smith-Waterman algorithm and Hidden Markov Model-based alignment.

Language models that accurately represent the statistical and syntactic patterns of a particular language are trained using monolingual data. These linguistic models help to maintain linguistic coherence and produce fluent translations. Depending on the required level of sophistication and the available computer resources, language models can be taught using approaches like n-gram models, RNNs, or transformer models.

The quality of translations can be significantly increased by using feature engineering techniques. The semantic and contextual information of words is encoded into low-dimensional vector representations by word embeddings, also referred to as dispersed word representations. In order to manage word meaning changes, synonyms, and polysemy, these embeddings enable machine translation systems, which eventually result in more accurate translations. The word embedding methods Word2Vec, GloVe, and FastText are all well-liked.

To improve translation quality, feature engineering also makes use of language-specific features. These features make use of linguistic details peculiar to a certain language, such as part-of-speech tags, syntactic constructions, or morphological data.[4] Such elements help machine translation models by adding more linguistic information and contextual signals, enabling more accurate translations and addressing language-specific issues.

Machine translation systems can achieve notable gains in translation quality by utilizing preprocessing stages like tokenization, sentence alignment, and language model training, as well as feature engineering approaches like word embeddings and language-specific features.

4.5 ARCHITECTURES OF NEURAL NETWORKS FOR MACHINE TRANSLATION

Refer to Figure 4.2 for the complete breakdown of the architectures of neural networks in machine translation.

RNNs: Machine translation frequently employs a family of neural network topologies called RNNs.[3] By keeping a concealed state that preserves the context of previously processed input, RNNs are made to process sequential data. RNNs may

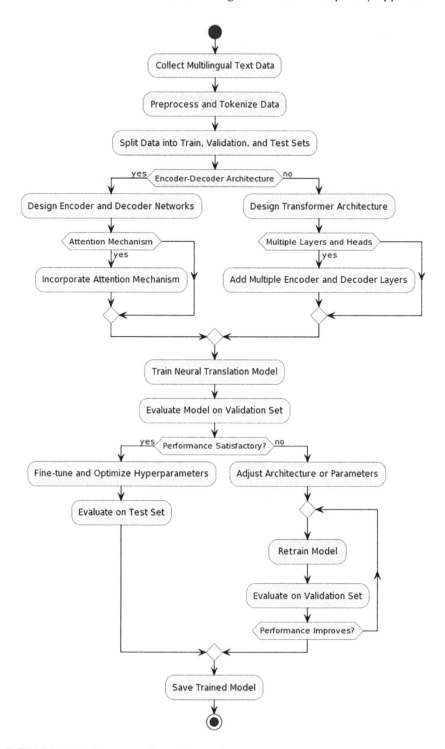

FIGURE 4.2   Architectures of neural networks.

produce a translation in the target language from a source language input sequence in the context of machine translation.

Contextual dependencies are captured by RNNs by propagating data from one time step to the next. The information about the previously viewed words and their context is encoded in the RNN's hidden state.

This enables the model to take into account the history of the input sequence and produce translations that are logical and appropriate for the context. Standard RNNs, however, experience the vanishing gradient problem, which might restrict their use.

Longest Short-Term Memory (LSTM) networks, a part of RNNs, were developed to overcome this drawback.[3] In order to more effectively capture long-term dependence, LSTMs contain memory cells and gating mechanisms.

While the gating mechanisms regulate the flow of information, the memory cells enable the model to selectively store an update information in the future time. Compared to simple RNNs, LSTMs have a better capacity to grasp long-term dependencies and increase translation accuracy.[3]

Transformer Models: Transformer models have become a ground-breaking machine translation architecture. Transformers rely on self-attention techniques to capture contextual dependencies as opposed to RNN-based systems, which analyze the input stream sequentially.

Using self-attention, each word in the input sequence pays attention to every other word to assess their relative value, is the fundamental concept of transformers. This enables the model to provide translations while taking the sentence's whole context into account.

Transformers perform simultaneous processing of the full input sequence, paying attention to various sections of the sequence to acquire data and make translation judgments. Through effective context modeling and the capturing of dependencies over the whole sequence, this parallel processing improves translation accuracy.

Transformers include a self-attention mechanism that enables the model to generate the translation while weighing the significance of various terms in the original text.

Transformers can better match the source and destination language information, resulting in more accurate translations, by paying attention to pertinent source language information.

Transformers also provide positional encoding to take into consideration the input sequence's sequential nature. The model can capture the word order and preserve the sentence structure during translation, thanks to positional encoding which offers information about the placement of each word in the sentence.

Role of Attention Mechanisms: The alignment of the information in the source and destination languages during translation depends critically on attention processes. When producing translations, attention enables the model to concentrate on particular segments of the input sequence, matching the pertinent source data with the intended result.

The ability of the model to identify which words in the source sentence are most pertinent to each word in the target phrase is provided by attention mechanisms in machine translation.[4]

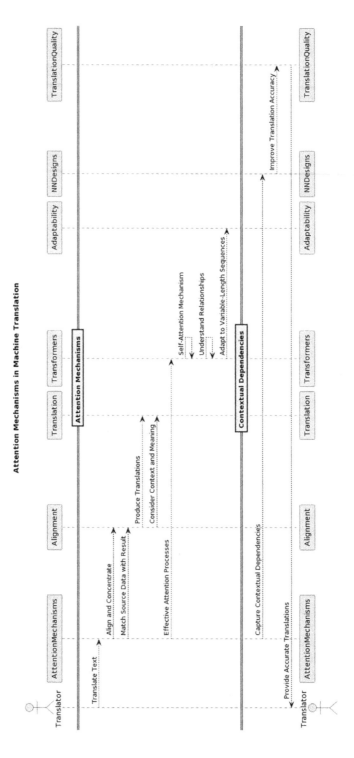

FIGURE 4.3 Attention mechanism in machine translation.

By taking into account the context and meaning of the original words, this align-ment aids the model in producing appropriate translations.

In order to translate one word from the source sentence into another in the target phrase, attention mechanisms compute attention weights for each word in the source sentence.

Figure 4.3 gives us a brief idea about the role of the attention mechanism.

Machine translation models based on transformers have shown to be especially good at using attention processes. Transformers include a self-attention mechanism that enables the model to understand the relationships between every word in the input sequence, leading to more precise alignment and context-aware translation.

The model is more versatile and adaptive to various translation tasks because of the attention mechanism's ability to manage variable-length input and output sequences.

In summary, by retaining hidden states, utilizing memory cells and gating mecha-nisms, and utilizing attention processes, neural network designs like RNNs, LSTMs, and transformers capture contextual dependencies in machine translation.[5]

These architectures have transformed the area of machine translation by making it possible to create models that can provide translations that are more accurate and contextually suitable.

4.6   TRAINING AND OPTIMIZATION

Training Process of Machine Translation Models: During the training phase of machine translation models, machine learning techniques are employed to improve the model parameters based on a training dataset.

The Following are the General Steps of the Training Process: The initial stage is to prepare the training data, which consists of parallel corpora with source language utterances and their corresponding target language translations. Usually, the data is preprocessed by tokenizing the sentences, dealing with unfamiliar words, and per-forming the appropriate cleaning procedures.[4]

The next step is to initialize the model's parameters. The weights and biases of the network layers may be among the parameters, depending on the neural network design being employed.

Forward Propagation: The model receives the input source sentence during train-ing and uses forward propagation to produce a translation in the target language. As a result, an output is generated once the input has been processed through the layers of the neural network.

Loss Computation: After comparing the produced and target translations, a loss function is used to determine how different they are from one another. Machine trans-lation frequently employs the loss functions cross-entropy loss and sequence-level loss.

Backward Propagation: To determine the model parameter gradients, the loss is backpropagated across the network. In this stage, the overall loss contribution from each parameter is calculated.

Model Parameter Update: Based on the computed gradients, optimization algo-rithms are utilized to update the model parameters. The goal is to reduce the loss function as much as possible while enhancing translation quality.

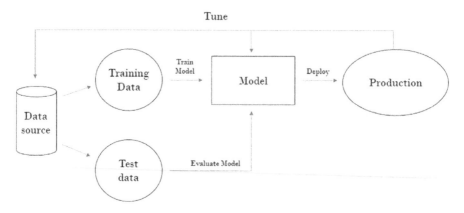

FIGURE 4.4 Optimization of algorithm.

Iterative Optimization: For several training samples, Steps c to f are performed iteratively to create epochs. A whole trip across the training dataset is represented by an epoch. Depending on how quickly the model converges, there may be different numbers of epochs.

Evaluation: To track the model's development and avoid overfitting, the model's performance is assessed on a distinct validation set at various points during the training phase. Using this evaluation, the best model can be chosen.

Optimization Algorithms: Stochastic Gradient Descent (SGD) is a popular machine learning optimization algorithm. It modifies the model parameters by computing the gradients on a randomly selected subset (mini-batch) of the training data. Because of this random selection, the method is computationally efficient and less prone to data noise. SGD updates are carried out in little stages, shifting the parameters to minimize the loss function.

Refer to Figure 4.4 for the understanding of the algorithm optimization process.

Adam (Adaptive Moment Estimation): Adam is an extension of SGD that modifies the learning rate for each model parameter in accordance with predictions of the first and second moments of the gradients. It provides faster convergence and better handling of sparse gradients by combining the advantages of the AdaGrad and RMSprop techniques.

The essential phases of the Adam optimization method are as follows:

i. **Initialization:** For each model parameter, Adam initializes the first and second moment variables (m and v) to zero.
ii. **Gradient Computation:** Based on the small batch of training examples, the gradients of the model parameters are computed during the forward propagation and backpropagation steps.
iii. **Moment Updates:** Adam determines the exponential moving averages of the first (m) and second (v) moments of the gradients. The decay rates used to calculate these moving averages are 1 and 2, respectively.
iv. **Bias Correction:** The moving average estimates may be biased toward zero because they are initialized with zeros, especially in the first training

iterations. By modifying the estimates with a bias correction term, Adam corrects for bias.

v. Adam changes the model parameters using the bias-corrected moment estimates and a learning rate after computing the estimates. The formula for updating a parameter is as follows: $\theta = \theta - (\alpha * m) \div (\sqrt{v} + \varepsilon)$, which is a minor constant introduced for numerical stability.

Based on the first and second moment estimations, Adam modifies the learning rate for each parameter, causing the model to converge more quickly and handle various gradients effectively.

4.7   EVALUATION AND METRICS

Evaluation Process for Machine Translation Systems: To gauge the effectiveness of machine translation systems and direct improvement efforts, quality evaluation is essential. Both manual and automatic measures are used in the machine translation evaluation process:

a. **Human Assessment:** In human assessment, translations produced by machine translation systems are evaluated by human judges. These judges frequently speak the target language fluently or bilingually. They evaluate the machine-generated translations in comparison to the reference translations and assign scores or rankings based on a number of factors, including fluency, sufficiency, grammaticality, and overall quality. The linguistic proficiency and naturalness of the translations are crucial insights gained via human inspection.

b. **Automated Metrics:** Automated metrics are impersonal measurements created to evaluate the accuracy of machine translations without the need for human interaction. These metrics measure the machine-translated texts against one or more reference translations and compare the results to predetermined standards. Large amounts of translated material can be evaluated quickly and effectively with the use of automated metrics. They are commonly used in machine translation system research, development, and benchmarking.

4.7.1   COMMONLY USED EVALUATION METRICS

BLEU (Bilingual Evaluation Understudy): BLEU is a well-liked assessment metric that is frequently employed in the study and improvement of machine translation. It is built on the idea of n-gram accuracy, which quantifies how closely the reference translations and machine translations match in terms of word sequences.

By measuring the number of matching n-grams in the machine-generated translation and the reference translations, BLEU determines the precision of various n-gram orders (usually unigrams, bigrams, trigrams, and occasionally higher orders). Additionally, it penalizes for producing more n-grams than the references contain. A weighted geometric mean is then used to aggregate the precision scores.

BLEU has some restrictions even if it is now a de facto standard. Fluency, adequacy, and word order are not taken into account by BLEU, which primarily concentrates on lexical similarity. Because it is sensitive to superficial similarities, translations that might not accurately convey the intended meaning often receive high marks. Furthermore, BLEU is domain-dependent, which means that its performance may vary across various text domains.

Metric for Evaluation of Translation with Explicit Ordering or METEOR: Another popular evaluation metric, METEOR, seeks to capture many facets of translation quality. It takes into account a variety of matching factors, such as unigrams, stemming, synonymy, word order, and more.

Considering the word alignment between the reference translations and the machine-generated translation, METEOR determines precision and recall values. In addition to a number of matching and penalty systems, the ultimate score is calculated using a harmonic mean of recall and precision.

METEOR has the advantage of handling word-order variations, accounting for synonyms, and stemming.[4] It can distinguish between variations in words' surface forms and offer more precise alignments. It has been demonstrated that METEOR performs well across a variety of language pairs and text domains. It does, however, have some restrictions. METEOR largely depends on the caliber of available linguistic resources, including word alignments, stemmers, and synonyms. Because of its complicated scoring system, it is challenging to evaluate and comprehend the precise contribution of each component.

TER (Translation Edit Rate): The Edit Distance between the Machine-Generated Translation and the Reference Translation (TER) is a measurement used in evaluation. It determines how many edits – including additions, subtractions, and substitutions – are necessary to turn the machine-generated translation into the reference translation.

TER concentrates on the surface-level alterations and offers a direct measurement of translation similarity.[4] Since it is linguistically neutral, it can be applied to other language combinations. A text that has been heavily edited or post-edited, where the emphasis is on the number of revisions done, can be evaluated well using TER.

TER does, however, have some restrictions. It does not take semantic equivalence or fluency into account and rather concentrates on the number of modifications. It may penalize translators for legitimate paraphrases or rearranging sentences to increase readability or flow. Additionally, because TER scores cannot fully capture the whole meaning or appropriateness of the translation, they may not be able to provide a comprehensive assessment of translation quality.

4.7.2 STRENGTHS AND WEAKNESSES OF EVALUATION METRICS

Each evaluation metric has its own advantages and disadvantages, and the degree to which they are correlated with human judgments depends on a number of variables. Here are some important details about these evaluation metrics' advantages and disadvantages:

4.7.2.1 BLEU

a. **Strengths:** BLEU is widely used, simple to implement, and effective computationally. It offers an immediate evaluation of translation quality and is simple to understand. For specific language pairs and text domains, BLEU scores have a fair amount of agreement with human assessments.
b. **Weakness:** BLEU's emphasis on lexical similarity and n-gram accuracy can produce high ratings for translations that may not accurately convey the intended meaning. Fluency, sufficiency, and word order – which are essential for assessing translation quality – are not taken into account. BLEU is susceptible to manipulation and is also perceptive to superficial similarities.

4.7.2.2 METEOR

Strengths: METEOR provides a more thorough assessment of translation quality by taking many linguistic factors like word order, stemming, and synonymy into account. It performs effectively in a variety of language and domain combinations. In comparison to BLEU, METEOR can tolerate variances in surface shapes and offer superior alignments.

Limitations: The effectiveness of METEOR significantly depends on the availability and caliber of linguistic resources like stemmers, synonyms, and word alignments. Its scoring system is intricate and may be difficult to understand. When linguistic resources are scarce or poorly matched to the target language, METEOR scores may not always match human judgments exactly.

4.7.2.3 TER

a. **Strengths:** TER provides an accurate comparison of similarity by measuring the edit distance between translations. It is not linguistically reliant and is less prone to fluency and adequacy problems. Since TER can detect significant translational changes, it is helpful for assessing heavily edited or post-edited text.
b. **Weaknesses:** TER does not take semantic equivalence into account and rather concentrates on the number of revisions. It may penalize translators for legitimate paraphrases or rearranging sentences to increase readability or flow. As TER scores do not fully capture the whole meaning or appropriateness of the translation, they may not be able to provide a thorough assessment of translation quality.

It's critical to realize that while these evaluation criteria provide quantitative assessments of translation quality, they do not fully account for human perception. In order to gain a thorough understanding of machine translation system performance, they should be utilized in conjunction with human review and other qualitative analyses. Additionally, depending on the language pair, text domain, and particular translation issues, the applicability and efficacy of these indicators may change.

4.8   METHODOLOGY

Machine learning techniques play a crucial role in machine translation since they have completely changed how we approach language translation tasks. The process for using machine learning in machine translation is described below, and refer to Figure 4.5 for brief information about the methodology:

1. **Issue Description:** Define the precise translation task, such as speech-to-text, image-to-text, or text translation from one language to another.
2. **Data Gathering and Preparation:** A mass of a sizable, parallel corpus of text or information in the target and source languages. By removing noise, special characters, and unnecessary information, clean up and preprocess the data. To construct a vocabulary, tokenize the text into words or subword units (like BPE or SentencePiece).
3. **Extracting Features:** You can encode words or subword units as numerical vectors by using methods like word embeddings (Word2Vec, GloVe, FastText), contextual embeddings (BERT, GPT, ELMo), or subword embeddings (WordPiece, Byte-Pair Encoding).
4. **Model Choice:** Select a machine translation-friendly machine learning model. Typical options include phrase-based SMT models are one type of SMT model. Models for NMT, such as attention-based sequence-to-sequence models. Models built on transformers (such BERT, GPT, and T5) have been honed for translation jobs.
5. **Post-Processing:** Use post-processing methods to improve the output of the model, such as capitalization, punctuation, and fluency.
6. **Deployment:** Use the trained machine translation model in applications and systems as an API, a service, or an integration where translation is needed.
7. **Constant Development:** Continually evaluate model performance in real-world circumstances and get user input. To enhance translation quality, repeat the training process with newer data and retrained models. To manage several languages, think about developing or improving multilingual models. Create specialized models for translations in fields like law, medicine, and technology. Continuously gather user feedback and monitor model performance in real-world scenarios.

4.9   ADVANCED TECHNIQUES AND RECENT DEVELOPMENTS

Advanced Techniques in Machine Translation: With the advent of several advanced methods, machine translation has made great strides in recent times. Here are some notable methods that have helped machine translation progress:

1. NMT models, especially those based on deep learning architectures such as RNNs and transformers, have revolutionized machine translation.[2]
2. These models effectively capture context and long-term interdependencies while learning to translate by analyzing large amounts of multilingual textual data.[2] Figure 4.6 gives us an example of the advanced techniques in the machine translation process.

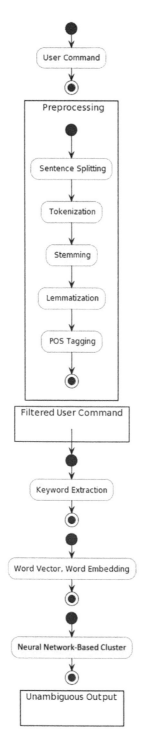

FIGURE 4.5 Methodology diagram for machine translation.

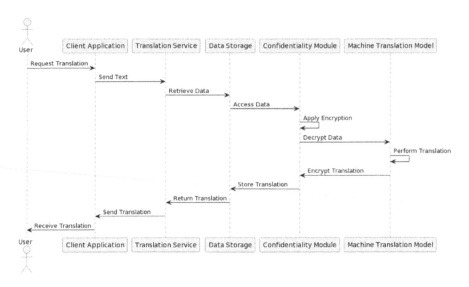

FIGURE 4.6   Machine translation and confidentiality.

Transition Learning: Transfer learning techniques make it possible to pre-train language models on large datasets and refine them for specific translation tasks. By using knowledge gained from huge volumes of data, this method helps to improve translation quality.

Attention Mechanism: Attention mechanisms improve the performance of machine translation models by allowing them to focus on relevant phrases from the source text during translation. Attention processes facilitate the copying of important information and improve the overall quality of the translation by assigning different weights to certain words or phrases.

Many machine translation methods use subword units, including subword embedding or byte pair encoding (BPE), rather than translating words at the word level.[2] Secondary word segmentation increases translation accuracy, especially for morphologically rich languages, by dealing with uncommon words, out-of-vocabulary terms, and rare words. Zero-Shot Translation and Multi-Language Translation:

Multilingual translation models can handle multiple languages at the same time, allowing efficient translation between different language pairs. This skill is extended by Zero Hit Translation, which allows translation between language pairs that are not directly visible during training.

Machine translation models can be improved using reinforcement learning strategies, such as reinforcement learning from human feedback. These methods aim to improve translation accuracy and fluency by using human-generated feedback to reinforce desired translation results.

Unattended Machine Translation: Without using a parallel corpus, unsupervised machine translation seeks to train translation models. Low-resource-intensive languages can be translated because unsupervised algorithms can train themselves to translate without concatenated versions using monolingual data from the source and target languages.

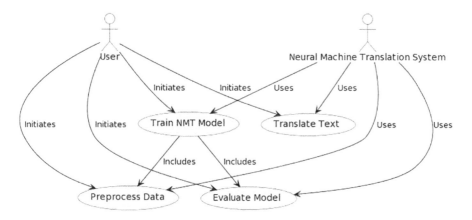

FIGURE 4.7   Neural machine translation with sequence-to-sequence RNN.

1. **Recent Developments in Neural Machine Translation:** NMT has recently made advances in unsupervised techniques and pre-trained language models, such as BERT (Bidirectional Encoder Representation from Transformers).[5] Here are some notable developments, and Figure 4.7 gives us an idea of a Sequential to Sequential Neural Machine Translation RNN.
2. **Pre-Trained Language Models for NMT:** A pre-trained language model that has been successfully applied to improve the performance of NMT is BERT. The pre-trained BERT integration, which contains detailed background information, can be used to initialize the NMT model instead of starting from scratch. This transfer learning strategy helps NMT models better understand the source language and produce more accurate translations.
3. **Contextual Embedding:** By using contextual embeddings provided by models such as BERT, the representation of words in NMT has been improved. In situations where it is important to define a word, these embeddings capture the context and meaning of the word based on the terms surrounding the word, resulting in more accurate translations.
4. **Multilingual Language Model:** To support NMT in multiple languages, multilingual language models, such as XLM (Multilingual Language Model), have been developed.[6] These models are pre-trained on huge amounts of multilingual data, facilitating knowledge transfer between languages and improving translation quality for under-resourced language pairs.
5. **Unattended Machine Translation (NMT):** NMT models are trained using unsupervised machine translation techniques that do not rely on parallel corpus. These methods use monolingual data from the source and target languages and use tools such as denoising encoders and automatic decompilers to learn to translate without concatenation problems. Unsupervised NMT has shown promising results, especially for low-resource languages where parallel training material is inadequate.

6. **Multilingual NMT:** Using a single model, multilingual NMT models can translate between multiple languages. These models take advantage of shared representations between languages, improving translation quality and maximizing resource usage.

4.10   CHALLENGES AND FUTURE DIRECTIONS

1. **Challenges:** The accuracy and quality of machine translation are hampered by a number of issues. Here are some pressing problems and their solutions, which are also represented by the flowchart in Figure 4.8:

   - **Languages with Few Resources:** The scarcity of parallel training data in low-resource languages makes it difficult to develop reliable translation models. The researchers looked at methods such as unsupervised machine translation, to solve this problem, training translation models using monolingual data from source and target languages. By applying lessons from high-resource languages and using multilingual models, translation quality for low-resource languages can also be improved.

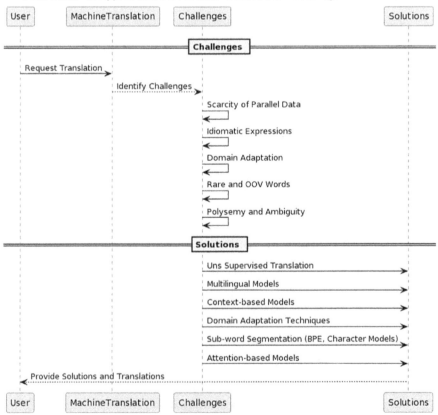

FIGURE 4.8   Challenges and solution.

- **Idiom Expressions:** Idioms are words or phrases that can be taken literally but also figuratively.[4] Since their meanings may not translate word for word correctly, it can be difficult to translate these expressions effectively. Knowledge of context is required to manage idiomatic languages, and attention-processing neural machine translation models have shown progress in capturing these nuances. Idioms can also be translated using strategies such as phrase-based translation and the use of bilingual dictionaries or phrase boards.
- **Domain Adaptation:** In specific fields, such as legal or medical translation, where specialized terminology and context are common, machine translation models often have difficulty performing well. Domain adaptation techniques can be used to improve or train models specific to certain domains.
- **Rare and Extra-Lexical Words:** When machine translation encounters rare or out-of-vocabulary (OOV) words that are not seen during training, problems can arise.[4] By dividing OOV words into sub-word units, sub-word segmentation algorithms such as BPE or character-based models can process them. These methods minimize the influence of OOV terms on translation quality and allow the translation model to handle rare words more efficiently.
- **Polysemy and Ambiguity:** When a term or phrase has multiple interpretations, the result is ambiguity. The phenomenon of a word having many similar meanings is called polysemy. For a translation to be honest, it is essential to remove ambiguity and polysemy. Attention-based neural machine translation models can help capture contextual information to distinguish words or phrases based on context.

2. **Future Directions:** Current machine translation research focuses on a number of intriguing directions and emerging trends. Here are some examples:
   - **Context Data:** An important area of research in machine translation is the incorporation of contextual data. More accurate and more contextual translations can be generated by models that take into account the surrounding context of the source sentence. Context-aware methods, such as those that use context information at the conversation or document level, are being explored in an effort to improve translation quality and consistency.
   - **Translations of Rare Words:** For accurate and fluent translation, it is essential to improve the translation of rare terms. Using sub-word units, morphological analysis, or context-based embedding, researchers are working on methods to better manage rare and infrequent words. The meaning and usage of uncommon words can be accurately captured by machine translation models, allowing them to generate more and maintain fluency.
   - Improving the consistency and fluency of machine translation results is an important area of research. More natural-sounding, stylistically consistent, and consistent translations are produced using methods

such as neural text-generation modeling, reinforcement learning, and iterative refinement. Ensuring that translated documents read smoothly and naturally is key to improving user experience and driving machine translation adoption.

- **Multi-Modal Translation:** Research focuses on integrating visual or audio information into machine translation models in response to the evolution of multimodal data (such as text accompanied by images or sounds). Multimodal translation attempts to handle translation tasks that require multiple methods and produce translations that are more contextual by including visual or spoken cues.

- **Improvements in Neural Architecture and Training:** To advance machine translation, researchers are working on improvements in neural architecture and training methods. The goal of methods such as knowledge distillation, multitasking learning, and model compression is to improve performance without sacrificing translation quality, model size, or efficiency. In addition, new designs such as transformer variants and sparse neural networks are being explored to overcome the limitations of translation efficiency and accuracy. Ongoing initiatives to improve translation quality, manage specific constraints, and create more accessible and reliable translation systems are exemplified by these evolving trends in machine translation and current research directions. Machine translation has the potential to be an even more powerful tool for breaking down language barriers and promoting effective cross-language communication.

4.11 CONCLUSION

The improvement in the quality, fluency, and accuracy of machine translations is mainly due to machine learning techniques. In terms of pattern recognition, translation models can be trained using machine learning methods to provide translations that are very similar to human-generated translations, understand context, and make decisions. Here are some important functions of a machine learning strategy in machine translation:

Pattern Recognition: Machine learning techniques allow translation models to learn from large amounts of multilingual textual data and identify patterns that contribute to accurate translations. The lexical, syntactic, and semantic patterns in the source language can be recognized by the models, which can then be used to generate equivalent translations in the target language.

Contextual Understanding: Translation models can understand the context of the source sentence more efficiently during translation through machine learning techniques such as neural networks. To manage idioms, distinguish words or phrases, and provide linguistically consistent and contextual translations, models can use contextual information.

Learn from Data: To discover language matches between source and target languages, machine translation models are mainly data-driven. Models can be trained on huge parallel corpus using supervised learning methods, where the source sentence and its corresponding translation are synchronized. Models can learn translation patterns using this data-driven method, generalize from versions, and improve translation quality over time.

Generalizability and Adaptability: Machine learning techniques make it easy to adapt translation models to other languages, domains, and styles. To support additional language pairs or specialized domains, models that have been trained on a language pair or domain can be adapted or extended. Machine translation systems can accommodate many translation requirements due to their flexibility, which also helps them perform better over time.

Machine learning algorithms are excellent at collecting complex patterns and dealing with language differences. Due to the ambiguities, idiomatic expressions, and variations that exist between languages, machine translation is inherently difficult. Rule-based systems often have difficulty successfully handling such complexities, while machine learning models can learn from huge volumes of data and adapt to that complexity.

Data-driven approach: Machine learning techniques rely on data-driven approaches and make translation decisions by learning from large volumes in parallel. Models can generalize from examples using this data-centric approach, adapting to different language and domain pairs, and improving over time. On the other hand, rule-based systems are less scalable and flexible because they require humans to build and maintain rules significantly.

Generalizability and Adaptability: By adapting or extending their training on specific data, machine learning models can easily generalize to new language, domain, or style pairs. Machine translation systems can now adapt to a wide variety of translation requirements without having to manually build or modify rules. Traditional rule-based methods have limited extensibility and generalization, as every single translation job requires extensive rule engineering and maintenance.

Transformer model and RNN are two machine learning models commonly used in machine translation. RNNs such as LSTM or closed-repetition units are commonly used in machine translation systems using a sequence-by-sequence model.

On the other hand, transforming toys have become a powerful alternative. The foundational article "Attention is all you need" introduced the design of the Transformer, which uses self-attention techniques to capture dependencies through the input string. Using this attention mechanism, Transformer models can pay attention to relevant source words during translation, increase translation accuracy, and handle long-range dependencies more efficiently.

REFERENCES

[1] Brown, Peter F., John Cocke, Stephen A. Della Pietra, Vincent J. Della Pietra, Frederick Jelinek, John Lafferty, Robert L. Mercer, and Paul S. Roossin. "A statistical approach to machine translation." *Computational Linguistics* 16, no. 2 (1990): 79–85.
[2] Zhao, Bei, and Wei Gao. "Machine Learning Based Text Classification Technology." In: 2022 *IEEE 2nd International Conference on Mobile Networks and Wireless Communications* (*ICMNWC*), IEEE, 2022, pp. 1–5.
[3] Sutskever, Ilya, Oriol Vinyals, and Quoc V. Le. "Sequence to sequence learning with neural networks." *Advances in Neural Information Processing Systems* 27 (2014).

[4] Sennrich, Rico, Barry Haddow, and Alexandra Birch. "Neural machine translation of rare words with subword units." (2015). *arXiv preprint arXiv:1508.07909.*

[5] Benkov, Lucia. "Neural machine translation as a novel approach to machine translation." In: *DIVAI 2020 The 13th International Scientific Conference on Distance Learning in Applied Informatics*, 2020, pp. 499–509.

[6] Bkassiny, Mario, Yang Li, and Sudharman K. Jayaweera. "A survey on machine-learning techniques in cognitive radios." *IEEE Communications Surveys & Tutorials* 15, no. 3 (2012): 1136–1159.

Section II

Data-Centric AI in Healthcare and Agriculture

5 Case Study Medical Images Analysis and Classification with Data-Centric Approach

Namrata N. Wasatkar and Pranali G. Chavhan

5.1 INTRODUCTION: BACKGROUND AND DRIVING FORCES

Medical image analysis plays a crucial role in modern healthcare, enabling accurate diagnosis, treatment planning, and monitoring of various medical conditions. With the advent of advanced technologies and the availability of large-scale medical image datasets, there is a growing need to develop efficient and reliable methods for analyzing and interpreting these images [1]. The data-centric approach in medical image analysis focuses on acquiring high-quality datasets, pre-processing the images to ensure accuracy, extracting meaningful features, and utilizing robust classification models [2,3]. By prioritizing data quality, this approach aims to optimize the performance and reliability of the analysis and classification process. Through the integration of machine learning, deep learning, and image processing techniques, the data-centric approach holds tremendous promise in enhancing medical imaging practices, improving healthcare decision-making, and ultimately benefiting patients worldwide [4]. Medical Images Analysis and Classification with a data-centric approach is a comprehensive and innovative field that leverages advanced techniques to extract valuable insights from medical images [4].

Medical image classification plays a critical role in modern healthcare, enabling accurate diagnosis, treatment planning, and patient management. With the rapid advancement of imaging technologies and the exponential growth of medical image data, there is an increasing need to develop efficient and reliable methods for classifying these images effectively [5]. The data-centric approach in medical image classification emphasizes the significance of acquiring high-quality datasets, pre-processing the images to enhance their quality and remove noise or artifacts, extracting relevant and discriminative features, and utilizing robust classification models [6].

By adopting a data-centric approach, healthcare practitioners and researchers can ensure that the classification process is optimized and based on accurate and representative data. The quality and diversity of the dataset are paramount to the success of the classification task, as it enables the model to learn and generalize patterns effectively. Acquiring a diverse dataset that covers various medical conditions,

DOI: 10.1201/9781003461500-7

imaging modalities, and patient demographics is essential to train a robust and reliable classifier [7]. Once the dataset is obtained, pre-processing techniques are applied to enhance the image quality and remove any inconsistencies or imperfections that may affect the classification accuracy. Pre-processing steps may involve resizing images, normalizing pixel values, applying filters, and handling missing data [8]. These steps ensure that the input images are in a suitable format for subsequent analysis and classification.

Feature extraction is a crucial step in medical image classification, as it involves converting the raw image data into meaningful and informative representations. Different techniques can be employed, ranging from traditional statistical features to more advanced deep learning-based approaches. These features aim to capture distinctive characteristics and patterns that are relevant to the classification task. By extracting discriminative features, the model can differentiate between different medical conditions accurately [9].

The selection of an appropriate classification model is another key aspect of the data-centric approach. Various models can be utilized, including traditional machine learning algorithms such as support vector machines, random forests, or more advanced deep learning architectures like convolutional neural networks (CNNs) [10]. The choice of the model depends on the complexity of the classification task, the available computational resources, and the interpretability of the results. It is crucial to select a model that strikes a balance between accuracy and computational efficiency.

Once the model is selected, it undergoes a training process using the pre-processed dataset. During training, the model learns to classify medical images based on the extracted features. The model's hyperparameters, such as learning rate, regularization, and architecture, are fine-tuned to optimize its performance. The trained model is then evaluated using appropriate metrics such as accuracy, precision, recall, and F1 score to assess its classification performance [11].

By leveraging the data-centric approach, medical image classification has the potential to significantly improve patient care. Accurate and reliable classification of medical images enables timely and appropriate treatment decisions, reduces the chances of misdiagnosis, and enhances overall healthcare outcomes. Furthermore, the continuous refinement and improvement of the classification process based on feedback from healthcare professionals and researchers can lead to advancements in medical imaging practices and contribute to the development of innovative diagnostic tools.

In supposition, the data-centric approach in medical image classification prioritizes the acquisition of high-quality datasets, pre-processing of images, extraction of meaningful features, and utilization of robust classification models [12]. By leveraging advanced techniques and placing an emphasis on data quality, this approach has the potential to revolutionize medical image classification, leading to improved patient care and advancing the field of medical imaging.

By employing a data-centric approach, this methodology focuses on acquiring high-quality datasets, pre-processing them to enhance their accuracy, extracting relevant features, and applying suitable classification models. This approach enables healthcare professionals and researchers to efficiently analyze and classify medical images, leading to improved diagnostic accuracy, treatment planning, and patient outcomes [13]. By combining cutting-edge technologies like machine learning, deep learning, and image processing, this approach holds tremendous potential in revolutionizing medical imaging practices and empowering healthcare practitioners with powerful tools for diagnosis and decision-making.

5.2 LITERATURE SURVEY

1. Bullock, J., Cuesta-Lázaro, C. and Quera-Bofarull, A., 2019, March. XNet: a CNN implementation for medical X-ray image segmentation suitable for small datasets.

    This paper presents a case study on the application of a data-centric approach to analyze and classify X-ray images for diagnosing lung diseases. The authors explore feature extraction techniques, feature selection methods, and model selection for accurate classification. They demonstrate the effectiveness of the data-centric approach in achieving high-accuracy rates for disease classification. With this approach, it provides overall accuracy of 92%, an F1 score of 0.92, and an AUC of 0.98, surpassing classical image processing techniques, such as clustering and entropy-based methods, while improving upon the output of existing neural networks used for segmentation in non-medical contexts.

2. Wang, J., Zhu, H., Wang, S.H. and Zhang, Y.D., 2021. A review of deep learning on medical image analysis. Mobile Networks and Applications, 26, pp.351–380.

    This comprehensive review discusses the use of deep learning techniques in medical image analysis. The authors present case studies on the application of deep learning models for tasks such as tumor detection, lesion segmentation, and disease classification in medical imaging.

3. Terzi, R., Azginoglu, N. and Terzi, D.S., 2022. False positive repression: Data centric pipeline for object detection in brain MRI. Concurrency and Computation: Practice and Experience, 34(20), p.e6821.

    This study presents a data-centric approach for brain tumor classification using MRI images. The authors present a case study on brain tumor classification, comparing the performance of different feature selection and classification algorithms, demonstrating the effectiveness of the data-centric approach in accurate tumor classification. The authors suggested pipeline outperformed the traditional pipeline by up to 18% on the Gazi Brains 2020 dataset and up to 24% on the BraTS 2020 dataset for mean specificity value without affecting the sensitivity measure significantly. This suggests that the suggested pipeline minimizes false positive rates caused by bias in real-world applications and can assist in reducing expert workload.

4. Swedhaasri, M., Parekh, T. and Sharma, A., 2021, August. A Multi-Stage Deep Transfer Learning Method for Classification of Diabetic Retinopathy in Retinal Images. In 2021 Second International Conference on Electronics and Sustainable Communication Systems (ICESC) (pp. 1143–1149). IEEE.

    This paper explores the application of a data-centric approach for retinal image analysis and the detection of diabetic retinopathy. The authors discuss various image Pre-processing techniques, feature extraction methods, and classification models. They present a case study on diabetic retinopathy detection using retinal fundus images, demonstrating the effectiveness of the data-centric approach in accurate disease classification. The authors proposed study effort proposes a multi-stage deep transfer learning approach that includes labeling using similar datasets, which is fundamentally distinct. The approach proposed in this study may be used as a screening tool for early identification of DR, with a sensitivity and specificity of 0.99 and a quadratic weighted kappa grade of 0.925466 of the blindness detection dataset.

This paper provides insights into the application of a data-centric approach in the analysis and classification of medical images for different healthcare scenarios. They cover various imaging modalities, pre-processing techniques, feature engineering methods, and classification models, highlighting the benefits and effectiveness of the data-centric approach in improving accuracy and performance in medical image analysis.

5. Chen, C.C., DaPonte, J.S. and Fox, M.D., 1989. Fractal feature analysis and classification in medical imaging. IEEE transactions on medical imaging, 8(2), pp.133–142.

In this article, there are two applications: (1) classification and (2) edge enhancement and detection. This estimate approach is used to define a normalized fractional Brownian motion feature vector for classification purposes. It represented the normalized average absolute intensity difference between pixel pairs on a scaled surface. The feature vector represents the statistical properties of the medial image surface with a small number of data items and is insensitive to linear intensity adjustment. A modified picture is created for edge enhancement and detection applications by computing the fractal dimension of each pixel throughout the whole medical image.

6. Mohan, G. and Subashini, M.M., 2018. MRI based medical image analysis: Survey on brain tumor grade classification. Biomedical Signal Processing and Control, 39, pp.139–161.

This is where digital image processing techniques and machine learning come into play, assisting with further diagnosis, therapy, before and post-surgical procedures, and bridging the gap between the radiologist and the computer. These hybrid approaches give radiologists a second viewpoint and support in comprehending medical pictures, hence boosting diagnosis accuracy. This article will look back at current advances in segmentation and classification in tumor-infected human brain MR images, with a focus on gliomas, including astrocytoma. The approaches for tumor extraction and grading that may be integrated into routine clinical imaging protocols are described.

5.3   IMPLEMENTATION-MEDICAL IMAGE ANALYSES

Step 1: Dataset Exploration and Pre-processing

Exploring and pre-processing a dataset with a data-centric approach involves understanding the data, handling missing values, dealing with outliers, and transforming the data to make it suitable for analysis [14].

Step 2: Data Visualization

Data visualization plays a crucial role in understanding and communicating insights from data. The data visualization process should be driven by the specific characteristics and requirements of data, as well as the objectives of the analysis. By adopting a data-centric approach, data visualizations effectively communicate insights and support data-driven decision-making.

Step 3: Feature Engineering

Feature engineering is an iterative process, and it requires a combination of analytical skills, domain knowledge, and creativity. By adopting a data-centric approach, we can uncover hidden patterns, improve model performance, and gain deeper insights from your data [15].

Step 4: Feature Selection

Feature selection is the process of identifying and selecting the most relevant and informative features from a dataset to improve model performance, reduce overfitting, and enhance interpretability. When approaching feature selection with a data-centric perspective, consider the following points:

- Define the Evaluation Metric
- Perform Initial Feature Exploration
- Filter Methods
- **Wrapper Methods**: Utilize wrapper methods that evaluate feature subsets by training models and measuring their performance [16, 17, 20].
- **Embedded Methods**: Leverage embedded methods that perform feature selection as part of the model training process [21].
- **Model-Based Evaluation**: Train your model using selected features and evaluate its performance using the defined evaluation metric [22].
- **Iterative Refinement**: Iterate the feature selection process by fine-tuning the selection criteria, exploring different methods, or incorporating domain knowledge.
- **Consider Dimensionality Reduction**: If dealing with high-dimensional datasets, consider dimensionality reduction techniques (e.g., Principal Component Analysis or t-SNE) to transform the data into a lower-dimensional space while retaining important information.

  Feature selection is a trade-off between model simplicity, interpretability, and predictive performance. A data-centric approach involves thoroughly evaluating different feature selection techniques, considering the specific requirements of your modeling task, and iteratively refining your feature selection process based on feedback and performance evaluation.

Step 5: Model Selection and Hyperparameter Tuning

It involves choosing the appropriate algorithm and optimizing its hyperparameters to achieve the best performance. When approaching model selection and hyperparameter tuning with a data-centric perspective. The data-centric approach involves an iterative process that considers the characteristics of the data, the specific modeling task, and the evaluation metrics [18]. By systematically exploring different models, tuning hyperparameters, and evaluating performance, we can select the best model and optimize its performance for our data.

Step 6: Model Evaluation

Model evaluation is a crucial step in the data modeling process to assess the performance and effectiveness of a trained model. Model evaluation is an ongoing process that requires careful consideration of the evaluation metrics, performance strategies, and the specific goals of your analysis. By adopting a data-centric approach, you can gain a deeper understanding of your model's performance, make informed decisions, and refine your modeling techniques to optimize results.

5.4   BREAST CANCER WISCONSIN DATASET

Implementing data-centric approach. However, we provided a code template that outlines the steps of the data-centric approach for the Breast Cancer Wisconsin dataset [19]. This code may need to modify and expand specific sections based on specific requirements and insights during the analysis.

The code as per Figures 5.1 and 5.2 provides a simplified example, and there are many more aspects to consider, such as hyperparameter tuning, cross-validation, and more in-depth feature engineering and analysis. This code snippet serves as a starting point to demonstrate the data-centric approach for the Breast Cancer Wisconsin dataset.

```
data = load_breast_cancer()
X = data.data
y= data.target
# Split the data into training and testing sets
X_train, X_test, y_train, y_test = train_test_split(X, y, test_size=0.2, random_state=42)
# Preprocess the data using StandardScaler
scaler = StandardScaler()
X_train = scaler.fit_transform(X_train)
X_test = scaler.transform(X_test)
# Logistic Regression
logistic_model = LogisticRegression()
logistic_model.fit(X_train, y_train)
y_logistic_pred = logistic_model.predict(X_test)
# Decision Tree Classifier
tree_model = DecisionTreeClassifier()
tree_model.fit(X_train, y_train)
y_tree_pred = tree_model.predict(X_test)
# Random Forest Classifier
forest_model = RandomForestClassifier()
forest_model.fit(X_train, y_train)
y_forest_pred = forest_model.predict(X_test)
# Calculate the accuracy for each model
accuracy_logistic = accuracy_score(y_test, y_logistic_pred)
accuracy_tree = accuracy_score(y_test, y_tree_pred)
accuracy_forest = accuracy_score(y_test, y_forest_pred)
print(f"Logistic Regression Accuracy: {accuracy_logistic * 100:.2f}%")
print(f"Decision Tree Classifier Accuracy: {accuracy_tree * 100:.2f}%")
print(f"Random Forest Classifier Accuracy: {accuracy_forest * 100:.2f}%")
```

```
Logistic Regression Accuracy: 97.37%
Decision Tree Classifier Accuracy: 94.74%
Random Forest Classifier Accuracy: 96.49%
```

FIGURE 5.1   Code for implementation of regression without preprocessing data.

```
# Load the Breast Cancer Wisconsin dataset
data = load_breast_cancer()
X = data.data
y = data.target
# Convert binary labels (0 and 1) to continuous values (0.0 and 1.0)
y_continuous = y.astype(float)
# Split the data into training and testing sets
X_train, X_test, y_train, y_test = train_test_split(X, y_continuous, test_size=0.2, random_state=42)
# Linear Regression
linear_model = LinearRegression()
linear_model.fit(X_train, y_train)
y_linear_pred = linear_model.predict(X_test)
# Decision Tree Regression
tree_model = DecisionTreeRegressor()
tree_model.fit(X_train, y_train)
y_tree_pred = tree_model.predict(X_test)
# Random Forest Regression
forest_model = RandomForestRegressor()
forest_model.fit(X_train, y_train)
y_forest_pred = forest_model.predict(X_test)
# Calculate the mean squared error for each model
mse_linear = mean_squared_error(y_test, y_linear_pred)
mse_tree = mean_squared_error(y_test, y_tree_pred)
mse_forest = mean_squared_error(y_test, y_forest_pred)
print(f"Linear Regression Mean Squared Error: {mse_linear:.4f}")
print(f"Decision Tree Regression Mean Squared Error: {mse_tree:.4f}")
print(f"Random Forest Regression Mean Squared Error: {mse_forest:.4f}")
```

```
Linear Regression Mean Squared Error: 0.0641
Decision Tree Regression Mean Squared Error: 0.0702
Random Forest Regression Mean Squared Error: 0.0341
```

FIGURE 5.2   Code for implementation of regression with preprocessing of data.

5.5   COMPARATIVE OF MODEL CENTRIC APPROACH

In the model-centric approach, the primary focus is on building and optimizing models, often with less emphasis on thorough data pre-processing and analysis. In the model-centric approach, the above code directly applies the model to the dataset without extensive data preprocessing. While this approach is quicker, it might lead to suboptimal results if the data is not properly prepared or if feature engineering is necessary.

Both approaches have their place depending on the available resources, and the complexity of the dataset. A balanced approach that incorporates elements from both strategies can often lead to the best results.

5.6   CONCLUSION

The case study emphasizes the importance of comprehensive and diverse datasets. The availability of a wide range of medical images representing different diseases and conditions enables the system to generalize and adapt to new cases effectively. Additionally, the inclusion of diverse patient populations helps to ensure that the developed algorithms are applicable across various demographics, thus reducing potential biases.

Furthermore, the case study highlights the need for robust and scalable infrastructure to support the analysis and classification of medical images. This includes powerful computing resources, storage capacity, and secure data management systems. Such infrastructure enables the efficient processing of large datasets and facilitates collaboration among healthcare professionals and researchers [23].

In conclusion, the case study underscores the transformative potential of a data-centric approach in the analysis and classification of medical images. By leveraging advanced algorithms, comprehensive datasets, and robust infrastructure, healthcare professionals can enhance diagnostic accuracy, improve patient outcomes, and accelerate medical research. The findings from this case study provide valuable insights and serve as a foundation for further advancements in the field of medical image analysis.

REFERENCES

[1] Roth, A., Wüstefeld, K. and Weichert, F., 2021. A data-centric augmentation approach for disturbed sensor image segmentation. *Journal of Imaging*, 7(10), p. 206.

[2] Bullock, J., Cuesta-Lázaro, C. and Quera-Bofarull, A., 2019. XNet: A convolutional neural network (CNN) implementation for medical x-ray image segmentation suitable for small datasets. In: *Medical Imaging 2019: Biomedical Applications in Molecular, Structural, and Functional Imaging* (Vol. 10953, pp. 453–463). SPIE, Bellingham, WA.

[3] Zahid, A., Poulsen, J.K., Sharma, R. and Wingreen, S.C., 2021. A systematic review o emerging information technologies for sustainable data-centric health-care. *International Journal of Medical Informatics*, 149, p. 104420.

[4] Kalyankar, P.A., Mulani, A.O., Thigale, S.P., Chavhan, P.G. and Jadhav, M.M., 2022. Scalable face image retrieval using AESC technique. *Journal of Algebraic Statistics*, 13(3), pp. 173–176.

[5] Shamshad, F., Khan, S., Zamir, S.W., Khan, M.H., Hayat, M., Khan, F.S. and Fu, H., 2023. Transformers in medical imaging: A survey. *Medical Image Analysis*, 88, p. 102802.

[6] Wang, L., Xue, W., Li, Y., Luo, M., Huang, J., Cui, W. and Huang, C., 2017. Automatic epileptic seizure detection in EEG signals using multi-domain feature extraction and nonlinear analysis. *Entropy*, 19(6), p. 222.

[7] Waugh, S.A., Purdie, C.A., Jordan, L.B., Vinnicombe, S., Lerski, R.A., Martin, P. and Thompson, A.M., 2016. Magnetic resonance imaging texture analysis classification of primary breast cancer. *European Radiology*, 26, pp. 322–330.

[8] Maharana, K., Mondal, S. and Nemade, B., 2022. A review: Data pre-processing and data augmentation techniques. *Global Transitions Proceedings*, 3(1), pp. 91–99.

[9] Preece, S.J., Goulermas, J.Y., Kenney, L.P. and Howard, D., 2008. A comparison of feature extraction methods for the classification of dynamic activities from accelerometer data. *IEEE Transactions on Biomedical Engineering*, 56(3), pp. 871–879.

[10] Aybike, U and Kilimci, Z.H., 2021. The prediction of chiral metamaterial resonance using convolutional neural networks and conventional machine learning algorithms. *International Journal of Computational and Experimental Science and Engineering*, 7(3), pp. 156–163.

[11] Dinh, A., Miertschin, S., Young, A. and Mohanty, S.D., 2019. A data-driven approach to predicting diabetes and cardiovascular disease with machine learning. *BMC Medical Informatics and Decision Making*, 19(1), pp. 1–15.

[12] Bhattacharya, S., Maddikunta, P.K.R., Pham, Q.V., Gadekallu, T.R., Chowdhary, C.L., Alazab, M. and Piran, M.J., 2021. Deep learning and medical image processing for coronavirus (COVID-19) pandemic: A survey. *Sustainable Cities and Society*, 65, p. 102589.

[13] Castaneda, C., Nalley, K., Mannion, C., Bhattacharyya, P., Blake, P., Pecora, A., Goy, A. and Suh, K.S., 2015. Clinical decision support systems for improving diagnostic accuracy and achieving precision medicine. *Journal of Clinical Bioinformatics*, 5(1), pp. 1–16.

[14] Whang, S.E., Roh, Y., Song, H. and Lee, J.G., 2023. Data collection and quality challenges in deep learning: A data-centric ai perspective. *The VLDB Journal*, 32(4), pp. 791–813.

[15] Hamid, O.H., 2023. Data-centric and model-centric AI: Twin drivers of compact and robust Industry 4.0 solutions. *Applied Sciences*, 13(5), p. 2753.

[16] Panthong, R. and Srivihok, A., 2015. Wrapper feature subset selection for dimension reduction based on ensemble learning algorithm. *Procedia Computer Science*, 72, pp. 162–169.

[17] Taylor, K.I., Staunton, H., Lipsmeier, F., Nobbs, D. and Lindemann, M., 2020. Outcome measures based on digital health technology sensor data: Data-and patient-centric approaches. *NPJ Digital Medicine*, 3(1), p. 97.

[18] Taylor, K.I., Staunton, H., Lipsmeier, F., Nobbs, D. and Lindemann, M., 2020. Outcome measures based on digital health technology sensor data: Data-and patient-centric approaches. *NPJ Digital Medicine*, 3(1), p. 97.

[19] Kumar, A. and Gautam, S., 2022. Improving medical diagnostics with machine learning: A study on data classification algorithms. *International Journal of Advanced Computer Research*, 12(61), p. 31.

[20] Chavhan, P.G., Ratil, R.V. and Mahalle, P.N., 2023. An investigative approach of context in internet of behaviours (IoB). In: *International Conference on Emerging Trends in Expert Applications & Security* (pp. 333–343). Springer, Singapore.

[21] Daphal, P., Pokale, S., Chavhan, P., Wasatkar, N., Rathi, S., Dongre, Y. and Kolekar, V., 2023. Human pose detection system using machine learning. *International Journal of Intelligent Systems and Applications in Engineering*, 11(3), pp. 553–561.

[22] Kharate, N., Patil, S., Shelke, P., Shinde, G., Mahalle, P., Sable, N. and Chavhan, P.G., 2023. Unveiling the resilience of image captioning models and the influence of pre-trained models on deep learning performance. *International Journal of Intelligent Systems and Applications in Engineering*, 11(9s), pp. 1–7.

[23] Mahalle, P.N., Shinde, G.R., Ingle, Y.S. and Wasatkar, N.N. (2023). Data-centric AI. In: *Data Centric Artificial Intelligence: A Beginner's Guide: Data-Intensive Research*. Springer, Singapore. doi:10.1007/978-981-99-6353-9_5

6 Comparative Analysis of Machine Learning Classification Techniques for Kidney Disease Prediction

Jayashri Bagade, Nilesh P. Sable, and Komal M. Birare

6.1 INTRODUCTION

The kidney's primary job is to filter the body's blood. Kidney disease is a silent killer because kidney failure can occur without any warning signs or symptoms. The definition of chronic renal disease is a deterioration in kidney function over months or years. Diabetes and high blood pressure are common contributors to kidney damage. Globally, chronic kidney disease (CKD) is a serious health issue that affects many people. People who can't afford therapy for chronic renal disease may suffer catastrophic effects if they don't receive it. The most accurate test to assess kidney function and the severity of CKD is the glomerular filtration rate (GFR). It can be calculated using the blood creatinine level, as well as factors like age, gender, and other details. Most of the time, becoming sick sooner is preferable. Consequently, it is feasible to avoid major diseases. The kidney function of people with CKD gradually deteriorates over time. It is a huge burden on the healthcare system due to its rising frequency and high risk of developing end-stage renal disease, which calls for dialysis or kidney transplantation. A major worldwide health concern, CKD also has a terrible prognosis for morbidity and mortality. However, CKD can be significantly slowed down and serious complications can be avoided with early detection and treatment. In order to effectively manage and treat the condition, it is imperative to be aware of the signs and symptoms of renal disease. By leading a healthy lifestyle, CKD can be prevented from progressing as quickly, by modifications like eating a balanced diet, exercising frequently, abstaining from smoking and excessive alcohol use, and managing underlying medical conditions like diabetes and hypertension. Regular kidney function tests (KFTs), such as urine and blood tests, can also identify CKD early on, allowing for quick management and intervention to stop further kidney damage. The major objective of this research is to investigate datasets, flow

DOI: 10.1201/9781003461500-8

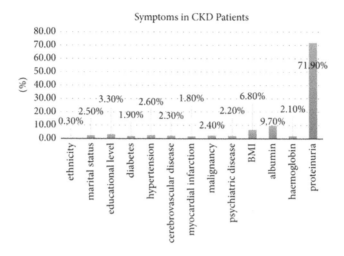

FIGURE 6.1   Symptoms in CKD patients.

diagrams, and block diagrams to employ different algorithms to predict the development of renal illness.

Early identification of renal disease can help prevent irreparable kidney damage, albeit it may not always be possible. It's critical to have a better understanding of kidney disease symptoms to accomplish this goal. To predict the occurrence of renal illness, the project involves analysing patient health and disease data, comparing them using various indices and using machine learning classification algorithms. Random Forests, K-nearest Neighbour, Support Vector Machine, ADA Boost, Gradient Boosting, Cat Boost, and Stochastic Gradient Boosting are some of the classification methods used [1]. The data is categorized by the machine classified into various classes, labels, and categories. Doctors often perform physical examinations, evaluate the patient's medical history, and then perform diagnostic tests and treatments to identify the underlying cause of symptoms to diagnose an illness.

With a fast-rising patient population, CKD is currently the leading cause of death, accounting for 1.7 million fatalities per year. Although there are many different diagnostic techniques, this study uses machine learning because of its high accuracy. Today, millions of people die from CKD, a condition that is quickly spreading and for which there is now no timely, effective treatment. Patients with chronic renal disease typically originate from middle- and low-income nations.

Exercise, drinking water, and avoiding junk food are all advised. Figure 6.1 depicts the typical signs of chronic renal disease.

6.2   LITERATURE REVIEW

Due to its potential to enhance diagnostic precision, prognostic prediction, and therapeutic outcomes, machine learning has attracted a lot of attention in recent years. For effective treatment and management of kidney diseases, early detection and precise disease progression prediction are essential. In 2015, Swathi Baby [2] suggested a system based on predictive data mining for the development of an analysis and prediction tool for renal illness. Data on renal disease collected and analysed by Weka and Orange software were used in the system. The study used a variety of machine learning methods to anticipate and statistically analyse the likelihood of renal sickness, including Naive Bayes, J48, AD Trees, K Star, and Random Forest. Performance indicators for each approach were computed and contrasted. The study's findings demonstrate that the K-star and Random Forest (RF) algorithms outperformed the opposition on the test dataset.

These methods have Receiver Operating Characteristic (ROC) values of 1 and 2, respectively, and were discovered to produce models more quickly. A million people perished in 2013 because of chronic renal disease. More people have CKD in developing nations, where there are 387.5 million CKD patients overall, 177.4 million of whom are men and 210.1 million of whom are women. These statistics demonstrate that a significant portion of the population in emerging nations has chronic renal disease and that this proportion is rising daily. For CKD to be treated at an early stage, a lot of work has been put into early diagnosis. In this paper, we emphasize accuracy while concentrating on machine learning prediction models for chronic renal disease. When both kidneys are destroyed, a common type of kidney illness known as CKD develops, and CKD patients must live with this condition for an extended period. Any renal issue that could impair kidney function is referred to here as kidney damage.

To forecast renal illnesses in 2015, Dayanand [3] suggested employing support vector machines (SVMs) and artificial neural networks (ANNs). The primary objective of this study was to compare the accuracy and execution times of these two algorithms. According to the experimental data, ANN is performed better than SVM in terms of accuracy. The Naive Bayes, SVM, and decision tree (DT) were used in different machine learning algorithms for classification, while RF, logistic regression, and linear regression were utilized in the medical sectors for regression and prediction. Due to early-stage diagnosis and prompt patient treatment, the death rate can be reduced by the effective application of these algorithms. Patients with chronic renal disease should maintain their clinical symptoms and engage in regular physical activity. Researchers Ganapathi Raju, K Gayathri Praharshitha, and K Prasanna Lakshmi completed a study in 2020 [4] that used different classification algorithms on patient medical information to diagnose chronic kidney illness. The primary objective of this study was to determine the classification algorithm that, based on the classification report and performance indicators, would be most useful for diagnosing CKD. In 2017, a team of researchers have used 14 attributes to predict CKD and achieved 0.991 accuracy with a multiclass decision forest [8].

A team of researchers used a multiclass decision forest in 2017 to predict CKD using 14 different attributes, and they were able to do so with an astounding accuracy of 0.991 [6]. To increase accuracy, the researchers eliminated instances with missing values and trained both a logistic regression model and a neural network. Overall accuracy for these models was 0.975 and 0.960, respectively. Correlations between the chosen attributes ranged from 0.2 to 0.8. From a medical standpoint, it's critical to consider the associations between characteristics and CKD. For instance, specific gravity has a correlation of 0.73 to the class and can both cause and be caused by CKD. Eliminating these characteristics might result in a drop in accuracy. In 2017, Sarica et al. [5] talked about the benefits of RF while considering any possible disadvantages. More study on comparisons between this method and other widely used classification systems is also encouraged, particularly in the early detection of the transition from mild cognitive impairment (MCI) to Alzheimer's disease (AD). This study recommends a procedure that involves preprocessing of the data, collaborative filtering for handling missing values, attribute selection, and CKD status prediction using clinical data. The additional tree and RF classifiers displayed the highest accuracy, obtaining 100% accuracy, with the least amount of bias towards the attributes.

In 2015, In 2021, Authors used the WEKA data mining tool to test eight machine learning models [7]. The Naive Bayes, Multi-layer Perception, and J48 algorithms performed the best with accuracy scores of 0.95, 0.99, and 0.99, respectively, and ROC scores of 1. The multilayer perceptron algorithm scored the highest in the study using Kappa statistics, with a score of 0.99, followed by the decision table and J48 algorithms with scores of 0.97. El-Houssainy et al. [8] examined the outcomes of various machine learning models and discovered that the Multiclass Decision Forest algorithm had the highest accuracy rate of about 99% for a condensed dataset with only 14 attributes. Supriya Aktar et al. [9] concentrated on using different machine learning classification algorithms to increase the CKD diagnosis' accuracy and shorten the diagnosis process. The goal of the study was to categorize various stages of CKD according to their severity. The performance of various algorithms, including radial basis function (RBF,) RF, and Basic Propagation Neural Network, was examined by the researchers. The analysis's findings demonstrated that, with an accuracy of 85.3%, the RBF algorithm performed better than the other classifiers. In a dataset of CKD, Dilli Arasu and Thirumalaiselvi [10] have worked on missing values. The accuracy of our model and the results of our predictions will both be lowered by missing values in the dataset. They came up with a solution to the issue that by performing a recalculation process on the CKD stages, they came up with unknown values.

They recalculated the values in place of the missing ones. With the aid of a machine learning algorithm, Salekin and Stankovic [11] employ a novel approach to detect CKD. They receive results based on a dataset with 400 records and 25 attributes that indicate whether a patient has CKD or not. To obtain results, they employ neural networks, RFs, and k-nearest neighbours. They use the wrapper method for feature reduction. For feature reduction, they use the wrapper method which detects CKD with high accuracy. The effects of class imbalance during data training for the development of neural network algorithms for the treatment of chronic renal disease are examined by Yildirim [12]. In the suggested work, comparative research was carried out using a sampling algorithm. This study demonstrates how sampling algorithms can help classification algorithms perform better. It also shows that the learning rate is a crucial factor that has a big influence on multilayer perceptron. Sharma et al. [13] tested 12 different classification algorithms on a dataset containing 400 records and 24 attributes. They have compared their estimated findings with the actual results to ascertain the precision of their forecasts. They used evaluation standards like precision, sensitivity, accuracy, and specificity. The DT approach offers a precision of 1, specificity of 1, and sensitivity of 0.9720 with an accuracy of up to 98.6%.

6.3   METHODS FOR CLASSIFICATION

In this study, the presence of chronic renal illness in people was predicted using several classification methods. The classifiers employed for classifications are SVM, K-Nearest Neighbour (KNN), ADA Boost (ADA), Cat Boost CAT, DT, and (RF. Each classifier projected the chance of the disease using the chronic kidney/renal disease dataset. After being evaluated for accuracy, precision, and F-measure, the classifier with the best performance was picked. The recommended approach makes use of a predictive data mining framework. The workflow is depicted in Figure 6.2.

Many hospitals and medical labs throughout the city provided the data for this investigation. The synthetic KFT dataset, which may be used to study various diseases, was made using these data. The dataset used in the study, which examined 401 cases, contained six variables including age, gender, urea, creatinine, and GFR. Data on renal diseases and how they impact kidney function are included in the KFT dataset. A dataset of patient medical details was used to test different classification techniques, and the effectiveness of each algorithm was compared. This analysis served as the foundation for the prediction. The model was trained and examined using a training dataset with 320 rows. The model's performance on an unknown dataset was assessed using the testing dataset, which had 80 rows. To predict the likelihood of the disease, the dataset for CKD was gathered and applied to each classifier. Based on the accuracy rate, precision, and F-measure values gleaned from the entire analysis, each classifier's performance was assessed. Quite a few algorithms, including SVM and KNN, are implemented in the project's architecture.

The choice to use an SVM was made based on the problem's nature, which may not be linearly separable. The SVM algorithm with a nonlinear kernel is a good choice in these circumstances. On the other hand, KNN is renowned for its

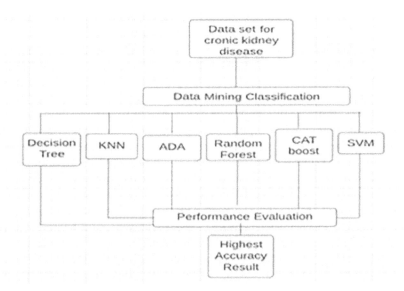

FIGURE 6.2   Workflow of experimentation.

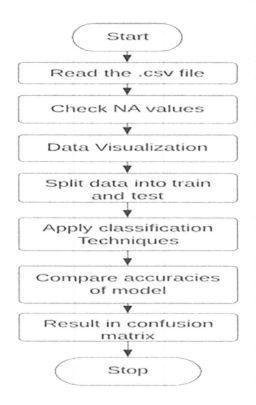

FIGURE 6.3 Algorithmic approach.

resistance to noise in training data, though its effectiveness might depend on the number of training examples used. The accuracy of the KNN algorithm depends on choosing the best value for the K parameter, which establishes the number of nearest neighbours and the distance metric to be applied. Calculations in machine learning can take a while, particularly when determining how far apart each instance is from all training instances. To handle categorical features of a dataset, RF, which is essentially a collection of DTs combined, can be used. Many training examples and high-dimensional spaces can both be handled by this algorithm. Certain criteria must be established to use RF. The algorithmic approach is shown in Figure 6.3.

6.3.1 SUPPORT VECTOR MACHINES (SVM)

The powerful, cutting-edge regression method SVM can be used with both linear and nonlinear data. SVM is utilized for binary and multiclass classification in Oracle Data Mining. The main benefit of SVM is its capacity to infer, implicitly, in a modified (nonlinear) feature space the distance between a molecule and the hyperplane without changing the original descriptors. This is feasible as a result of the "kernel trick." The most popular Gaussian kernel, also referred to as the radial basis function kernel, was used in this study. The SVM algorithm's objective is to establish the optimal decision boundary or line that can divide n-dimensional space into classes so that we may quickly place.

6.3.2 K-Nearest Neighbour (KNN)

The K-Nearest Neighbour algorithm (K-NN) is a nonparametric pattern recognition model for classification and regression. It operates by finding the K closest training instances in the feature space, regardless of whether the input is for classification or regression. KNN is an illustration of instance-based learning. The algorithm outputs a class membership for KNN classification, where a 75% vote of neighbours is necessary for classification, when K=3, the class contains only the three nearest neighbours. Each neighbour is given a weight of 1/d in a traditional weighting system, where d is the distance from the data points. The Euclidean distance, or the shortest distance in a straight line between two neighbours, is calculated by the K-NN algorithm. K-NN's lack of sensitivity to the data's local configuration values is a disadvantage, though. Before using the K-NN method in the feature space, feature extraction is done to turn raw data into a set of features.

The k-nearest neighbours' algorithm, sometimes referred to as KNN or K-NN, is a supervised learning classifier that employs proximity to produce classifications or predictions about the grouping of a single data point. Although it can be applied to classification or regression issues, it is commonly employed as a classification algorithm because it relies on the idea that comparable points can be discovered close to one another.

6.3.3 ADA Boost Technique

Popular and effective, ADA has been used extensively in a variety of industries, including computer vision, natural language processing, and bioinformatics. The algorithm has become a useful tool for resolving challenging issues because of its propensity to adapt to changing data and enhance performance over time. Its use in ensemble methods has also improved the robustness and accuracy of machine learning models. Many researchers and practitioners in the field rely on the ADA algorithm because of its adaptability and efficiency.

6.3.4 Cat Boost Technique

A brand-new open-source machine learning algorithm called Cat Boost was created by Yandex in 2017. This algorithm, which is based on the idea of trees and gradient boosting, is particularly helpful for categorical boosting, application ranking, and various recommendation systems. The Cat Boost algorithm is well-known for being simple to implement and simple to use, and it is frequently used to solve classification and regression problems. This algorithm also has the benefit of being effective with small and heterogeneous datasets. The Cat Boost algorithm's capacity to handle categorical features automatically and effectively is perhaps its most noteworthy benefit, making it a useful tool for data analysis in a variety of contexts. Both categorical and numerical features can be handled by the gradient boosting variation known as Cat Boost. To transform categorical data into numerical features, there is no need for feature encoding methods like One-Hot Encoder or Label Encoder.

6.3.5 DECISION TREE

One common supervised learning method for both classification and regression tasks is the DT algorithm. Although it can be used to solve regression issues, classification tasks are where it is most frequently applied. The algorithm uses a classifier structure resembling a tree, with internal nodes denoting dataset features and internal branches denoting decision rules. DTs use an inquiry-based approach, in which questions are posed to ascertain whether or not a specific attribute is present. The data are then divided into subtrees and further examined for classification or regression tasks using the results.

6.3.6 RANDOM FOREST

The popular machine learning algorithm RF is a part of the supervised learning methodology. It can be applied to ML issues involving both classification and regression. It is predicated on the idea of ensemble learning, which is the act of integrating various classifiers to address a complicated issue and enhance the model's performance. According to what its name implies, "Random Forest is a classifier that contains a number of DTs on various subsets of the given dataset and takes the average to improve the predictive accuracy of that dataset." Instead of depending on a single DT, the RF uses forecasts from each tree and predicts the result based on the votes of the majority of predictions.

Higher accuracy and overfitting are prevented by the larger number of trees in the forest. Some DTs may predict the correct output, while others may not because the RF combines numerous trees to forecast the class of the dataset. But when all the trees are combined, they forecast the right result. For the dataset's feature variable to predict true outcomes rather than a speculated result, there should be some actual values in the dataset. Each tree's predictions must have extremely low correlations.

6.4 RESULT

The effectiveness of each algorithm was assessed after a study was conducted using a variety of algorithms. The accuracy values for each algorithm are displayed on a graph that was made to help convey this information in an understandable and concise manner. The graph gives a visual representation of how each algorithm performs, making it simple to compare them and determine which algorithm is the most accurate for the given dataset.

Data analysis frequently employs this method of presenting findings through graphs because it makes complex information easier to understand. It is simpler to spot patterns and trends. Graphs can also aid in the simplification of complex information to make it more understandable to a wider audience.

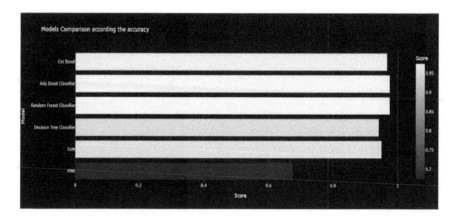

FIGURE 6.4   Comparison of accuracy of models.

TABLE 6.1
Performance Comparison of Models

Sr. No	Classification Model	Accuracy		Precision	Recall	F1 Score
		Training	Testing			
1	KNN	0.77	0.67	0.74	0.71	0.72
2	SVM	0.94	0.95	0.99	0.93	0.96
3	Random forest	1.0	0.975	0.96	0.94	0.98
4	Decision tree	0.97	0.94	0.93	0.97	0.95
5	ADA Boost	1.0	0.97	0.96	1.00	0.98
6	Cat Boost	1.0	0.966	0.96	0.99	0.97

In this situation, the graph showing the accuracy values for each algorithm can assist academics and medical professionals in deciding which algorithm is best for identifying a specific disease or condition. The development of more precise diagnostic tools or an improvement in patient care for the specific condition can both benefit from this information. Overall, the effectiveness of data analysis in healthcare and other fields can be greatly improved using graphs and other visual aids when data is presented visually than when it is presented in its raw form.

The machine learning models are trained on the KFT dataset to validate the performance of the model. The models trained on 320 data records are used to test 80 unseen data records. Performance of the models is evaluated using four evaluation parameters namely accuracy, precision, recall, and F1 score. The results are presented in Table 6.1. A comparison of the accuracy of the model is shown in Figure 6.4.

6.5   CONCLUSIONS AND FUTURE SCOPE

In the medical field, data mining and machine learning have found uses, including in the prognosis of CKD. To predict the likelihood of CKD, this study introduces a novel decision support system that makes use of machine learning classifiers. The classifiers were successful in predicting other diseases in addition to CKD. The effectiveness of three different classifiers used in the study to predict the presence of CKD was compared. The findings demonstrated that in terms of predicting CKD, the ADA Boost and RF classifiers performed better than the SVM, DT, KNN, and CAT Boost classifiers. Overall, the study has overcome earlier shortcomings and increased the precision of CKD prediction. The study's results are encouraging and serve as a foundation for additional study in this area.

The current techniques for anticipating chronic renal disease are deemed sufficient, despite some drawbacks. However, as the table below illustrates, research is still being done to increase the precision of kidney disorder prediction and identification. A more advanced CKD prediction system is still needed despite current initiatives. Given that this area of research is still largely unexplored, a decision support system that can aid in the early detection of chronic renal disease is especially necessary.

This study uses a variety of classification methods to identify CKD including RFs, KNN, SVM, ADA Boost, DT, and Cat Boost. These classifiers' performance can be evaluated and contrasted with that of other classifiers. For prompt treatment to begin and to stop the disease from worsening, early detection of CKD is essential. Therefore, early disease detection and prompt treatment are crucial for the medical industry. Alternative classifiers can be investigated and assessed in upcoming studies to find better approaches to objective function problems.

REFERENCES

[1] Konstantina Kourou, Themis P. Exarchosa, Konstantinos P. Exarchos, Michalis V. Karamouzis, Dimitrios I. Fotiadis: "Machine learning applications in cancer prognosis and prediction", *Computational and Structural Biotechnology Journal*, Vol. 13, pp. 8–17 (2015).

[2] P. Swathi Baby, T. Panduranga Vital: "Statistical analysis and predicting kidney diseases using machine learning algorithms" *International Journal of Engineering Research and Technology*, Vol. 4, (2015).

[3] S. Vijayarani, S. Dhayanand: "Kidney disease prediction using SVM and ANN algorithms", International Journal of Computing and Business Research, Vol. 6, (2015).

[4] Ganapathi Raju, K. Gayathri Praharshitha, K. Prasanna Lakshmi: "Prediction of chronic kidney disease (CKD) using data science", International Conference on Intelligent Computing and Control Systems (ICCS) (2019).

[5] Alessia Sarica, Antonio Cerasa, Aldo Quattrone: "Random forest algorithm for the classification of neuroimaging data in alzheimer's disease", *Front Aging Neurosci*. 2017 Oct 6; 9: 329. doi: 10.3389/fnagi.2017.00329. PMID: 29056906; PMCID: PMC5635046 (2017).

[6] N.V. Ganapathi Raju, K. Prasanna Lakshmi, K. Gayathri Praharshitha: "Prediction of chronic kidney disease (CKD) Using data science", International Conference on Intelligent Computing and Control Systems (ICCS) (2017).

[7] Gazi Mohammed Ifraz, Muhammad Hasnath Rashid, Tahia Tazin, Sami Bourouis, Mohammad Monirujjaman Khan: "Comparative analysis for prediction of kidney disease using intelligent machine learning methods" *Comput Math Methods Med*. 2021 Dec 3; 2021: 6141470. doi: 10.1155/2021/6141470. Retraction in: Comput Math Methods Med. 2023 Nov 1; 2023: 9864519. PMID: 34899968; PMCID: PMC8664508, (2021).

[8] El-Houssainy A. Ready, Ayman S. Anwar: "Prediction of kidney disease stages using data mining". *Informatics in Medicine Unlocked*, Vol. 15 (2019).

[9] Suraiya Aktar, Abhijit Pathak, Abrar Hossain Tasin: "Chronic kidney disease (CKD) Prediction using data mining techniques", In book: *Advances in Intelligent Systems and Computing* (pp. 976–988). Publisher: Springer, Cham. (2021).

[10] S Dilli Arasu, R Thirumalaiselvi: "Review of chronic kidney disease based on data mining techniques", *International Journal of Applied Engineering Research* ISSN 0973-4562 Volume 12, Number 23 pp. 13498–13505 (2017).

[11] Asif Salekin, John Stankovic: "Detection of Chronic Kidney Disease and Selecting Important Predictive Attributes", 2016 IEEE International Conference on Healthcare Informatics (ICHI), (2016).

[12] Elias Dritsas, Maria Trigka: "Machine learning techniques for chronic kidney disease risk prediction." Pinar Yildirim: "Chronic Kidney Disease Prediction on Imbalanced Data by Multilayer Perceptron: Chronic Kidney Disease Prediction", IEEE 41st Annual Computer Software and Applications Conference (COMPSAC), (2017).

[13] Sahil Sharma, Vinod Sharma, Atul Sharma: "Performance Based Evaluation of Various Machine Learning Classification Techniques for Chronic Kidney Disease Diagnosis", *International Journal of Modern Computer Science (IJMCS)*, Vol. 4, (2016).

7 Fusion of Multi-Modal Lumber Spine Scans Using Convolutional Neural Networks

Bhakti Palkar

7.1 INTRODUCTION: BACKGROUND AND DRIVING FORCES

The spine supports all the activities like lifting, walking, sitting and standing. Number of spine patients is rising across the globe. In India, more than 200,000 spine patients are treated in a year. More than 30,000 cases are of only spinal cord injury due to accidents [1]. Earlier, back pain used to be a problem for only elderly people, but nowadays, we observe back pain in children and young adults also. It is mainly because of an unhealthy lifestyle. Earlier kids and young adults used to play sports outside, but now they are glued to television or mobile phones and frequently in an abnormal posture on a couch and consuming a lot of junk food. This causes lower back problems. Back muscles support the spine and its strength is important to the human body. When we lift something heavy, major stress is handled by the back muscles. If the back muscles are weak, then the stress is transferred to the spine vertebras and discs. This leads to various spine-related diseases like degenerative spine diseases, spine Spondylosis, Sciatica and scoliosis. World Spine Day is observed on 16 October every year. In 2017, a major metropolitan four-city survey was conducted in India to identify categories and types of spine patients. Nearly 75% of patients of the surveyed people suffered from lower back pain and the age group of these people was 16–34 [2]. The patients are increasing rapidly and so is the quantity of medical scans. The rapid growth in the quantity of medical images being captured worldwide is also because companies like GE Healthcare, Siemens and Philips are coming up with technically advanced, easy and user-friendly devices. Magnetic resonance imaging (MRI), X-ray, computed tomography (CT), ultrasound, mammograms, positron emission tomography (PET), Single-photon emission computed tomography (SPECT) PET, SPECT are some common medical imaging techniques. Each technique has its own traits. Depending on the body organ being observed, imaging modality is prescribed by a doctor. In some situations where one imaging modality is not enough to arrive at some conclusion, doctors suggest multiple modality images. The pervasiveness of medical images influences the necessity of accurate analysis

DOI: 10.1201/9781003461500-9

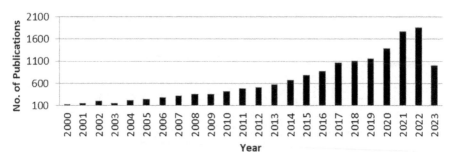

FIGURE 7.1   Quantity of papers available in PubMed database on "medical image fusion".

Source: PubMed Dataset.

of these images. The research area "medical image fusion" is growing vastly [3]. In Figure 7.1, we can observe the increasing number of publications based on "Medical Image Fusion" in PubMed database from year the 2000 to June 2023.

Key Contribution: In this research work, lumbar spine diseases of 12 different types are considered for fusion. A novel deep learning and wavelet-based approach is used for CT and MRI fusion of spine images to generate one image that contains details from both MR and CT images.

7.2   RELATED WORK

Image fusion is a very broad term. It is applied on any two images to integrate their contents into one image. All the methods of fusion are generally sorted into four categories: (1) Spatial domain; (2) Pyramid based; (3) Frequency domain transforms; (4) Neural network.

A variety of spatial domain techniques like simple average, minimum selection, maximum selection, Max-Min, simple block replace, weighted averaging, intensity-hue-saturation, Brovey, principal component analysis (PCA) and guided filtering are used for fusion. Being simple and easy to implement is the main distinguishing factor of these methods. However, these methods may show blurred output, sometimes making them not suitable for medical applications. In this category, only intensity-hue-saturation combined with PCA is applied on PET and MR images of brain to detect Alzheimer's [4].

Pyramid-based fusion techniques [5–16] generate images of decent quality. These techniques have been applied mostly on general images. The output depends on the number of decomposition levels. The higher the number of decomposition levels, the better would be the output here. Only a morphological pyramid in this category is used on CT and MR images of the human brain for tumour diagnosis [16]. Sometimes, pyramid-based fusion methods show blocky effect on output images. To deal with this problem, the Laplacian pyramid is combined with a Discrete Cosine Transform, and then, it is applied on MRIs and CT scans of the brain [17].

The third category of fusion methods is "frequency domain-Transform based fusion". The most extensively used transform in the medical domain is discrete wavelet transform (DWT). It is typically applied on CT and MR images of the brain [18–25]. It is also combined with PCA as a fusion rule to detect brain cancer cells using CT and MR images [26]. We can generate wavelets using other transforms and use them for fusion in place of DWT [27,28]. In spite of providing a better signal-to-noise ratio, DWT is sometimes not preferred by researchers because it lacks phase information and it is a shift variant. Complex wavelet transform is also quite popular among researchers. The dual tree complex wavelet transform (DT-CWT) overcomes the drawbacks of DWT but it requires more processing power, and more memory than DWT because of the dual trees [29]. DT-CWT is combined with particle swarm optimization for brain diagnosis using CT and MR images [30,31]. Rotated wavelet transform (RWT) is slightly different from DWT. It preserves texture and displays high contrast. However, edge orientations are limited in the output of RWT. It is also applied to CT-MR images of the brain [32]. Stationary wavelet transform (SWT) removes "shift variance" drawback of DWT like DT-CWT. But its computational complexity is very high and it needs larger storage space. SWT has been used to fuse CT and MR images of the brain [33]. Lifting wavelet transform reduces the memory requirement of DWT but it is very time-consuming. It has been tested on CT-MRI, MRI-PET and CT-SPECT scans of brain [34]. All the variants of wavelet transform cannot extract curves very efficiently. Curvelet transform efficiently represents curves of the edges with a lesser number of coefficients. However, it generates redundant features and requires a much longer time to calculate coefficients. Curvelet transform has been applied to CT-MR images of the brain, abdomen and CT-mammograms of the breast [35]. Contourlet transform is good at capturing geometric structures in images. It lacks shift-invariance, results in ringing artefact and cannot deal with mis-registration which in turn results in image distortion. Contourlet transform has been applied to CT-MR images of lungs, T1MRI-T2MRI of knees and X-Ray-CT of eyes [36,37]. Non-subsampled contourlet transform (NSCT) deals with the problems of "mis-registration", but it is very time-consuming. NSCT has been applied to MRI-PET images of the brain [38]. The fourth category of fusion methods is "neural network based fusion" [39]. Artificial neural network is mostly clubbed with other methods like wavelet and fuzzy logic for fusion [40]. Pulse-coupled neural network (PCNN) does not require any training and it produces a minimal number of features even for large images. It faces difficulty in estimating the optimum values for its large number of parameters. It is applied to CT-MR images of the brain [41]. PCNN is combined with non-subsampled shearlet transform [42], ripplet transform [43] and also with NCST [44] for CT and T2–MR fusion. In the past 4 years, people have been using deep networks to extract features [45,46]. Finding a good fusion algorithm in the medical domain is still a challenge because a fusion method that works for one combination of multi-modal images may fail completely for other modalities. It is also observed that "brain" is the most researched organ in this research area. Almost little-to-no attention is paid to "spine" which is also a crucial body part.

7.3   PROPOSED WORK

This section introduces a new method to fuse multi-modal images using two very much known deep learning frameworks – VGG19 and AlexNet. These deep frameworks are used in combination with 2D-DWT.

7.3.1   2D-Discrete Wavelet Transform

In the first step, the Image goes through the low pass filter and the high pass filter separately. The outputs are then downsampled column-wise thereby reducing the number of columns by half. The downsampled images are then sent through the low pass filter and the high pass filter separately, and then again, the outputs are downsampled row-wise. This process generates four different images which are one-fourth of the original image in size. One image shows approximation coefficients and the other three images show horizontal, vertical and diagonal features. Figure 7.2 shows the result of applying 2D-DWT on the CT image.

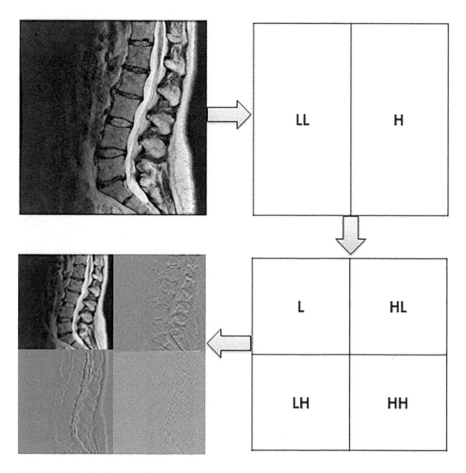

FIGURE 7.2   2D- DWT of CT image of the lumber spine.

7.3.2 VISUAL GEOMETRY GROUP (VGG)-19 NETWORK

The visual geometry group (VGG) network came out in 2014 as the second winner of a competition. Vgg19 is one of the variants of VGG. The number 19 is the number of convolution layers used in the network. Each convolution layer has a RELU activation function with it. The layers are divided into five sets. Very tiny filters of size 3×3 are used in each layer. The size of the convolution layer is doubled with each passing set. After each set of convolution layer, a 2×2 max pool layer is used with stride 2. It reduces the image size by half. After the last set of convolution layer, the image size reduces to 7×7. The image is then flattened and three fully connected layers are used.

We can use pre trained VGG-19 network trained on billions of images of ImageNet dataset [47]. It can detect 1000 different classes. All the images are of size 224×224. Since the network is trained over a variety of images, it has learned very rich features from the images. That is the main reason it is used in the transfer learning approach. Figure 7.3 shows VGG19 architecture.

7.3.3 ALEXNET NETWORK

AlexNet is also a convolutional neural network like VGG[48]. Alexnet is the winner of the ILSVRC competition held in 2012. Figure 7.4 shows AlexNet architecture.

It is much smaller in size than VGG-19 with just five convolutional layers and three fully connected layers. Each Convolutional layer has a RELU activation function with it except the last layer. Max-pooling layer is used after the first, second and fifth convolutional layers which are of size 3×3 with stride 2. It has three fully connected layers at the end. Like VGG19, AlexNet is also trained over the ImageNet dataset.

7.3.4 WAVELET+DEEP FUSION

Figure 7.5 shows the proposed "Wavelet+Deep Fusion" Architecture.

CT and MRI images of the lumber spine are first aligned with each other and then they are used for fusion. Both the images are decomposed into four different images - approximation coefficient (LL), horizontal coefficient (LH), vertical coefficient (LV) and diagonal coefficient (LD) using 2D-DWT. A convolutional neural network is used to fuse similar coefficients of the two images. So, "Deep Fusion" is invoked four times to fuse the four different coefficients. Once the four different fused images are obtained, inverse DWT is used on them to get the final fused image. Figure 7.6 demonstrates how "Deep Fusion" is used to fuse two images.

7.4 RESULT AND DISCUSSION

All techniques experimented with in the research work have used the SpineWeb data set [49]. It contains CT and MR images of the lumber spine of 20 patients. The dataset covers various degenerative lumber spine diseases. Each CT image is registered (aligned) with an MR image of the same pair using a landmark-based registration

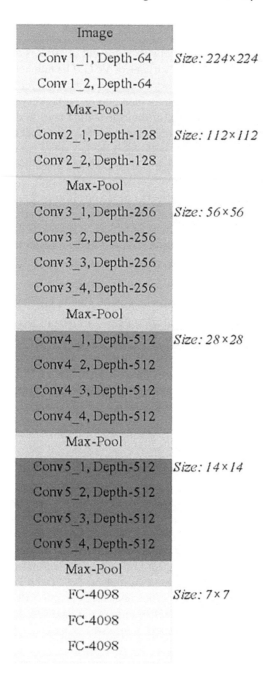

FIGURE 7.3   VGG19 architecture.

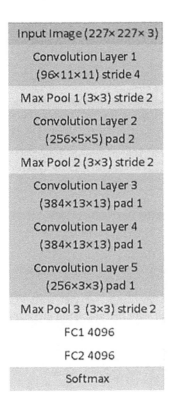

FIGURE 7.4 AlexNet architecture.

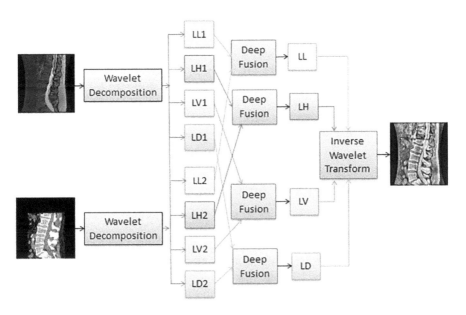

FIGURE 7.5 Wavelet+deep CNN architecture.

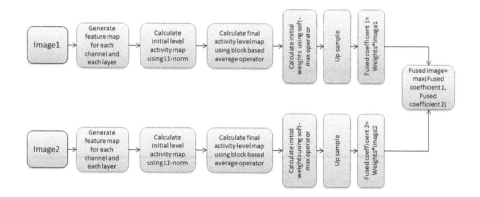

FIGURE 7.6   Deep fusion.

technique. Lumbar spine fusion using "wavelet with VGG-19" and "Wavelet with Alexnet" have been compared with the following conventional methods.

1. Spatial Domain Technique-Simple Average
2. Discrete Cosine Transform (DCT)
3. Hybrid Wavelet Transform (HWT)
4. Stationery Wavelet Transform (SWT)
5. Dual Tree-Complex Wavelet Transform (DT-CWT)
6. Discrete Cosine Transform-Laplacian Pyramid (DCT-LP)

7.4.1   FUSED IMAGES

Patient 1: Figure 7.7 shows how the CT image is aligned with the MR image for Patient 1, and Figure 7.8 shows fused images generated using the CT and MRI of Patient 1.

Patient 2: Figure 7.9 shows how the CT image is aligned with the MR image for Patient 2, and Figure 7.10 shows fused images generated using CT and MRI of the same patient.

7.4.2   QUANTITATIVE ANALYSIS OF ALL TECHNIQUES

The quality of all fused images is judged using three performance metrics: entropy, spatial frequency and standard deviation [50]. Entropy indicates information content. Tables 7.1–7.3 show values of entropy, standard deviation and spatial frequency, respectively for five patients using all the methods.

The high value of entropy indicates that the image has a good amount of information. High value of standard deviation indicates that the image has very good contrast.

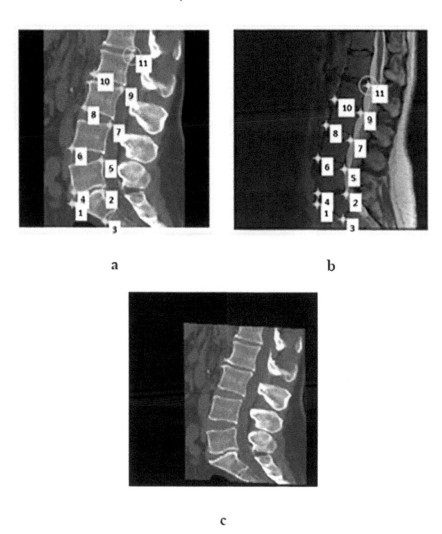

a   b

c

FIGURE 7.7   (a) Moving image (CT)-control point selection, (b) fixed image (MR)-control point selection, and (c) CT registered with MR image.

The high value of spatial frequency indicates good quality. "Wavelet+Vgg19" technique showed the best values (shown in bold in every row) for all the patients.

7.5 CONCLUSION

Lumber Spine CT and MRI scans are merged into one image to observe L1, L2, L3, L4 and L5 vertebras, discs, spinal cord, nerves and tissues in one image. A novel technique based on wavelet and CNN is introduced in this research work. VGG19

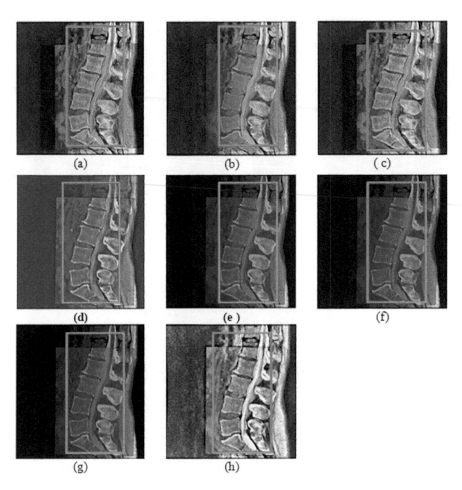

FIGURE 7.8   Patient 1 fused images: (a) simple average, (b) DCT, (c) hybrid wavelet transform, (d) wavelet+alexnet, (e) SWT, (f) DCT-LP, (g) DT-CWT, and (h) Wavelet+VGG19.

and Alexnet are combined with 2D-DWT to generate a fused image. Extensive experimentation is done to observe difference in fused images generated using eight different techniques, of which six are conventional techniques and two are novel techniques. Registration of CT with MRI is done using a landmark-based registration technique, and then it is fused with MRI. Three evaluation performance metrics – entropy, spatial frequency and standard deviation are used to compare all the methods. It is observed that fused images generated using Wavelet+VGG19 technique showed the highest values for all three parameters which indicate that this fused image has at most information content, better contrast and quality than all the other images. Medical experts can look at this image only instead of looking at CT and MRI images of the spine. VGG19 can be replaced by other convolutional neural networks like RESNET and GoogleNet to observe the difference in fused images.

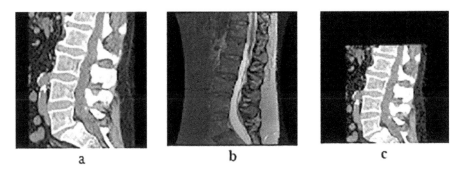

FIGURE 7.9   (a) CT, (b) MRI and (c) CT registered with MR image.

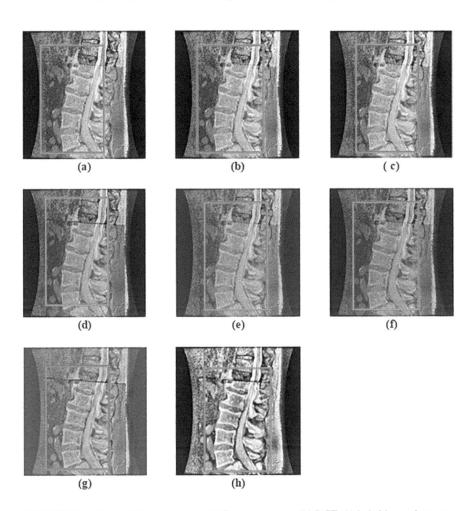

FIGURE 7.10   Patient 2 fused images. (a) Simple average, (b) DCT, (c) hybrid wavelet transform, (d) wavelet+alexnet, (e) SWT, (f) DCT-LP, (g) DT-CWT, and (h) wavelet+VGG19.

TABLE 7.1

Entropy

Patient No.	Simple Average	DCT	HWT	Wavelet+AlexNet	SWT	DCT-LP	DT-CWT	Wavelet+VGG19
1	7.30	7.30	7.30	7.31	7.52	7.34	7.28	7.74
2	7.56	7.56	7.56	7.58	7.78	7.60	7.55	7.85
3	7.27	7.27	7.27	7.28	7.44	7.29	7.29	7.80
4	7.55	7.55	7.55	7.55	7.41	7.57	7.53	7.72
5	7.06	7.06	7.06	7.08	7.37	7.09	7.07	7.43

TABLE 7.2

Standard Deviation

Patient No.	Simple Average	DCT	HWT	Wavelet+AlexNet	SWT	DCT-LP	DT-CWT	Wavelet+VGG19
1	51.16	50.52	51.16	48.42	62.03	49.58	53.04	63.53
2	47.00	63.07	47.07	47.57	62.09	48.28	46.81	64.29
3	42.30	46.39	42.35	42.35	54.12	42.38	42.56	60.63
4	58.80	59.82	58.87	58.88	72.47	59.12	59.05	73.23
5	35.59	46.36	35.66	36.01	47.08	36.28	35.53	48.99

TABLE 7.3

Spatial Frequency

Patient No.	Simple Average	DCT	HWT	Wavelet+AlexNet	SWT	DCT-LP	DT-CWT	Wavelet+VGG19
1	7.00	7.08	7.00	5.24	5.88	5.55	3.56	9.96
2	13.42	13.45	13.44	11.15	10.86	12.31	6.49	14.35
3	5.23	5.34	5.24	2.94	4.86	3.10	2.87	9.71
4	9.07	9.09	9.08	6.03	7.64	6.63	4.85	11.62
5	6.98	7.01	7.00	6.10	5.69	6.56	3.39	7.53

REFERENCES

[1] http://timesofindia.indiatimes.com/articleshow/64992298.cms?utm_source=contentofinterest&utm_medium=text&utm_campaign=cppst

[2] https://timesofindia.indiatimes.com/city/mumbai/73-patients-with-spine-problems-have-lower-back-complaint-survey/articleshow/61137025.cms

[3] https://pubmed.ncbi.nlm.nih.gov/?term=medical+image+fusion

[4] Changtao He, Quanxi Liu, Hongliang Li, Haixu Wang, Multimodal medical image fusion based on IHS and PCA, *Procedia Engineering*, 7, 2010, pp. 280–285.

[5] Mahesh Malviya, Sanju Kumari, Srikant Lade, Image fusion techniques based on pyramid decomposition, *International Journal of Artificial Intelligence and Mechatronics*, 4, 2014, pp. 127–130.

[6] P. Burt, E. Adelson, Laplacian pyramid as a compact image code, *IEEE Transactions on Communications*, 31, 1983, pp. 532–5407.

[7] Jianguo Sun, Qilong Han, Liang Kou, Liguo Zhang, Kejia Zhang, and Zilong Jin, Multi-focus image fusion algorithm based on Laplacian pyramids, *Journal of the Optical Society of America* 35, 2018, pp. 480–490.

[8] H. Olkkonen, P. Pesola, Gaussian pyramid wavelet transform for multiresolution analysis of images, *Graphical Models and Image Processing*, 58, 1996, pp. 394–398.

[9] P. Burt, A gradient pyramid basis for pattern selective image fusion, *The Society for Information Displays (SID) International Symposium Digest of Technical Papers*, 23, 1992, pp. 467–470.

[10] A. Toet, Image fusion by a ratio of low-pass pyramid, *Pattern Recognition Letters*, 9, 1996, pp. 245–253.

[11] H. Anderson, A filter-subtract-decimate hierarchical pyramid signal analyzing and synthesizing technique, U.S. Patent 718–104, 1987.

[12] L. C. Ramac, M. K. Uner, P. K. Varshney, Morphological filters and wavelet based image fusion for concealed weapon detection, *Proceedings of SPIE*, 3376, 1998, pp. 110–119.

[13] M. D. Jasiunas, D. A. Kearney, J. Hopf, Image fusion for uninhabited airborne vehicles, In: *Proceedings of IEEE International Conference on Field Programmable Technology*, 2002, pp. 348–351.

[14] S. Marshall, G. Matsopoulos, Morphological data fusion in medical imaging, In: *IEEE Winter Workshop on Nonlinear Digital Signal Processing*, IEEE, 1993, pp. 6–1.

[15] K. Mikoajczyk, J. Owczarczyk, W. Recko, A test-bed for computer-assisted fusion of multi-modality medical images, In: Chetverikov, D., Kropatsch, W.G. (eds) *Computer Analysis of Images and Patterns*. CAIP 1993. Lecture Notes in Computer Science, vol 719, Springer, 1993, pp. 664–668.

[16] G. Matsopoulos, S. Marshall, J. Brunt, Multiresolution morphological fusion of MR and CT images of the human brain, In: *Vision, Image and Signal Processing, IEE Proceedings*, vol. 141, IET, 1994, pp. 137–142.

[17] V. P. S. Naidu, Bindu Elias, A novel image fusion technique using DCT based Laplacian pyramid, *International Journal of Inventive Engineering and* Sciences (IJIES), 1, 2, 2013, pp. 1–18.

[18] S. G. Mallat, A theory for multiresolution signal decomposition, the wavelet representation, *IEEE Transaction on Pattern Analysis and Machine Intelligence*, 11, 7, 1989, pp. 674–693.

[19] Yong Yang, Dong Sun Park, Shuying Huang, Zhijun Fang, Zhengyou Wang, *Wavelet Based Approach for Fusing Computed Tomography and Magnetic Resonance Images*, IEEE, 2009, pp. 5770–5772.

[20] Yong Yang, Dong Sun Park, Shuying Huang, Nini Rao, Medical image fusion via an effective wavelet based approach, Journal on Advances in Signal Processing, 579341 2010, 44.

[21] Guihong Qu, Dali Zhang, Pingfan Yan, Medical image fusion using two-dimensional discrete wavelet transform, In: *Proc. SPIE 4556, Data Mining and Applications*, 2001. doi:10.1117/12.440275

[22] J. Teng, X. Wang, J. Zhang, S. Wang, P. Huo, A multimodality medical image fusion algorithm based on wavelet transform, In: Tan, Y., Shi, Y., Tan, K.C. (eds) *Advances in Swarm Intelligence*. ICSI 2010. Lecture Notes in Computer Science, 6146. 2010, pp. 627–633.

[23] B. Alfano, M. Ciampi, G. D. Pietro, A wavelet-based algorithm for multimodal medical image fusion, In: Falcidieno, B., Spagnuolo, M., Avrithis, Y., Kompatsiaris, I., Buitelaar, P. (eds) *Semantic Multimedia*. SAMT 2007. Lecture Notes in Computer Science, vol 4816, pp. 117–120.

[24] X. Li, X. Tian, Y. Sun, Z. Tang, Medical image fusion by multi-resolution analysis of wavelets transform, In: *Wavelet Analysis and Applications*, Springer, 2007, pp. 389–396.

[25] Rajiv Singh, Ashish Khare, Multiscale medical image fusion in wavelet domain, *The Scientific World Journal*, 2013, p. 521034, doi:10.1155/2013/521034

[26] Abhinav Krishn, Vikrant Bhateja, Himanshi, Akanksha Sahu, Medical image fusion using combination of PCA and wavelet analysis, *International Conference on Advances in Computing, Communications and Informatics (ICACCI)*, Delhi, India, 2014, pp. 986–991.

[27] H. B. Kekre, Archana Athawale, Dipali Sadavarti, Algorithm to generate Kekres wavelet transform from Kekres transform, *International Journal of Engineering Science and Technology*, 2, 5, 2010, pp. 756–767.

[28] Bhakti Palkar, Dhirendra Mishra, Fusion of multi-modal lumbar spine images using Kekre's hybrid wavelet transform, IET Image Processing, 13, 12, 2019, pp. 2271–2280.

[29] W. Selesnick, R. G. Baraniuk, N. G. Kingsbury, The dual-tree complex wavelet transform, *IEEE Signal Processing Magazine*, 22, 6, 2005, pp. 123–151.

[30] J. Tao, S. Li, B. Yang, Multimodal image fusion algorithm using dual-tree complex wavelet transform and particle swarm optimization, In: Huang, DS., McGinnity, M., Heutte, L., Zhang, XP. (eds) *Advanced Intelligent Computing Theories and Applications*. ICIC 2010. Communications in Computer and Information Science, vol. 93. Springer, 2010. pp. 296–303.

[31] Rajiv Singh, Richa Srivastava, Om Prakash, Ashish Khare, Multimodal Medical Image Fusion in Dual Tree Complex Wavelet Transform Domain Using Maximum and Average Fusion Rules, *Journal of Medical Imaging and Health Informatics*, 2, 2, 2012, pp. 168–173.

[32] Pusit Borwonwatanadelok, Wirat Rattanapitak, Somkait Udomhunsakul, Multi-focus image fusion based on stationary wavelet transform, I. *International Conference on Electronic Computer Technology*, Macau, China, 2009, pp. 77–81.

[33] R. Asokan, T. C. Kalaiselvi, M. Tamilarasi, Medical image fusion using stationary wavelet transform with different wavelet families, *Pakistan Journal of Biotechnology*, 13, 2016, pp. 10–14.

[34] Wei Li, Xuefeng Zhu, Shaocheng Wu, A novel approach to fast medical image fusion based on lifting wavelet transform, In: *Proceedings of the 6th World Congress on Intelligent Control and Automation*, June 21–23, 2006, Dalian, China.

[35] Deron Ray Rodrigues, Curvelet based image fusion techniques for medical images, *International Journal for Research in Applied Science & Engineering Technology*, 3, III, 2015, pp. 310–316.

[36] M. N. Do, M. Vetterli, Contourlets, a directional multi-resolution image representation, *Proceedings of IEEE International Conference on Image Processing*, 1, 2002, pp. I-357–I-360.

[37] Jyoti Agarwal, Sarabjeet Singh Bedi: Implementation of hybrid image fusion technique for feature enhancement in medical diagnosis, *Human-centric Computing and Information Sciences*, 5, 2015, p. 3.

[38] T. Li, Y. Wang, Biological image fusion using a NSCT based variable-weight method, *Information Fusion*, 12, 2, 2011, pp. 85–92.

[39] H. Szu, I. Kopriva, P. Hoekstra, N. Diakides, M. Diakides, J. Buss, J. Lupo, Early tumor detection by multiple infrared unsupervised neural nets fusion, In: *Engineering in Medicine and Biology Society, Proceedings of the 25th Annual International Conference of the IEEE*, vol. 2, IEEE, 2003, pp. 1133–1136.

[40] Y.-P. Wang, J.-W. Dang, Q. Li, S. Li, Multimodal medical image fusion using fuzzy radial basis function neural networks, In: *International Conference on Wavelet Analysis and Pattern Recognition, ICWAPR07*, vol. 2, IEEE, 2007, pp. 778–782.

[41] W. Li, X.-F. Zhu, A new algorithm of multi-modality medical image fusion based on pulse-coupled neural networks, In: Wang, L., Chen, K., Ong, Y.S. (eds) *Advances in Natural Computation*, Springer, 2005, pp. 995–1001.

[42] Sharma Dileepkumar Ramlal, Jainy Sachdeva, Chirag Kamal Ahuja, Niranjan Khandelwal, Multimodal medical image fusion using non-subsampled shearlet transform and pulse coupled neural network incorporated with morphological gradient, *Signal, Image and Video Processing*, 12, 8, 2018. pp. 1479–1487.

[43] C.T. Kavitha a, C.Chellamuthu b, R. Rajesh, Multimodal Medical Image Fusion Using Discrete Ripplet Transform and Intersecting Cortical Model, Procedia Engineering 38, 2012, pp. 1409–1414.

[44] Sudeb Das, M. K. Kindu, NSCT-based multimodal medical image fusion using pulse coupled neural network and modified spatial frequency, *Medical & Biological Engineering & Computing*, 50, 10, 2012, pp. 1105–1114, doi:10.1007/s11517-012-0943-3.

[45] Y. Liu, X. Chen, R. K. Ward et al., Image fusion with convolutional sparse representation, *IEEE Signal Processing Letters*, 23, 12, 2016, pp. 1882–1886.

[46] Yu Liu, Xun Chen, Juan Cheng, Hu Peng, A medical image fusion method based on convolutional neural networks, In: *20th International Conference on Information Fusion Xian*, China, 10–13 July 2017.

[47] https://www.image-net.org/

[48] https://www.oreilly.com/library/view/advanced-deep-learning/9781789956177/b2258a a6-2c18-449c-ac00-939e812f5a4a.xhtml.
https://www.oreilly.com/library/view/advanced-deep-learning/9781789956177/b2258a a6-2c18-449c-ac00-939e812f5a4a.xhtml

[49] http://spineweb.digitalimaginggroup.ca

[50] Dhirendra Mishra, Bhakti Palkar. Article: Image fusion techniques: Review. *International Journal of Computer Applications*, 130, 9, 2015, pp. 7–13.

8 Medical Image Analysis and Classification for Varicose Veins

Jyoti Yogesh Deshmukh, Vijay U. Rathod, Yogesh Kisan Mali, and Rachna Sable

8.1 INTRODUCTION

Digital imaging and medicine are getting more and more integrated into society as science and technology advance. Recent innovations in technology, such as image processing and virtual reality, are rapidly finding their way into the medical industry. The field of digital medicine has advanced quickly in recent years as interdisciplinary medical research combines with digital art.

The current healthcare system understands that while clinical procedures must be efficient, patient safety is of utmost importance. These conditions are not at all exclusive of one another. For instance, when local or regional anaesthesia is used during surgery rather than more intensive general anaesthesia, both patient safety and economic effectiveness are maximized. It is still a difficult and open challenge to objectively evaluate the safety of clinical procedures while taking patient comfort and financial expenses into account major diseases in India caused by a bad lifestyle! Between 2005 and 2015, India's proportion of overweight and obese people increased. 21.7% of women and 19.6% of males between the ages of 17 and 41 were not set in stone to be overweight or large. Corpulence is lethal! Joint inflammation, malignant growth, barrenness, coronary illness, back agony, diabetes, and stroke are the seven sicknesses most often connected to heftiness. Poor psychological wellness, respiratory issues, irregular chemical characteristics, and food sensitivities are also normal. Stoutness, which was once broad in major league salary nations, is currently present and deteriorating in low- and centre-pay nations. Obesity is mostly caused by an inability to compensate for all of the energy consumed. Fat is created from this additional energy. Fighting infectious diseases requires levying higher costs on unhealthy foods, accurate labelling, and the development of environments that promote physical activity. With a few notable exceptions, current therapies for obesity have largely demonstrated just moderate success, and preventative strategies are relatively ineffectual. Therefore, a fuller knowledge of the factors that contribute to severe or morbid obesity is urgently needed. This understanding could result in novel and creative intervention strategies.

Accurate analysis of medical data will benefit in the early detection of illnesses, patient care, and community services as machine learning in biomedicine and healthcare quickly improves. The quantity and quality of unreported and inferior medical data, on the other hand, jeopardizes disease analysis accuracy.

DOI: 10.1201/9781003461500-10

In order to identify obese people, this study provides an obesity detection algorithm that is specifically designed for the Indian population. Additionally, based on the set of symptoms entered into the system, it predicts which diseases the person is most likely to get. Even if you feel healthy, it can tell you if you are at high or low risk. The system certifies that a person's health is within acceptable bounds and provides the option to evaluate and monitor their health via email. Documents that patients (or maybe doctors) need to examine or recover as needed can also be uploaded and accessed easily.

The most prevalent peripheral vascular disease is varicose veins in the lower limbs. There are now more than 25 million adults who have varicose veins in their lower limbs, which affects about 23% of adults. Over 8% of Chinese people have varicose veins. In addition to compromising aesthetics, varicose veins can induce thrombophlebitis, venous oedema, cutaneous varicose veins, and an increased risk of deep vein thrombosis. This could lead to disability and a decrease in employment capacity. The direct annual cost of treating chronic venous disease in the USA is estimated to be between $2.5 and $2 billion. Varicose vein treatment costs in the UK make up 2% of all national health care spending. Conservative therapy and surgical therapy are the two most common conventional treatments for varicose veins; however, roughly one-third of cases return within 10 years of surgery. Treatments with a low level of invasiveness are being created. As a result, research into the molecular and cellular mechanisms underlying fungal pathogenesis will be crucial in the future for discovering novel treatment targets and creating novel therapeutic approaches.

Hemodynamic variations are directly sensed by vascular endothelial cells (VECs), the unbroken monolayer layer that lines the lining of blood vessels between the blood flow and the vessel wall. It is a mechanical barrier that serves a variety of important roles in the body's physiological and pathological processes, including substance transport, auto crime, and paracrime. In many illnesses, particularly in the lower extremities, its structure and function are aberrant. It is essential for the growth and spread of varicose veins. The method proposed using harsh words in patients with varicose veins to improve diagnosis accuracy through fundamental information processing [1]. Images of vascular endothelial cells can be classified using this method based on various illness situations. Ajitha [2] classified a number of noteworthy traits using a range of pattern classifiers before using an artificial neural network to photos of leg veins. Shi et al.'s [3] excellent classification of pictures of vascular endothelial cells using support vector machines improved early detection of this disease. Zhu et al. [1] proposed employing a grip sensation-based responsive and predictive brain control method to investigate lower extremity varicose veins. Veinidis et al. used 3D mesh sequences to construct an unsupervised human motion search technique to assess whether lower extremities have varicose veins. The aforementioned algorithm, meanwhile, has several drawbacks. B. Vascular endothelial cell data are sparse, network training is challenging, and the adaptive effect is weak. Through consecutive iterations of the training process, deep learning uses a hierarchical feature extraction structure to abstract the input image from low level to high level, identifying the most crucial file attributes. Extract more in-depth and broader features. In order to extract characteristics and classify them, this article makes use of deep learning algorithms. In this study, lower extremity varicose veins are detected and classified using features extracted from images of vascular endothelial cell inflammation using multi-scale deep learning algorithms. Multiple convolutional layers were used to extract multi-scale characteristics from photos of vascular endothelial cells. In addition, we develop a competitive strategy that can lower the network layer parameters while extracting more compact features by using the MFM activation function rather than the ReLU activation function. For dimensionality reduction, this network employs a method of 3 * 2 convolution kernel and 1 * 2 convolution kernels. This can be applied to strengthen the network's ability to extract features and further optimize the network's parameters.

8.1.1 KEY CONTRIBUTIONS

In this chapter, we have focussed on identifying varicose veins disease and its possible data science methods to detect it. Some of the key contributions of this chapter are as follows:

- How and why varicose veins affect the human legs?
- How it differs from normal veins of human legs?
- Use of multi-scale technology to detect the stage or level of varicose vein problem.
- Notable characterization and recognition of disease with deep convolutional neural network (D-CNN).
- Activation function and pooling methods are used to have fine categorization of the varicose veins.
- It has a detailed experimental set-up with the use of the convolutional neural network (CNN) for detecting the severity of the disease.
- Data science statistical methods are used to give evolutionary results of the experiments.
- Metrics performance assessment will be done of all referred data science statistical methods.

8.2 RELATED WORKS

To determine whether a lesion is present in the human body as well as to identify and classify the lesion, doctors diagnose medical images. The programmed characterization and acknowledgement of clinical pictures have so collected a great deal of consideration. Since the fiery peculiarity of vascular endothelial cells is firmly connected with varicose veins in the lower furthest points, this article proposes a vascular endothelial cell-based venous framework to accomplish the programmed order and identification of provocative pictures and various pictures of varicose veins in the lower limits. We offer a method for locating aneurysms. First, we photographed the vascular endothelial cells in both healthy people and people with varicose veins. Numerous convolutional layers are employed to extract multi-scale information from the image of vascular endothelial cells. Because of this, we extract more condensed features using the max-feature-map (MFM) activation function as opposed to the ReLU activation function, and we also incorporate a competing method to reduce the network layer parameters. In order to further optimize the network parameters, the network also uses a 1 * 2 convolution kernel for dimensionality reduction and a 3 * 2 convolution kernel to improve the network's ability to extract features.

The clinical tissue classification system for identifying varicose veins using medical imaging is suggested in this article. Over 90% of all cases of the many varieties of varicose veins are ulcers. The system outlined in the proposed study can be used to recognize and categorize varicose veins at any stage. The taxonomy is divided into two sections in this article:

Texture features like homogeneity, energy, entropy, contrast, mean, dissimilarity, and variance are extracted during the feature extraction stage. To distinguish between various twisting phases, these collected features are categorized using a K-nearest neighbour classifier and a support vector machine.

A significant fraction of people are affected by chronic venous insufficiency (CVI), which cannot be treated without medical treatment. However, a lot of patients don't get their medical advice right away. Physicians also require methods to categorize patients based on the severity of their CVI at the same time. To help doctors and patients, we suggest an automated categorization technique dubbed the CVI classifier. An idea classifier in this strategy first guides low-level picture highlights to medium-level semantic elements prior to building a multi-scale semantic model to develop a semantically rich picture portrayal. Second, a scene classifier is prepared to gauge CVI seriousness utilizing the streamlined element subsets obtained by the high-request reliance-based include determination approach. Classification performance is measured using the F1 score, kappa coefficient, and classification accuracy.

Routine outpatient varicose vein surgery is commonly performed under local anaesthesia. Despite the fact that local anaesthesia is affordable and can reduce patient risk, some patients endure discomfort during surgery. Thus, the careful group should decide if to utilize general or neighbourhood sedation in light of an emotional subjective evaluation of the patient's nervousness and torment responsiveness. It is absolutely impossible to confirm. To make sense of the relationship between cardiovascular reaction change and agony during varicose vein a medical procedure, we foster a three-layered polynomial surface fitting of physiological information and patient mathematical agony evaluations. Pulse changeability information was dissected for ghostly and underlying intricacy highlights as torment markers in no time before 18 varicose vein systems. The aggravation expectation model that came about was approved once, with a kappa coefficient of 0.82 (virtual arrangement) and a region under the beneficiary working bend of 0.98 (close to consummate exactness). This evidence of idea study shows the capacity of exactly evaluating torment awareness and science [4], allowing practitioners to prescribe the safest and least expensive anaesthetic drugs to specific individuals in an unbiased manner.

By creating a cutting-edge system to optimize machine learning algorithms for accurately predicting obesity and related disorders among the Indian population, this work seeks to address the aforementioned constraints. Unhealthy manufactured foods are readily available, thanks to federal food restriction restrictions. More so among younger generations, India's increasingly career-focused lifestyle has led to an unpredictable biological pattern that favours indoor play over outside recreation. The emergence of obesity nowadays is influenced by behavioural and socio-psychological factors as sleep, stress, race, and hormone imbalances [5].

Capillary blood pressure (CBP) is the main driver of fluid exchange between microvessels. Prior to apparent peripheral oedema, asymptomatic systemic venous congestion can have a direct impact on peripheral CBP. Therefore, in a range of clinical diseases including heart failure, venous insufficiency, etc., CBP assessment can provide early oedema control. At this time, CBP measurements can only be performed in invasive and difficult experimental circumstances [6]. We adjusted the frequently utilized oscillometric strategy in this study's home blood vessel pulse screens and fostered an opto-mechanical gadget to empower harmless and programmed CBP estimation. To quantify skin slender throbs, his proposed CBP framework is equipped with a blue-light photoplethysmogram sensor embedded in a finger/toe sleeve.

8.3   GAP ANALYSIS

Doctors diagnose medical images to evaluate whether a lesion is present in the human body, as well as to identify and classify the lesion. There has been a great deal of interest in the programmed grouping and acknowledgement of clinical pictures. Lower appendage varicose veins request programmed characterization and distinguishing proof because of their immediate relationship to the fiery cycles of vascular endothelial cells. This exploration made a historic hypothesis known as MSD-CNN, a varicose vein discovery strategy in view of pictures of vascular endothelial cell irritation and multi-scale profound learning, to forestall such a phase of clinical disappointment.

8.4   THE PROPOSED WORK

A. Overview of Lower Extremity of Varicose Veins Case

Varicose veins are now a highly frequent ailment as a result of society's ongoing advancement and improvements in living standards. The top layer of skin is unaffected by human varicose veins in their early stages. Some disorders are also readily disregarded by patients and receive little attention from the general public. When venous valves in the legs are clogged for an extended period of time, varicose veins can form Ref. [7]. Blood silting from blood backflow leads to thrombosis, which happens as the condition slowly spreads. After calf oedema and thrombosis, varicose veins in the legs are brought on by a gradual darkening of the skin on the outer layer of the calf. If medical attention is postponed, amputations and even cancers could develop. A dangerous illness called thrombosis can significantly affect a patient's quality of life and length of life. Figure 8.1 compares varicose veins and healthy veins.

Most vascular sicknesses are brought about by lower furthest point varicose veins, which are continuous venous illnesses in vascular medical procedures. Eczema, a gradual loss of pigmentation, swelling, and distortion of the superficial veins in the lower extremities – veins that are vulnerable to chronic varicose veins, thrombophlebitis, and other consequences – are the clinical signs. These complications can affect the patient's ability to work and lead a normal life has an adverse effect on.

Vascular endothelial cell inflammation is frequently a crucial connection or expression of the onset of many cardiovascular, cerebrovascular, and peripheral vascular disorders. One of the most prevalent vascular illnesses

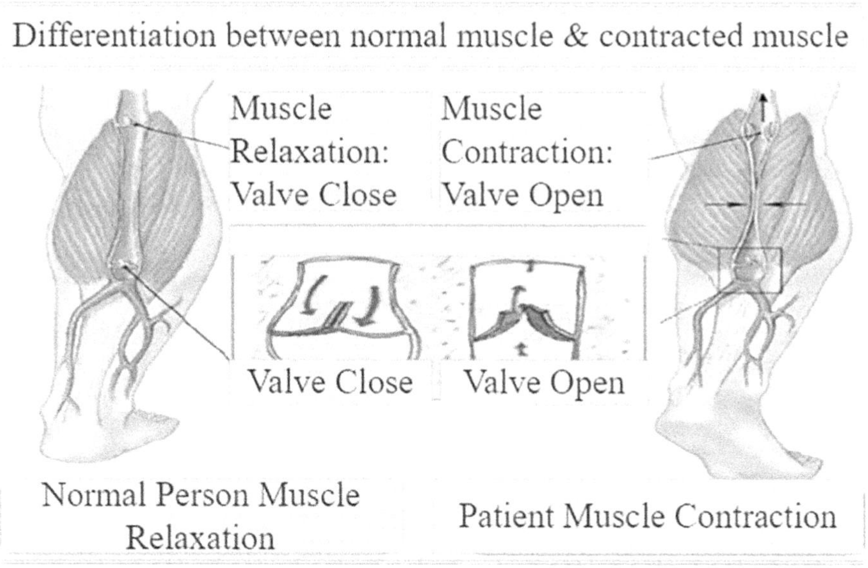

Differentiation between normal muscle & contracted muscle

Muscle Relaxation: Valve Close

Muscle Contraction: Valve Open

Valve Close   Valve Open

Normal Person Muscle Relaxation

Patient Muscle Contraction

FIGURE 8.1   Distinguish between varicose veins and normal veins.

is varicose veins of the lower extremities, which can cause leg oedema, distorted superficial vein dilation, severe varicose vein development, localized bleeding, or infection. Varicose veins in the lower legs have been linked favourably to vascular endothelial cell inflammation. The purpose of this article is to identify and detect leg varicose veins by concentrating on vascular endothelial cells and extracting attributes from cell images.

B. Multi-Scale Image Technology Method

Multi-scale picture innovation is a strategy for communicating pictures with different goals. The method involved with handling pictures at different scales is known as multi-scale division after that.

Removing all highlights on a solitary scale in numerous visual imaging applications could challenge. In this study, we present a multi-scale technique to facilitate feature extraction and improve feature extraction performance. The key tasks when employing multi-scale picture technology are expressing images in multi-scale settings and figuring out how scales relate to one another. A common example of a multi-scale depiction of a picture among them is an image pyramid.

Scale-based analysis is a method that uses the picture pyramid. This reflects the transform resolution for the identical image's layers precisely. With the biggest picture at the base and the littlest picture at the top, the image size is commonly expanded and diminished in a pyramidal example. Like the human visual framework, picture pyramid designs can address pictures at a few scales and depict the full picture at different scales. Pyramidal pictures are developed utilizing down testing. Subsequently, the picture order ascends as more picture detail is lost and the picture goal drops. However, as demonstrated in Figure 8.2, photographs with lower quality

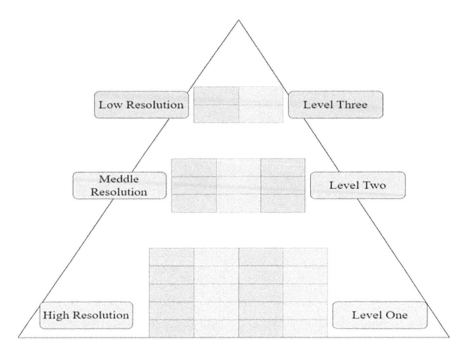

FIGURE 8.2   Image pyramid.

and size could include more generic elements. The resolution of vascular endothelial cells, for instance, decreases with decreasing size and increases in the sharpness of outlines and features following multi-scale processing of the pictures of vascular endothelial cells. Vascular endothelial cell images get more detailed and greater in size as the resolution of the endothelial cells increases. By removing features from multi-scale images, image pyramid structures can achieve the goal of condensing multi-scale information, improving the relevance and depth of feature representation. Below is a basic illustration of the many image pyramid types and structures.

1. Sub-Sampling Pyramid

    Image pyramids can be used to graphically portray multi-scale structures. Pyramiding is a common technique that involves applying a low pass filter to smooth out an image and then down-sampling the outcome. One method for lowering the size of the image and improving the resolution of the two adjacent layers is down-sampling. This method mostly involves removing the horizontal and vertical pixels from the image. Scale-space theory states that the image size should be decreased using the proper smoothing filtering. The resulting pyramid is a subsampled pyramid if no filter smoothing is applied. An image that has been successfully downscaled using a subsampling pyramid has a much lower resolution. To create thumbnail images that are only one-fourth the size of the actual image, the pixels and columns are primarily sampled pixel by pixel for an image subsampling pyramid. This procedure is repeated until the required number of photographs is obtained. The tiers of the built-up pyramid satisfy the experiment's requirements.

The top and bottom images' size ratios are always set to 1 when creating an image pyramid. By down-sampling the image of the subsequent layer, the image of the preceding layer is produced. The following organizing principles apply to the photo pyramid: The original image is down-sampled, and the layer with the lowest resolution is at the top, the resolution of the layers behind it is down-sampled, and the resolution of the image continuously decreases from the bottom to the top. It has the quality of being vulnerable. They are separated in half. The visual organization is more pronounced in the photo pyramid as image resolution decreases. With each lower level, the image's resolution rises and its local features and details are richly improved.

2. Gaussian Pyramid

Depending on the kind of filter employed, a low-pass filter can be used to smooth images when creating image pyramids. Pyramids of many shapes and sizes are produced. An average filter, for instance, results in an average pyramid. A Gaussian smoothing filter is used to create a Gaussian pyramid. The quality of the subsampled image and whether the preceding image's pixels can accurately reflect the values of the pixels in the subsequent level will determine which filter is used. The basic principle behind the Gaussian Pyramid is to convolution the base picture with a Gaussian kernel, test the subsequent picture to get the past picture, and afterwards input the new picture to rehash the convolution cycle with. The down-inspecting approach is likewise done various times to develop an information structure.

The expression for the Gaussian smoothing filter is as follows:

$$g(x) = \frac{1}{\sqrt{2\pi}\sigma} e^{-\left(x^2/2\sigma 2\right)} \tag{8.1}$$

The standard deviation is the variable, and its magnitude affects how smooth the signal is. Using the example of the 5 * 3 Gaussian kernels, we may obtain the Gaussian kernel for convolution after discretizing the Gaussian function.

The standard deviation formula is:

$$w = \frac{1}{256} \begin{bmatrix} 1\ 2\ 6\ 4\ 16\ 24\ 6\ 24\ 36\ 4\ 1\ 16\ 4\ 24\ 6 \end{bmatrix} \tag{8.2}$$

3. The Pyramid of Gaussian Difference

The distinction of two Gaussian capabilities with contrasting fluctuations by the Laplace-Gaussian, a band-pass filter that reflects is an approximation of the Gaussian difference. The filter function's formula is as follows:

$$D(x,y,\sigma 1,\sigma 2) = (G(x,y,\sigma 1)) - G(x,y,\sigma 2)) * I(x,y) = L(x,y,\sigma 1) - L(x,y,\sigma 2) \tag{8.3}$$

C. The Deep Convolutional Neural Network (D-CNN)

Artificial neural theory is the foundation of deep learning. It can focus on nonlinear transformation of data, have a network structure with more layers, and represent more abstract properties of images by optimizing the learning method in comparison to typical neural networks. In the fields of picture categorization and recognition, machine vision is widely used and has achieved some notable recognition results. Speaking recognition, target detection and tracking, computer advertising, recommender systems, target classification, and image segmentation are just a few of the areas where deep learning technology has achieved significant advancements. The primary focal point of numerous universities, research foundations, and organizations is innovation research. Profound learning can be utilized generally speaking where traditional man-made consciousness innovations fizzle since it can advance significant level theoretical properties from low-level information, like picture pixels. Online directed and solo learning procedures are utilized in profound learning. The profound convolutional brain networks with start-to-finish learning capacities and solid grouping and forecast execution are one of them, and they address administered learning. An auto encoder is a portrayal of unaided learning and it is equipped for remaking the first info picture. The highlights of the picture are addressed by the centre organization layer. Unsupervised deep learning networks select pictures that might not be used on the study day by giving the network a lot of pre-training with irrelevant pictures. Your information can be gotten to the next level. An immense number of picture assets are presently accessible as a result of the Web and online entertainment, which benefitted from the improvement of PC innovation and large information organizations. How much managed profound learning research has developed? Individuals are especially worried about research on profound convolutional brain organizations. Profound convolutional brain network's major areas of strength for models' speculation execution, which has been trained on databases with a size of over 1 million, accurately capture their classification and discriminating abilities.

1. The neural network's convolutional structure.

Convolutional brain organizations (CNN) are the most generally utilized profound learning network structure. Furthermore, it fundamentally affects various fields, including picture handling. When contrasted with conventional picture handling techniques, CNNs offer the upside of utilizing start-to-finish learning capacities to involve the real picture as info directly and avoid image pre-processing with little-to-no user involvement. CNN offers the advantage of adopting local connection architecture over standard neural networks, and it is distinguished by simple model construction. The training weight parameter controls the size of the convolution kernel because a weight distribution method is employed to distribute weight across the neurons. Due to the fact that it is unrelated to the quantity of neurons in the hidden layer, this further limits the trainable parameters. The CNN network still has great feature extraction abilities despite a significant decrease in the weight parameter.

Convolutional layers' nodes are only hazily linked to one another and to neighbouring network levels. A convolution kernel can extract features. To add more features, one can use convolution kernels. A feature map is the term used to describe this feature produced via convolutional kernel mapping. Usually, each layer is made up of several feature maps. Each feature map is made up of several nodes that are squarely organized. The same weight parameter or shared weight is inherited by nodes with the same feature level. The initialization of a tiny value matrix is typically randomized by convolution kernels during training. The final training is given the right amount of weight thanks to ongoing learning. The likelihood that a CNN will over fit the training set is decreased for each shared weight in a convolutional kernel that can lower connectivity between neighbouring network layers. A down-sampling layer is another name for a pooling layer. The two tactics of average pooling and maximal pooling are widely used by him. The first one is actually used. It has a wide range of applications. CNNs' convolutional and pooling layers significantly lower the network's complexity and parameters. In a CNN, there are two components.

Convolution, activation, and pooling are methods used in feature extraction and feature mapping. Finally, a softmax classifier is used to categorize it. Figure 8.3 depicts the elements of a standard CNN structure: a picture input layer, a convolutional layer, an enactment layer, a pooling layer, a completely associated layer, a softmax classifier, and a layer of convolutions.

Each understood unit can interface a restricted piece of the constant district of the information picture in light of nearby identification limitations on associations among certain input units forced by the convolutional layers of a convolutional brain organization. Convolutional layer weight boundaries are comprised of a few convolution parts. In the wake of playing out a joint convolution procedure on the whole picture, a component map is extracted in a convolution check.

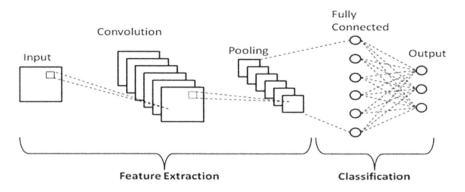

FIGURE 8.3   Structure of CNN.

Following is the formula to show how the convolution kernel functions:

$$S(i,j) = (X*W)(i,j) + b = \sum_{k=1}^{M}(X_k + W_k)(i,j) + b \qquad (8.4)$$

The quantity of information pictures is shown by the variable M, where X_k is the kth picture and W_k is the kth convolution portion. The variable b is the counterbalanced. A 3 * 4 convolution part and one convolution step equivalent to one pixel are delivered when a 5 * 6 info network is utilized. $S(i, j)$ means the worth of the relating position component in the element map comparing to the convolution part W in the component map S, where S is the element map relating to the convolution portion W. Figure 8.4 shows the convolution process in action.

1. Activation Function

CNNs may tackle linear atomicity problems largely using nonlinear formulas that are provided by activation functions. CNNs include activation functions as a fundamental component. Regardless of whether the organization order is a solitary layer organization, the organization can direct straight planning without a trace of an initiation capability. Enactment capabilities can be partitioned into two significant classifications: piecewise direct capabilities and nonlinear capabilities with a dramatic construction (Figure 8.5).

The most typical kind of activation function is the sigmoid function with exponential shape, and its functional formula is:

$$f(x) = \frac{1}{\left(1+e^{-x}\right)} \qquad (8.5)$$

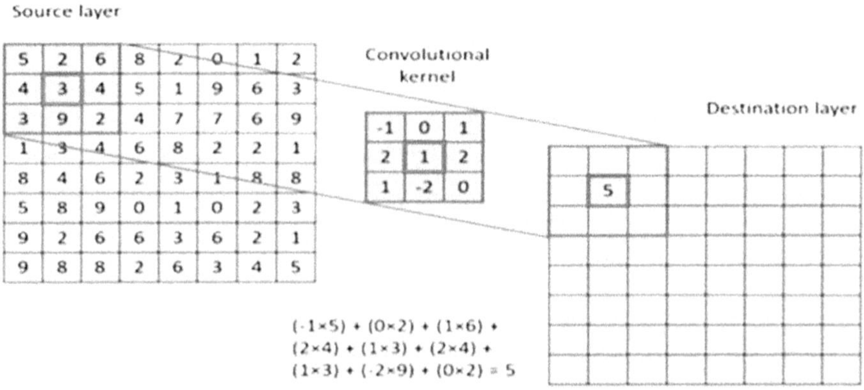

FIGURE 8.4   Schematic diagram of convolution operation.

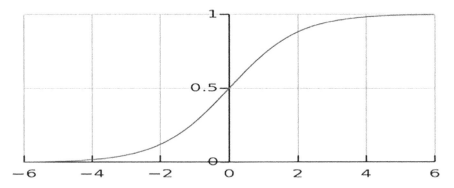

FIGURE 8.5 Schematic diagram of sigmoid function.

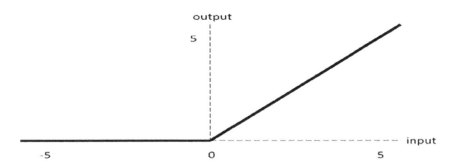

FIGURE 8.6 Schematic diagram of ReLU activation function.

Another typical exponential shape activation function is the Tanh capability (exaggerated digression), [−1, 1] is its scope and capability articulation. The formula for the exponential shape activation function is as follows:

$$f(x) = \left(1 - e^{-2x}\right) / \left(1 + e^{-2x}\right) \tag{8.6}$$

The Tanh function exhibits soft saturation, a feature that is similar to the sigmoid function and can easily lead to gradient dispersion, the sigmoid function converges more slowly than it does, though. The piecewise linear function of the ReLU linear correcting unit is written as:

$$f(x) = max(x, 0) \tag{8.7}$$

The chart of the ReLU enactment capability is displayed in Figure 8.6. At the point when $x > 0$, ReLU can safeguard the slope without lessening, settling the angle scattering issue and enabling direct, supervised training of the deep network.

2. Pooling Layer

Sampling is the core of a pooling layer. In order to extract the essential aspects of the input feature map while lowering the network parameters for improved characterization, the feature map is somehow compressed. Decreased network parameters are also helpful in avoiding over-fitting.

There are two common pooling techniques. The best and typical pooling. See the maximum 2 * 2 pooling with a 2-pixel step size in Figures 8.7 and 8.8. Only one of these pooling convolution part loads can go over 1, while the rest can go under 0. The convolution bit will be set where 1 signifies the most noteworthy worth of every component on the element map.

In augmentations of two pixels, the convolution bit travels through the component map. The component map is diminished to

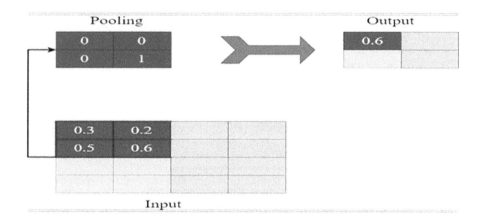

FIGURE 8.7 Max pooling.

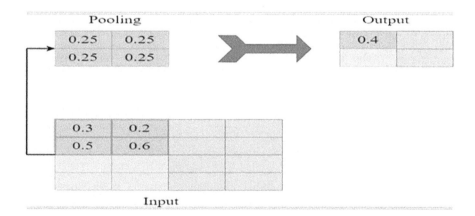

FIGURE 8.8 Mean pooling.

one-fourth of its unique size subsequent to testing the best worth. With the exemption that the normal of the things in the inclusion zone of the component map is recovered and used as the result, normal pooling is indistinguishable from the maximum example procedure. The convolution piece's sliding step size decides the size of the last result map. The generated feature map will be one-fourth the size of the original image, using 2 pixels as an example.

8.5   RESULT AND DISCUSSION

A. Feature Extraction

Identifying the components that are most important for pattern identification is made possible by feature extraction, one of the most important procedures in image processing. When a subset of characteristics enables the creation of patterns with similarities within classes and differences between other classes, it is considered to be a good subset of features. In the segmented image, varicose vein texture features are retrieved.

1. Texture characteristics

Texture refers to the spatial organization of colours or intensities inside an image or specific regions of an image. We can presume the texture of the image for natural situations that were caught in photograph picture segmentation is supported by the usage of picture textures (Figure 8.9).

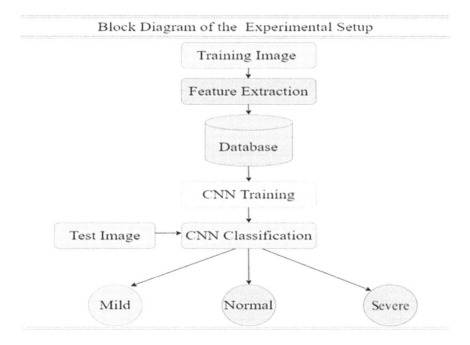

FIGURE 8.9   Block diagram of the experimental work.

- **Homogeneity**: The degree of dispersion can be measured using the concept of homogeneity. It adjusts regional variances in image textures while reflecting their local uniformity. A high uniformity rating indicates that the local distribution of the image texture is homogeneous, with no variance occurring within the area. The Formula to calculate the degree of dispersion to measure homogeneity is as follows:

$$\sum_{i,j-0}^{N-1} \frac{Pi,j}{1+(i-j)^2} \tag{8.8}$$

- **Energy**: Energy can be thought of as an indicator of how often pixel pairings are repeated. It checks the homogeneity of the image. The energy value will be high if the pixels are highly similar. The energy can be calculated using the following formula:

$$\sum_{i,j-0}^{n-i} (Pi,j)^2 \tag{8.9}$$

- **Entropy**: The texture of the input image is described by entropy, a measure of randomness. When all components of the coexistence matrix are equal, it's worth is at its highest. The formula for entropy calculation is as follows:

$$\sum_{i,j=0}^{N-1} -ln(pi,j)\,pij \tag{8.10}$$

- **Contrast**: Finding the intensity difference between a pixel and its neighbours throughout the image is known as contrast, used to enhance the quality of images. The variation in hue that makes an object stand out is called contrast. Differences in hue and brightness between things and other objects in the same field of vision are visual indicators of contrast. The formula to find the contrast between pixels is as follows:

$$\sum_{i}^{N} \sum_{j}^{N} (i-j)^2 (P(i,j)) \tag{8.11}$$

- **Mean**: By averaging every pixel value in the image, average is determined. The average values show how each pixel's intensity contributed to the overall image. The mean of every pixel will be calculated with the following formula:

$$\mu = \sum_{j=1}^{N} j\,(p)_{ij} = \sum_{i=1}^{N} i\,(p)_{ij} \tag{8.12}$$

- **Dissimilarity**: The numerical scale for comparing the similarity or difference of two data from 0 (objects are alike) to ∞ (objects are different). To calculate dissimilarity, the following formula is referred:

$$\sum_{i=1}^{N}\sum_{j=1}^{N} P_{ij} \, |i-j| \tag{8.13}$$

- **Variance**: Variance is typically used to categorize images into distinct regions by determining how each pixel differs from the centre or nearby pixels. The categorization of images will calculate with variance and its formula is as follows:

$$V = V_i \sum_{i=1}^{N}\sum_{j=1}^{N} (1-\mu i)^2 \, P_{i,j} \tag{8.14}$$

B. Metrics for Performance Assessment

The proportion of accurately diagnosed varicose vein stages, or True Positives, is used to gauge the suggested method's sensitivity. It is calculated with the following formula:

$$= \frac{\text{Sensitivity No of cases matched with clinicians report}}{\text{No of cases matched with clinicians report} + \text{No of cases not matched with clinicians report}} * 100 \tag{8.15}$$

Utilizing predictions of false positives, specificity is evaluated. The percentage of varicose vein stages that the technology detected but the doctor did not report is known as the false positive rate. Rarely may clinicians misinterpret the correct stage with the aid of specificity. Specificity is evaluated with following formula:

$$\text{Specificity} = 1 - \frac{\text{No. of cases identified by the system}}{\text{No. of cases reported by the clinicians}} * 100 \tag{8.16}$$

Accuracy is a measure of a system's ability to anticipate outcomes in terms of genuine positive, genuine negative, misleading positive, and misleading negative values. The formula to calculate system's ability accuracy is as follows:

$$\text{Accuracy} = \frac{\text{True Positive+True Negative}}{\text{True Positive+True Negative+False Positive+False Negative}} \tag{8.17}$$

The suggested system is measured using these three separate metrics. Thirty-three photos in total were needed to train the system. Thirty different photographs were utilized in a test set that was created using a random sampling technique (Tables 8.1 and 8.2).

TABLE 8.1

Confusion Matrix for the CNN Classifier's Test Set

Test Set	Genuine Positive	Misleading Positive	Genuine Negative	Misleading Negative
T1	14	7	34	6
T2	15	6	33	5
T3	14	7	35	7

TABLE 8.2

Statistical Performance Analysis of CNN and SVM Classifier

	CNN Classifier		SVM Classifier	
Test set	Sensitivity	Specificity	Sensitivity	Specificity
T1	0.772929	0.764768	0.896825	0.884729
T2	0.888889	0.955555	1	0.926833
T3	0.823576	0.968254	0.552632	1

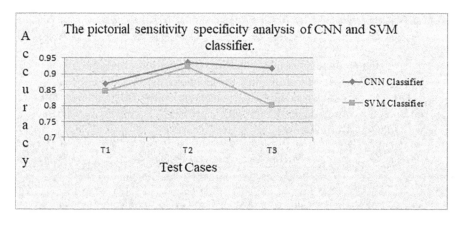

FIGURE 8.10 The pictorial sensitivity specificity analysis of KNN and SVM classifier.

The results of the testing phase were used to calculate the aforementioned performance metrics. Figure 8.10 shows the image sensitivity specificity analyses for the CNN and SVM classifiers. Table 8.3 presents the findings of the accuracy analysis. Experiment results reveal that the SVM classifier offers sensitivity (77.94%), specificity (86.78%), and accuracy (78.84%) while the CNN classifier of the suggested approach offers sensitivity (72.46%), specificity (85.17%), and accuracy (80.95%).

TABLE 8.3
Accuracy Analysis of KNN and SVM Classifier

Test set	CNN Classifier Accuracy	SVM Classifier Accuracy
T1	0.869542	0.845654
T2	0.936488	0.92238
T3	0.918635	0.801268

8.6 CONCLUSION

Now more than ever, early detection and treatment of varicose veins require computer-assisted image analysis for histological classification. The suggested model extracts textural information that is extremely helpful for classifying different phases of wounding. He also uses two classifiers in this strategy; thus, the efficacy of both classifiers will aid in the discovery of a more accurate classifier in subsequent research. The results for the classifier to identify varicose vein stages will be increasingly accurate as more datasets and processing steps are added to the approach in the future.

REFERENCES

1. Zhu, Ruizong, Huiping Niu, Ningning Yin, Tianjiao Wu, and Yapei Zhao. "Analysis of varicose veins of lower extremities based on vascular endothelial cell inflammation images and multi-scale deep learning." *IEEE Access* 7 (2019): 174345–174358.
2. Ajitha, K. "SVM VS KNN for classification of histopathological images of varicose ulcer", *Advances in Engineering: an International Journal (ADEIJ)* 3, no. 2 (2020): 19–28.
3. Shi, Qiang, Weiya Chen, Ye Pan, Shan Yin, Yan Fu, Jiacai Mei, and Zhidong Xue. "An automatic classification method on chronic venous insufficiency images." *Scientific Reports* 8, no. 1 (2018): 17952.
4. Barulina, Marina, Askhat Sanbaev, Sergey Okunkov, Ivan Ulitin, and Ivan Okoneshnikov. "Deep learning approaches to automatic chronic venous disease classification." *Mathematics* 10, no. 19 (2022): 3571.
5. Adjei, Tricia, Wilhelm Von Rosenberg, Valentin Goverdovsky, Katarzyna Powezka, Usman Jaffer, and Danilo P. Mandic. "Pain prediction from ECG in vascular surgery." *IEEE Journal of Translational Engineering in Health and Medicine* 5 (2017): 1–10.
6. Pereira, Naomi Christianne, Jessica D'souza, Parth Rana, and Supriya Solaskar. "Obesity related disease prediction from healthcare communities using machine learning." In: *2019 10th International Conference on Computing, Communication and Networking Technologies (ICCCNT)*, pp. 1–7. IEEE, 2019.
7. Liu, Jing, Bryan Yan, Shih-Chi Chen, Yuan-Ting Zhang, Charles Sodini, and Ni Zhao. "Non-invasive capillary blood pressure measurement enabling early detection and classification of venous congestion." *IEEE Journal of Biomedical and Health Informatics* 25, no. 8 (2021): 2877–2886.

9 Brain Tumor Detection Using CNN

Paras Bhat, Sarthak Turki, Vedyant Bhat,
Gitanjali R. Shinde, Parikshit N. Mahalle,
Nilesh P. Sable, Riddhi Mirajkar,
and Pranali Kshirsagar

9.1 INTRODUCTION

The human body is a combination of interrelated parts or networks where each part is interconnected to the other, and dysfunction in one part shows the impact on the overall body of the individual. Being such a complex system nature has provided it with an inbuilt processor which manages all its work and responds to every stimulus in a reasonable manner. Humans have named it as brain, the most important organ of human beings. Our existence is immensely dependent on the proper functioning of the brain that performs most of our tasks, be it controlling voluntary movement, creating and managing memories, developing thoughts, etc. [1].

Now-a-days, due to processed foods, the use of plastics in our day-to-day life, the consumption of adulterant drinks, the increase in smoking among youth, etc., have made this disease of cancer spread like a forest fire which is increasing at a very fast pace [2]. Some of the brain cancers are depicted in Figure 9.1.

A brain tumor is such a kind of tumor in which the tissues inside the brain start to grow abnormally creating an extra piece of mass inside the brain which takes away the nutrients of its surrounding cells, thus resulting in brain failure. The disease is curable if it is identified at an early stage, which is the most challenging part of this process as it mildly shows any symptoms at its early stage and often gets skipped away by doctors. In order to help the live saviors, i.e. doctors to predict this problem at an early stage, here this project aims to provide some more time for the doctors to think and curate this problem as early as possible. We have tried to build a machine that uses CNN and many more algorithms to detect the brain tumor at its early stage. Our machine identifies a tumor from a picture and returns the result of whether the tumor is positive or negative, which makes it useful in situations when we need to be certain of the tumor status.

The primary goal of brain tumor detection is to classify various tumor forms in addition to just detecting them. It also serves the purpose of identifying a tumor from a picture and gives the output of whether the disease is present or not, which makes it useful in situations when an infected person needs to be certain of the tumor's status. This project is focused on developing a system that can recognize tumor blocks in MRI scans of various patients and prevent the damage it causes in a patient's life.

DOI: 10.1201/9781003461500-11

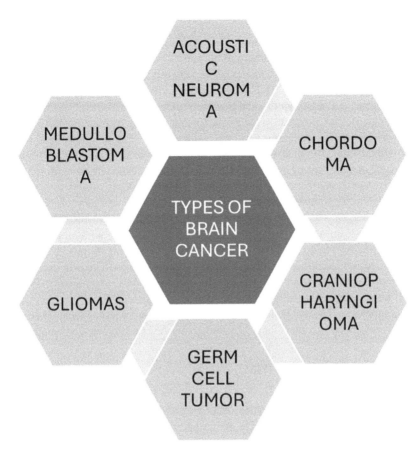

FIGURE 9.1 Types of brain cancer [3].

9.2 LITERATURE SURVEY

Sasikala et al. [4] suggested some new self-activating tumor detection methods with the help of Deep Neural Network (DNN) for proficient glioblastoma detection. It uses a final layer that implements fast segmentation on the order of 24 s–3 min across the lung area. Jyothi et al. [5] proposed eight different kinds of MRI scans out of which seven represent different tumor kinds and one represents basic brain tumor. The method of Deep CNN and SVM uses it in a collection of standard data items intended to facilitate systematic measurement comparison in order to achieve a precision of 92.17% with a correctness of 93%. Joshi et al. [6] focused on brain tumor segmentation. Only quantitative measures of disease modeling allow process monitoring and recovery. The model is more susceptible for detecting defects related to brain and stroke, brain tumors or infections.

Kiranmayee et al. [7] proposed a prototype which consists of both testing and training phases and implements the enhancement of service by combining health and network support emotionally in the area of health service and improving its quality. Arya et al. [8] have given an overview of different image preprocessing and division methods, which contain picture filtering methods, noise-removing methods, usage of graphs and algorithms like watershed. Siar et al. [9] proposed the method of CNN while reaching an accuracy of 98.66% and also used the radial basis function and Decision Tree classifier. The SoftMax Fully Connected Plate used for image classification had a classification accuracy of 98.57%.

Deepak et al. [10] proposed the methods that were used: GoogleNet and CNN, and he also describes the advantage of CNN-based classifier systems is that they do not require manually segmented tumor regions and provide a fully automated classifier. Demiharan et al. [11] suggested a segmentation technique for categorizing brain tumor MRIs. Using station wavelet transform, learning vector quantization, cerebral spinal fluid (CSF), edema, white matter (WM), and grey matter were on the order of 0.87 for grey matter, 0.96 for CSf, and 0.77 for edema. WM was discovered in 0.91%. Aneja et al. [12] suggested a segmentation algorithm that uses fuzzy C-means (FCM) clusters for noise figures as well as a fuzzy clustering averaging technique. The cluster validity function, run time, and convergence error rate of 0.537% are used to evaluate segmentation values.

Yang et al. [13] used discrete wavelength transform (DWT) with an accuracy of 93.9% and an objective prediction of 6.9%. Badza et al. [14] proposed their own CNN architecture for three types of brain tumor classification. The proposed model is more straightforward than the existing pre-trained models. They used T1W-MRI data for the training and testing with tenfold cross-validation.

These approaches have suggested many ways in which the model has achieved efficient ways to diagnose a brain tumor. Table 9.1 summarizes the literature work on brain cancer.

9.3   PROPOSED ALGORITHM

The brain being the most important and delicate part is also the most complex organ of the body of a human. Understanding the functioning of the brain in itself is a tedious task, but through our project, we have tried to understand its complex behavior and developed a project which uses convolutional neural network architecture to detect the region accumulated by tumor by processing its MRI images, that too at an early stage. The main purpose is to help doctors in predicting diseases at an early stage and save the lives of people.

The working of the CNN model is shown in Figure 9.2; details of the CNN layers are as follows:

- **The Convolution Layer:** The main layer of CNN is a convolution layer which consists of kernels or filters present in it whose size is smaller than the actual image. The convolution layer has the function of extracting the features of the input image given to it and returning the output in matrix form.
- **Activation:** The activation layer consists of an activation function inside the layer. For our model, we have chosen the activation function ReLU. The purpose of ReLU activation function is that it will give the output as negative if the input is negative and will give the same output if the input is positive.
- **Max Pooling:** The max pooling layer reduces the dimensions of the image by taking out the largest element present in the matrix on which pooling is used.
- **Flatten:** Flatten is another layer present in CNN which is used to convert the pooled feature matrix into a list. The output given by the flatten layer is taken as the input to the fully connected neural network.
- **Dense:** The dense has the function of connecting the fully connected layer to the neural network.

TABLE 9.1
Summary of Literature Work on Brain Cancer

Research work	Used Methods	Used Dataset	Obtained accuracy	Advantages	Discussion
Wentao et. al. [1]	Methods used were SVM and deep CNN	BraTS 2014 and BraTS 2016	CNN 87.57% and SVM 86.04%	Faster segmentation	Need improvement in accuracy
S et al. [4]	Methods used are neural networks, K-means and fuzzy logic	BraTS 2010	FCM in WM, GM, CSF 30.01, 31.04, 28.04	Enhancement of picture with noise that too with least error	Need of updation in misclassification error
Jyoti et al. [5]	Methods used are deep CNN and SVM	OASIS	92.17% Precision, 93% correctness, 92% recall and 91% f1-score	Multi-class classification shows great significance	Size of the model is evanescently small and can't handle big datasets
Joshi et al. [6]	Methods used are image segmentation, restoration and enhancement of images	30 research papers from 2000–2015	HSOM scans 110 abnormal and 62 normal axial MRI images with a 92.41% accuracy	Problem of image restoration and enhancement of images has been resolved and explained with proper methodologies.	Algorithm could solve particular research problems only.
Kiranmayee et al. [7]	Detecting brain tumor consisting of training and testing phase			The outcomes gained demonstrate that the combination of emotionally supportive networks with medical services can improve the quality of services.	It was on a prototype stage

(Continued)

TABLE 9.1 (*Continued*)
Summary of Literature Work on Brain Cancer

Research work	Used Methods	Used Dataset	Obtained accuracy	Advantages	Discussion
Deepak et al. [10]	Methods used were GoogleNet and deep CNN	Figshare	DCNN 91.2% and SVM Classifier 0.98%	Stable and efficient	Lack of accuracy in transfer model
Demirahan et al. [11]	Methods used are neural networks, self-organizing maps and Wavelets	IBSR 2015 and BraTS 2012	WM 90%, GM 87%, hydrops 76%, tumor 60% and CSF 95%	Enhancement of efficiency in WM.GM and edema	Can't be applied on newly generated dataset
Aneja et al. [12]	Method used is fuzzy clustering mean algorithm	NSL–KDD	FCM 1.173, T2FCM 0.951 and IFCM 0.436	Reduction of disturbances in training set & size clot	Need of updation in misclassification error
Yang et al. [13]	Methods used is DWT	GE Healthcare	Collected reliability of 93.9% and an objective error rate of 6.9%	More work on deduction on SVM	Crises of Model handling
Badza et al. [14]	Method used is CNN	BRATS and CBICA	Repeating the Fitting procedure 10 times we get the punctuality of 95.08%	Could be used for differential datasets	Heavy run-time

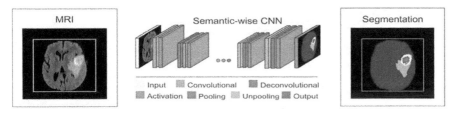

FIGURE 9.2   CNN model working for brain tumor detection.

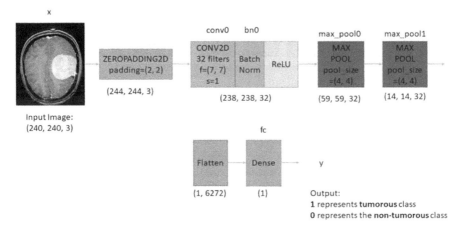

FIGURE 9.3   Architecture of CNN model.

The dataset is taken from github, 253 MRI images with 155 positive instances and 98 negative samples. The neural network couldn't be trained because the dataset was too little. In order to address the problem of data imbalance, data augmentation proved helpful. Data augmentation is used to increase the dataset. The dataset now has 1085 positive examples and 980 negative examples, for a total 2065 example photos, following data augmentation.

The following pre-processing processes were used for each image:

Images are resized such that they only show the brain in one section (which is the most important part of the image). The neural network accepts images of the same sizes, hence image shapes are kept as 240, 240, 3 = (image width, image height, number of channels). The value of pixels can be scaled using Normalization to a range of 0–1.

The data were divided as follows:

- Training was done with 70% of the data
- To validate, 15% of the data
- Test will use 15% of the data

9.3.1   NEURAL NETWORK ARCHITECTURE

The system architecture is shown in Figure 9.3; let's discuss each layer of the architecture in detail:

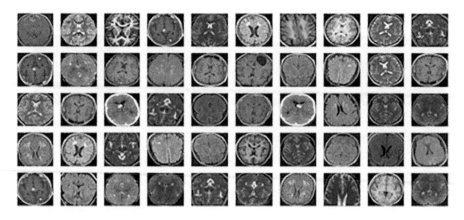

FIGURE 9.4 MRI images without tumor.

The first step involves giving the input to the neural network. The neural network is given an input image with a shape of (240, 240, 3) for each input image x. When the image is given as input to the neural network, it traverses the following layers:

The first layer it traverses is the zero-padding layer which is of the size of (2,2). Then followed by the zero-padding layer, there is a convolutional layer which consists of 32 filters, with a stride of 1 and the filter with the size of (7,7). After the convolution layer, there is a normalization layer which helps in normalizing the pixel values in a batch to speed up computation. After the normalization layer, there is the activation layer which consists of the activation function. The activation function we used is the ReLU activation function. After the activation layer, there is a max pooling layer with a filter size of 4 and a stride of 4. Then again, there is an identical layer of Max Pooling with $f = 4$ and $s = 4$. After the pooling layers, there is a flatten layer which converts the three-dimensional matrix into a vector with only one dimension. After the flatten layer, there is a dense layer in which one neuron is in a dense, fully linked layer with an output unit that has sigmoid activity.

MRI images without brain tumor and having brain tumor are shown in Figures 9.4 and 9.5, respectively.

9.4   RESULT AND DISCUSSION

The result was generated through continuous testing of the model which was done as follows: First, load the model and we are doing that by using the file path: model = load_model (filepath='models/cnn-parameters-improvement-23-0.91.model'). So we have a model.metrics_names, the purpose at the time of compilation is to check against the monitored quantities which are very important in the callback. To see if the model is performing well, it becomes essential to evaluate it against the test model. A test model is based upon a pre-processed dataset using data preparations. We obtain the correctness based on the F-measure on the test model, and the result we achieved is: For loss, it is 11.3%, and for the accuracy, it is 88.7%, f1-score is 0.88.

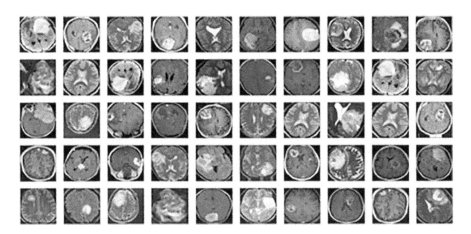

FIGURE 9.5 MRI images with tumor.

Let's keep in mind the ratio of positive to negative examples: Start by declaring the variables m and n_positive for the size of the dataset and the quantity of positive examples, respectively. Now, we can compute the total examples that are negative i.e. n_negetive=m-n_positive

Number of examples: 2065
Positive Examples as Percentage: 52.54237288135593%
Number of positive examples: 1085
Negative Examples as Percentage: 47.4576271186440%
Number of negative examples: 980

Training Data:

So, the Percentage of Positive and Negative data is 52.8719723183391% and 47.1280276816609% respectively while the Number of Positive and Negative samples are 764 and 681

Validation Data:

Number of Examples: 310
Consequently, the ratio of positive to negative samples is from 54.83870967741935% to 45.16129032258065%.
We get 170 positive samples and 140 negative samples

Testing Data:

Number of Examples: 310
Positive samples as a Percentage is 48.70967741935484% while as a number it is 151. Negative Sample as a percentage is 51.29032258064516% while as a number it is 159

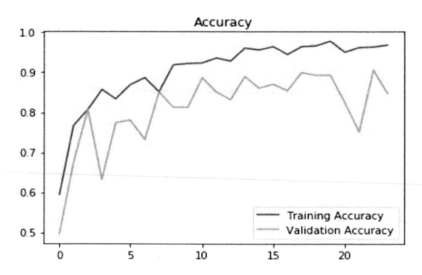

FIGURE 9.6   Graph of training and validation accuracy.

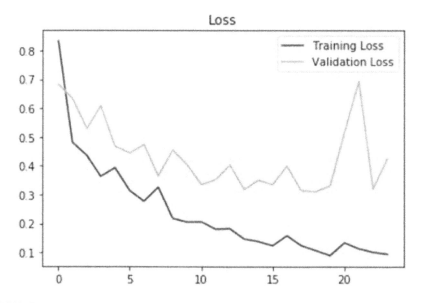

FIGURE 9.7   Graph of training and validation loss.

Graphs shown in Figures 9.6 and 9.7 show that with the increase in the testing data of the model, its training and validation accuracy is increasing continuously while the training and validation loss is being continuously reduced which is shown in Figures 9.6 and 9.7.

9.5 CONCLUSION

In this work, we reviewed the available feature-based research in the literature. We have implemented the CNN model with 88.7% accuracy on the test set and a score of 0.88 on the test set for f1. This model can detect brain cancer, and the results are satisfactory when you consider how balanced the data is. This will help the doctors to predetermine the disease and save more lives.

REFERENCES

1. Wu, Wentao et al. (2020). An intelligent diagnosis method of brain MRI tumor segmentation using deep convolutional neural network and SVM algorithm. *Computational and Mathematical Methods in Medicine*, Volume 2020, Special issue.
2. Deepa, S. A. (2016) Review of brain tumor detection from tomography. In: *International Conference on Computing for Sustainable Global Development (INDIACom)*. (pp. 3997–4000). IEEE.
3. Siar, M., & Teshnehlab, M. (2019, October). Brain tumor detection using deep neural network and machine learning algorithm. In *2019 9th international conference on computer and knowledge engineering (ICCKE)* (pp. 363–368). IEEE. https://www.zeeva.in/know-everything-about-brain-cancer/
4. Sasikala, S., Bharathi, M., & Sowmiya, B. R. (2018). Lung cancer detection and classification using deep CNN. *International Journal of Innovative Technology and Exploring Engineering*, 8(25), 259–262.
5. Jyothi, P., & Singh, A. R. (2022). Deep learning models and traditional automated techniques for brain tumor segmentation in MRI: a review. *Artificial Intelligence Review*, 56(4), 2923–2969.
6. Joshi, D., & Goyal, R. (2017). Review of tumor detection in brain MRI images. In: *2019 International Conference on Innovative Trends and Advances in Engineering and Technology (ICITAET)* (pp. 206–209). IEEE.
7. Kiranmayee, B. V., Rajinikanth, T. V., & Nagini, S. (2017, September). Explorative data analytics of brain tumour data using R. In: *2017 International Conference on Current Trends in Computer, Electrical, Electronics and Communication (CTCEEC)* (pp. 1182–1187). IEEE.
8. Arya, M., & Sharma, R. (2016). Brain tumor detection through MR images: a review of segmentation techniques. *International Journal of Computer Applications*, 975, 8887.
9. Siar, M., & Teshnehlab, M. (2019). Brain tumor detection using deep neural network and machine learning algorithm. In: *2019 9th International Conference on Computer and Knowledge Engineering (ICCKE)* (pp. 363–368). IEEE.
10. Deepak, S., & Ameer, P. M. (2019). Brain tumor classification using deep CNN features via transfer learning. *Computers in Biology and Medicine*, 111, 103345.
11. Demirhan, A., Törü, M., & Güler, I. (2014). Segmentation of tumor and edema along with healthy tissues of brain using wavelets and neural networks. *IEEE Journal of Biomedical and Health Informatics*, 19(4), 1451–1458.
12. Aneja, D., & Rawat, T. K. (2013). Fuzzy clustering algorithms for effective medical image segmentation. *International Journal of Intelligent Systems and Applications*, 5(11), 55–61.
13. Yang, G., Nawaz, T., Barrick, T. R., Howe, F. A., & Slabaugh, G. (2015). Discrete wavelet transform-based whole-spectral and subspectral analysis for improved brain tumor clustering using single voxel MR spectroscopy. *IEEE Transactions on Biomedical Engineering*, 62(12), 2860–2866.
14. Badža, M. M., & Barjaktarović, M. Č. (2020). Classification of brain tumors from MRI images using a convolutional neural network. *Applied Sciences*, 10(6), 1999.

10 Explainable Artificial Intelligence in the Healthcare

An Era of Commercialization for AI Solutions

Prasad Raghunath Mutkule, Nilesh Popat Sable, Parikshit N. Mahalle, and Gitanjali R. Shinde

10.1 INTRODUCTION

The significance of explainable artificial intelligence (XAI) is a term encompassing techniques that render AI systems interpretable and comprehensible to end-users. The importance of XAI is underscored by its applicability in numerous fields. In areas such as healthcare, ensuring the reliability of AI models is paramount. Furthermore, AI explainability can lead to new insights in fields such as Physics, Mathematics, and Chemistry. Equally important is the need for everyday users of AI to understand its decision-making processes. Additionally, XAI can aid neuroscience research in the testing and explanation of hypotheses related to brain activity and learning mechanisms. Apart from explicating the importance of XAI, this chapter delves into two XAI methods – model-agnostic and model-specific. The universal applicability and sensitivity analysis feature of model-agnostic methods positions them as suitable for any ML model. Conversely, model-specific methods are tied to certain ML models, employing techniques such as activation maximization and deep network understanding and visualization. XAI solutions adhere to specific criteria, such as trustworthiness, transferability, causality, and interactivity, that provide a framework for assessing the quality and efficiency of XAI methods. Through this investigation of XAI and its significance, it seeks to demystify AI systems, making them more transparent and interpretable.

Machine learning (ML) algorithms can produce findings that are understandable to humans with the help of XAI. An XAI model predicts an impact and its biases. It assists in decision-making aided by AI by evaluating correctness, fairness, and transparency. A company's ability to explain AI is crucial when it comes to bringing AI models into production. A responsible AI development strategy can also be

DOI: 10.1201/9781003461500-12

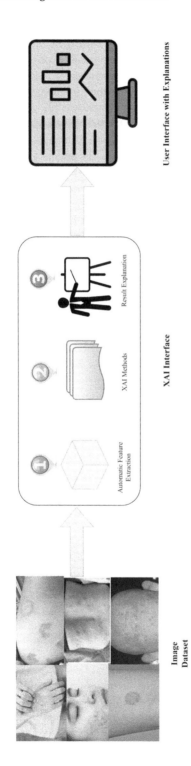

FIGURE 10.1 XAI overview.

implemented when AI is explainable. The ability to understand and retrace how a computer arrives at a conclusion will become more difficult as AI advances. A "black box" is created to represent the entire mathematical process, which makes it difficult to understand. These black-box models are constructed using data [1]. A lot of times, even the people who created the algorithm don't understand what's going on inside them or how it came up with a particular conclusion [2]. According to the business world, XAI identifies patterns and predicts desirable behaviours that lead to improved outcomes. With XAI, the firm owner can directly manage AI operations, since he already understands what the machine does. By understanding and understanding how AI systems work, stakeholders can build trusting relationships with you. It also ensures the company's safety, as all operations should follow safety regulations. It takes commitment to comply with new security regulations. Under the existing Right to Justify statute, all choices taken quickly are prohibited. Figure 10.1 gives an overview of XAI.

10.2   PRINCIPLES OF EXPLAINABLE AI

AI systems must consider how the information will be received by humans as they formulate these principles [3]. All factors will affect which explanation is appropriate for a given situation, including the requirements of the situation, the task at hand, and the consumer. Regulations and laws, quality control of AI systems, and customer relations are a few examples of these situations. Motives, reasons, and perspectives are captured by the four principles.

It is important to note that XAI is based on four principles:

10.2.1   EXPLANATION

There is an explanation or reasoning accompanying all outputs. AI systems must provide proof, support, and rationale in support of each output under the Explanation principle. Essentially, this theory implies that an explanation can be provided by a system without it necessarily being justified, appropriate, or instructive in and of itself; the only requirement is that the system can provide a rational explanation [4,5]. In the current state of technology, this type of XAI technique is being developed and validated extensively. There are a number of technologies and methods being developed and implemented at the moment. Their explanations are not subject to any quality criterion.

10.2.2   MEANINGFUL

System explanations are understandable by individual users. A meaningful system is one that is understood by the recipient of its explanations. A user meets this concept when the explanation is understood by them and/or helpful to them in completing a task. A one-size-fits-all approach may not be the best answer based on this principle. It may be necessary to provide different explanations to different groups of users for the same system. Users may receive explanations tailored to their needs due to the Meaningful principle [6–8]. There are many large groups of people in the world, such as developers versus users, lawyers versus judges, etc. There may be some differences between the objectives and desires of these two groups. The importance of certain factors may differ between forensic practitioners and juries. It is also possible to personalize explanations for individuals using this concept as well. It is found that there is sometimes a difference in perception between individuals who are observing the output of the same AI system, for a variety of reasons.

10.2.3 EXPLANATION ACCURACY

It is accurate to describe the output generation process of the system in the description. Explanations that are meaningful to users can only be generated by systems if they are applied together with the Meaningful principle. System output generation processes are not required to be accurately explained in order to comply with these two principles. Providing accurate explanations is essential to the Explanation Accuracy principle. Correctness of explanation is different from decision accuracy. Decision accuracy refers to the system's ability to make the right decision when making decisions. Although the system may make an accurate judgement regarding the situation, the accompanying explanation may not accurately explain how the results were reached, no matter how accurate the judgment may be [9]. It has been established by AI researchers to create standard metrics that measure the accuracy of algorithms and systems. It is understood that there is no performance metric that can be used to measure the accuracy of explanations, although there are reliable measurement methods available.

10.2.4 KNOWLEDGE LIMITS

In order for a system to work properly, it has to operate under conditions that lead to the output of the system being reliable under those conditions. System boundaries are implied by the preceding concepts. In light of this Knowledge Limits concept, it is argued that systems are capable of detecting situations that are beyond the scope of their design or approvals. In this approach, we identify and express limitations of knowledge so that we don't make judgements when we don't need to. With the Knowledge Limits Principle, you can build trust in a system by eliminating deceptive, harmful, or unfair decisions or outcomes. One of two approaches can be taken when dealing with a system's knowledge limitations [10–12]. First, it could be that the inquiry isn't within the purview of the system. Users can upload pictures of apples to bird species categorization systems, for instance. If the system was unable to locate any birds in the supplied image, then it might provide an answer indicating that it was unable to provide an answer because it could not locate any birds in the image. I am going to respond to your question as well as explain my reasoning [13]. Based on a threshold of internal confidence, one may be able to determine which of the two methods has the most likely response, but the second method may have reached a knowledge limit in working with a limited amount of data. For example, a bird classification system may not be able to establish the species of a bird based solely on the input image of the bird. Despite the fact that this image is of poor quality, the algorithm may still be able to recognize that it is of a bird in this example [14,15].

10.3 NEED OF AI FOR EXPLANATION

There are some AI systems that do not require explanation. Occasionally, we will need an explanation only in cases where we are the ones who require it. Making a system that requires an explanation requires knowledge of which system needs one. Developers can then use a strategy that is appropriate for their situation [16]. In order to figure out when our system must explain something, we need to take into account the following points listed below:

10.3.1 THE NEED FOR FAIRNESS

There are certain forms of fairness within the system that are mandatory, and people cannot compromise when it comes to fairness. Statistical predictions are critical to the success of any project and are able to have an impact that is irreplaceable and lasting in the long term. Depending on the situation, a physician may recommend an operation, suggest receiving hospice care for the patient, etc. The system has the obligation to explain when there is a high cost associated with a mistake, where the system is required to produce the right result in response to the mistake [6,17]. In the event it is incorrectly predicted, it can have serious consequences, including life and death. As an example, if malignant tumours are misclassified as benign tumours, this can pose a great risk to the health of the individual.

10.3.2 PERFORMING AT PEAK LEVELS

There is a need to have a high level of performance from a system or model. General Data Protection Regulation (GDPR) is one example of compliance that should be explained when compliance is needed.

10.3.3 THE NEED FOR TRUST

It is essential that the system explains how it generates a particular output when gaining the trust and confidence of the user. This feature, parameter, and model used in the application should be identified in the description.

10.4 VARIOUS XAI ALGORITHMS

While there are many XAI algorithms that explain ML models, the following are three examples:

10.4.1 SHAPLEY ADDITIVE EXPLANATIONS (SHAP)

SHapley Additive exPlanations (SHAP) aims to provide a comprehensive understanding of the technique designed to quantify the contribution of each feature to a model's prediction. Through an in-depth analysis of how predictions shift when examining all imaginable outcomes, it assigns SHAP values to individual features, thereby allowing straightforward explanations of individual predictions and overall feature importance [18]. The significant advantage of the SHAP approach has been extensively explored here, which lies in its ability to offer both local and global interpretability creating a unified model explanation. This trait makes SHAP an instrumental tool for understanding complex prediction models.

10.4.2   LOCAL INTERPRETABLE MODEL-AGNOSTIC EXPLANATIONS

It delves into the application of the Locally Interpretable Model-Agnostic Explanations (LIME) for explicating ML models, addressing the challenges of SHAP's computational intensity and time-extensive nature. LIME enhances these through the generation of a data points sample around the predicted data point, followed by constructing a linear regression model utilizing this weighted sample to discern the impact of features on prediction [19]. However, it should be noted that LIME's inability to maintain global faithfulness is due to its structure that builds explanations solely based on data point samples adjacent to the instance it explains. The core focus is the construction and analysis of sparse linear models surrounding individual instances or predictions done via LIME.

10.4.3   INTEGRATED GRADIENTS

The theory and application of Integrated Gradients is an innovative method for deciphering the predictions of a deep learning (DL) model. The application of Integrated Gradients involves observing changes in the model's prediction compared to a baseline or masked instance by progressively turning on discrete input features [11,20]. The objective of this method is to identify pivotal features and examine their influence on the predictions made by the model. Integrated Gradients offer an optimized approach by delivering faster computations than SHAP values, holding particular suitability for DL models. However, this procedure requires the model to possess differentiability for successful implementation. Future research should aim to expand the applicability of Integrated Gradients to a broader range of models and prediction tasks [21].

10.5   BEST WORKING ALGORITHM

The short comparative study of two model-explaining algorithms, LIME and SHAP, is mentioned in the previous section. The evaluation framework used throughout the research highlights the strengths and weaknesses of each algorithm, helping readers to ascertain the best fit based on their requirements and constraints. LIME is identified as a preferable choice for scenarios with restricted resources or where immediate predictions are necessary, due to its primary focus on single data point analysis [22]. In contrast, SHAP emerges as a more efficient tool for those seeking a comprehensive, global explanation harmonized with specific local predictions. It underscores the pivotal role of an in-depth understanding of the underlying data, model intricacies, and situational nuances in choosing the optimal algorithm.

10.6 EXPLAINABLE AI FOR DECISION-MAKERS

This delves into the realm of XAI and its significance in rendering ML models more comprehensible and efficacious for a non-specialist audience. The research spotlights the ambiguity in the definitions of interpretability and explainability in AI literature and explores the increasing appeal of XAI as it presents a solution to the AI 'black box' riddle. It further ventures into the potential uses of AI in the healthcare sector, particularly highlighting its role in refining treatment regimens and disease monitoring, while underscoring that most AI models in this field are still in the nascent stage of development. The document assesses the stakes involved in complex models and underscores the crucial requirement for transparency and inter-pretability, especially when the outcomes are pivotal, as in medical decision-making scenarios. It evaluates the different explainability techniques, elaborating on their respective aims and inherent restrictions. The chapter accentuates the relevance of XAI frameworks such as LIME, SHAP, and PDP in offering both local and global insights into the model while stressing the dearth of research on information neces-sary for AI-driven decision-making in healthcare. The different authors explore the continual tension between complexity and interpretability in XAI designs, reveal-ing the necessity for a multiplicity of explanation methods and a more formalized approach in this arena [23–26]. This also seeks to illuminate the influence XAI holds on the conception, acceptance, and utilization of AI-based instruments in the healthcare sector.

10.7 NEED OF XAI IN HEALTHCARE

Some use cases within the healthcare industry need to be explained in order to avoid confusion. The black-box function of many AI systems is acceptable for most fields, except the healthcare industry. Many users wish to keep their logic secret and private, so they do not want their system to reveal the logic. Black-box functions, however, are not acceptable to doctors and patients in healthcare, where mistakes can lead to dangerous outcomes. In addition to being trained in identifying diseases and providing treatment, doctors are well-equipped to treat them. The AI system cannot diagnose patients if it hasn't been trained on the correct data. Due to this, users can-not be sure of the results of the system, which makes it hard to trust it. In order to support XAI's basic principles, transparency, fairness, etc., we must overcompensate for ML's opaque nature [27–32].

A system that detects cancer in Caucasian skin is an example of an AI system that performs better than one that detects cancer in darker-skinned people. Dark skin can be missed by this method, thus potentially resulting in cancerous lesions. This system provides biased results, so they recognize it. Some subpopulations may be at risk of death as a result of this misjudged output. Insufficient data is later found to be responsible for this bias. There is not much information about dark skin in the data set that was used to train the system. Hence, the result, data, and predic-tion model of our system need to be more transparent and explained in a clear and concise manner [33–36].

10.8 APPLICATIONS OF XAI IN HEALTHCARE

A great deal of advances in AI have been made in the healthcare industry over the past few years, and they have proven to be a boon to the industry, including the detection of genetic links, the use of robotic surgery, and even improving hospital efficiency due to the use of AI. Figure 10.2 depicts applications of XAI in healthcare.

10.8.1 CLINICAL DECISION SUPPORT

A health professional must take into account every crucial detail when diagnosing a patient. Due to this, medical records often contain unstructured notes that are difficult to sift through. If there was even the slightest mistake in monitoring even a single relevant fact, the life of a patient could be put at risk. In order to narrow down all relevant information from patient reports, doctors are able to take advantage of

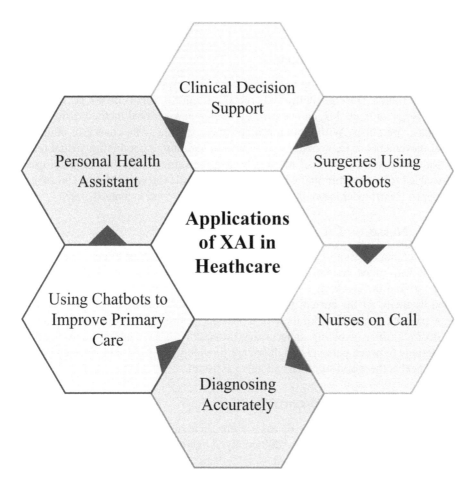

FIGURE 10.2 Applications of XAI in healthcare.

Natural Language Processing (NLP) with the assistance of NLP. With AI, technology can process and store large quantities of information, which will enable database knowledge to be built and may improve clinical decision support through facilitating examinations and recommendations for each patient.

10.8.2 Using Chatbots to Improve Primary Care

In many cases, it is common for people to schedule appointments with their general physicians, which may turn out to be a false alarm or a condition that could be treated by self-treatment. By automating primary care, AI allows doctors to handle more crucial and dire cases, without having to worry about mundane administrative tasks. Using medical chatbots, which are AI-powered services with smart algorithms, patients can save money on avoidable doctor's appointments, thereby saving time and money on unnecessary doctor's visits. They provide immediate answers to health-related questions and concerns as well as tips on how to handle any potential problems they may encounter.

10.8.3 Surgeries Using Robots

Incisions made with precision and speed have been revolutionized by AI and collaborative robots. During lengthy and crucial procedures, robots do not get tired, so fatigue is not an issue. ML can be used to develop new surgical methods using data from past operations. With these machines, there is little or no chance of unintentional movements or tremors during surgery. In addition to combining virtual reality with AI-enabled robots for minimally invasive surgery, vicarious surgical uses AI-enabled robots for minimally invasive surgery, while Carnegie Mellon University developed Heartlander, a small mobile robot designed to aid in heart therapy.

10.8.4 Nurses on Call

Virtual nursing assistants can direct patients to the best and most effective care units with the help of AI systems. Almost all queries can be answered by these virtual nurses around the clock, as well as examinations and instant solutions can be provided by them. At the current time, there are many AI-powered applications that allow patients to interact with their care providers more regularly between visits to the doctor's office, avoiding unnecessary hospital visits by enabling more regular interactions between patients and their care providers. With AI and voice controls, Care Angel is the world's first virtual nurse assistant.

10.8.5 Diagnosing Accurately

With AI, doctors can diagnose diseases more accurately, predict them more effectively, and diagnose them faster. Additionally, AI algorithms have been proven to be effective and cost-effective in diagnosing diabetic retinopathy as well as detecting other diseases. ML will help pathologists make better diagnoses, for example, thanks to PathAI. Cancer diagnosis mistakes are being reduced and methods for treating patients individually are being developed by the company.

10.9 AI IN HEALTHCARE: THREATS AND OPPORTUNITIES

It is important to be aware of different risks related to AI in healthcare according to a report that was released by the Brookings Institution. According to the Institution's report, the following threats have been identified as part of the risk management program all are given in Figure 10.3.

10.9.1 INJURY/ERROR

There is a significant risk that AI in healthcare will at times be wrong, as it might suggest the wrong treatment to a patient or make the wrong diagnosis on a radiology scan, resulting in injury or dire health consequences to the patient. For instance, it might suggest the wrong medication to a patient or make a mistake in locating the tumour on a radiology scan. At least two reasons may be involved in the difference between AI errors and human errors. The significance of this is that an AI system error may cause injury to thousands of patients, while human medical professionals may also make errors.

10.9.2 AVAILABILITY OF THE DATA

The fragmented data, coupled with the patient's tendency to switch insurers and providers, causes the data to become more complicated and less understandable, which increases the possibility of error and increases the total cost.

FIGURE 10.3 Threats of XAI in healthcare.

10.9.3 Security

Many patients believe that data is being collected and exchanged between health systems and AI developers for the purpose of enabling AI systems, leading them to sue. AI systems can also predict private information about patients even if they have not disclosed it themselves. This raises another issue regarding the use of AI systems.

10.9.4 Inequality and Bias

The biases in the available data can also be absorbed by AI systems since they adapt to the available data. The AI systems are less likely to be aware, and therefore less likely to treat if the data is primarily collected from academic medical centres.

10.9.5 Changing Professions

Medical professions may undergo significant changes in the future as a result of AI systems' use. Most of the work in areas such as radiology is automated. The high amount of AI use raises the concern that humans will become increasingly unable to detect AI errors and develop medical knowledge as a result of a decline in human knowledge and capacity over time.

10.10 HEALTHCARE BENEFITS OF XAI

AI systems in healthcare are rapidly being adopted due to XAI. In the face of Big Data, a human has difficulty making decisions because AI systems identify patterns and make decisions based on it. Some features that are provided by XAI are described in Figure 10.4.

- **Transparency**: The key to XAI is transparency. User-friendly algorithms, models, and features make XAI accessible. The requirements for transparency may differ from one user to the next. Suitable users will find it helpful.
- **Fidelity**: An explanation is provided by the system. The performance of the model should be in line with what is expected.
- **Domain sense**: As a result of the system, a user can find an explanation that is easily understandable to him or her as well as relevant to the domain. There is a proper context in which it is explained.
- **Consistency**: In order to avoid confusing the user, explanations should be consistent for all predictions.
- **Generalizability**: A general explanation should be provided by the system. However, it should not be too general.
- **Parsimony**: There shouldn't be a lot of complexity in explaining the system. There should be a maximum amount of simplicity in this process.
- **Reasonable**: As a result, it explains why AI systems work the way they do.
- **Traceable**: Data and logic can be tracked by XAI. By knowing how the data contributed to the output, users are able to make informed decisions. By tracking logic or data problems, users can solve them in a more logical or data-driven manner.

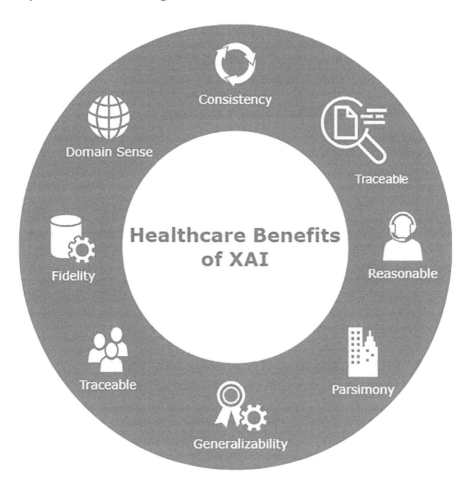

FIGURE 10.4 Benefits of XAI in healthcare.

10.11   CHALLENGE OF XAI IN HEALTHCARE

10.11.1   User-Centric Explanations

Critically examines the challenges involved in creating transparent and explainable ML models for healthcare systems. It delves into some of the key barriers to this process, such as the necessity for understanding advanced mathematics and statistics, inadequate systems design suitable for ML model deployment, the discrepancy between interpretable explanations and complex ML processes, and difficulties surrounding the tracking of model training. It also describes the limitations of XAI methods in identifying relevant features, the essential requirement for a thorough evaluation of these explanations, and uncertainties regarding the reliability of XAI methods. It underscores the crucial role of end-users, specifically clinicians, in the development and assessment of ML models intended for healthcare settings. However, it also recognizes the difficulties associated with engaging time-constrained clinicians and the discord between the preferences of ML experts and clinicians for different types of explanations. This advocates effective resolution for these challenges to establish more dependable and transparent ML models in healthcare systems, thus ensuring their broader acceptability and application.

10.11.2 Performance vs. Transparency Trade-off

The ramifications of utilizing XAI has been done for enhancing comprehension of ML models used in healthcare. It discusses the intricate equilibrium between model complexity and accuracy and elucidates how heightened model transparency can augment decision analysis. While black-box AI models such as DL and ensembles tend to lack transparency and hence inhibit fair decision-making and trust, grey-box AI models, such as statistical models, strike a delicate balance between transparency and comprehensibility. On the contrary, white-box AI models like graphical models, linear models, rule-based models, and decision trees tend to offer heightened explainability at the expense of decreased performance. An optimal model is one that offers high explainability while maintaining satisfactory performance, even in the face of the inevitable trade-off of uncovering patterns against attaining data-fitting accuracy. The necessity of discussing this trade-off with end-users to comprehend the clinical and human implications of misclassification is also brought to light.

10.11.3 Balancing Requirements of Interpretability

The intricate concept of interpretability in ML systems, specifically within the realm of healthcare is explored. The focus lies on the quest to decipher a universal definition, the requisites for an optimal interpretable ML model in healthcare, and the striking balance between model performance and user comprehension. Delve into the challenges encountered in realizing soundness, intelligibility, and scope, alongside instilling trust regarding the modus operandi of both black and grey box AI models. The scope of the model is also considered for explanations on both local (instance-based) and global levels. Furthermore, how the delicate equilibrium between soundness and comprehension can be impacted by the specificity of the application domain and the degree of interpretability anticipated by the end-user. This seeks to provide a comprehensive understanding of navigational strategies within the complex landscape of ML system interpretability in healthcare applications.

10.11.4 Assistive Intelligence

The role and limitations of ML algorithms in critical domains, such as healthcare, is explored. While ML aims to automate decision-making processes, it is highlighted that human supervision remains essential, particularly in safety-critical applications. It asserts while ML systems can function as beneficial medical assistants, they should not be entrusted entirely with patient care due to the need for accurate data and human intervention. Accordingly, this would lead to arguments for a human-in-the-loop framework in healthcare and stresses the need for the development of XAI mechanisms to ensure transparency and accountability in ML systems used in healthcare.

10.12   XAI OVER AI: HOW TO OVERCOME CHALLENGES

Customer trust is one of the biggest challenges in AI systems. An opaque AI system is one in which the system's output is not accompanied by any explanation or hypothesis. The healthcare system is an example of where customers find it challenging to trust machines that do not explain. Medical practitioners and patients do not adopt opaque AI systems due to their incompetence. This is reduced by XAI.

10.12.1   Trust and Confidence

In the AI system, doctors and patients can become wary of it because it is opaque. For various reasons, users seek explanations of the system in order to gain a better understanding of the logic of the model, as well as to give an explanation to others as to why the system works and to provide the reasoning behind making a decision. XAI builds users' trust and confidence by providing them with explanations.

10.12.2   Detect and Remove Bias

Because of its lack of transparency, the system cannot provide users with a clear view of its defects and biases. As a result, the detection and removal of bias and the provision of safeguards against bias become difficult.

10.12.3   Model Performance

The model's behaviour cannot be tracked due to the lack of awareness among model users.

10.12.4   Regulatory Standards

Regulatory standards cannot be recognized by users. As a result, the system would be harmed.

10.12.5   Risk and Vulnerability

Risk management systems must be able to explain how they deal with risks. Particularly, when the environment is unknown to the user, it can be detected early and action can be taken with XAI. What if the system is unable to provide the user with information about how they can mitigate the risks associated with it?

10.13   FUTURE PROSPECTS

Models can be used to simplify complex systems that are intractable. ML capabilities may be underutilized if DNNs with many parameters are not exploited in order to extract quality data using DNNs. A new, more complex component can be added to an existing model with the intent of gaining new insights. Just as it was with the earlier models and demonstrations, it's very important to discuss why the additional components correlate with other insights. In some industries, there are still a number of techniques that are embedded deeply into the culture, yet powerful ML algorithms are finding new applications in these fields. Fragmented and experimental implementations of existing or custom-developed interpretable techniques exist in the nascent field of medical ML, which is still in its infancy. In spite of the current focus on improving feature selection and extraction accuracy and performance, interpretability research may still have large untapped potential.

10.14   CONCLUSION

This chapter has significantly explored the profound relevance of XAI in healthcare, underlining its critical role in high-stakes decision-making processes that pervade the medical field. In light of potentially severe consequences arising from incorrect predictions by AI models, this underscores the need for the development and adoption of techniques for building AI applications that aid users in comprehending the model's output and predictions. The chapter detailed various methods, assigning them into six categories, and thoroughly examined diverse tools and techniques specific to healthcare's unique demands. Moreover, the chapter sheds light on the irrefutable demand for integrated explainability tools combining XAI, ML, and DL, especially for delicate medical procedures that call for utmost precision. Recognizing the increasing demand for trustworthy and transparent AI models among medical professionals, the call for enhanced collaboration between data scientists and medical experts for the design and successful development of efficient XAI systems is indispensable. Successfully harnessing this alliance can lead to an enhanced understanding of diseases' causation, better measurement of medication influences, and overall improved patient satisfaction. Finally, the chapter excelled in providing further research sources, reinforcing its arguments and providing groundwork for future exploration in the realm of XAI in healthcare. Such ingenuity creates an opportunity to delve deeper into the concept and critically analyze areas such as ethics and the engagement of user-centred design in AI developments. This ultimately paves the way for the potential maximization of the use of AI, particularly XAI in healthcare, advancing medical practices towards remarkable progress and efficiency.

REFERENCES

1. Arrieta AB, Díaz-Rodríguez N, Del Ser J, Bennetot A, Tabik S, Barbado A et al. Explainable artificial intelligence (XAI): Concepts, taxonomies, opportunities and challenges toward responsible AI. *Information Fusion*. 2020;58:82–115.
2. Angelov PP, Soares EA, Jiang R, Arnold NI, Atkinson PM. Explainable artificial intelligence: An analytical review. *Wiley Interdisciplinary Reviews: Data Mining and Knowledge Discovery*. 2021;11(5):e1424.
3. Samek W, Wiegand T, Müller K-R. Towards explainable artificial intelligence, Explainable AI: Interpreting, Explaining and Visualizing Deep Learning, pp. 5–22. doi:10.1007/978-3-030-28954-6_1. 2017.
4. Ribeiro MT, Singh S, Guestrin C, editors. Why should i trust you? Explaining the predictions of any classifier. In: *Proceedings of the 22nd ACM SIGKDD international Conference on Knowledge Discovery and Data Mining*, 2016. San Francisco, USA.

5. Zhou B, Khosla A, Lapedriza A, Oliva A, Torralba A, editors. Learning deep features for discriminative localization. In: *Proceedings of the IEEE Conference on Computer Vision and Pattern Recognition*, 2016. Las Vegas, NV, USA.

6. Selvaraju RR, Cogswell M, Das A, Vedantam R, Parikh D, Batra D, editors. Grad-cam: Visual explanations from deep networks via gradient-based localization. In: *Proceedings of the IEEE International Conference on Computer Vision*, 2017. Venice, Italy.

7. Chattopadhay A, Sarkar A, Howlader P, Balasubramanian VN, editors. Grad-cam++: Generalized gradient-based visual explanations for deep convolutional networks. In: *2018 IEEE Winter Conference on Applications of Computer Vision (WACV)*, IEEE, 2018. Lake Tahoe, NV, USA.

8. Cirqueira D, Nedbal D, Helfert M, Bezbradica M, editors. Scenario-based requirements elicitation for user-centric explainable AI: A case in fraud detection. In: *Machine Learning and Knowledge Extraction: 4th IFIP TC 5, TC 12, WG 84, WG 89, WG 129 International Cross-Domain Conference, CD-MAKE 2020, Proceedings 4*, Dublin, Ireland, August 25–28, 2020, Springer, 2020.

9. Alicioglu G, Sun B. A survey of visual analytics for explainable artificial intelligence methods. *Computers & Graphics*. 2022;102:502–20.

10. Kim B, Wattenberg M, Gilmer J, Cai C, Wexler J, Viegas F, editors. Interpretability beyond feature attribution: Quantitative testing with concept activation vectors (tcav). In: *International Conference on Machine Learning, PMLR*, 2018. Stockholm Sweden.

11. Raghunath MP, Ankayarkanni B. An empirical review on brain tumor classification approaches. *Information Systems and Management Science*, 2022;12:15–27.

12. Noh H, Hong S, Han B, editors. Learning deconvolution network for semantic segmentation. In: *Proceedings of the IEEE International Conference on Computer Vision*, 2015., pp. 114–123, vol-07.

13. Watson D. The rhetoric and reality of anthropomorphism in artificial intelligence. *Minds and Machines*. 2019;29(3):417–40.

14. Guidotti R, Monreale A, Ruggieri S, Turini F, Giannotti F, Pedreschi D. A survey of methods for explaining black box models. *ACM Computing Surveys (CSUR)*. 2018; 51(5):1–42.

15. Misztal-Radecka J, Indurkhya B, editors. Getting to know your neighbors (KYN). Explaining item similarity in nearest neighbors collaborative filtering recommendations. In: *Adjunct Publication of the 28th ACM Conference on User Modeling, Adaptation and Personalization,* 2020. Italy.

16. Thommandru, A., Mutkule, P., Bandi, A., and Tongkachok, K. Towards applicability of artificial intelligence in healthcare, banking and education sector. *ECS Transactions*. 2022;107(1):16665–16671.

17. Nimmy SF, Hussain OK, Chakrabortty RK, Hussain FK, Saberi M. Explainability in supply chain operational risk management: A systematic literature review. *Knowledge-Based Systems*. 2022;235:107587.

18. Saeed W, Omlin C. Explainable ai (xai): A systematic meta-survey of current challenges and future opportunities. *Knowledge-Based Systems*. 2023;110273.

19. Egger J, Pepe A, Gsaxner C, Jin Y, Li J, Kern R. Deep learning-a first meta-survey of selected reviews across scientific disciplines, their commonalities, challenges and research impact. *PeerJ Computer Science*. 2021;7:e773. 56.

20 Gritzalis D, Iseppi G, Mylonas A, Stavrou V. Exiting the risk assessment maze: A meta-survey. *ACM Computing Surveys (CSUR)*. 2018;51(1):1–30.

21. Došilović FK, Brčić M, Hlupić N, editors. Explainable artificial intelligence: A survey. In: *2018 41st International Convention on Information and Communication Technology, Electronics and Microelectronics (MIPRO)*, IEEE, 2018.

22. Kolli CS, Raghunath MP, Meenakshi S, Maheswari K, Britto CF, Kushwaha S, 2022. Efficient development of supervised learning algorithm for kidney stone prediction. In: *2022 International Conference on Inventive Computation Technologies (ICICT)*. Nepal.

23. Das A, Rad P. Opportunities and challenges in explainable artificial intelligence (xai): A survey (2020) pp. 229–239, vol-11.

24. Alonso JM, Catala A, editors. *Proceedings of the 1st Workshop on Interactive Natural Language Technology for Explainable Artificial Intelligence (NL4XAI 2019). Proceedings of the 1st Workshop on Interactive Natural Language Technology for Explainable Artificial Intelligence (NL4XAI 2019)* (2019). Turkey.

25. Almasri A, Alkhawaldeh RS, Çelebi E. Clustering-based EMT model for predicting student performance. *Arabian Journal for Science and Engineering.* 2020;45:10067–78.

26. Warman A, Warman PI, Sharma A, Parikh P, Warman R, Viswanadhan N et al. Interpretable artificial intelligence for COVID-19 diagnosis from chest CT reveals specificity of ground-glass opacities (2020). doi:10.1101/2020.05.16.20103408.

27. Zhu S, Fan W, Yang S, Pardalos PM. Scheduling operating rooms of multiple hospitals considering transportation and deterioration in mass-casualty incidents. *Annals of Operations Research.* 2023;321(1-2):717–53.

28. Lan S, Fan W, Shao K, Yang S, Pardalos PM, editors. *Medical Staff Scheduling Problem in Chinese Mobile Cabin Hospitals During Covid-19 Outbreak. Learning and Intelligent Optimization: 15th International Conference, LION 15,* Athens, Greece, June 20–25, 2021, *Revised Selected Papers* 15, Springer, 2021.

29. Lan S, Fan W, Yang S, Pardalos PM, Mladenovic N. A survey on the applications of variable neighborhood search algorithm in healthcare management. *Annals of Mathematics and Artificial Intelligence.* 2021;12:1–35.

30. Anand L, Rane, K.P., Bewoor, L.A., Bangare, J.L., Surve, J., Raghunath, M.P., Sankaran, K.S., and Osei, B., 2022. Development of machine learning and medical enabled multimodal for segmentation and classification of brain tumor using MRI images. *Computational Intelligence and Neuroscience,* 2022;29:1–8.

31. Fan W, Liu J, Zhu S, Pardalos PM. Investigating the impacting factors for the healthcare professionals to adopt artificial intelligence-based medical diagnosis support system (AIMDSS). *Annals of Operations Research.* 2020;294:567– 92.

32. Abidin, S., Prasad Raghunath, M., Rajasekar, P., Kumar, A., Ghosal, D., and Ishrat, M., 2022. Identification of disease based on symptoms by employing ML. In: *2022 International Conference on Inventive Computation Technologies,* Nepal *(ICICT).*

33. Horáček J, Koucký V, Hladík M. Novel approach to computerized breath detection in lung function diagnostics. *Computers in Biology and Medicine.* 2018;101:1–6.

34. Pardalos, P. M., Georgiev, P. G., Papajorgji, P., and Neugaard, B. (eds.). *Systems analysis tools for better health care delivery.* Springer Science & Business Media, 2013; vol. 74.

35. Alves, C.J., Pardalos, P.M., and Vicente, L.N. (Eds.). *Optimization in medicine.* Springer Science & Business Media, 2007; vol. 12.

36 Roshanzamir, M. et al. (2023) Quantifying uncertainty in automated detection of alzheimer's patients using Deep Neural Network [Preprint]. doi:10.20944/preprints 202301.0148.v1.

11 Role of Data-Centric Artificial Intelligence in Agriculture

Rajkumar Patil, Nilesh Popat Sable,
Parikshit N. Mahalle, Gitanjali R. Shinde,
Prashant Dhotre, and Pankaj Chandre

11.1 INTRODUCTION

Indian agriculture has traversed a remarkable journey from an era where farmers relied on age-old techniques and manual labor to the present, characterized by the integration of modern tools and technology. In the past, agricultural practices were deeply rooted in traditional wisdom, with manual plowing, hand sowing, and rudimentary irrigation methods being the norm. As time progressed, the Green Revolution introduced improved seeds, fertilizers, and mechanized equipment, catapulting productivity. Today, precision agriculture, satellite imagery, IoT devices, and data-driven insights have reshaped Indian farming, enhancing efficiency and sustainability while bridging the gap between historical practices and cutting-edge innovation [1].

The realm of agriculture is undergoing a transformative evolution, powered by the synergistic integration of Data-Centric Artificial Intelligence (AI) [2–4]. This convergence holds the promise of addressing pressing challenges in food production, resource allocation, and sustainability. With an ever-growing global population and the escalating impact of climate change, the need for innovative solutions in agriculture has never been more critical.

The advent of AI has revolutionized the way we perceive and harness data. Agriculture, a sector deeply rooted in empirical knowledge and practice, is now embracing the data-driven paradigm. Data, often referred to as the new "oil," has become a valuable asset for decision-makers across the agricultural spectrum. By capturing and analyzing a wealth of information ranging from climate patterns, soil health, crop growth, and market trends, AI empowers stakeholders with insights that were once beyond reach [5]. The introduction of AI in agriculture is not merely a technological shift, but a strategic shift in the very fabric of farming practices. Traditional approaches, while valuable, often grapple with inefficiencies and uncertainties that can limit productivity. In contrast, Data-Centric AI offers the potential to enhance precision, optimize resource utilization, and minimize environmental impact. Through advanced predictive models, decision support systems (DSSs), and smart automation, AI-enabled agriculture holds the promise of achieving higher yields while conserving resources and minimizing waste [6].

The objective of this chapter is to examine the crucial part that data-centric AI plays in agriculture. It delves into the various dimensions of this transformation, starting with the convergence of AI and Agriculture, highlighting the paramount importance of data in modern agriculture. After that, it examines several approaches of gathering data in agriculture, including sensor technology, Internet of Things (IoT) applications, remote sensing, satellite images, and aerial surveillance. Further exploration of the complex procedures for data preparation, cleaning, and application of machine learning (ML) methods – particularly deep learning (DL) for image analysis – is provided in this chapter. The chapter next looks at the use of predictive modeling in agriculture, discussing forecasts for crop production, pest and disease outbreaks, and the effect of weather on agriculture. The adoption of smart agricultural equipment, variable rate technology, precise irrigation and fertilization, and resource optimization are all covered in-depth. The chapter also looks at the creation of warnings, recommender systems for agricultural practices, risk assessment, and mitigation, as well as DSSs for real-time monitoring. Lastly, it acknowledges the challenges and future directions in Data-Centric AI in agriculture, touching upon concerns related to data privacy and security, integration with traditional farming knowledge, and the scalability of AI solutions for smallholder farmers. The chapter concludes with a recap of the benefits and opportunities presented by Data-Centric AI in agriculture, accompanied by a call to action for future development in this field.

11.1.1 THE CONVERGENCE OF AI AND AGRICULTURE

The convergence of AI and agriculture is an innovative synergy that has the potential to transform how we produce food, manage resources, and tackle the urgent problems of feeding a growing global population while minimizing environmental impacts. Agriculture is being improved in every way by the use of AI technologies like ML, computer vision, and data analytics. In precision agriculture, large datasets from sensors, satellites, and drones are analyzed by AI-driven algorithms to improve crop management [7]. In order to maximize yields and optimize resource use, farmers can make data-driven decisions about planting, irrigation, and pest control [8]. Robotic systems that are AI-powered are also creating a name for themselves by automating labor-intensive operations like weeding and harvesting, lowering labor costs, and boosting output [9]. Additionally, AI-driven models which predict weather patterns and crop diseases give farmers the ability to plan and act in advance, eventually protecting their livelihoods [10]. In this era of convergence, AI is not only increasing output but also supporting sustainability by lowering chemical inputs, conserving water, and reducing waste. It's promoting a new era of "smart farming," in which automated systems and data-driven insights enable farmers to adapt to shifting environmental circumstances and maximize resource utilization. However, issues still exist, such as ensuring that small-scale farmers have equitable access to AI tools and resolving data privacy issues. Despite this, the combination of AI and agriculture has great potential for creating food production systems that are more effective, robust, and sustainable while using fewer resources to fulfill the needs of the world's rising population. Figure 11.1 shows the potential application of AI in Agriculture.

The coronavirus epidemic and the Ukraine War, which were both exacerbated by a labor shortage, had a negative impact on the record levels of crop production in 2022 [11]. According to the researcher's findings in Ref. [12], the widespread adoption of AI and Precision Agriculture tools has the potential to significantly lower operating expenses as a percentage of revenue, from 42% to 33%. A potential $67 billion market opportunity could arise from this. Figure 11.2 shows global annual operating cost compared with the use of AI for the year 2022 for Corn, Wheat, and Soybean. Also, when autonomous technology becomes more widely used in agriculture, businesses may be able to create recurring revenue streams with margins comparable to software-as-a-service business models. It's crucial to remember that, even

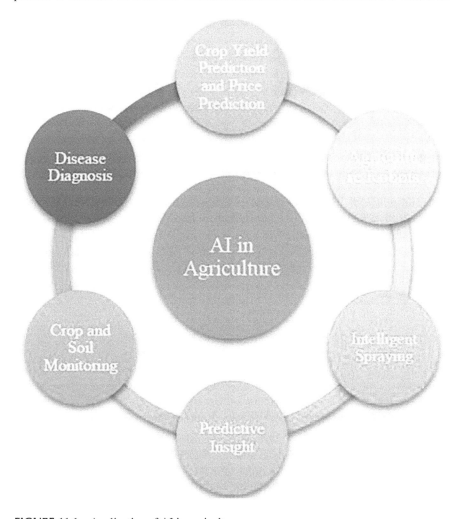

FIGURE 11.1   Application of AI in agriculture.

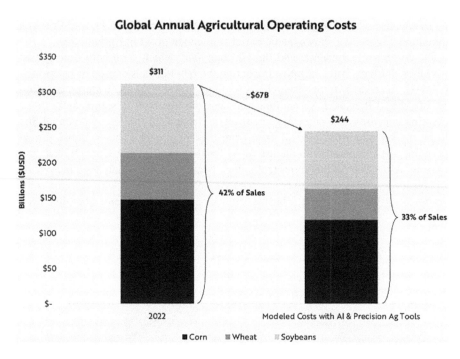

FIGURE 11.2 Global annual agricultural operating cost. *Source*: ARK Investment Management LLC, 2023, based on data from USDA as of July 12, 2023 [12].

though the emphasis has been on cost reduction, autonomous solutions can increase crop yields by reducing the need for human labor, particularly at night or during crucial agronomic periods. Due to labor constraints, many farmers sometimes struggle to procure labor-dependent machinery for field activities. Autonomous technologies have the potential to dramatically improve crop output prospects while addressing this difficulty.

We hold the belief that AI and Precision Agriculture have the potential to bring about the most significant advancements in agriculture since the introduction of the tractor a century ago. In our perspective, these innovations have the capacity to boost farm profitability, reduce food costs, and meet the growing global need for crops, ultimately enhancing the efficiency and sustainability of farming on a global scale within the next 5–10 years.

11.1.2   IMPORTANCE OF DATA IN MODERN AGRICULTURE

Data is essential to modern agriculture and has transformed the sector in several ways. Farmers can now gather and analyze a ton of data from sensors, drones, and satellites due to precision agriculture in order to make wise decisions. This data-driven strategy enables exact resource allocation, optimizing the use of pesticides, fertilizers, and water, while minimizing waste and adverse environmental effects. Data also helps with better pest management, disease outbreak prediction, and crop health monitoring. It improves logistics along the supply chain, assuring prompt deliveries and cutting down on food waste. In the end, data-driven agriculture promotes sustainability, boosts yields, and aids in feeding a growing world population while minimizing negative environmental effects. In Ref. [13], the author highlights the pivotal role of efficient data management in driving the exponential growth of Smart Farming in modern agriculture. It emphasizes the use of data in supporting producers' crucial decisions, with a focus on maximizing productivity and sustainability through unbiased data gathered from sensors. It has been demonstrated that the future of sustainable agriculture will be built on the integration of AI and data-driven tactics with robotic solutions. The review thoroughly examines the entire range of advanced farm management systems, from data collection in crop fields to variable rate applications, highlighting their potential to improve resource utilization, lessen environmental impact, and revolutionize food production to address the challenges of impending population growth.

The primary data collected from crops must be processed efficiently to transform numerous images into meaningful and clear-cut information. Farmers in traditional settings rely on visual inspections to make crop management decisions based on their experience without the use of technological technology. Farms with cutting-edge technology tend to adopt a more data-driven strategy. Sensors are used to gather factual information about the environment, the soil, and the crops. To help farmers make wise decisions, the data is subsequently processed using AI algorithms and filtering techniques. Throughout the information-based management cycle for advanced agriculture shown in Figure 11.3, this cycle – from data gathering to action – continues and comes to an end after harvest. The way that farmer maximizes their crop yields and resource management has been revolutionized by precision agriculture.

11.2   DATA COLLECTION IN AGRICULTURE

Modern farming practices rely heavily on data collecting that helps farmers and researchers make educated decisions, and increase productivity while minimizing resource wastage. Data on soil, weather, crop growth, and livestock health are all systematically gathered as part of this process. The ideal circumstances for planting and fertilizing crops can be determined using information about the soil, including its pH, nutrient content, and moisture levels. The ability to predict weather patterns and make prompt decisions about irrigation and pest management is made possible by weather data such as temperature, precipitation, and humidity. Sensor and drone data on crop growth are used to track the health of plants, their rates of expansion, and any possible problems like disease or nutritional deficiencies. The tracking of an animal's weight, health, and reproductive habits is included in livestock statistics. Data collecting in agriculture has improved in accuracy and efficiency with the introduction of cutting-edge technology like IoT sensors, remote sensing, and ML. These data-driven insights help farmers use resources more efficiently, lessen their impact on the environment, and improve yields, all of which improve the viability and profitability of agricultural practices. Additionally, c data sharing and collaboration within the agricultural community are essential to harness the full potential of data collection, allowing farmers to adapt to changing conditions and global challenges like climate change and food security. In summary, agricultural data collecting has

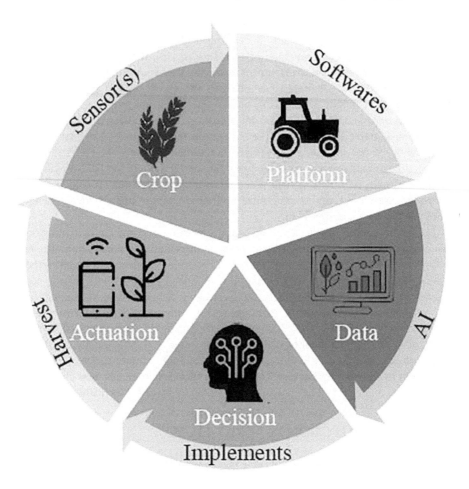

FIGURE 11.3   Information-based management cycle for advanced agriculture.

transformed into a crucial instrument for modern farming, fostering innovation and efficiency in a sector entrusted with feeding a growing global population while contending with a variety of environmental and economic concerns.

11.2.1   INTERNET OF THINGS: COLLECTING INFORMATION

In the realm of agriculture, the Internet of Things (IoT) involves the deployment of sensors and various devices to transform every aspect and activity of farming into valuable data. Approximately 10%–15% of farmers in the United States are reportedly utilizing IoT solutions on their farms, covering an impressive 1.2 billion ha and encompassing 250,000 farms [14]. IoT plays a pivotal role in Agriculture 4.0, and it's a driving force behind the collection of significant data in agriculture [15]. The agricultural sector is poised to undergo substantial transformation owing to advancements in IoT technologies [16]. Projections indicate that, with the adoption of new techniques, IoT has the potential to boost agricultural productivity by a remarkable

70% by the year 2050 [17]. This is particularly crucial as the world faces the challenge of increasing global food production by 60% by 2050 to support a growing population expected to reach over nine billion [18].

One of the primary benefits of IoT implementation is the achievement of higher crop yields and cost reduction. For instance, studies conducted by OnFarm revealed that, on average, farms using IoT experience a 1.75% increase in crop yields, while energy costs decrease by $17–$32 per ha, and the water usage for irrigation diminishes by 8% [15].

A. Sensor Technologies

Sensor technologies have played a significant role in revolutionizing agriculture by enabling farmers to monitor and manage their crops, livestock, and overall farm operations more efficiently. These sensors gather data on many environmental aspects and offer insightful analysis to enhance decision-making and optimize resource allocation [19]. In agriculture, the following prominent sensor technologies are employed:

1. Soil Sensors
   a. Soil Moisture Sensors: Let farmers decide when and how much to irrigate crops, therefore saving water and enhancing crop development. These sensors assess the moisture content in the soil.
   b. Soil pH Sensors: Measure the acidity or alkalinity of the soil, which is important for managing nutrients and choosing the right crops.
2. Weather Stations
   a. Weather Stations: Include numerous sensors including temperature, humidity, wind speed, and rainfall detectors. Weather stations also incorporate other types of sensors. For accurate weather forecasts and administration of farming activities, they offer real-time weather data.
3. Crop Health Sensors
   a. Remote Sensing: To track crop health, find illnesses, and determine nutrient levels, satellite- or drone-based sensors collect photos and data.
   b. Hyper spectral Imaging: This cutting-edge technique examines the light reflected from crops to detect minute changes in plant health.
4. Livestock Monitoring Sensors
   a. RFID Tags and GPS: Used in the location and movement monitoring of cattle. Information on breeding and health can also be stored on RFID tags.
   b. Wearable Sensors: To keep checks on an animal's health, behavior, and well-being, sensors like accelerometers and temperature gauges can be fastened to it.
5. Environmental Sensors
   a. Air Quality Sensors: Measure factors such as air temperature, humidity, and gas concentrations to ensure optimal conditions for livestock and crops.

b. Water Quality Sensors: Check the purity of water sources before using them for irrigation or animal use.

6. Nutrient Management Sensors

a. Nitrate and Phosphate Sensors: Enable farmers apply fertilizer accurately to avoid excess or underuse by measuring nutrient levels in soil or water.

7. Pest and Disease Monitoring

a. Pest Traps and Sensors: These tools enable focused interventions by assisting in the detection and monitoring of pest and disease activity in crops.

B. Drones and Aerial Surveillance

Aerial surveillance and drone technology have revolutionized agriculture by allowing for more precise and effective crop management. The high-resolution cameras and a variety of sensors on board these unmanned aerial vehicles give farmers crucial information for streamlining their operations. Drones give farmers the ability to make data-driven choices about anything from crop health monitoring and insect infestation detection to determining irrigation requirements and yield estimates. Aerial surveillance helps in early problem identification, enables prompt response, decreases crop losses, and reduces the need for pesticides and water resources [20]. Drones are also useful for mapping fields and producing in-depth 3D models, which helps with land management and boosts overall production. Drones and aerial surveillance are turning into increasingly important tools for modern farmers as they strive to increase yields, cut costs, and promote environmentally friendly farming practices as the agricultural sector continues to face challenges like climate change and the need for sustainable practices.

In Figure 11.4, the integration of sensor technologies, drones, and aerial surveillance exemplifies their pivotal roles in IoT-driven smart agriculture. By gathering data on crop health, weather, and soil moisture in real time,

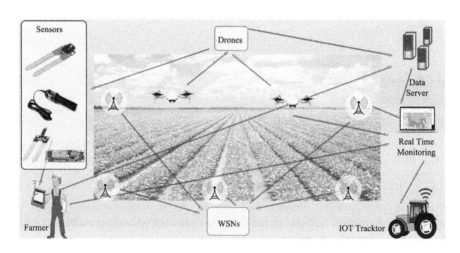

FIGURE 11.4   IoT-based smart agriculture. *Source*: From ref. [20].

these technologies improve precision farming and help farmers manage resources more effectively and produce more food.

11.3   DATA PROCESSING AND ANALYSIS

Data processing and analysis in agriculture play a pivotal role in modern farming practices, contributing to increased productivity, resource optimization, and informed decision-making discussed in Section 11.1 in detail. Farmers and agricultural professionals utilize various data sources, including weather data, soil quality measurements, crop yields, and remote sensing imagery, to gather valuable information about their fields discussed in Section 11.2 in detail. Through advanced technologies such as IoT sensors, drones, and satellite imaging, these data are collected in real time or at regular intervals discussed in Section 11.2.1 in detail. Subsequently, this raw data is processed using specialized software and algorithms to extract meaningful insights. Analysis of this processed data helps farmers make informed choices about crop planting, irrigation, fertilizer application, and pest control. It also enables the prediction of disease outbreaks and adverse weather events, thus allowing for proactive measures. Ultimately, data processing and analysis empower agriculture with data-driven precision, leading to more sustainable and efficient farming practices while ensuring environmental conservation.

11.3.1   DATA PREPROCESSING

Preprocessing the data is an essential stage in agricultural data analysis because it guarantees that the information that will be used for decision-making and analysis is correct, dependable, and consistent. Figure 11.5 illustrates some key steps and factors involved in preprocessing of data for agricultural purposes.

Integration of Data: To build a single dataset, combine information from several sources, such as weather, soil, and crop yield data. Ensure that the data is consistent with respect to time, place, and other important properties [21].

Transformation of Data: To bring all variables to a common scale, we normalize or scale the data. If distributions of data are skewed, use transformations like logarithms to handle them. Use of one-hot encoding to convert category variables into numerical representation [22].

Feature Engineering: Improve the performance of the model by developing additional features that are based on domain knowledge. Extract the information that is pertinent from the raw data, such as generating vegetation indices from satellite images or heat stress indices [23].

Dimensionality Reduction: Reduce the amount of features in order to avoid the "curse of dimensionality" and boost the overall efficiency of the model. In order to accomplish this goal, one may make use of methods such as principal component analysis [24].

Data Cleaning: Deal with missing data by either assuming their values or interpolating between them. Eliminate any outliers that can bias the outcomes of the study or modeling. Find and fix any inaccuracies in the measurements or data entries [25].

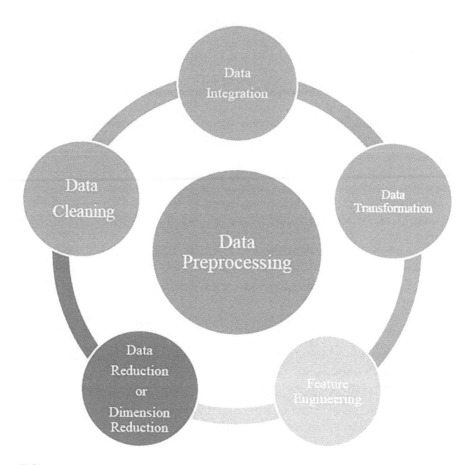

FIGURE 11.5 Key steps for data preprocessing.

The process of preprocessing data is iterative, and the choice of preprocessing processes will rely on the particular agricultural application as well as the features of the data. An efficient preprocessing of data can result in better predictions and insights, which can, in turn, lead to improvements in agricultural decision-making, whether the prediction is for crop production, disease detection, or resource allocation.

11.3.2 ML AND DL TECHNIQUES IN AGRICULTURE

The management of crops, the prediction of yields, and the efficient use of resources have all been transformed by ML and DL. By providing farmers with data-driven insights, these innovative solutions are promoting sustainable and effective agricultural practices. ML algorithms like Random Forests, Support Vector Machines, and Decision Trees are invaluable tools for tasks such as disease detection, pest monitoring, and yield prediction. As a result, farmers are able to proactively address problems and improve their agricultural operations. They do this by using past data to find trends and make predictions. For instance, ML models can assist in early disease detection, enabling prompt action, and minimizing agricultural losses by analyzing data on crop health and environmental conditions. DL, with its neural network architectures, has made significant strides in agriculture. Convolutional neural networks (CNNs) are excellent in image analysis, which makes them the best choice for identifying plant diseases. CNNs can quickly and effectively identify illnesses by studying images of leaves or fruits, eliminating the need for manual checks and resulting in healthier crops [26]. Figure 11.6 shows the architecture of ML and DL in agriculture.

Another DL method used in agriculture for time series data analyzing, such as weather forecasting, is recurrent neural networks (RNNs). RNN can analyze huge amounts of historical meteorological data to predict future circumstances, assisting farmers in making well-informed choices about when to sow, irrigate, and harvest. This enhances resource allocation and minimizes the impact of weather-related risks on crop yields [27]. Generative adversarial networks (GANs) play a unique role by generating synthetic data to simulate various environmental conditions. Without the requirement for actual field testing, this synthetic data helps with crop planning and scenario testing. For optimal production and resource efficiency, farmers can utilize GANs to optimize resource allocation, irrigation plans, and crop rotation techniques [28]. Figure 11.7 illustrates the agricultural challenges addressed by various research projects, along with the AI-powered solutions employed for each of these endeavors. These projects differ in their goals, approaches, and the materials utilized [29].

Due to the tremendous capabilities that ML and DL technologies have given farmers for decision-making and resource optimization, agriculture has undergone a revolution. These innovations improve weather forecasting, disease detection, yield prediction, and crop management. Farmers may contribute to sustainable agricultural practices that are essential for feeding a growing world population by utilizing the potential of ML and DL, which can also help them enhance production and minimize resource waste.

Figure 11.7 shows the Conceptualization of the several agricultural operations and AI-related technologies of the European research projects.

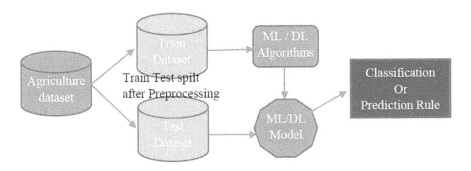

FIGURE 11.6   Basic architecture of ML and DL for agriculture.

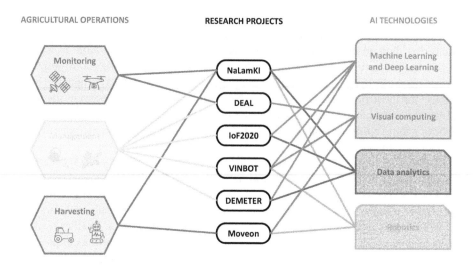

FIGURE 11.7   Conceptualization of the several agricultural operations and AI-related technologies of the European research projects described in [29].

11.4   DECISION SUPPORT SYSTEMS

The integration of Data-Centric AI and DSSs has become a transformational force in the field of modern agriculture. By offering real-time monitoring and alerts, enabling effective recommender systems for agricultural practices, and boosting risk assessment and mitigation tactics, these technologies provide farmers with invaluable tools [30]. The development of sensor technology and remote monitoring tools has made it possible for DSS to continually gather and analyze information about crop health, soil moisture, weather patterns, and equipment status. Farmers can now make quick decisions about irrigation, pest management, and resource allocation. Additionally, DSSs may notify farmers via alerts and notifications of prospective problems like unfavorable weather patterns or disease outbreaks, allowing for prompt measures to safeguard crops and increase yields. Figure 11.8 presents two categories of DSS the initial category enables data representation through visualizations like maps or graphs, while the second category focuses on forecasting future events (predictive). In the second phase that Data-centric AI plays a crucial role, they possess the capacity to glean insights from extensive historical data [30].

AI-powered recommender systems are essential for improving farming methods. These systems can provide specific suggestions to farmers by compiling information on soil quality, previous crop performance, market trends, and weather forecasts. This might involve suggestions for planting seasons, crop rotation, and even crop price predictions from the market. Farmers may maximize resource use and raise overall production by implementing these tips.

Risk assessment and mitigation are critical components of DSS in agriculture. AI systems can examine historical data to find trends in crop diseases, insect infestations, or extreme weather occurrences. Armed with this information, farmers may

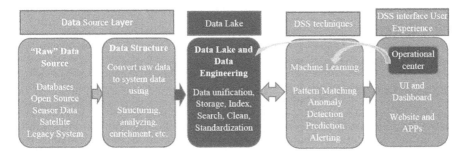

FIGURE 11.8   Architecture of DSS and data-centric AI for smart agriculture.

proactively employ risk mitigation techniques, such as modifying planting dates, selecting crop types that are disease-resistant, or spending money on protective infrastructure. In addition to reducing potential losses, this proactive strategy supports resilient and sustainable agricultural methods [31,32].

Data-Centric AI in agriculture, supported by DSSs, has revolutionized the industry. These technologies provide real-time data, personalized advice, and sophisticated risk assessment capabilities to farmers. To ensure food security for a growing global population while reducing environmental impact, agribusiness may advance toward more effective, lucrative, and sustainable practices by utilizing the potential of AI-driven DSS.

11.5   CHALLENGES AND FUTURE DIRECTIONS

As agriculture transitions to the digital era, data-centric AI has enormous potential to transform the sector. To realize its full potential, a number of significant issues and future initiatives must be addressed.

11.5.1   DATA PRIVACY AND SECURITY CONCERNS

The biggest difficulty faced in data-centric AI for agriculture is how to protect the growing troves of sensitive data. In the modern farming environment, a wide range of IoT devices, drones, and satellite technologies come together to collect intricate data about crops and soil conditions. However, the influx of such priceless data raises the unsettling possibility of privacy invasions, exposing the susceptibility of personal agricultural information to malicious actors. A determined effort is required to address this critical problem, including the development and implementation of powerful data encryption, access control, and anonymization solutions. These technological fortifications will serve as an indomitable bulwark against the perils of data exposure. Furthermore, ensuring data privacy and security across the agriculture sector depends on the development of thorough rules and industry standards. We can protect farmers' interests while ensuring the continued development and innovation of data-centric AI in agriculture by creating a strong framework of rules and standards. We may strive to leverage the transformational potential of data-driven agriculture while protecting the sensitive data that drives its development in this harmonic synergy of technology, legislation, and monitoring [33].

11.5.2 INTEGRATION WITH TRADITIONAL FARMING KNOWLEDGE

The integration of AI and data-driven technology offers intriguing potential in the constantly changing world of agriculture, but it is crucial that these developments live in harmony with the research of conventional agricultural knowledge. The invaluable practical insights and expertise of generations of farmers must not be relegated to the periphery. Instead of replacing these time-honored talents, AI should be seen as a potent ally that enhances and perfects them. The establishment of user-friendly AI systems that are meticulously developed to promote interaction between the agricultural community and technology specialists is necessary in order to recognize this symbiotic connection. Such collaboration acts as a link between the concrete reality of on-the-ground farming practices and data-driven insights.

The effective integration of these two realms, where AI complements rather than replaces human knowledge, is essential for contemporary agriculture. We can achieve levels of efficiency, sustainability, and resilience in farming that have never before been possible by creating a harmonic alliance between tradition and innovation. The preservation of ancestors' wisdom and the use of cutting-edge technology are intertwined in this communal journey, offering a better future for agriculture.

11.5.3 SCALING AI SOLUTIONS FOR SMALLHOLDER FARMERS

Smallholder farmers make up an important percentage of the global agricultural population; they face resource constraints and limited access to cutting-edge technologies. Data-driven AI must be both scalable and cost-effective for it to benefit everyone. As a result, affordable AI solutions must be developed that are especially suited to the unique requirements and constraints of small-scale agriculture.

The development of streamlined user interfaces that increase smallholder farmers' access to AI tools is one strategy for reaching this objective. Additionally, as mobile devices are frequently more common than conventional PCs in rural regions, leveraging the power of mobile technology might be crucial in this endeavor. We can provide farmers access to tools at their fingertips by creating AI programmers that can operate on mobile devices.

Additionally, providing thorough training and assistance is essential. Smallholder farmers might not be as comfortable with technology as larger businesses. Therefore, focused training initiatives and continuing support can close this knowledge gap, enabling these farmers to successfully embrace and apply AI solutions to improve their farming methods. Democratizing AI in agriculture depends on making technology accessible, inexpensive, and usable for smallholder farmers throughout the world, who are the group that needs it most.

"Empowering smallholder farmers with AI solutions is not just about scaling technology; it's about scaling hope, resilience, and prosperity on the world's most important growth frontier."

11.6   AI SUCCESS STORIES IN AGRICULTURE

Telangana is the success story of Indian agritech. AI tools, soil testing, e-commerce & more [34]: Telangana's use of agritech is a shining example of an incredible achievement in Indian agriculture. The state has used AI to transform the farming industry. By 2025, the state hopes to offer agritech services to 100,000 farmers according to a detailed plan it has established. This forward-thinking strategy combines the establishment of public infrastructure with smart partnerships, well-designed initiatives, and progressive legislation. The structure for public–private partnerships in the state has encouraged collaboration between the federal and state governments and technological firms, promoting the quick uptake of innovative solutions. Telangana has also made the restructuring of the agro value chain, encouraging effectiveness and sustainability in the industry.

Initiatives like the Agriculture Data Exchange (ADEx), which offers a platform for experimentation and data exchange, and the Agritech Sandbox have fostered agritech innovation. Additionally, the creation of an agriculture data management system guarantees that important data is tapped for well-informed choices.

Success in agritech in Telangana goes beyond local achievement; it provides a repeatable paradigm for other nations and regions seeking to digitally alter their agricultural industries. Telangana's story provides a ray of light, illustrating technology may be a driver for sustainable and wealthy agricultural futures as global agriculture faces increasing difficulties.

AI-Powered Agriculture: Revolutionizing Farming Practices [35]: Agerris, an Australian start-up, has transformed agriculture with its autonomous robot, Swagbot. Using AI and ML, Swagbot navigates rugged terrain, analyzes crop data, and makes real-time decisions, increasing efficiency and profits for farmers. Agerris is also pioneering AI systems for crop monitoring, disease detection, and yield prediction, further enhancing farming practices. This success story showcases AI's potential to address global challenges like food security and climate change while optimizing resource use. Agerris exemplifies how AI is revolutionizing agriculture, promising a sustainable and prosperous future for farmers and the planet.

11.7   CONCLUSION

This chapter has explored the pivotal role of data-centric AI in agriculture. The convergence of AI and agriculture is a promising frontier with enormous potential to change how we think about modern farming. Effective use of AI technology depends on an understanding of the significance of data in contemporary agriculture. We explored the crucial components of data collection, highlighting the IoT's contribution to the collection of important data from agricultural activities. Once gathered, this data goes through a substantial modification known as data preprocessing, which makes it possible to use ML and DL algorithms designed particularly for agriculture on it. DSSs have developed as an essential AI use in agriculture, offering farmers insightful information and suggestions for improving their farming methods. We also talked about the difficulties that must be overcome in order to fully realize AI's promise in agriculture, such as issues with data security and privacy, integration with conventional agricultural expertise, and the requirement for scaling AI solutions for smallholder farmers.

We also looked at real-world examples of AI being successfully used in agriculture, with Telangana serving as a shining example of how AI can improve agricultural practices. We also discussed the major advancements being made in this industry by Australian start-ups. The application of data-centric AI in agriculture has the potential to revolutionize the sector by presenting fresh approaches to venerable problems. In order to ensure sustainable and effective agricultural production in the years to come, it will be essential to handle the difficulties and seize the potential given by AI in agriculture.

REFERENCES

1. Rozenstein, O., Cohen, Y., Alchanatis, V., et al. "Data-driven agriculture and sustainable farming: friends or foes?" *Precision Agric volume* (2023). doi:10.1007/s11119-023-10061-5

2. Singh, P. "Systematic review of data-centric approaches in artificial intelligence and machine learning." *Data Science and Management* 6, no. 3 (2023): 144–157. doi:10.1016/j.dsm.2023.06.001.

3. Zha, D., Bhat, Z.P., Lai, K.H., Yang, F., Jiang, Z., Zhong, S., and Hu, X. "Data-centric artificial intelligence: a survey." (2023). arXiv preprint arXiv:2303.10158.

4. Salehi, S., and Schmeink, A. "Data-centric green artificial intelligence: a survey." *IEEE Transactions on Artificial Intelligence.* doi:10.1109/TAI.2023.3315272.

5. AlZubi, A.A., and Galyna, K. "Artificial intelligence and internet of things for Sustainable Farming and Smart Agriculture." *IEEE Access* 11 (2023): 78686–78692. doi:10.1109/ACCESS.2023.3298215.

6. Elbasi, E. et al. "Artificial intelligence technology in the agricultural sector: a systematic literature review." *IEEE Access* 11 (2023): 171–202. doi:10.1109/ACCESS.2022.3232485.

7. Kobayashi, T., Yokogawa, T., Igawa, N., Sato, Y., Fujii, S., and Arimoto, K. "A Compact low power AI module mounted on drone for plant monitor system." In: *2019 8th International Congress on Advanced Applied Informatics (IIAI-AAI)*, Toyama, Japan, 2019, pp. 1081–1082. doi:10.1109/IIAI-AAI.2019.00236.

8. Tantalaki, N., Souravlas, S., and Roumeliotis, M. "Data-driven decision making in precision agriculture: the rise of big data in agricultural systems." *Journal of Agricultural & Food Information* 20, no. 4 (2019): 344–380. doi:10.1080/10496505.2019.1638264

9. Wakchaure, M., Patle, B.K., and Mahindrakar, A.K. "Application of AI techniques and robotics in agriculture: a review." *Artificial Intelligence in the Life Sciences* 3 (2023): 100057. doi:10.1016/j.ailsci.2023.100057.

10. Dilmurat, K., Sagan, V., and Moose, S. "AI-driven maize yield forecasting using unmanned aerial vehicle-based hyperspectral and lidar data fusion." *ISPRS Annals of the Photogrammetry, Remote Sensing and Spatial Information Sciences* 3 (2022): 193–199. doi:10.5194/isprs-annals-V-3-2022-193-2022.

11. U.S. Senate Committee on Agriculture, Nutrition, and Forestry. "Revisiting farm production expenses." https://www.agriculture.senate.gov/newsroom/minority-blog/revisiting-farm-production-expenses (accessed September 9, 2023).

12. ARK Invest. "Will the convergence between artificial intelligence and precision agriculture lower farming costs?" *ARK Invest* (2023). https://ark-invest.com/articles/analyst-research/will-the-convergence-between-artificial-intelligence-and-precision-agriculture-lower-farming-costs/ (accessed September 9, 2023).

13. Saiz-Rubio, V., and Rovira-Más, F. "From smart farming towards agriculture 5.0: a review on crop data management." *Agronomy* 10, no. 2 (2020): 207. https://doi.org/10.3390/agronomy10020207.

14. Brown, A. "What is IoT in agriculture? Farmers aren't quite sure despite $4bn US opportunity-report." *AgFunderNews* (accessed September 2, 2023). https://agfundernews.com/iot-agriculture-farmers-arent-quite-sure-despite-4bn-us-opportunity.html.

15. Gralla, P. "Precision agriculture yields higher profits, lower risks." *HPE Insights* (June 2018). https://www.hpe.com/us/en/insights/articles/precision-agriculture-yields-higher-profits-lower-risks-1806.html (accessed September 2, 2023).

16. Tzounis, A., Katsoulas, N., Bartzanas, T., and Kittas, C. "Internet of things in agriculture, recent advances and future challenges." *Biosystems Engineering* 164 (2017): 31–48. doi:10.1016/j.biosystemseng.2017.09.007

17. Sarni, W., Mariani, J., and Kaji, J. "From dirt to data: the second green revolution and IoT." *Deloitte Insights*. https://www2.deloitte.com/insights/us/en/deloitte-review/issue-18/second-green-revolution-and-internet-of-things.html (accessed September 2, 2023).

18. Mykleby, M., Doherty, P., and Makower, J. *The New Grand Strategy: Restoring America's Prosperity, Security, and Sustainability in the 21st Century*. St. Martin's Press (2016).

19. Shaikh, F.K., Karim, S., Zeadally, S., and Nebhen, J. "Recent trends in internet-of-things-enabled sensor technologies for smart agriculture." *IEEE Internet of Things Journal* 9, no. 23 (2022): 23583–23598. doi:10.1109/JIOT.2022.3210154.

20. Shafi, U., Mumtaz, R., García-Nieto, J., Hassan, S.A., Zaidi, S.A.R., and Iqbal, N. "Precision agriculture techniques and practices: from considerations to applications." *Sensors* 19, no. 17 (2019): 3796. doi:10.3390/s19173796.

21. Nachankar, M. "Challenges of big data in agriculture: data collection and integration." International School of Advanced Management. https://isam.education/en/challenges-of-big-data-in-agriculture-data-collection-and-integration (accessed September 2, 2023).

22. Wijaya, R., and Pudjoatmodjo, B. "An overview and implementation of extraction-transformation-loading (ETL) process in data warehouse (case study: department of agriculture)." In: *2015 3rd International Conference on Information and Communication Technology (ICoICT)*, 70–74. Nusa Dua, Bali, Indonesia, 2015. doi:10.1109/ICoICT.2015.7231399.

23. Bocca, F.F., and Rodrigues, L.H.A. "The effect of tuning, feature engineering, and feature selection in data mining applied to rainfed sugarcane yield modeling." *Computers and Electronics in Agriculture* 128 (2016): 67–76. doi:10.1016/j.compag.2016.08.015.

24. Sabarina, K., and Priya, N. "Lowering data dimensionality in big data for the benefit of precision agriculture." *Procedia Computer Science* 48 (2015): 548–554. doi:10.1016/j.procs.2015.04.1345.

25. Yanwei, Y., Ling, X., Fuhua, J., Dafang, G., Sa, A., and Kang, N. "Experimental optimization of big data cleaning method for agricultural machinery." *Nongye Jixie Xuebao Transactions of the Chinese Society of Agricultural Machinery* 52, no. 6 (2021). https://nyjxxb.net/index.php/journal/article/view/1190

26. Durai, S.K.S., and Shamili, M.D. "Smart farming using machine learning and deep learning techniques." *Decision Analytics Journal* 3 (2022): 100041. doi:10.1016/j.dajour.2022.100041.

27. Saini, U., Kumar, R., Jain, V., and Krishnajith, M.U. "Univariant time series forecasting of agriculture load by using LSTM and GRU RNNs." In: *2020 IEEE Students Conference on Engineering & Systems (SCES)*, Prayagraj, India, pp. 1–6, 2020. doi:10.1109/SCES50439.2020.9236695.

28. Lu, Y., Chen, D., Olaniyi, E., and Huang, Y. "Generative adversarial networks (GANs) for image augmentation in agriculture: a systematic review." *Computers and Electronics in Agriculture* 200 (2022): 107208. doi:10.1016/j.compag.2022.107208.

29. Linaza, M.T. et al. 2021. "Data-driven artificial intelligence applications for sustainable precision agriculture." *Agronomy* 11 (6): 1227. doi:10.3390/agronomy11061227.

30. Borrero, J.D., and Mariscal, J. "A case study of a digital data platform for the agricultural sector: a valuable decision support system for small farmers." *Agriculture* 12, no. 6 (2022): 767. doi:10.3390/agriculture12060767.

31. Nikhil, R., Anisha, B.S., and Kumar, P.R. "Real-time monitoring of agricultural land with crop prediction and animal intrusion prevention using internet of things and machine learning at edge." In: *2020 IEEE International Conference on Electronics, Computing and Communication Technologies (CONECCT)*, Bangalore, India, pp. 1–6, 2020. doi:10.1109/CONECCT50063.2020.9198508.

32. Lafont, M., Dupont, S., Cousin, P., Vallauri, A., and Dupont, C. "Back to the future: IoT to improve aquaculture - real-time monitoring and algorithmic prediction of water parameters for aquaculture needs." In: *2019 Global IoT Summit (GIoTS)*, Aarhus, Denmark, IEEE, 2019. doi:10.1109/GIOTS.2019.8766436.

33. Kumar, P., Gupta, G.P., and Tripathi, R. "PEFL: deep privacy-encoding-based federated learning framework for smart agriculture." *IEEE Micro* 42, no. 1 (2022): 33–40. doi:10.1109/MM.2021.3112476.

34. Neo, G.H., and Rama Rao, K.T. "Telangana is the success story of Indian agritech: AI tools, soil testing, E-commerce & more." 2023. https://theprint.in/economy/telangana-is-the-success-story-of-indian-agritech-ai-tools-soil-testing-e-commerce-more/1630359/ (accessed September 2, 2023).

35. Ajayi, O. "AI-powered agriculture: revolutionizing farming practices." 2023. https://www.linkedin.com/pulse/ai-powered-agriculture-revolutionizing-farming-practices-ajayi/ (accessed September 2, 2023)

12 Detection and Classification of Mango Fruit-Based on Feature Extraction Applying Optimized Hybrid LA-FF Algorithms

*Mukesh Kumar Tripathi, M. Neelakantappa,
Parikshit N. Mahalle, Shylesha V. Channapattana,
Ganesh Deshmukh, and Ghongade Prashant*

12.1 INTRODUCTION

India is capable of producing a variety of horticulture products owing to its land territory resilience. The overall horticultural output includes 90% of the fruit and vegetables. The production of fruit and vegetables is 33% [1]. India is the leading producer of mangoes. However, India is currently witnessing negative growth of −0.86%. This is due to estimation loss during post-harvest. Improper assessment, wrong field handling, transportation, mechanical damage during harvesting, and disease cause quality losses in fruits. [2–5]. This is a serious issue that requires proper attention. Mango fruits usually perish quickly, especially if stored in low temperatures of 7°C –13°C. Another cause for fruit losses is the traditional grading approach [6,7]. This is more time-consuming and labor intensive. This loss can be minimized through proper framework and supply chain management with participants and other entities. An optimal harvest time and the selection of quality are beneficial.

Customers power the fruit industry. The public trust in the fruit industry has been diminished. Humans are more health conscious and vigilant. The definitions and aspects of "quality" vary from the fruit class, the target audience, the requirements, and the applicability. The assessment and grading of fruit quality is a progressively complex task. In the past, determining fruit's internal and external attributes was challenging and time-consuming. This is because of traditional evaluation methods and a need for more research. The traditional approach uses tone to detect the quality based on flavor. Yellow spots on the skin surface are another common form to iden-tify the disease. Much of the experiment also focused on external characteristics and fruit deficiencies that could contribute to inaccuracies. Manual assessment relies upon human activity. Research is based on the conventional technique for selecting a high-quality fruit in mango fruits [8]. In post-harvest processing, this approach could be more realistic. Demand for high-quality fruit is growing, and non-destructive automated techniques with a neutrosophic machine-learning framework are also desirable.

In today's era, only a few studies have also been conducted for the quality evalu-ation of mangoes. Therefore, the suggested method is to grade the quality of mango fruits based on external and internal characteristics. The destructive and non-destruc-tive framework for quality grading is the most suitable solution. Our proposed system can be further investigated for mango fruit quality assessment and grading with a machine-learning framework. Fruits are essential parts of the diet [9]. Fruits con-tain vital nutrients, fiber, energy, ascorbic acid, and proteins necessary for a healthy human body [10]. Fruits are consumed in various forms as food or supplementary to food. This mango is widely accepted due to its high nutrient value, taste, and flavor. Mango is consumed in raw form or ripe form. The worldwide market for mango is 55 million tonnes [11].

High-quality mangoes have increased day by day. Therefore, assessment and grading are essential. Some internal features include soluble solids content (SSC), total acid content (TAC), P_H, physiological features, weight, dryness, firmness, mois-ture, and maturity [12–15]. Combining all these physical and biochemical param-eters defines the quality of mangoes. The grading based on external attributes could be more efficient and accurate. Near-infrared spectroscopy (NIRS) has excellent potential for internal quality assessment and grading of mangoes. Further, to expand the mango fruit market, it is necessary to develop an alternative framework to grade the quality of mangoes [16–18]. This paper investigated the grading for mango fruit quality with a neuromorphic approach-based intelligent system. Then, hyperspectral imaging is employed to estimate the internal attributes of the mangoes with machine learning techniques.

12.2   RELATED WORK

Quality assessment is essential for a high-quality product after harvest, as it is pos-sible to assess and grade fruit quality according to external and internal attributes. Appearance is a critical perception in the assessment and grading of fruits. The appearance will influence market value as well as consumer preference. However, internal attributes are more essential to the grading of fruits. A methodology to assess the quality of mango during the ripening process stage [19,20] is studied. The image processing technique is applied for preprocessing and background subtraction. Also, the ranked search method ranks the attributes of images belonging to information gain. Finally, in the training and testing phases, C4.5 algorithms are implemented, and a 96% accuracy rate is achieved overall. This framework is based on external attributes. However, these studies have not considered internal attributes for grading.

Maturity is one of the critical aspects of the quality of fruit. During the ripening process, dry matter (DM) content is utilized to show the maturity level of mango fruit. A robust and practical approach to recognize the spectral image and assess the maturity level of mango fruit [21] is explored. They have implemented classification and regression modeling to detect the mango and evaluate the quantity of DM. The results show that for the Partial least squares regression (PLSR) model, $R^2 = 0.580$ for the CNN model. However, the system is unstable under natural light.

A random forest (RF)-based model to evaluate the internal attributes of mango [22] is investigated. The two categories of mango, namely "Nam Dakoi" and "Irwin" at different temperatures are studied. L* a* b* color space is employed to identify the color of the mango peel. The internal features such as Total soluble solid (TSS) and ascorbic acid are calculated through destructive techniques. A RF based model is utilized to grade the internal quality of mango. However, this model has utilized destructive techniques.

NIRS techniques have gained attention as they are non-destructive, fast, and cost-effective. NIRS-based wavelength selection for calibration model [23] is studied. This wavelength selection method has high consistency. Two different databases are used to predict the effectiveness of the prediction model. The experiment combined the wavelength selection method with standard sample calibration transfer methods. The proposed method is applicable only in a high range of wavelengths of spectra.

A framework for the total acidity prediction of mango [24] by NIRS is presented. This method utilized three regression approaches: Partial least squares regression (PLSR), Support Vector Machine (SVM), and artificial neural networks (ANNs). Spectra acquired in a wavelength range from 1000 to 2500 nm. Further, total acidity is predicted. The calibration and prediction models achieved more than 90% accuracy with the ANN model. However, handling spectra dimension is complex.

A hyperspectral imaging system to estimate moisture content [25] is studied. Visible-near infrared is applied for spectra with a wavelength range between 400 and 1000 nm, and second, NIR is employed with a wavelength range between 880 and 1720 nm. PLS is utilized for calibration and prediction models. Results show that for mango samples in the spectral wavelength range between 400 and 1000 nm, the accuracy rate is 43.70%, whereas an 87.15% accuracy rate has been achieved with NIR-based spectra wavelength range between 880 and 1720 nm.

Detection of firmness attribute framework for mango [25] based on NIRS is explored. In this framework, both destructive and non-destructive methodologies are implemented to evaluate the internal quality of mangoes. Vis-NIR extracts the spectra with a wavelength range of 400–1050 nm. Subsequently, the PLS model builds the relationship between spectra and internal parameters. Further, genetic algorithms are used to estimate the firmness level of mango fruit. Mango fruit image is a combination of different internal biochemicals, and sometimes, it is difficult to estimate the parameters based on a regression model. These challenges can be avoided by utilizing NIRS with machine learning techniques.

The internal attributes of fruit are evaluated by applying destructive and non-destructive methods. Destructive approaches are time-consuming and costly in deciding the quality of the features, such as carotenoid materials, chlorophyll, phenolic acids, and sugars. Research has therefore concentrated on developing and applying non-destructive techniques to quality assessment and evaluation of mature stages in real time [26]. The benefit of non-destructive techniques is that we can track the same fruit for an extended period, refine calculations, and gain a more profound image of the actual properties of the fruit. These non-destructive techniques have been shown as efficient and proposed for evaluating quality grading in the fruit industry [27].

NIRS has the advantage of extracting important internal attributes of fruits. It has successfully tracked the production of disorders such as early detection injury in the mango [28]. One limitation of the NIRS application is that it is costly. However, NIRS is practical and usable for quality grading of fruits based on internal features [29,30]. The critical problem of NIRS is the robustness of the calibration mode [31] for fruit quality evaluation. Furthermore, the robustness of NIRS models [32,33] often depends on fruit cultivation and harvest season. The non-destructive process with infrared spectroscopy is used to estimate the internal attributes of the quality of the mango. The development of an automated assessment and grading system is a complex task. In this framework, extracting the feature of image data is difficult, followed by a training and classification

TABLE 12.1

Application of Machine Vision for Fruit Grading

Application	Preprocessing	Feature Extraction	Data Analysis	Accuracy	References
Sorting of mango	Ostu Threshold Techniques	Color and Size	Fuzzy rule	94.97	[23]
Grading of date fruit	Binary Threshold Techniques	Shape, Size, Intensity	BPNN	80	[24]
Grading of mango	Binary Threshold Techniques	Mass	Statics analysis	97	[25]
Sorting of mango	Gamma curve fitting	Color	Coefficient of determination	98	[26]
Sorting of mango	Convolution Filter	Color, volume	ANN	80	[27]
Grading of Mango	Threshold-Techniques	Size	Caliber model	89.5	[28]
Grading of Mango	HSI	Texture	Neural Network	93.33	[29]
Grading of Mango	Binaries adaptive threshold	Color, shape	PCA	92	[30]
Classification of mango	Ostu Threshold-Techniques	Region	Bayes classifier	90.01	[31]
Sorting of mango	Threshold-Techniques	Mass and volume	Regression model	91.76	[32]

process. With the above point, developing an accurate and efficient quality grading model-based approach is necessary.

After reviewing the data in Table 12.1, we observed that an accurate and efficient quality grading model-based approach is needed based on machine learning techniques. Developing innovation in consolidating the physicochemical and biochemical data with machine vision conveys an effort towards a coordinated framework for the agriculture industry. These goals will take care of the issues, yet they will likewise give legitimate knowledge of internal and external parameters in the machine vision framework.

12.3   PROPOSED MODEL

The diagrammatic progression of the proposed mango reviewing model is given in Figure 12.1. This suggested work is chiefly expected to present a cleverly programmed mango reviewing model with four stages, for example, (1) Preprocessing, (2) Element Extraction, (3) Ideal Component Determination, and (4) Characterization. In the pre-handling stage, the accompanying system occurs, like picture resizing, commotion evacuation, and division. Picture resizing is essential to increment or lessen the all-out number of pixels. Commotion evacuation calculation is the method involved with eliminating or diminishing the clamor from the picture. The picture is divided into numerous sections, otherwise called picture objects.

The subsequent stage is component extraction, separating the shape, variety, and surface highlights. Some of the conditions utilized in this work are minutes, form region, shape edge, form guess, raised structure, looking at convexity, bouncing square shape most miniature encasing circle, fitting an oval, and fitting a line.

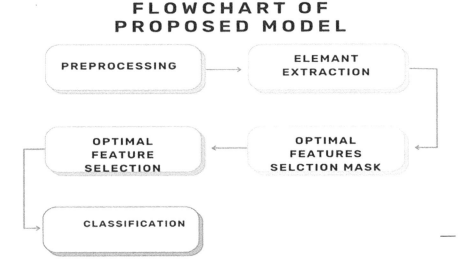

FIGURE 12.1   The diagrammatic flow of proposed mango grading model.

Before removing the condition, the info picture is entirely changed to a dim-scale picture. The variety highlights like histogram, mean, middle, standard deviation, most excellent variety recurrence, and negligible variety recurrence are removed. Before this component extraction, the RGB picture is changed over entirely to an LAB (laboratory) image.

12.4 RESULTS AND DISCUSSION

The executed mango reviewing model is assessed utilizing Python. However, the dataset comprises pictures of covered class names; we have coordinated to obtain 748 images of mangoes of various class marks. Among them, 169 views have a place with solid mangoes, 34 sick mangoes, 192 ready mangoes, 164 unripe mangoes, 97 major mangoes, 41 medium-sized mangoes, and 49 highly enormous mangoes. The investigation is performed for the executed Streamlined Profound CNN model with ideal elements over other ordinary models and regular highlights, and the outcomes are plotted.

Table 12.2 makes sense of the investigation of executed CNN against the regular CNN model with all elements and the applicable highlights, Auto Encoder+ All highlights RNN+ All highlights. The Unripe classification, the proposed model with ideal highlights has achieved advancement for FDR (minimization measure), which is 35.21% and 75.68% better than traditional CNN with all elements and regular CNN with highlights in, Auto Encoder+ All endlessly includes RNN+ All elements separately. The investigation subsequently made sense of the predominant exhibition of the proposed CNN model with ideal elements against customary CNN.

TABLE 12.2

Comparison Performance Measure of All Categories of Mango with Respect to All Method

Test cases	Measures	CNN+ All Features	CNN+ FIS Features	Auto Encoder+ All Features	RNN+ All Features	Optimized CNN+ Optimal Features
HD	FOR	0.085	0.123	0.24	0	0.942
	FPR	0.901	0	0	0.5117	0
	FNR	0.2	1	0.8	0	0.9
	FDR	0.871	0	0	0.587	0
RU	FOR	0.087	0	0.24	0.57	0.0574
	FPR	0.257	1	0	0	0.547
	FNR	0.052	0	0.548	0.39	0.031
	FDR	0.125	0.578	0	0	0.134
BMV	FOR	0	0.1475	0.185	0.139	0.15
	FPR	0.85	0	0	0	0
	FNR	0	1	0.758	0.3433	0.7
	FDR	0.758	0	0	0	0

12.5 CONCLUSION

An automated grading system is designed to speed up the process of classifying the mango images and facilitate quality evaluation in the industrial sector. A new hybrid optimization algorithm, LA-FF, is introduced to overcome the slow convergence. The grading is evaluated based on healthy–diseased (HD), Ripe Unripe (RU), and Big medium very big (BMV) categories, and in all test cases, our proposed methodology achieves higher accuracy than conventional methods. Similarly, the proposed Optimized CNN reaches the least False omission rate (FOR), False positive predictive value (FPR), False Negative predictive value (FNR), and False discovery rate (FDR) values than the traditional method.

REFERENCES

[1] Nandi, C.S., Tudu, B., and Koley, C.: A machine vision technique for grading of harvested mangoes based on maturity and quality, *IEEE Sensors Journal* 2016, 16(16), 6387–6396.
[2] Nambi, V.E., Thangavel, K., Jesudas, D.M.: Scientific classification of ripening period and development of colour grade chart for Indian mangoes (*Mangifera indica* L.) using multivariate cluster analysis, *Scientia Horticulturae* 2015, 193, 90–98.
[3] Tripathi, M.K., and Dhananjay D.M.: A role of computer vision in fruits and vegetables among various horticulture products of agriculture fields: A survey, *Information Processing in Agriculture* 2020, 7(2), 183–203.
[4] Anurekha, D., and Sankaran, R.A.: Efficient classification and grading of MANGOES with GANFIS for improved performance, *Multimedia Tools and Applications* 2019, 79, 1–16.
[5] Wang, F., Zheng, J., Tian, X., Wang, J., and Feng, W.: An automatic sorting system for fresh white button mushrooms based on image processing, *Computers and Electronics in Agriculture* 2018, 151, 416–425.
[6] Tripathi, M.K., and Maktedar, D.D.: Recent machine learning based approaches for disease detection and classification of agricultural products, In: *2016 International Conference on Computing Communication Control and Automation (ICCUBEA)*, IEEE, 2016, pp. 1–6.
[7] Bhatt, A.K., and Pant, D.: Automatic apple grading model development based on back propagation neural network and machine vision, and its performance evaluation, *AI & Society* 2015, 30(1), 45–56.
[8] Chiranjeevi, K., Tripathi, M.K., and Maktedar, D.D.: Block chain technology in agriculture product supply chain, In: *2021 International Conference on Artificial Intelligence and Smart Systems (ICAIS)*, IEEE, 2021, pp. 1325–1329.
[9] Mohammadi, V., Kheiralipour, K., and Varnamkhasti, M.G.: Detecting maturity of persimmon fruit based on image processing technique, *Scientia Horticulturae* 2015, 184, 123–128.
[10] Mohapatra, A., Shanmugasundaram, S., and Malmathanraj, R.: Grading of ripening stages of red banana using dielectric properties changes and image processing approach, *Computers and Electronics in Agriculture* 2017, 143, 100–110.
[11] Tripathi, M.K., and Dhananjay, D.M.: Optimized deep learning model for mango grading: Hybridizing lion plus firefly algorithm, *IET Image Processing* 2021, 15(9), 1940–1956.

[12] Chen, X., Li, Z., Wang, Y., and Liu, J.: Effect of fruit and hand characteristics on thumb-index finger power-grasp stability during manual fruit sorting, *Computers and Electronics in Agriculture* 2019, 157, 479–487.

[13] Tripathi, M.K., and Dhananjay, D.M.: A framework with OTSUS thresholding method for fruits and vegetables image segmentation, *International Journal of Computer Applications* 2018, 975, 8887.

[14] Zhang, Y., Lee, W.S., Li, M., Zheng, L., Ritenour, M.A.: Non-destructive recognition and classification of citrus fruit blemishes based on ant colony optimized spectral information, *Postharvest Biology and Technology* 2018, 143, 119–128.

[15] Tripathi, M.K., and Maktedar, D.D.: Detection of various categories of fruits and vegetables through various descriptors using machine learning techniques, *International Journal of Computational Intelligence Studies* 2021, 10(1), 36–73.

[16] Zhang, Y., Wang, S., Ji, G., Phillips, P.: Fruit classification using computer vision and feedforward neural network, *Journal of Food Engineering* 2014, 143, 167–177.

[17] Taghipour, A., and Frayret, J.-M.: Coordination of operations planning in supply chains: a review, *International Journal of Business Performance and Supply Chain Modelling* 2013, 5(3), 272–307.

[18] Channapattana, S.V., Srinidhi, C., Madhusudhan, A., Notla, S., Arkerimath, R., and Tripathi, M.K.: Energy analysis of DI-CI engine with nickel oxide nanoparticle added *Azadirachta indica* biofuel at different static injection timing based on exergy. *Energy* 2023, 267, 126622.

[19] Alavi, N.: Quality determination of Mozafati dates using Mamdani fuzzy inference system, *Journal of the Saudi Society of Agricultural Sciences* 2013, 12(2), 137–142.

[20] Gandomi, A.H., Yang, X.-S., Talatahari, S and Alavi, A.H.: Firefly algorithm with chaos, *Commun Nonlinear Sci Numer Simulat* 2013, 18, 89–98.

[21] Utai, K., Nagle, M., Hämmerle, S., Spreer, W., Mahayothee, B., Müller, J.: Mass estimation of mango fruits (*Mangifera indica* L., cv. Nam Dokmai) by linking image processing and artificial neural network, *Engineering in Agriculture, Environment and Food* 2019, 12(1), 103–110.

[22] Shivendra, K.C., and Tripathi, M.K.: Detection of fruits image applying decision tree classifier techniques. In: *Computational Intelligence and Data Analytics: Proceedings of ICCIDA 2022*, Springer Nature Singapore, Singapore, 2022, pp. 127–139.

[23] Saad, F.S.A., Ibrahim, M.F., Shakaff, A.Y.M., Zakaria, A., Abdullah, M.Z.: Shape and weight grading of mangoes using visible imaging, *Computers and Electronics in Agriculture* 2015, 115, 51–56.

[24] Schulze, K., Nagle, M., Spreer, W., Mahayothee, B., Müller, J.: Development and assessment of different modeling approaches for size-mass estimation of mango fruits (*Mangifera indica* L., cv. Nam Dokmai), *Computers and Electronics in Agriculture* 2015, 114, 269–276.

[25] Tripathi, M.K., and Maktedar, D.D.: Internal quality assessment of mango fruit: an automated grading system with ensemble classifier, *The Imaging Science Journal* 2022, 70(4), 253–272.

[26] Mizushima, A., Lu, R.: An image segmentation method for apple sorting and grading using support vector machine and Otsu method, *Computers and Electronics in Agriculture* 2013, 94, 29–37.

[27] Gurubelli, Y., Ramanathan, M., Ponnusamy, P.: Fractional fuzzy 2DLDA approach for pomegranate fruit grade classification, *Computers and Electronics in Agriculture*, 2019, 162, 95–105.

[28] Nyalala, I., Okinda, C., Nyalala, L., Makange, N., Chao, Q., Chao, L., Yousaf, K., Chen, K.: Tomato volume and mass estimation using computer vision and machine learning algorithms: Cherry tomato model, *Journal of Food Engineering* 2019, 263, 288–298.

[29] Tripathi, M.K., Maktedar, D., Vasundhara, D.N., Moorthy, C., and Patil, P.: Residual life assessment (RLA) analysis of apple disease based on multimodal deep learning model, *International Journal of Intelligent Systems and Applications in Engineering* 2023, 11(3), 1042–1050.

[30] Luo, F., Zhang, L., Du, B. and Zhang, L.: 2020. Dimensionality reduction with enhanced hybrid-graph discriminant learning for hyperspectral image classification. *IEEE Transactions on Geoscience and Remote Sensing*, 58(8), 5336–5353.

[31] Tripathi, M.K., Neelakantapp, M., Nagesh Kaulage, A., Nabilal, K.V., Patil, S.N., and Bamane, K.D.: Breast cancer image analysis and classification framework by applying machine learning techniques, *International Journal of Intelligent Systems and Applications in Engineering* 2023, 11(3), 930–941.

[32] LeCun, Y., Kavukvuoglu, K., and Farabet, C.: Convolutional networks and applications in vision, In: *Proceedings of 2010 IEEE international symposium on circuits and systems*, 2010, pp. 253–256.

[33] Boothalingam, R.: Optimization using lion algorithm: a biological inspiration from lions social behavior, *Evolutionary Intelligence* 2018, 11(1-2), 31–52.

Section III

Building AI with Quality Data
for Multidisciplinary Domains

13 Guiding Your Way
Solving Student Admission Woes

Snehal Rathi, Shekhar Chaugule,
Manisha Mali, Gitanjali R. Shinde,
and Swati Patil

13.1 INTRODUCTION

Our research paper focuses on addressing the challenges encountered by students during the admission process for engineering colleges. The project, "Guiding Your Way," aims to alleviate the difficulties and provide a streamlined solution for students seeking admission to these institutions. We understand the complexities and obstacles that students face during this critical phase and have developed this project with the intention of making the process smoother and more efficient. The admission process for engineering colleges entails enrolling on a dedicated website where the percentage obtained in the diploma exams plays a crucial role. Once all students have completed the enrollment, a comprehensive list is generated of the percentage and rank of each student among all Maharashtra State Board of Technical Education (MSBTE) candidates. The rank obtained becomes instrumental in determining the cutoff list for various colleges. Our motivation for developing this project stemmed from personal experiences, where we encountered similar challenges during our own admissions. While I had a rank within the range of 700–750, allowing me to easily identify the top ten colleges I could potentially be allotted to, some of my friends faced a more daunting situation with ranks like 15,000 or 18,000. They were unsure which colleges would consider their rank for admission. One significant hurdle they faced was the cumbersome process of scrolling through a lengthy PDF document containing hundreds of college listings. It became impractical and time-consuming to manually identify the colleges suitable for their rank. This inspired us to create a solution that could provide a comprehensive list of colleges with a single click.

Our proposed solution involves the development of an application [1] that allows students to input their preferred department, category, and admission criteria (rank or percentage). By specifying a minimum and maximum rank, the application generates a list of colleges with cutoffs falling within the given rank range. This feature not only saves students from the anxiety and effort of manually searching through extensive PDF documents but also significantly reduces the time required to obtain a suitable list of colleges. Our project aims to alleviate the stress and uncertainty faced by students during the admission process. By providing a user-friendly platform that streamlines

DOI: 10.1201/9781003461500-16

the search for eligible colleges, we hope to empower students with the information they need to make informed decisions about their educational future [2,3].

13.2 LITERATURE REVIEW

In this section, we describe the related concepts used in the specific literature and also adapted in the proposed application.

CollegeDunia.com website reveals valuable insights into its features, services, and impact on the college selection process. CollegeDunia.com is a popular platform that provides comprehensive information about various colleges, courses, admission processes, and other related details.

Additionally, the literature survey emphasizes the need for accurate and reliable college predictions, especially for diploma students seeking admission to engineering colleges. However, it is noted that CollegeDunia.com currently does not provide college prediction services specifically for diploma students [4,5].

Careers360 is a prominent online platform that offers comprehensive information and guidance to students seeking admission to colleges in India. The website provides extensive details about various colleges, courses, fees, admission processes, and counseling services, making it a valuable resource for students and parents alike. One notable feature of Careers360 is its extensive collection of student reviews and ratings. These reviews provide firsthand experiences and opinions shared by current and former students, offering valuable insights into the quality of education, facilities, and overall college environment. Career360.com is a valuable resource for students seeking higher education in India. With its extensive database of colleges and courses, the website provides students with reliable and accurate information to make informed decisions regarding their academic pursuits. However, the college prediction feature for diploma students is currently not available on the website and will be provided on the Guiding Your Way website [6].

Shiksha.com is a renowned education portal in India that provides a comprehensive platform for students to explore and gather information about various colleges and courses across multiple disciplines. The literature survey highlights the significance of Shiksha.com as a valuable resource for students seeking admission to medical, engineering, design, and other fieldshiksha.com incorporates virtual assistants into its system, enhancing the user experience and providing personalized guidance. Virtual assistants [7,8], powered by artificial intelligence, offer real-time assistance to users, addressing their queries and helping them navigate the website effectively. This feature demonstrates Shiksha.com's commitment to leveraging technology to support students in their educational pursuits [9,10].

One such website we analyzed was CollegeDekho.com, a popular platform that offers comprehensive details about colleges, courses, and admission procedures. However, during our analysis, we identified certain features that were not present in CollegeDekho.com but were crucial for Diploma holder students. One prominent feature lacking in CollegeDekho.com was the ability to find colleges based on rank and caste, especially for Diploma holder students. While CollegeDekho.com provides information about colleges and their cutoffs, it does not cater to the specific needs of Diploma students who have unique criteria for admission. Diploma holders often face challenges in finding suitable colleges based on their rank and caste category, as their admission process differs from that of other students.

To address this gap, our project, Guiding Your Way, focuses on incorporating this essential feature. We have developed an application that allows Diploma holder students to easily search for colleges based on their rank range and caste category. This feature streamlines the college selection process for Diploma students and provides them with relevant and personalized options [11].

One key feature that is missing in IndiaCollegesHub.com is the ability to find colleges based on rank and caste, especially for Diploma holder students. While the website offers general information about colleges, it does not cater to the unique requirements of Diploma students when it comes to college selection. Diploma holders face challenges in finding suitable colleges based on their rank range and caste category, which is different from the admission process for other students. Through our literature survey, we have identified the limitation of IndiaCollegesHub.com in meeting the specific needs of Diploma holder students. Our project aims to bridge this gap and provide a comprehensive solution that allows Diploma students to find suitable colleges based on their rank and caste category. By incorporating this feature, Guiding Your Way offers a unique tool to facilitate the admission process for Diploma holder students [12,13].

IndCareer.com primarily focuses on providing information about the hospitality of colleges, scholarships, and event details, along with general education system information [14]. However, our analysis revealed a significant gap in terms of a specific feature that is vital for Diploma holder students. One crucial feature that is absent in IndCareer.com is the ability to find colleges based on rank and castes specifically for Diploma holder students. While the website offers valuable information about the hospitality sector and scholarships, it does not cater to the unique needs of Diploma students when it comes to college selection. Diploma holders face challenges in finding suitable colleges based on their rank range and caste category, which is distinct from other students' admission criteria [15].

13.3 TECHNOLOGY USED

The "Guiding Your Way" project utilized a range of technologies to develop an efficient and user-friendly web-based application for assisting students in the admission process for engineering colleges. Python served as the primary programming language due to its versatility and extensive libraries. Flask, a lightweight web framework, was employed to handle the backend development, including routing and data processing. To collect data from the result website, BeautifulSoup, a web scraping library, was used in conjunction with Selenium, an automation tool for web browsers. This allowed for the extraction of relevant information from the website and its subsequent conversion into an Excel spreadsheet format using the openpyxl library. In this following technologies are used as follows:

Python scripts were then developed to further convert the data into JSON format, enabling easier manipulation and integration with the application. HTML, CSS, and JavaScript were used for the front-end development, ensuring a visually appealing and interactive user interface. The Git version control system was utilized to manage the source code, facilitating collaboration and efficient tracking of code changes. These technologies collectively enabled the development of a robust and efficient web-based application that streamlined the admission process for engineering colleges.

- **Python**: Python programming language was used as the primary language for the development of the "Guiding Your Way" project. Python's versatility, extensive libraries, and ease of use made it suitable for web scraping,
- **Flask**: Flask is a lightweight and flexible web framework in Python. It is used to handle routing, request handling, and data processing.
- **openpyxl**: openpyxl is a Python library specifically designed for reading and writing Excel files.
- **HTML**: Hypertext Markup Language (HTML) is the standard markup language for creating web pages. It was used in conjunction with Flask to develop the frontend interface.
- **JavaScript**: JavaScript is a widely used programming language that allows for interactive and dynamic elements on web pages. It was utilized to add interactivity and functionality to the "Guiding Your Way" application, enabling features such as form validation and real-time updates.
- **JSON**: JavaScript Object Notation (JSON) is a lightweight data interchange format. After converting the collected data from the website into Excel format, a Python script was developed to further convert it into JSON format. JSON allowed for easier data manipulation and integration with the application.

13.4   METHODOLOGY

The college selection and admission process can be overwhelming for students due to the vast amount of information available and the complexity of decision-making. To address these challenges, this research paper presents a proposed system called "Guiding Your Way." This innovative web-based application aims to revolutionize the college selection and admission process by providing students with accurate information, personalized recommendations, and efficient tools for decision-making [8].

Comprehensive College Comparison: "Guiding Your Way" provides a comprehensive college comparison feature that allows students to evaluate multiple colleges based on various parameters such as infrastructure, faculty, placement records, and academic programs. This enables students to make well-informed decisions by considering their specific preferences and priorities.

- **Data Collection**: The data required for the project was collected from the result website, which provides information about students' ranks and the cutoff lists of various engineering colleges. The data collection process involved scraping the website to extract the necessary information
- **Data Conversion**: The collected data was initially in a website format. To analyze and manipulate the data effectively, it was converted into an Excel spreadsheet format. Python programming language was utilized to develop a web scraping script using libraries such as BeautifulSoup and Selenium to extract the data from the website and store it in the Excel file (Figure 13.1).

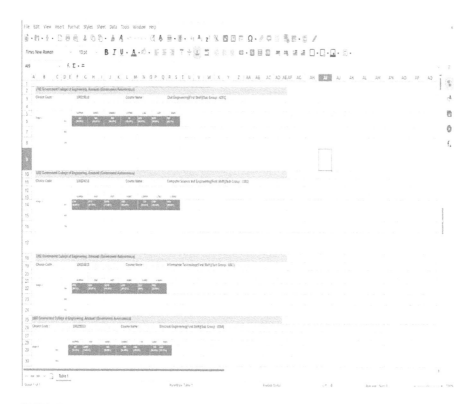

FIGURE 13.1   Converted dataset.

- **Data Transformation**: Once the data was in the Excel format, a Python script using the openpyxl library was developed to convert the Excel data into JSON format. This step was crucial as it allowed for easier data manipulation and integration with the "Guiding Your Way" application (Figure 13.2).

In the above system, work begins with data collection from the internet in the form of PDF files. These files contain valuable information about colleges, including rankings, courses, and other relevant details. To facilitate easy data manipulation, a PDF-to-Excel converter is employed to convert the PDF files into an Excel format. Once in Excel format, the system creates a dataset by organizing the data into columns and rows. This dataset includes crucial information such as college names, rankings, branches, and percentages. To enable further processing, an Excel to JSON transformation is performed using a Python automation script. This script parses the Excel file and converts the data into a JSON file, which offers a structured representation suitable for filtering and querying.

When a user interacts with the system, they input their desired criteria, such as rank, branch, and percentage. The system then applies filtering mechanisms to the JSON data, narrowing down the options to colleges that meet the user's specified requirements.

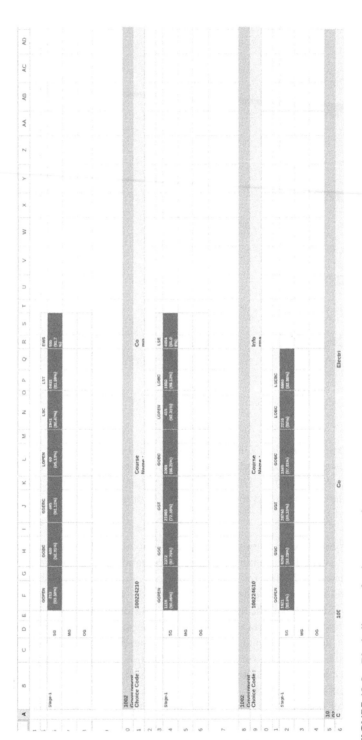

FIGURE 13.2　Block diagram for the proposed system.

After the system displays the college's list.

- **Application Development**: The application development process involves using a combination of programming languages and frameworks. Python, Flask, and openpyxl were used to handle the backend functionalities of the application. HTML, CSS, and JavaScript were employed for the front-end development to create an interactive and user-friendly interface.
- **Testing and Evaluation**: To ensure the reliability and accuracy of the "Guiding Your Way" application, extensive testing was conducted. This included unit testing of individual components and integration testing to verify the interaction between different modules. User testing was also performed to gather feedback and evaluate the usability of the application.
- **Ethical Considerations**: Throughout the project, ethical considerations were taken into account, particularly regarding data privacy and security. Measures were implemented to safeguard any personal or sensitive information collected during the data scraping process.
- **Evaluation of Results**: The results were evaluated by comparing the generated JSON data with the original data from the website to ensure accuracy and integrity. Additionally, the performance of the application was assessed based on factors such as response time, user satisfaction, and system efficiency.

13.5   CHALLENGES IN THE PRESENT SYSTEM

The present system of education websites, such as Shiksha, CollegeDunia, and Careers360, play a vital role in assisting students with information regarding colleges, courses, and admission processes. However, despite their usefulness, these platforms face several challenges that hinder their effectiveness. This research paper aims to identify and address these challenges by proposing a novel system called "Guiding Your Way."

Limited Information: The existing education websites often provide limited information, making it difficult for students to make informed decisions regarding their college choices. "Guiding Your Way" aims to overcome this challenge by offering comprehensive and up-to-date information about colleges, including cutoff ranks, courses offered, and eligibility criteria.

Inadequate Data Integration: The existing systems struggle with integrating data from various sources, leading to inconsistencies and outdated information. The proposed system will address this challenge by employing robust data integration techniques to ensure accurate and real-time data from reliable sources.

Inefficient College Comparison: The current websites often lack effective tools for comparing different colleges based on various parameters such as infrastructure, faculty, and placement records. The proposed system will incorporate a comprehensive college comparison feature, enabling students to make informed decisions.

Inadequate Support for Diploma Students: Many existing platforms do not cater specifically to diploma students seeking admission to engineering colleges. "Guiding Your Way" will address this gap by providing specialized support and guidance for diploma students, considering their unique requirements.

Lack of Career Guidance: The current education websites often overlook the crucial aspect of career guidance. The proposed system will integrate career guidance resources, providing students with valuable insights into various career options associated with different courses and colleges.

13.6   RESULTS AND ANALYSIS

We present the results obtained from the evaluation of the Guiding Way system and analyze its performance and effectiveness in addressing the challenges of the admission process for engineering colleges. The analysis focuses on various aspects, including data accuracy, system efficiency, and user satisfaction (Figure 13.3).

Study Content for the Syllabus of the Diploma Course:

- The Guiding Way project successfully retrieved study content for the syllabus of the Diploma course from reliable sources.
  Finding Best Colleges based on Percentage Range:
- The Guiding Way system effectively processed the percentage range provided by students and generated a list of colleges matching the criteria.
- The algorithm compared the student's percentage with the cutoff lists of various colleges and identified the ones where admission was possible (Figure 13.4).

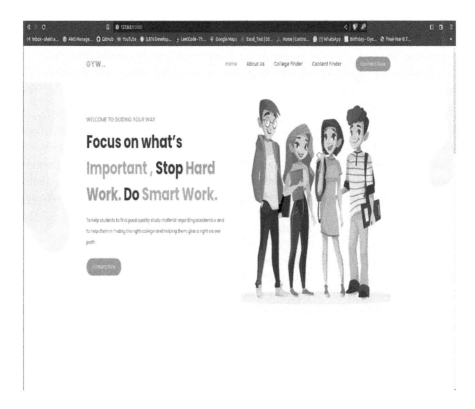

FIGURE 13.3   Home page.

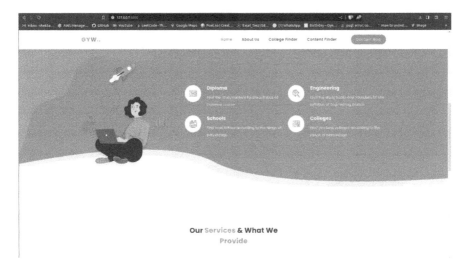

FIGURE 13.4   About us page.

We aimed to address the challenges faced by students during the admission process for engineering colleges. We developed this project with the intention of solving these problems and ensuring that no student encounters the same difficulties we experienced. The admission process for engineering colleges involves enrolling on a website and considering the aggregate percentage obtained in the final year exams of the Diploma course. Once all students have enrolled, a comprehensive list is generated, which includes the percentage and rank of each student among all MSBTE students.

We observed that the use of rank is crucial in this process. By referring to the previous year's cutoff list, students can compare their rank and estimate the colleges they may be allotted. However, we encountered a problem where students with higher ranks, such as 15,000 or 18,000, struggled to identify the colleges they were eligible for due to the large number of options listed in a PDF document.

To address this issue, we developed an application called Guiding Your Way. This application allows students to select a particular department and their admission category and choose between rank and percentage as the criteria. By entering a minimum rank of 7000 and a maximum rank of 8000, for example, the application generates a list of colleges with a cutoff between the specified rank range. This functionality saves students time and effort by providing a comprehensive list with just a single click (Figures 13.5–13.7).

13.7   ADVANTAGE OF THE PROPOSED SYSTEM OVER THE EXISTING SYSTEM

Firstly, Guiding Way provides a more streamlined and efficient process for students seeking admission to engineering colleges. By automating the process of converting data from the result website into a JSON file, Guiding Way eliminates the need for

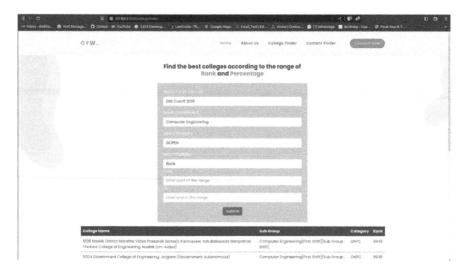

FIGURE 13.5   Cutoff find page.

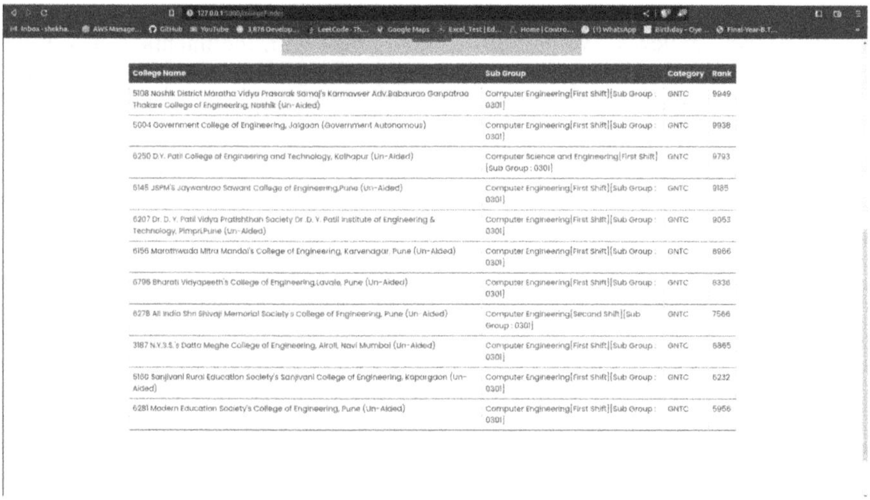

FIGURE 13.6   Result page.

students to manually sift through lengthy PDF documents. This not only saves time but also reduces the chances of errors. Guiding Way offers personalized guidance to students based on their rank and preferences. The system suggests a list of colleges that the student is eligible for, based on their rank and desired course. This helps students make informed decisions and increases their chances of getting admitted to their preferred college. Guiding Way provides a user-friendly interface that is easy to navigate, even for those with limited technical knowledge. The system is designed to be intuitive and user-centric, with clear instructions and helpful tips. Guiding Way

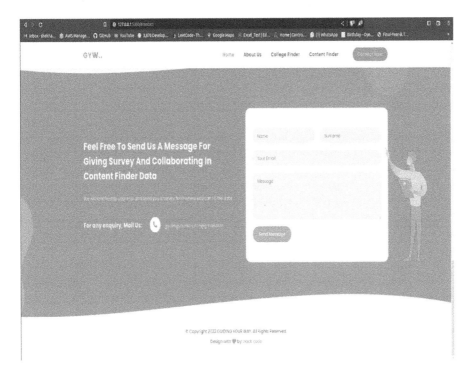

FIGURE 13.7   Contact us page.

is a comprehensive solution that addresses all the major challenges faced by students during the admission process. From providing information on colleges to helping students make choices based on their preferences, the system offers end-to-end guidance and support.

13.8   HARDWARE REQUIREMENTS

   a. Computer: 256 GB HDD 4 GB RAM
   b. Intel i3 processor

13.9   SOFTWARE REQUIREMENTS

   a. Browser (Chrome, Mozilla, edge)
   b. Vs.code

13.10   CONCLUSION AND FUTURE WORKS

In conclusion, the proposed system "Guiding Way" has successfully addressed the challenges faced by students during the admission process for engineering colleges. By leveraging web scraping techniques and data processing using Python, we have developed a user-friendly web application that simplifies the college selection process.

We have demonstrated the effectiveness of our system in providing accurate and comprehensive information about college cutoff ranks and percentages. Our system has proven to be a valuable tool for students, eliminating the need to manually search through lengthy PDF documents and providing a streamlined interface to access relevant information. The inclusion of features such as filtering by rank or percentage has further enhanced the usability of the application.

Overall, the "Guiding Way" system has demonstrated its potential to alleviate the challenges faced by students during the admission process. Its accurate and efficient college selection mechanism, coupled with its user-friendly interface, makes it a valuable resource for students seeking admission to engineering colleges. Future work could involve expanding the system's database to include more colleges and integrating real-time updates for cutoff ranks and percentages to ensure up-to-date information for users.

13.11   LIMITATION

However, we acknowledge several limitations in our current research. First, while our project offers a useful application for students seeking admission to engineering colleges, it does not introduce any novel methodologies. The lack of novel techniques may limit the originality and potential impact of the work. Future research should explore opportunities to incorporate innovative methodologies to further enhance the project's effectiveness and relevance. Secondly, "Guiding Your Way" currently relies on data provided by the MSBTE enrollment website. Any discrepancies or inaccuracies in the data from the source may affect the application's output. Therefore, continuous efforts to validate and update the data sources are essential to ensure the reliability of our application.

REFERENCES

[1] KularbPhettong, K. and Limphoemsuk, N. 2017. The effective of learning by augmented reality on Android platform. In: *E-Learning, E-Education, and Online Training*, Springer, Cham, pp. 111–118.
[2] Sahin, D. and Yilmaz, R.M. 2020. The effect of Augmented Reality Technology on middle school students' achievements and attitudes towards science education. *Computers & Education* 144, 103710.
[3] Friendsickness in the Transition to College: Precollege Predictors and College Adjustment Correlates. https://www.proquest.com/openview/8f3984886702e757f2d29 bcaa7276a9e/1?pq-origsite=gscholar&cbl=18750
[4] This System Website Provide the Details about the College Site and Counseling System. https://collegedunia.com/ and https://www.careers360.com/]
[5] Von Ah D, Ebert S, Ngamvitroj A, Park N, Kang DH. 2005. Predictors of health behaviours in college students. *Journal of Advanced Nursing* 48(5),463-474. doi: 10.1111/ j.1365-2648.2004.03229.x. PMID: 15533084.
[6] Osadchyi, V.V., Valko, N.V. and Kuzmich, L.V., 2021, March. Using augmented reality technologies for STEM education organizations. *Journal of Physics: Conference Series* 1840(1), 012027.

[7] Fan, M., Antle, A.N. and Warren, J.L., 2020. Augmented reality for early language learning: A systematic review of augmented reality application design, instructional strategies, and evaluation outcomes. *Journal of Educational Computing Research* 58(6), 1059–1100.

[8] Ghulamani, S. and Zareen, S., 2018, March. Educating students in remote areas using augmented reality. In: *2018 International Conference on Computing, Mathematics and Engineering Technologies (iCoMET)*, IEEE, pp. 1–6.

[9] Rathi, S., Deshpande, Y., Nagaral, S., Narkhede, A., Sajwani, R. and Takalikar, V. 2021. Analysis of user's learning styles and academic emotions through web usage mining. In: *2021 International Conference on Emerging Smart Computing and Informatics (ESCI)*, Pune, India, pp. 159–164. doi:10.1109/ESCI50559.2021.9397037.

[10] Adrianto, D., Hidajat, M. and Yesmaya, V., 2016, December. Augmented reality using Vuforia for marketing residence. In: *2016 1st International Conference on Game, Game Art, and Gamification (ICGGAG)*, IEEE, pp. 1–5.

[11] Radosavljevic, S., Radosavljevic, V. and Grgurovic, B. 2020. The potential of implementing augmented reality into vocational higher education through mobile learning. *Interactive Learning Environments* 28(4), 404–418.

[12] Aneena Aley Abraham (2023). Ranking System of Indian Universities and Colleges. Retrieved February 12, 2024, from https://www.shiksha.com/science/ranking/top-universities-colleges-in-india/121-2-0-0-0

[13] Gomes, C., Chanchal, S., Desai, T. and Jadhav, D., 2020. Class student management system using facial recognition. *ITM Web of Conferences* 32, 02001.

[14] Raju, K.C., Yugandhar, K., Bharathi, D.V.N. and Vegesna, N., 2018, November. Third based modern education system using augmented reality. In: *2018 IEEE 6th International Conference on MOOCs, Innovation and Technology in Education (MITE)*, IEEE, pp. 37–42.

[15] Živčić-Bećirević, I., Smojver-Ažić, S., & Dorčić, T. M. 2017. Predictors of university students' academic achievement: A prospective study. Društvena Istraživanja, 26(4), 457–476

14 Melodic Pattern Recognition for Ornamentation Features in Music Computing

Makarand Ramesh Velankar,
Sneha Kiran Thombre, and
Harshad Suryakant Wadkar

14.1 INTRODUCTION

Technology has made inroads in creative art domains such as music, drawing, etc. Automatic pattern recognition in music is a challenging problem due to the complex nature of music. Modeling and recognition of prosodic components such as ornamentation in music makes it more challenging. Examples of prosodic features used in speech are tone, stressed word, or voice modulation. They are experienced in audio, but cannot be represented in the corresponding text matter. Traditionally, different pattern recognition (PR) paradigms for music pattern analysis include statistical and structural approaches for a specific predefined task. A statistical approach based on probabilistic models with efficient use of machine learning algorithms for different applications in music information retrieval (MIR) is common among researchers. The structural or symbolic approach based on formal grammar helps model melodic or rhythmic structures in the music. The use of neural networks for PR now extends to deep neural networks for efficient prediction. The boundaries between different paradigms are fuzzy and fading. Combined approaches are also gaining popularity as they share the same goals.

The statistical approach attempts to extract numerical values from the data as a source for classification. This technique has gained more acceptance and popularity in the research community due to different machine learning and classification algorithms applied to the numerical data extracted from the digital objects under study. Self-repetitive pattern identification is a topic of interest from music summary or content-based MIR. A comparative study of Chroma features, Constant Q transforms features, and MFCC features was performed. Results were compared with ground truth obtained from human expert annotation for identifying repetitive patterns [1]. The ground truth used in most of the systems is input from human experts.

It is not easy to get the ground truth for large datasets with duration in hours for audio files. The challenge is to generate and evaluate ground truth for massive

DOI: 10.1201/9781003461500-17

musical data, which can evaluate different machine learning algorithms. The vector space model was used for melodic pattern extraction of the raga in Indian art music, and the results were assessed for diverse classification strategies [2]. The statistical PR approach using vector representation is suitable for machine learning algorithms. They typically require input data in feature values. Modeling appropriate features of the music, which we interpret as structures, is the challenge in music computing. The structural approach thus becomes necessary for melodic or rhythmic patterns, perceived on a timeline as a sequence.

Structural or syntactic PR is generally applied for melodic or rhythmic PR. In melodic patterns, the note sequence pattern is usually represented as an ordered list of notes with string-type data structure. A monophonic musical pattern is described by using notes as the fundamental unit for the representation. The hierarchical tree structure can be used to represent the pattern at different granularity levels. The directed graph structure is another representation of the notes' transition in melody. Induction and matching of sequential melodic patterns pose several computational challenges but are helpful for musically interesting retrieval tasks [3]. Time series symbolic pattern representation of music is a challenge, as the data are multidimensional and real valued, with patterns rarely repeating precisely. Data margins and fuzziness are used considering the perception of patterns. Pattern segmentation for processing can be done using perceptually grouped melodic phrases. Pitch transcription, rhythmic meter, or tempo information may not be the only helpful information for structural pattern analysis.

The use of timbre information with string-matching techniques can be more beneficial for polyphonic music [4]. The music structural pattern representation plays a significant role in the automatic conversion from a sheet printed music for the performance (interpretation) or vice versa (transcription). Evaluation of accuracies related to optical music recognition systems used for structural musical interpretation is a challenge [5]. A graphical structure can represent music scores. The terminal nodes directly describe the content of the music, the internal nodes represent its incremental summary, and the arc represents its relationship.

The similarity between two melodies can be calculated by analyzing the structure of the graph and finding the shortest path between corresponding nodes in the graph [6]. Due to the effective modeling of sequential patterns for the time-variant music and human perception of musical patterns, a structural approach is suitable for melodic patterns. Therefore, more robust music knowledge representation systems are possible with this paradigm. Human brains process musical patterns for different interpretations, and a neural network-based approach attempts to model the same.

The artificial neural network (NN) is a computing model composed of interconnections of artificial neuron units to simulate the human brain. Different problems in music have been successfully addressed with the help of different variants of NN. For example, the use of dynamic programming and recurrent NN with hidden states or memory units for chord recognition is found better than the hidden Markov model [7]. Convolutional Neural Network (CNN) trained on a mel-scaled spectrogram produced promising results for automatic boundary detection for musical structures [8]. Research indicates that NN can be trained to identify statistical inconsistencies across audio features to predict valence/arousal values for emotion classification [9].

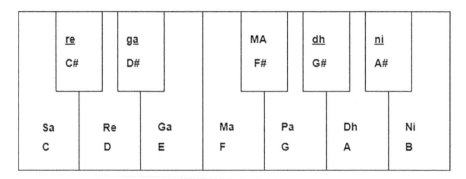

FIGURE 14.1   Indian and Western music notation mapping.

Deep neural network models for solving PR problems are becoming increasingly popular. They can primarily learn complex non-linear input and output relationships, have almost no dependence on domain-specific knowledge, and the availability of practical models. For the effective implementation of this strategy, a vast training dataset is required. Datasets provide the foundation for machine learning Algorithms.

Indian music is represented using either Western or Indian notations. For example, piano or harmonium as wind instruments with reeds representing the notes shows similarity and mapping of both notations. The mapping is as shown in Figure 14.1. The melodic patterns are described using a sequence of notes such as C D E in Western form with equivalent Indian notations as Sa Re Ga. The notation representation of songs is helpful for composers or performers to play songs during recording or live shows. Traditionally, Indian classical music (ICM) uses various music ornamentation forms to convey specific rasa or mood during raga performance. Music ornamentation is integrated into melodic and rhythmic patterns to add esthetic appeal during the performance. Various ornamentation forms include kan swar, meend, khatka, murkhi, Andolan, and gamaka. This ornamentation is used in Indian film songs as a natural extension due to the influence of ICM. As per the inputs from the performers [10], kan swar or grace note (tiny duration note) is used prominently in Indian music for conveying emotional appeal. kan swar is sung or played before or after the main note during the melody. A grace note is a similar notion used in Western music ornamentation.

During the computational study of ornaments in Hindustani music [11], kan swar or grace note was observed as a subtle change (delicate and difficult to analyze). Other ornaments such as meend (glide from one note to another or glissando) or krintan (kan swar followed by a meend) represent a variety of music ornaments used in Indian music. The rate of change in frequency and amplitude constitutes ornamentation's fundamental nature of the computational aspects.

The chapter is organized in the following manner. A detailed survey related to data-driven melodic PR and specific to music ornamentation feature is covered in Section 2. Research gaps are presented in Section 3. Methodology along with an exploratory learning algorithm used is explained in Section 4. Section 5 covers results and discussions with future directions.

14.2　RELATED WORK

14.2.1　DATA-DRIVEN MELODIC PR

Data-driven PR approaches are successfully applied in various domains. The detailed survey has shown great promise for future developments of data-driven models [12]. Data-driven modeling using computational intelligence is likely to complement or replace knowledge-driven models [13]. Deep learning data-driven models are successfully implemented in domains such as healthcare [14], e-commerce [15], bio-medical research for DNA sequence [16], and Cyber security [17]. In music computing, the data-driven approach is explored for various applications. Handwritten music notation recognition [18], melodic PR [19], genre classification [20], music recommendation [21], automatic transcription [22], and music generation [23] are some of the applications explored by researchers using data-driven approach. For melodic PR, attempts have been made for tasks such as automatic chord recognition [24], F–0 or tonic estimation [25], and vocal melody extraction [26]. For ICM, melody extraction using a data-driven approach is attempted for raga motif identification [27], raga recognition [28], emotion classification [29], and genre classification [30]. For Indian music ornamentation features, the challenges of using the data-driven model are presented by researchers [31].

14.2.2　ROLE OF MUSIC ORNAMENTATION

Traditionally, Hindustani classical music uses various music ornamentation forms to convey specific rasa or mood during raga performance. Various ornamentation forms include kan swar, meend, khatka, murkhi, Andolan, and gamaka [32]. These ornamentations are used in Indian film songs as a natural reflection because of the classical music background of various composers and singers. As per the inputs from the performers, kan swar (a tiny duration note) is used prominently in Indian music for conveying emotional appeal.

Kan swar is sung or played before or after the main note during the melody. During the Computational Study of Ornaments in Hindustani Music [11], it was observed that, in kan swar presentation, the change is subtle (delicate and difficult to analyze). Kan swar followed by a glide/meend from one note to another (glissando) termed Krintan. Classification of melodic sequences into 17 different clusters depending on various ornamentation features was proposed. It was also proposed that the rate of change in frequency and amplitude domains together constitutes the fundamental nature of ornamentation. A grace note in Western music is a similar notion as kan swar in Indian music. Grace note was considered an Atemporal event in Western music with the addition of dummy silence if required for alignment during real-time music to score alignment [33]. During the study of the timing of 11 grace notes in 45 piano performances, the grace notes with a longer mean duration tended to deviate significantly from proportional duration, whilst shorter grace notes were roughly invariant over tempo [34]. Features were numerically extracted from score data in MusicXML and performance data in MIDI [35]. The number of notes preceding and following it is presented as a time signature 4D vector as a feature for the grace note. The role of ornamentation features, especially grace notes or kan swar, was prominent in conveying emotions [10]. Further, such feature dimensions may be associated with different emotion classes. Therefore, successfully capturing the expressive features of ornamentation and its association with emotion can improve the accuracy of Music Emotion recognition classification. Performers use ornamentation to provide a different experience to listeners during the performances.

14.2.3 MUSIC ORNAMENTATION

Musical ornamentation is the way the performers or music arrangers add value to the original musical composition to convey meaning [11]. Music ornamentation plays a significant role in conveying the intended meaning and experience to the listener. Different genres of music forms have varied ornamentation specific to the genre with the cultural impact. Indian music consists of various musical ornaments such as grace notes, vibrato, glides, and variations [32]. Many ornamentations use subtle acoustic parameters such as timbre, intensity, and pitch. They are challenging to capture, considering the nature of change and relativeness. In the case of Western music, a majority of the ornaments are well-documented with sheet music notations [33]. Western music performance guided by sheet music has a fixed format and relatively less scope for improvisations. Jazz music has a similarity with Indian music considering the improvisation aspect in both. In speech communication, pauses, stress on different words, voice modulation, and repetition of specific words or phrases convey content effectively. Similarly, in musical performance, these clues are used along with musical embodiment, referred to as music prosody.

Music prosody is the non-verbal clues used to convey musical meaning in the case of vocal performances. In the instrumental version, the clues used are specific to the instrument by utilizing the features and capabilities associated with the instrument. Every performer attempts to convey the message in their style and interpretation. One can notice that the performance by different artists for the same musical piece or same artist at different times does have variations, and modeling these aspects is a challenging task considering its subtle nature.

Indian music has various forms such as classical, regional, and traditional folk, in popular. The ornamentation and prosodic elements used to differ with these forms. Indian music is traditionally an orally transmitted teaching-learning system, and Pandit Bhatkhande and Pandit Paluskar introduced formal notations during the beginning of the nineteenth century. It was probably the first sincere attempt of music documentation in the form of notations which many musicians and composers then adopted. These notations attempt to capture some of the ornamentation, such as glides and vibrato which guides the performer. Thus, the performers have more liberty within the musical framework of Indian music.

14.3 GAP ANALYSIS

As per the discussions with renowned performers [10], the grace note (kan svar) is considered one of the critical ornamentations used across different music traditions to convey emotions.

The gaps identified from the survey and discussions with researchers are as follows:

1. As per the literature survey related to Indian music, it was observed that very little work has been done so far to model and identify the music ornamental features.
2. The annotated dataset for ornamental features is not readily available.

The need was felt to apply PR algorithms. For data-driven approaches such as deep learning, the annotated dataset required is quite large. Thus, the initial approach used was exploratory learning with a small annotated dataset to identify the challenges likely to be faced which need to be addressed for data-driven methods.

14.4 METHODOLOGY

In our first attempt to explore the music embodiment of ornaments as prosodic features, we have developed an algorithm to capture this ornamentation feature using an exploratory learning approach. The exploratory learning algorithm is developed to identify "grace note", a source for inducing emotion as per performers. The experimentation was carried out with the help of annotations provided by domain experts. Due to no fixed rules and boundaries documented for ornamentation with flexibility for interpretations, the annotations provided by experts for the same musical piece had some variations. A grace note is an ornamentation, defined as a short-duration note presented before or after a steady note. The duration of a grace note and steady note is not fixed and is relative as per the perception or interpretations of domain experts. Manual annotations are a time-consuming process and have limitations due to time availability by domain experts.

The annotated audio sample with waveform and annotated notes marked before the main note is as shown in Figure 14.2. The audio sample has eight grace notes sung before the main notes. The grace notes are of very small duration visible in

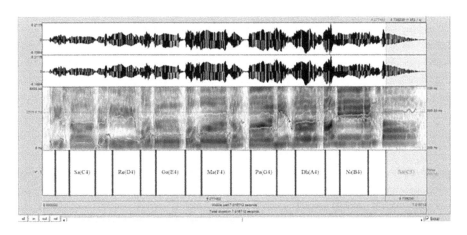

FIGURE 14.2   Annotated grace notes for audio sample.

the figure in blue line spikes. The main notes are represented in Indian, and their counterpart Western note format is shown in brackets as SA (C4), Re (D4), respectively. That is, a note in Indian notation SA is shown in Western notation as C4 in the bracket. It can be noticed from the vertical bars in blue that the main note durations are relatively long compared to a small duration grace note appearing before them.

Grace notes (in bracket) annotated before the main notes in the Sargam as per Indian notations are

(Re) Sa, (Ga)Re, (Ma)Ga, (Pa)Ma, (Dh)Pa, (Ni)Dh, (Sa') Ni, (Re') Sa'

The equivalent representation using western notations is

(D4) C4, (E4) D4, (F4) E4, (G4) F4, (A4) G4, (A#4) A4, (C5) B4, (D5) C5.

The following example demonstrates the grace notes identified using the developed algorithm. Results are obtained with possible grace notes identified with the note and duration. "gn" stands for the grace note identified, mentioned before the grace note identified. Results show notes followed by relative durations and grace notes as small relative durations, such as 1, 2, or 3. Whereas, the main notes have longer relative durations, such as 13, 15, and 16.

['gn', ' D4', 2, 'C4', 13, 'gn', 'E4', 2, 'D4', 13, 'gn', 'F4', 3, 'E4', 16, 'gn', 'G4', 2, 'F4', 15, 'gn', 'A4', 2, 'G4', 15, 'gn', 'A#4', 2, 'A4', 16, 'gn', 'C5', 1, 'B4', 15, 'gn', 'D5', 2, 'C5', 16]

The result shows that eight grace notes are correctly identified out of a total of eight grace notes annotated for the sample shown. The algorithm was further tested for other samples. The results obtained are used to fine-tune the algorithm to correctly identify grace notes for different test samples. The results from 20 annotated short samples were obtained using the developed algorithm and were discussed with expert annotators for further improvements in the algorithm.

Algorithm for Grace note identification

```
// Initialization
I = 1//sample number initialized to the first sample
// Time instance  of the sample I − T[I]
// Intensity of the sample I   − A[I]
// Pitch of the sample I − P[I]
// Identification maximum Intensity and minimum intensity
MaxI = A[0]// Maximum Intensity audio sample initialization
i = 1
while(End of samples i)// begin of loop 1
{
        If(MaxI < A[i])
        MaxI = A[i]
} // end of loop 1
MinI = MaxI− 30// Defines Audible Intensity range
// Intensity below MinI considered as silence
i = 0
// Convert pitch info to notes N[ ] a ray
while(End of samples n)// begin of loop 2
{
        Read P[i]
```

```
        Identify the Western note(WN) from the pitch range//
Pitch range covers All audible frequencies
        Write N[WN] // Notes in Western notation format which
covers an entire audible range
} // end of loop 2
i = 0\\ NSGN[] with grace notes identified
while(end of NewC)
{
        Read 4 samples as NS[i], NS[i +1], NS[i +2] and NS[i +3]
        FN = NS[i]\\ first note
        FD = NS[i +1]\\ first note relative duration
        SN = NS[i +2]\\ second note
        SD = NS[i +3]\\ second note relative duration
        if(FD < SD)
        {
           PD = 0.2 * SD
        }
        if (FD < PD and FD <3)\\ Grace note identification
        {
           Add NS[i], NS[i +1], NS[i +2] and NS[i +3] to NSGN[]
           Append NSGN[] GNP
           i = i +4\\ Previous note as grace notes
        }
           else IF(FD > SD and SD <3)
        {
ND = 0.2 * FD
        }
        if(SD < ND)\\ Grace note
        {
           Add NS[i], NS[i +1], NS[i +2] and NS[i +3] to NSGN[]
           Append NSGN[] gn
           i = i +4\\ Next note as grace note
        }
        else
        {
           i = i +2
        }
}\\
NSGN[] contains grace note info
```

The samples used for training and testing the algorithm were containing grace notes as the only ornamentation feature. Further, it was advised to test the algorithm for audio samples with the presence of other ornamentation patterns such as glides. It was observed that the algorithm provided the wrong output on a few occasions due to overlap. Overlap of grace notes and confusion with glides was one of the significant issues observed, as shown in Figure 14.3. Grace notes here are predicted as (A#4) A4 and (C4) B4, which are observed as false positives compared with human annotations. Although the grace note is visible, it is referred to as glide by domain experts. Thus, the algorithm misjudged the glide with grace note as it was not modeled for other ornamentation features such as glide.

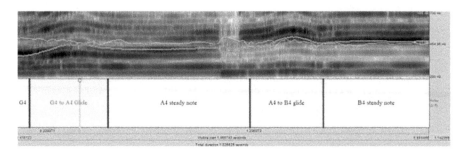

FIGURE 14.3   Grace notes confusion with glide.

The results showed reasonably good accuracy for samples; however, the algorithm misinterpreted some instances. It is due to the overlap of ornamentation patterns such as glides and grace notes.

14.5   RESULT AND DISCUSSION

Following were the critical observations from the result analysis and discussion with the experts.

- Challenges observed to tackle false-positive or true-negative identification cases.
- The role of intensity and timbral characteristics need to be studied.
- Pitch range considerations need to be revisited along with 12-pitch octave representation using the equal-tempered scale.
- Need to study other ornaments such as glide, jerk, murki, Andolan vs. grace note.
- Identification of grace notes in isolation without considering other ornamentation leads to errors as glides are also identified as grace notes in some cases.
- Data-driven approach with unsupervised or semi-supervised learning looks promising approach to identify ornamentation patterns.

It was observed that although the algorithm developed has provided reasonably good accuracy, it is still far away from practical use in applications. The rule-based approach has limitations for ornamentation patterns due to the complex nature of the data. Experts did not annotate the grace notes identified by algorithms in some cases. The algorithm failed to capture some grace notes, annotated by experts. Non-standardization of duration leads to some discrepancies among expert opinions. Annotation and agreement among the experts is a challenging issue. The need felt to standardize the duration of grace notes with experimentation and opinions of domain experts. More experimentation and a huge annotated dataset are needed for enhancing the algorithm and utilizing the ornamentation features for any application. Music recommendation is a prominent application in music computing considering online music consumption.

Annotating a large dataset for ornamental features is a very time-consuming task for humans. A data-driven approach combining CNN and RNN may prove to be a useful approach. CNN for the image analysis of the audio waveforms and RNN with sequence modeling are suitable for ornamental feature identification. Semi-supervised or unsupervised or reinforcement learning approach to train a model need to be explored with a data-driven approach to identifying melodic patterns with respect to ornamentation features.

Deep belief network (DBN) is one of the best possible alternatives one can explore. It has a stack-restricted Boltzmann machine or RBM, which identifies hidden patterns effectively in unsupervised learning methodology. The model can be trained using a semi-supervised learning approach with a small number of annotated samples. The pretraining of the model makes it different from typical neural network models. For music ornamentation features or patterns, DBN looks as a promising alternative as having large labeled data for ornamentation patterns is very unlikely considering the human efforts required. DBN with the feature of pretraining requires small annotated data or labeled samples and thus it matches the requirement of the suitable model for the task. The data-centric or data-driven model training happens in the hidden layers of DBN and is the most promising approach identified for ornamentation pattern identification in computational music. A data-driven approach to identify musical embodiment or ornamentation in the performance will be useful for musicians and music learners.

REFERENCES

[1] Lu, L., Wang, M., and Zhang, H.-J. (2004). Repeating pattern discovery and structure analysis from acoustic music data. In: *Proceedings of the 6th ACM SIGMM international workshop on Multimedia information retrieval*, New York, NY, USA, pp. 275–282.

[2] Gulati, S., Serra, J., Ishwar, V., Senturk, S., and Serra, X. (2016). Phrase-based raga recognition using vector space modeling. In: *2016 IEEE International Conference on Acoustics, Speech and Signal Processing (ICASSP)*, IEEE, pp. 66–70.

[3] Klapuri, A. (2010). Pattern induction and matching in music signals. In: Mitsuko Aramaki, Mathieu Barthet, Richard Kronland-Martinet, Sølvi Ystad (eds.) *International Symposium on Computer Music Modeling and Retrieval*, Springer, New York, pp. 188–204.

[4] Aucouturier, J.-J., and Sandler, M. (2002). Finding repeating patterns in acoustic musical signals: Applications for audio thumb nailing. In: Jyri Huopaniemi (ed.) *Audio Engineering Society Conference: 22nd International Conference: Virtual, Synthetic, and Entertainment Audio,* Audio Engineering Society.

[5] Bainbridge, D., and Bell, T. (2001). The challenge of optical music recognition. *Computers and the Humanities*, 35(2), 95–121.

[6] Orio, N., and Roda, A. (2009). A measure of melodic similarity based on a graph representation of the music structure. In: *ISMIR*, Kobe, Japan, pp. 543–548.

[7] Boulanger-Lewandowski, N., Bengio, Y., and Vincent, P. (2013). Audio chord recognition with recurrent neural networks. In: *ISMIR*, Citeseer, pp. 335–340.

[8] Ullrich, K., Schl¨uter, J., and Grill, T. (2014). Boundary detection in music structure analysis using convolutional neural networks. In: ISMIR, Taipei, Taiwan. pp. 417–422.

[9] Vempala, N. N., and Russo. F. A. (2012). Predicting emotion from music audio features using neural networks. In: *Proceedings of the 9th International Symposium on Computer Music Modeling and Retrieval (CMMR), Lecture Notes in Computer Science*, London, UK, pp. 336–343.

[10] Personal Discussions (2012–2013). Personal discussions with renowned vocalist Veena Saharabuddhe, Pandit Sanjeev Abhyankar and flute player Pandit Keshav Ginde.

[11] Narayan, A. A. (2018). Computational study of ornaments in Hindustani music. PhD thesis, International Institute of Information Technology, Hyderabad.

[12] Bai, X., Wang, X., Liu, X., Liu, Q., Song, J., Sebe, N., and Kim, B. (2021). Explainable deep learning for efficient and robust pattern recognition: A survey of recent developments. *Pattern Recognition*, 120, 108102.

[13] Solomatine, D. P., and Ostfeld, A. (2008). Data-driven modeling: some past experiences and new approaches. *Journal of Hydro Informatics*, 10(1), 3–22.

[14] Chen, Y. W., and Jain, L. C. (2020). *Deep Learning in Healthcare: Paradigms and Applications*, Springer, Heidelberg.

[15] Zhang, Q., Yang, L. T., Chen, Z., and Li, P. (2018). A survey on deep learning for big data. *Information Fusion*, 42, 146–157.

[16] Busia, A., Dahl, G. E., Fannjiang, C., Alexander, D. H., Dorfman, E., Poplin, R., and DePristo, M. (2018). A deep learning approach to pattern recognition for short DNA sequences. BioRxiv, 353474.

[17] Sarker, I. H. (2021). Deep cybersecurity: a comprehensive overview from neural network and deep learning perspective. *SN Computer Science*, 2(3), 154.

[18] Calvo-Zaragoza, J., Toselli, A. H., and Vidal, E. (2019). Handwritten music recognition for mensural notation with convolutional recurrent neural networks. *Pattern Recognition Letters*, 128, 115–121.

[19] Velankar, M., and Kulkarni, P. (2022). Melodic pattern recognition and similarity modeling: a systematic survey in music computing. *Journal of Trends in Computer Science and Smart Technology*, 4(4), 272–290.

[20] Elbir, A., and Aydin, N. (2020). Music genre classification and music recommendation by using deep learning. *Electronics Letters*, 56(12), 627–629.

[21] Van den Oord, A., Dieleman, S., and Schrauwen, B. (2013). Deep content-based music recommendation. In: C.J. Burges and L. Bottou and M. Welling and Z. Ghahramani and K.Q. Weinberger (eds.) *Advances in Neural Information Processing Systems*, NeurIPS Proceedings, 26.

[22] Benetos, E., Dixon, S., Duan, Z., and Ewert, S. (2018). Automatic music transcription: An overview. *IEEE Signal Processing Magazine*, 36(1), 20–30.

[23] Briot, J. P., and Pachet, F. (2020). Deep learning for music generation: challenges and directions. *Neural Computing and Applications*, 32(4), 981–993.

[24] Micchi, G., Kosta, K., Medeot, G., and Chanquion, P. (2021). A deep learning method for enforcing coherence in automatic chord recognition. In: *ISMIR*, pp. 443–451.

[25] Bittner, R. M., McFee, B., Salamon, J., Li, P., and Bello, J. P. (2017, October). Deep salience representations for F0 estimation in polyphonic music. In: *ISMIR*, Suzhou (China) pp. 63–70.

[26] Su, L. (2018, April). Vocal melody extraction using patch-based CNN. In: *2018 IEEE International Conference on Acoustics, Speech and Signal Processing (ICASSP)*, IEEE, Calgary, AB, Canada. pp. 371–375.

[27] Sharma, A. K., Aggarwal, G., Bhardwaj, S., Chakrabarti, P., Chakrabarti, T., Abawajy, J. H., and Mahdin, H. (2021). Classification of Indian classical music with time-series matching deep learning approach. *IEEE Access*, 9, 102041–102052.

[28] Shah, D. P., Jagtap, N. M., Talekar, P. T., and Gawande, K. (2021). Raga recognition in Indian classical music using deep learning. In: *Artificial Intelligence in Music, Sound, Art and Design: 10th International Conference, EvoMUSART 2021, Held as Part of EvoStar 2021, Proceedings 10, Virtual Event* April 7–9, 2021, Springer, New York, pp. 248–263.

[29] Nag, S., Basu, M., Sanyal, S., Banerjee, A., and Ghosh, D. (2022). On the application of deep learning and multi-fractal techniques to classify emotions and instruments using Indian Classical Music. *Physica A: Statistical Mechanics and its Applications*, 597, 127261.

[30] Singh, Y., and Biswas, A. (2022). Robustness of musical features on deep learning models for music genre classification. *Expert Systems with Applications*, 199, 116879.

[31] Velankar, M., Thombre, S., and Wadkar, H. (2022). Evaluating deep learning models for music emotion recognition. *International Journal of Engineering Applied Sciences and Technology*, 7(6), 252–259.

[32] Pudaruth, S. K. (2016). A reflection on the aesthetics of Indian music, with special reference to Hindustani raga-Sangita. *Sage Open*, 6(4), 2158244016674512

[33] Cont, A. (2010). A coupled duration-focused architecture for real-time music-to score alignment. *IEEE Transactions on Pattern Analysis and Machine Intelligence*, 32(6), 974–987.

[34] Windsor, Luke, Aarts, Rinus, Desain, Peter, Heijink, Hank, and Timmers, Renee. (2001). The timing of grace notes in skilled musical performance at different tempi: A preliminary case study. *Psychology of Music*, 29(2), 149–169.

[35] Jeong, Dasaem, Kwon, Taegyun, Kim, Yoojin, and Nam, Juhan. (2019). Score and performance features for rendering expressive music performances. In: *Music Encoding Conference*, Music Encoding Initiative Vienna, Austria, pp. 1–6.

15 Content Analysis Framework for Skill Assessment

Abhishek Kabade, Harshad Jagadale,
Anurag Bharde, and S. P. Sonavane

15.1 INTRODUCTION

The education sector has undergone significant changes due to advancements in technology, resulting in a need for innovative learning and skill assessment methods. This book chapter delves into a cutting-edge system that harnesses the power of the Internet of Things (IoT), machine learning, artificial intelligence (AI), blockchain, and RFID technology to address these challenges.

In today's fast-paced world, educational institutions must teach students theoretical knowledge and practical skills that are relevant to the industry. Traditional assessment methods may often fail to capture students' abilities. Therefore, there is a growing demand for a robust system that can accurately assess skills while fostering collaboration between academia and industry. The system presented in this chapter revolves around an AI-based learning environment, incorporating an academic chatbot and a central database to facilitate seamless communication between students and industry professionals. The effectiveness of this system is demonstrated through a case study conducted at an academic institution, Walchand College of Engineering (WCE) in Sangli (MS), India.

At the core of the system lies the integration of RFID technology. Each student is assigned a unique identity through an RFID card that stores comprehensive information, including personal details, academic performance, and skill indices. These skill indices represent the students' abilities, encompassing both relative and absolute skill levels. Stored in separate blocks within a blockchain network, these indices ensure data integrity and security while granting industry professionals access to relevant information. The system also employs machine learning algorithms along with natural language processing techniques to extract meaningful content from diverse sources such as text and audio materials. This content analysis enables the system to provide intelligent responses to student queries and offer personalized recommendations for skill improvement.

The book chapter is divided into three parts to provide a comprehensive understanding of the system.

Part I focuses on the infrastructure of the WCE campus network, highlighting the academic chatbot, central database, and wireless RFID connections that form the foundation of the system.

DOI: 10.1201/9781003461500-18

Part II delves into the intent behind industry queries, referencing query processing from Part I and introduces the content analyzer. The contents are selected from documents, and for experimentation, the student resume document is taken as input to extract skill-indicating tokens resulting in Resume Analyzer [1]. This component calculates skill indices based on the data stored on RFID cards. This section demonstrates how the system offers a comprehensive overview of students' skills, assisting both academia and industry in identifying suitable talent.

Part III explores the mechanism of recommending study materials and educational resources tailored to each student's specific skill improvement needs.

By integrating IoT, machine learning, AI, blockchain, and RFID technology, this system offers a holistic approach to content learning and analysis for skill assessment. It promotes effective collaboration between academia and industry, enhances skill evaluation, and provides personalized opportunities for skill development. The subsequent sections of the chapter delve into the intricate details of the system, highlighting its potential to revolutionize the educational landscape and meet the evolving demands of the modern world.

i. Developed framework
ii. Connected with the cloud
iii. Integrated RFID
iv. AI/ML Block
v. Result Analysis

15.2   RELATED WORK

Chatbots have emerged as powerful conversational agents facilitating interactive and personalized interactions between humans and computer systems. With their ability to understand natural language input and generate contextually relevant responses, chatbots have found applications in various domains, including customer service, virtual assistants, and information retrieval systems. Chatbots [2] seem to hold great promise when it comes to providing fast and convenient support to users by delivering targeted answers to their questions. There's a massive popularity for chatbots in the recent phase within business organizations, technology firms, etc. which has been attributed to their cost-saving potential and has unlocked new abilities to handle multiple requests simultaneously. Chatbots have completely evolved beyond being mere assistants and now have established themselves as companions through their interactive responses and conversation styles. According to a research study, customer service chatbots on various social platforms often encounter requests that are emotional and sentimental to their health. Many intelligent agents have emerged as powerful and highly promising tools for better mental health therapy [3]. Studies have promisingly demonstrated the effectiveness of simple innovations such as engaging in deep breathing practices, acts of kindness, increasing and improving positive emotions, and reducing negative emotions. Most of the time [4], students have had to physically visit universities or colleges to collect various information like tuition fees, term schedules, and other relevant details during their admission process or as per their daily needs. This process is very tedious and time-consuming, also it requires manpower in providing the required information to visitors.

To address these challenges, a chatbot can be developed. The chatbot aims to facilitate interaction between users and a chatbot that can be accessed anytime and anywhere. By integrating the chatbot seamlessly into the university or college website through simple language conversions, it becomes readily available to provide a wide range of information related to the institution and student-specific queries. The chatbot serves as a valuable resource for anyone accessing the university's website, allowing users to ask questions pertaining to the university and receive corresponding responses generated by an algorithm after processing the input message. Job search [5] from the online portal is one of the most upcoming and efficient job search methods for both the job seeker and the job provider. The solutions for these new-age technologies are still the traditional and time-taking methods are still the same. The answers are driven by manual rules like searching and reading the complete resume which takes a huge mental power and time also hinging a bit with the effectiveness and frustration. Job finding is a type of recommender system. The Recommender system was first introduced by Resnick and Varian [6] who pointed out that in a typical recommender system, people provide recommendations as inputs, which the system then aggregates and directs to appropriate recipients. For job matching, many research works have been conducted to invent different recommender systems for job recruiting [7]. Among all of them, Malinowski et al. [8] proposed bilateral matching recommendation systems for bringing people together with jobs using an Expectation Maximization algorithm, while Golec and Kahya [9] portray a fuzzy model for competency-based employee evaluation and selection with fuzzy rules. Paparrizos et al. [10] used Decision Table/Naive Bayes as a hybrid classifier.

15.3 PROPOSED SYSTEM

The overall system's block diagram is demonstrated in Figure 15.1, where the WCE network is connected to the cloud, facilitating the sharing and receiving of

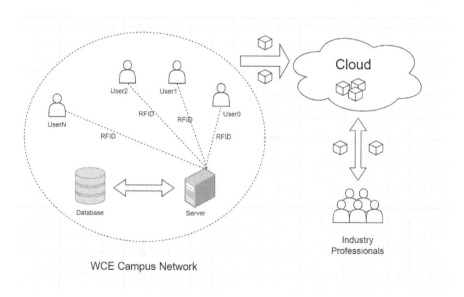

FIGURE 15.1 Institutional level content learning and analysis for skill assessment.

information with industry professionals. Within the institutional campus network, the server is connected to the database and also to the users, each of whom has their own RFID. These RFID devices are linked to industry peers through the cloud, utilizing blockchain technology.

15.4   PART I: CHATBOT

This book chapter introduces a comprehensive methodology for harnessing natural language processing (NLP) techniques in developing an academic chatbot as part of an IoT-based learning system.

NLP, a field within AI, aims to empower computers with the ability to comprehend, interpret, and generate human language. By incorporating NLP techniques, the chatbot becomes proficient in understanding the intent behind queries and delivering meaningful responses. These techniques encompass various aspects of language understanding and processing, including tokenization, stemming, named entity recognition (NER) (identifying entities like names, organizations, and locations), sentiment analysis (determining the expressed sentiment in text), and language modeling (predicting word sequences).

By implementing NLP techniques in the academic chatbot, the IoT-based learning system offers students an interactive and intelligent interface for resolving queries and receiving skill improvement recommendations. This integration enhances the system's ability to understand and process language, resulting in a more effective and user-friendly experience for students.

15.4.1   NLP IMPLEMENTATION

The implementation of the chatbot involves the use of Natural Language Toolkit (NLTK), a widely adopted open-source library in Python for NLP tasks. Figure 2 indicates the flow of implementation. The following steps outline the implementation process:

1. **Importing Corpus**: This step entails accessing and uploading the data files required to train and evaluate the NLP models. The system retrieves the necessary data files, which serve as the dataset for training the chatbot. The corpus may consist of various textual data such as documents, conversations, or any relevant content.
2. **Preprocessing Data**: Data preprocessing is a critical step that involves cleaning and modifying the raw text to make it suitable for analysis. It includes operations such as removing punctuation, converting all letters to lowercase, eliminating stop words (commonly used words like "a," "the," and "is" that carry little meaning), and handling special characters or symbols.
3. **Test Case Processing**: Test case processing involves preparing and managing test cases to evaluate the chatbot's functionality. Test cases comprise input patterns and their corresponding expected responses, used to validate the accuracy and validity of the chatbot's replies. These test cases cover different scenarios and user queries to ensure the chatbot performs as intended.

4. **Tokenization**: Tokenization involves breaking the text into smaller units which are also known as tokens. Tokens typically represent words or phrases, serving as the fundamental building blocks of the text. The tokenization step segments the text based on specific rules or patterns, such as whitespace or punctuation marks, to separate individual words or phrases. Tokenization enables the chatbot to process and understand the meaning of each token, facilitating further analysis.

5. **Stemming:** The technique of reducing words into their base or root forms is called Stemming. It removes the suffixes or prefixes associated with the words, focusing on the core part that represents the essence of the word. Stemming helps consolidate words with similar meanings, reduces word size, and improves the efficiency of text analysis tasks like sentiment analysis or information retrieval.

6. **Bag of Words (BoW):** The BoW model is a widely used representation technique in NLP. It treats each document as a "bag" containing its words, without considering grammar and word order. By constructing a vocabulary of unique words in the corpus, the model represents each document as a vector. Each dimension in the vector corresponds to a word in the vocabulary. The values assigned to each dimension indicate the frequency or presence of the respective word in the document. The BoW representation proves valuable for various NLP tasks, including text classification, topic modeling, and information retrieval.

7. **One-Hot Coding:** One-hot coding is a technique employed to numerically represent categorical variables. In NLP, it can be used to represent words or entities as binary vectors. Each word is assigned a unique index, and its vector representation has a value of 1 for the corresponding index and 0 elsewhere.

By following these detailed steps, including data import, preprocessing, test case processing, tokenization, stemming, BoW, and one-hot coding, the NLP-based chatbot can effectively process and analyze textual data, generating precise and relevant responses to user inquiries, depicted in Figure 15.2.

15.4.2 Block Diagram

15.4.3 Algorithm and Code: Chatbot Response Generation Using TF-IDF and Cosine Similarity

The code implements a chatbot that uses TF-IDF and cosine similarity to find the most similar sentence to the user's response. It generates a response based on the similarity, and if there is no understanding, it responds with a default message. The TF-IDF matrix is used to represent the importance of words in the sentences and to measure the similarity between the user's response and previous sentences cosine similarity is used.

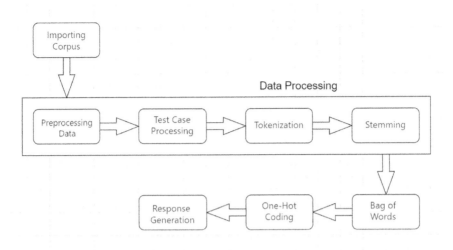

FIGURE 15.2 Block diagram for NLP implementation.

Algorithm

1. Start the response (user_response) function.
2. Initialize an empty string variable robo_response to store the chatbot's response.
3. Append the user's response to the list of sentence tokens.
4. Create a TfidfVectorizer object with a custom tokenizer (lem_normalize) and English stop words.
5. Compute the TF-IDF matrix for all the sentence tokens using the vectorizer.
6. Calculate the cosine similarity between the user's response and all other sentences in the TF-IDF matrix.
7. Find the index of the most similar sentence based on the cosine similarity.
8. Flatten and sort the cosine similarity values in ascending order.
9. Retrieve the second-highest cosine similarity value.
10. If the similarity value is zero, set robo_response as "Sorry, I don't understand you."
11. Otherwise, retrieve the most similar sentence from the sentence_tokens list using the obtained index and append it to robo_response.
12. Return the robo_response as the chatbot's response.

Program Code

```
def response(user_response):
    robo_response = ''
# Initialize the response variable for the chatbot
```

```
# Append the user's response to the sentence tokens
    sentence_tokens.append(user_response)
# Create a TF-IDF vectorizer with a custom tokenizer and stop
words
    vectorizer = TfidfVectorizer(tokenizer=lem_normalize,
stop_words='english')
# Compute the TF-IDF matrix for the sentence tokens
    tfidf = vectorizer.fit_transform(sentence_tokens)
# Compute the cosine similarity between the user's response
and all other sentences
    values = cosine_similarity(tfidf[-1], tfidf)
# Find the index of the most similar sentence
    idx = values.argsort()[0][-2]
# Flatten and sort the cosine similarity values
    flat = values.flatten()
    flat.sort()
# Get the second highest cosine similarity value
    req_tfidf = flat[-2]
# Check if the similarity is zero, indicating no understanding
    if req_tfidf == 0:
        robo_response = '{} Sorry, I don\'t understand you'.
format(robo_response)
    else:
# Retrieve the most similar sentence as the chatbot's response
        robo_response = robo_response + sentence_tokens[idx]
return robo_response
```

In the provided code snippet, cosine similarity is utilized to find the most similar sentence to the user's input. Cosine similarity is a metric which is used to measure the similarity between two vectors, particularly in high-dimensional spaces.

How it helps in generating responses to the chatbot:

1. **Sentence Tokenization**: The user's input and other sentences are tokenized, which means they are split into individual words or phrases.
2. **TF-IDF Vectorization**: The TfidfVectorizer from the 'sklearn.feature_extraction.text' module is used to convert the tokenized sentences to numerical representations called TF-IDF vectors. TF-IDF, which stands for Term Frequency-Inverse Document Frequency, is a technique commonly utilized in information retrieval and text mining. Based on the frequency and rarity of the words in the entire corpus, it assigns corresponding weights.
3. **Cosine Similarity Calculation**: The TF-IDF vector for the user's input is compared with the TF-IDF vectors of all the other sentences in the 'sentence_tokens' list. The cosine similarity is calculated between the vectors using the 'cosine_similarity' function from the 'sklearn.metrics.pairwise' module.

    The cosine similarity between two vectors can be determined by evaluating the dot product of the vectors and dividing it by the product of their

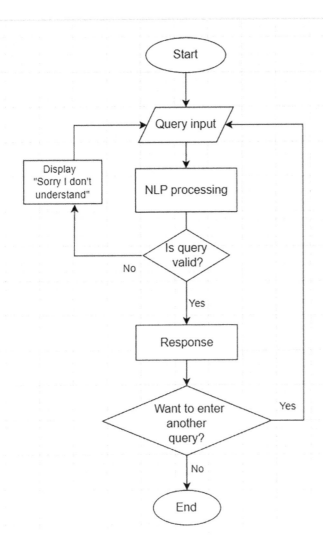

FIGURE 15.3   Flowchart depicting the workflow of the chatbot.

magnitudes. Given two vectors A and B, the cosine similarity (similarity score) is computed as follows:

$$\text{Cosine Similarity} \ = \ A{\cdot}B \ / \left(\|A\| * \|B\|\right) \tag{15.1}$$

where $A \cdot B$ represents the dot product of vectors A and B. ǁAǁ denotes the magnitude (Euclidean norm) of vector A. ǁBǁ denotes the magnitude (Euclidean norm) of vector B. The dot product of two vectors A and B is the sum of the products of their corresponding components:

$$A \cdot B = A1 * B1 + A2 * B2 + \ldots + An * Bn \qquad (15.2)$$

The magnitude (Euclidean norm) of a vector A is calculated as the square root of the sum of the squares of its components:

$$\| A \| = sqrt(A1^2 + A2^2 + \ldots + An^2) \qquad (15.3)$$

By dividing the dot product of Vectors A and B by the product of their magnitudes, the cosine similarity value is obtained. This value falls within the range of –1 to 1, with 1 indicating strong similarity, 0 indicating no similarity, and –1 indicating dissimilarity or oppositeness.

4. **Finding the Most Similar Sentence:** The index of the sentence with the highest cosine similarity to the user's input is obtained using the "argsort" function. The response associated with that index is then selected as the generated response for the chatbot.

    By using cosine similarity, the chatbot identifies the sentence from the existing dataset that is most similar to the user's input. This allows the chatbot to provide a response that is relevant and contextually appropriate to the user's query or statement

15.5 PART II: RESUME ANALYZER

The Resume Analyzer, which is discussed in Part 1 regarding query processing, elevates skill assessment to a new level by leveraging the data stored on RFID cards [11]. This section offers a detailed explanation of how the Resume Analyzer precisely calculates skill indices based on the information extracted from the cards, thereby providing a comprehensive overview of students' skills.

The proposed system consists of two dashboards: one for users and another for the admin. The system accepts resumes in PDF format, which are then extracted into plain text. This extraction process utilizes the PDFMiner library to convert the PDF resume into plain text format [12]. Next, Pyresparser is employed to extract keywords from the resume, encompassing both technical and non-technical terms. These keywords are stored in an array.

Additionally [13], the system allows the recruiter to specify their skillset requirements, which are stored in a separate array. The system then matches these requirements with the skills possessed by the candidates [14]. The percentage of requirements fulfilled by each candidate is calculated by the system. Furthermore, the system assigns a score to each uploaded resume based on various factors such as projects, achievements, hobbies, positions of responsibility, and educational details mentioned in the resume [15]. This score is intended to evaluate the overall quality and suitability of the resume.

In the context of resume analysis, the Resume Analyzer performs six essential functions.

1. **Standardization**: A resume parser automatically extracts information from resumes and transforms it into a consistent format, enabling effortless searching, sorting, and comparison.
2. **Keyword Extraction**: This is a process performed by a resume parser that identifies important keywords and phrases from a resume. These extracted keywords and phrases can then be utilized to filter and rank candidates according to their skills and qualifications.
3. **Skills Matching**: A resume parser matches the skills and qualifications listed on the resume with the job description. This functionality assists recruiters in identifying the candidates who are more suitable for the job post based on the specific requirements [16].
4. **Blockchain Integration**: Blockchain technology can enhance the security and immutability of the Resume Analyzer system. The candidate's resume data, including parsed information and Analyzed results, can be stored on the blockchain network. This ensures that the information remains tamper-proof, transparent, and accessible only to the authorized parties.
5. **Contact Extraction**: A resume parser captures the candidate's personal details such as name, contact number, and email.
6. **Qualification Matching**: In the process of resume parsing, the system extracts details related to the candidate's work history, educational background, certifications, and other pertinent qualifications, allowing for effective qualification matching.
7. **Data Analysis**: Data obtained from resumes is analyzed to detect patterns and trends, enabling organizations to enhance their recruitment procedures and identify potential areas for optimization.

Algorithm of Pyresparser

Algorithm

13. Parse the resume document using the appropriate parser for the file format (e.g., PyPDF2 for PDF).
14. Preprocess the parsed text to clean and normalize it.
15. Segment the preprocessed text into sentences.
16. Use spaCy's NER module to identify entities (names, addresses, and phone number) in each sentence.
17. Add the identified entities to the list of extracted entities.
18. Use pattern-matching techniques to extract specific information (educational qualifications, work experience, and skills) from the parsed text.
19. Add the extracted information to the list of extracted entities.
20. Convert the list of extracted entities into a structured format like JSON or DataFrame.
21. Return the parsed resume information in the chosen structured format.

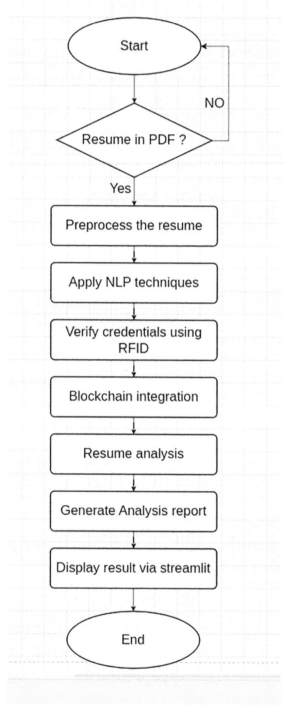

FIGURE 15.4   Flowchart illustrating the Resume Analyzer process.

15.5.1 Flow of Application

Application working shown in flowchart 15.4

The proposed model has five steps:

- Resume collections.
- Keywords searching and skills extraction.
- Matching skills with industry requirements.
- Calculating percentage requirement fulfilled by the candidates.
- Creating QR code of the uploaded resume and a self-introductory video of the user.
- Using Blockchain technology for data privacy and security

15.5.2 Resume Collection

Different machine learning algorithms are employed to suggest a shortlist of resumes to recruiters from a large pool of resumes. However, these decisions rely on the assumption that the data provided in the resumes is structured and standardized within the same field.

For instance, if a company requires "Docker" skill, the system can search for the keyword "Docker" in the resumes of the candidates. However, this method is not able to give any insight into the candidate's proficiency level in that specific field. It is unable to determine the candidate's level of expertise or competence in that particular area.

15.5.3 Blockchain Implementation

In the proposed Figure 15.5, the process initiates with a request being initialized. This request triggers the creation of a block that contains the student's resume. After the formation of the block, it is transmitted to peer industries within the network. The block node then undergoes validation to ensure its authenticity and integrity. If the block successfully passes the validation process, it is added to the existing Blockchain, expanding the chain with the new block. Finally, the request reaches the industry, marking the completion of the cycle. This diagram visually represents the sequential flow of the request and highlights the crucial steps involved in the creation and dissemination of blocks within the Blockchain network.

15.6 PART III MECHANISM OF RECOMMENDING EDUCATIONAL RESOURCES

This section explores the mechanism of recommending study materials and educational resources tailored to each student's specific skill improvement needs within the IoT-based learning framework.

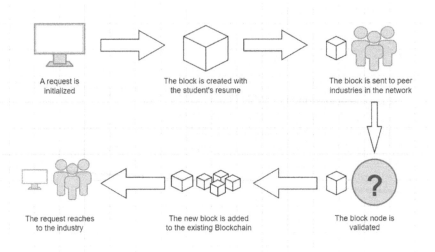

FIGURE 15.5   Resume transaction through blockchain.

The algorithms are written in the Python language. These algorithms are used for keywords searching and extraction. Extracted data is stored in MySQL database. Stored data is fetched whenever required for matching with the given or mandatory skill set of the industry. According to the candidate's skills, the system will generate his interested field. The framework suggests the candidate for the online courses and YouTube channels as per his interest derived by the framework.

Based on his score, the framework classify them into three groups:

1. Fresher
2. Intermediate
3. Experienced

The score is calculated as the sum of percentage skills matched and the score obtained for the mentioning other important details such as projects, achievements, educational details, etc.

The candidates and companies will interact through web-based interface developed using "Streamlit" library. The percentage marks are divided by 2 to scale it in terms of 50, and other 50 marks are for the mentioning of other important resume details.

15.7 FLOWCHART OF QR CODE

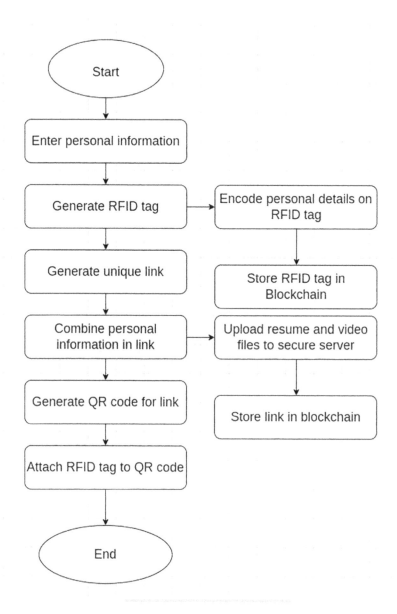

FIGURE 15.6 Flowchart of QR code implementation using blockchain and RFID.

15.8   IMPLEMENTATION OVERVIEW

The work related to all the modules has been implemented using the web interface. Below are some of the modules. Streamlit library is used for web hosting
purposes. MySQL database is used to store data and fetch that data from the
database.

In Figure 15.7, Candidate resume. Here, he can upload his resume pdf.

Then, keywords are extracted from the resume and keywords are matched with
the required skill set of the company and the percentage requirement fulfilled is calculated as shown in Figure 15.8.

In Figure 15.9, the candidate can create his QR code for the link containing resume soft copy with the self-introductory video of Figure 15.10, the
Admin (Recruiter) get to know about all the uploaded resumes, their scores,

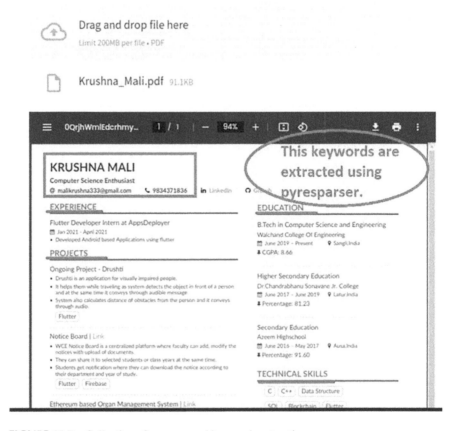

FIGURE 15.7   Collection of resumes and keywords extraction.

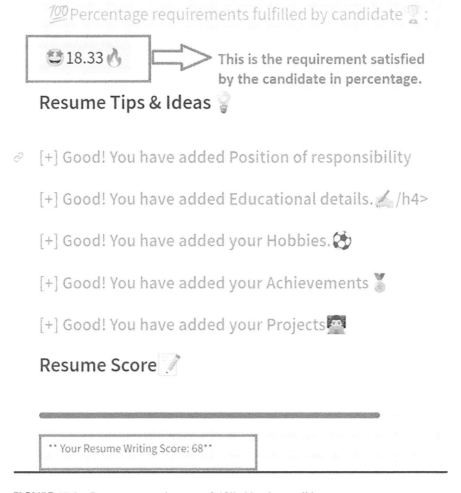

FIGURE 15.8 Percentage requirements fulfilled by the candidate.

recommended fields, name of the candidate, etc. Admin is also provided with a pie chart showing recommended fields for the candidates depicting the percentage share of each field.

In Figure 15.11, Company can add or delete skills from the skill set that the candidate needs to have. Recruiter can add manually also. These skill set are then matched with the skills of the candidate. The score is calculated from the percentage skills matched with the company's required skill set. The candidate's extracted skill set and the company's skill set are stored in two different arrays. Their intersection is taken to calculate the percentage score.

Home

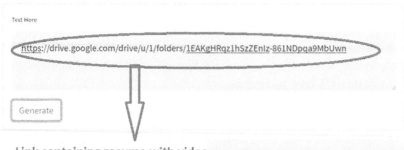

Text Here

https://drive.google.com/drive/u/1/folders/1EAKgHRqz1hSzZEnIz-861NDpqa9MbUwn

Generate

Link containing resume with video Original Text

https://drive.google.com/drive/u/1/folders/1EAKgH
Rqz1hSzZEnIz-861NDpqa9MbUwn

FIGURE 15.9   QR code generation.

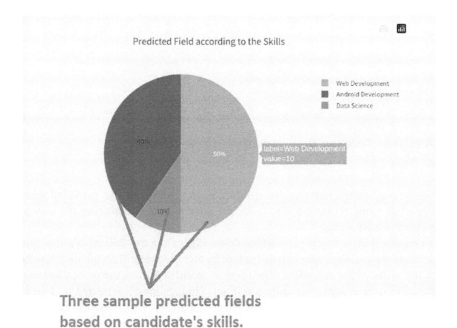

Predicted Field according to the Skills

- Web Development
- Android Development
- Data Science

40%

50%

label=Web Development
value=10

10%

**Three sample predicted fields
based on candidate's skills.**

FIGURE 15.10   Pie-chart depicting the percentage of the candidate interested in each field.

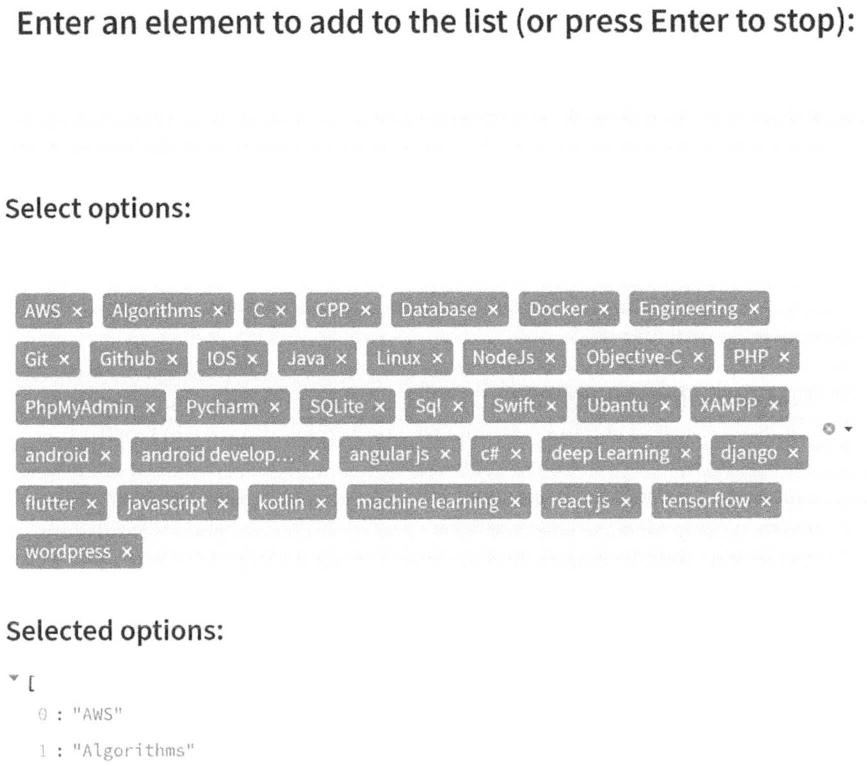

Enter an element to add to the list (or press Enter to stop):

Select options:

AWS × | Algorithms × | C × | CPP × | Database × | Docker × | Engineering ×

Git × | Github × | IOS × | Java × | Linux × | NodeJs × | Objective-C × | PHP ×

PhpMyAdmin × | Pycharm × | SQLite × | Sql × | Swift × | Ubantu × | XAMPP ×

android × | android develop... × | angular js × | c# × | deep Learning × | django ×

flutter × | javascript × | kotlin × | machine learning × | react js × | tensorflow ×

wordpress ×

Selected options:

```
▼ [
    0 : "AWS"
    1 : "Algorithms"
```

FIGURE 15.11   Company's required skill-set figure enlarged.

15.9   REMARK

This book chapter explores an innovative IoT-based learning system that integrates machine learning, AI, blockchain, and RFID technology. The system aims to bridge the gap between academia and industry by providing a comprehensive solution for skill assessment and collaboration between the two sectors. The chapter discusses the implementation details, with a particular focus on the development of an academic chatbot by the use of NLP algorithms. The chatbot's ability to get the language and generate human-like language enables meaningful interactions and personalized recommendations for skill improvement.

The integration of blockchain technology in the Resume Analyzer module, along with NLP techniques, enhances security, privacy, and trust in the resume verification process. It enables efficient text processing and addresses the challenges associated with natural language extraction. However, the system may face difficulties in disambiguating similar words with different meanings. Despite this, it serves as a primary tool for identifying eligible candidates for job opportunities.

Additionally, the use of QR codes for recruiters streamlines the hiring process, saving time and providing convenience. However, it is important to carefully evaluate the challenges and limitations associated with blockchain technology in the resume analysis system. Factors such as complexity, scalability, and integration efforts should be considered based on the specific requirements and goals of the application.

15.10   FUTURE WORK

The future work in the Chatbot and Resume Analyzer system aims to focus on several key factors, including scalability enhancement, network capability improvement, block integrity, training set enhancement, and evaluation of proficiency of the candidate in a particular field.

1. **Scalability Enhancement:** Using various methods such as shading, sidechains, or Layer-2 solutions to enhance the system's capacity in handling an increasing number of resumes and users.
2. **Network Capability Improvement:** Collaboration with network engineers is undertaken to upgrade hardware, improve network protocols, and ensure the seamless and efficient transmission of data between network components.
3. **Block Integrity Assurance:** Using hashing algorithms in conjunction with digital signatures allows us to verify the authenticity of resumes and prevent any tampering or unauthorized modifications.
4. **Proficiency Assessment:** If a candidate mentions "Java" in their resume, our system can determine that they have knowledge of "Java". However, the system does not estimate their proficiency level. To address this, we can develop a chatbot function integrated with the Resume Analyzer. This chatbot function will interact with the candidate and evaluate their proficiency in specific technical keywords.

REFERENCES

1. Resume Screening Using LSTM, *International Journal of Research Publication and Reviews*, 3(4), 2567–2569, https://ijrpr.com/uploads/V3ISSUE4/IJRPR3705.pdf
2. Adamopoulou, E., and Moussiades, L. (2020). An overview of chatbot technology. In: Maglogiannis I., Iliadis L., Pimenidis E. (eds), *Artificial Intelligence Applications and Innovations. AIAI 2020. IFIP Advances in Information and Communication Technology*, vol. 584, Springer, Cham. https://www.researchgate.net/publication/341730184_An_Overview_of_Chatbot_Technology
3. Ghandeharioun, A., McDuff, D., Czerwinski, M., and Rowan, K. (2019). EMMA: An emotion-aware wellbeing chatbot. In: *2019 8th International Conference on Affective Computing and Intelligent Interaction (ACII)*, Cambridge, UK, 2019, pp. 1–7, doi:10.1109/ACII.2019.8925455. https://ieeexplore.ieee.org/abstract/document/8925455
4. Patel, N. P., Parikh, D. R., Patel, D. A., and Patel, R. R. (2019). AI and web-based human-like interactive university chatbot (UNIBOT). In: *2019 3rd International Conference on Electronics, Communication and Aerospace Technology (ICECA)*, Coimbatore, India, 2019, pp. 148–150, doi:10.1109/ICECA.2019.8822176. https://ieeexplore.ieee.org/abstract/document/8822176

5. Lin, Y., Lei, H., Addo, P. C., and Li, X. (2016). Machine learned resume-job matching solution. https://arxiv.org/abs/1607.07657

6. Resnick, P., and Varian, H. R. (1997). Recommender systems. *Communications of the ACM*, 40(3), 56–58. doi:10.1145/245108.245121

7. Al-Otaibi, S. T., and Ykhlef, M. (2012). A survey of job recommender systems. *International Journal of the Physical Sciences*, 7(29), 5127–5142. https://academicjournals.org/journal/IJPS/article-full-text-pdf/B19DCA416592.pdf

8. Malinowski, J., Keim, T., Wendt, O., and Weitzel, T. (2006). Matching people and jobs: A bilateral recommendation approach. https://www.researchgate.net/publication/232615527_Matching_People_and_Jobs_A_Bilateral_Recommendation_Approach

9. Golec, A., and Kahya, E. (2007). A fuzzy model for competency-based employee evaluation and selection. *Computers & Industrial Engineering*, 52(1), 143–161. https://www.researchgate.net/publication/222332549_A_fuzzy_model_for_competencybased_employee_evaluation_and_selection

10. Paparrizos, I., Cambazoglu, B. B., and Gionis, A. (2011). Machine learned job recommendation. In: *Proceedings of the Fifth ACM Conference on Recommender Systems,* ACM, New York, pp. 325–328. https://www.researchgate.net/publication/221141098_Machine_learned_job_recommendation

11. Bojars, U., and Breslin, J. G. ResumeRDF: Expressing skill information on the semantic web. https://www.researchgate.net/publication/266448089_ResumeRDF_Expressing_skill_information_on_the_Semantic_Web

12. (2015). Resume analyzer an automated solution to recruitment process. *International Journal of Engineering nd Technical Research*, 3(8). https://www.erpublication.org/published_paper/IJETR032886.pdf

13. Bojars, U. Extending FOAF with resume information. https://www.w3.org/2001/sw/Europe/events/foaf-galway/papers/pp/extending_foaf_with_resume/

14. Verma, M. (2017). Cluster based ranking index for enhancing recruitment process using text mining and machine learning. *International Journal of Computer Applications*, 157(9). https://www.researchgate.net/publication/312518297_Cluster_based_Ranking_Index_for_Enhancing_Recruitment_Process_using_Text_Mining_and_Machine_Learning

15. Jurka, T. P., Collingwood, L., Boydstun, A. E., Grossman, E., and van Atteveldt, W. (2013). A supervised learning package for text classification. *The R Journal*. https://journal.r-project.org/archive/2013/RJ-2013-001/index.html

16. Li, L., Chu, W., Langford, J., and Schapire, R. E. (2010). A contextual-bandit approach to personalized news article recommendation. In: *Proceedings of the Nineteenth International Conference on World Wide Web*. https://arxiv.org/pdf/1003.0146.pdf

16 Machine-Learning Techniques for Effective Text Mining

*Shivam Singh, Chandrakant D. Kokane,
Vilas Deotare, and Tushar Waykole*

16.1 INTRODUCTION TO TEXT MINING AND MACHINE LEARNING

16.1.1 DEFINITION AND SCOPE OF TEXT MINING

Text mining is the process of collecting valuable information, patterns, and insights from unstructured textual data. It is also known as text data mining or text analytics. Unstructured text data includes a wide range of sources such as emails, social media posts, news articles, research papers, customer reviews, and more.[1] Unlike structured data, which is organized in a predefined format (e.g., databases, spreadsheets), unstructured text lacks a clear and uniform structure, making it challenging to analyze using traditional methods.

The Definition of Text Mining: Text mining involves the application of various computational techniques, natural language processing (NLP) algorithms, and machine-learning methods to process, understand, and analyze unstructured textual data. The ultimate goal of text mining is to convert the raw text into structured, actionable information, enabling users to uncover hidden patterns, trends, sentiments, relationships, and other valuable insights within the data.[2]

The Scope of Text Mining: The scope of text mining is extensive, and it finds applications in diverse fields due to the widespread availability of textual data. Some key areas where text mining is applied include:

1. **Information Retrieval:** Text mining is used to build search engines and information retrieval systems that can efficiently retrieve relevant documents or information based on user queries.
2. **Sentiment Analysis:** Sentiment analysis, often known as opinion mining, is a subset of text mining that focuses on determining a text's sentiment or emotional tone. It is extensively used in social media monitoring, market research, and client feedback analysis.
3. **Text Classification:** Text mining allows for the classification of texts based on their content into predetermined groupings or categories. This has uses in spam identification, topic tagging, document organizing, and other areas.

DOI: 10.1201/9781003461500-19

4. **Named Entity Recognition (NER):** NER is the process of identifying and categorizing named entities in text, such as people's names, organizations' names, locations, dates, and other specified phrases. It is useful in the extraction of information and the building of knowledge graphs.
5. **Topic Modeling:** Topic modeling is a technique for identifying and extracting hidden topics or themes in a big collection of texts. It finds use in content recommendation systems, content analysis, and document clustering.
6. **Language Translation:** Text mining techniques can be used in machine translation systems to automatically translate text from one language to another.
7. **Text summarizing:** Automatic text summarizing is the process of producing succinct summaries of lengthy documents or articles, allowing users to grasp the important points without having to read the entire text.
8. **Fraud Detection:** Text mining can be applied in fraud detection and prevention, such as identifying suspicious text patterns in emails or financial reports.
9. **Healthcare and Biomedical Applications:** Text mining plays a vital role in extracting useful information from medical records, research articles, and clinical notes, enabling better decision-making in healthcare.
10. **News Analysis:** Text mining is used to scan news articles and social media feeds in order to find patterns, sentiment around specific topics, and public opinion.

The scope of text mining is continually expanding as researchers and practitioners develop new techniques and adapt existing ones to address emerging challenges and domains. However, it's important to note that text mining also presents certain challenges, such as dealing with noisy data, language complexities, privacy concerns, and ethical considerations, which need to be carefully addressed in its applications.[4] The operational process of text mining is illustrated in Figure 16.1.

16.1.2 Importance of Machine Learning in Text Mining

Machine learning is critical in text mining because it allows for effective analysis and extraction of useful insights from unstructured text data.[1] The following major characteristics help to understand the significance of machine learning in text mining:

1. **Handling Unstructured Data:** Text data is typically unstructured and lacks a predefined format, making it challenging to process and analyze using traditional methods. Machine-learning algorithms are well-suited to handle unstructured data and can automatically learn patterns and structures from textual information, transforming it into a structured format for further analysis.
2. **Feature Extraction and Representation:** Machine-learning techniques provide various feature extraction and representation methods that help convert raw text into meaningful numerical representations.[2] These methods, such as Bag-of-Words (BoW), Term Frequency-Inverse Document

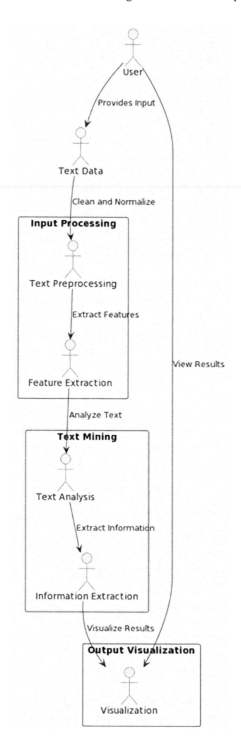

FIGURE 16.1 Text mining working.

Frequency (TF-IDF), and Word Embeddings, capture the semantic meaning and context of words, making it easier for algorithms to understand and analyze textual data effectively.

3. **Text Classification and Categorization:** Machine-learning algorithms excel in text classification tasks where documents are categorized into predefined classes or categories. Whether it's categorizing news articles, sentiment analysis of customer reviews, or spam detection in emails, machine-learning models can automatically learn from labeled data and classify new text data accurately.

4. **Sentiment Analysis and Opinion Mining:** Extracting sentiment and views from text is a difficult undertaking that necessitates a thorough grasp of the context and emotional tone. SVMs and Recurrent Neural Networks (RNNs) are strong sentiment analysis models that allow businesses to glean useful insights from consumer feedback, social media posts, and other sources.

5. **Named Entity Recognition (NER):** In NER, machine-learning approaches are frequently used to detect and categorize named entities in text, such as names of people, organizations, locations, and dates. NER is required for a variety of applications such as information extraction, knowledge graph generation, and data connecting.

6. **Topic Modeling:** Topic modeling methods, such as Latent Dirichlet Allocation (LDA) and Non-negative Matrix Factorization (NMF), are a subset of machine learning that aid in the discovery of hidden topics or themes within a huge collection of texts. This aids in the organization and comprehension of big text corpora, and it is useful for content suggestion and analysis.

7. **Text Clustering:** Unsupervised machine-learning methods such as K-means and Hierarchical Clustering are used for text clustering, which groups similar documents together based on their content. Text clustering assists in organizing and summarizing massive document collections, allowing for more effective information retrieval.

8. **Deep Learning for Text:** Deep learning models, particularly recurrent and convolutional neural networks (CNNs), have performed admirably in a variety of NLP applications. They can learn complicated patterns and hierarchical representations from text input automatically, resulting in cutting-edge performance in tasks such as machine translation, text summarization, and question answering.

9. **Continuous Improvement:** Machine-learning models can be trained iteratively, allowing them to improve over time as they encounter new data. This adaptability is valuable in dynamic text mining scenarios, where data distribution and characteristics may change.

10. **Task Automation:** Machine learning automates a variety of text mining operations, decreasing manual labor and enhancing efficiency. This automation is especially important when dealing with vast amounts of text data that would be impossible to evaluate manually.

In summary, machine learning enables text mining by providing sophisticated tools and algorithms capable of extracting valuable information, patterns, and insights from unstructured text data, allowing businesses, researchers, and analysts to make more informed decisions and gain a deeper understanding of the textual information at their disposal.

16.1.3 KEY CONTRIBUTIONS

1. **Holistic Overview**: This chapter furnishes an all-encompassing understanding of machine-learning methods specifically designed for text mining. It equips readers with a solid foundation in the subject's essentials.
2. **Practical Significance**: The chapter underscores the practical importance of text mining across diverse domains, from marketing to healthcare, emphasizing its role in informed decision-making.
3. **Challenges and Opportunities**: By outlining the challenges and potential in text mining, this chapter prepares readers for navigating the intricacies of the field.
4. **Preprocessing Profundity**: Emphasizing the role of preprocessing, the chapter delineates techniques like normalization and NER, offering insights into data enhancement.
5. **Feature Extraction Focus**: Through the elucidation of BoW, TF-IDF, and word embeddings, the chapter underscores the essence of feature extraction for meaningful text analysis.
6. **Supervised Learning Clarity**: With a focus on techniques like Naive Bayes, SVM, and decision trees, the chapter provides a clear path to understanding supervised text classification.
7. **Unveiling Unsupervised Techniques**: Exploration of the K-means, hierarchical clustering, and LDA techniques demystifies unsupervised text clustering and topic modeling.
8. **Sentiment and Opinion Discernment**: Specific attention to sentiment analysis, from lexicon-based methods to deep learning models, equips readers with tools to comprehend public sentiment.
9. **Advanced Applications:** Through real-world applications and advanced techniques like text summarization, text generation, and question-answering systems, readers gain insights into text mining's diverse applications.[5]
10. **Ethics and Future Prospects:** Ethical considerations, privacy concerns, and future trends are explored, shaping responsible and forward-looking text mining practices.

By encapsulating these contributions, this chapter empowers readers, be they researchers, practitioners, or students, with a robust toolkit for harnessing machine learning's capabilities in text mining. It's not merely a theoretical discourse but a pragmatic guide to extract valuable insights from textual data and pave the way for impactful decision-making.

16.2   PREPROCESSING AND TEXT REPRESENTATION

Text mining requires preprocessing and text representation, which include translating raw unstructured text input into a structured format suitable for analysis using machine-learning techniques.[3] These stages aid in the reduction of noise, the extraction of useful information, and the representation of textual data in a numerical format that can be fed into machine-learning models. Let's take a closer look at each of these steps:

16.2.1   DATA CLEANING AND NORMALIZATION

- Data cleaning involves removing any irrelevant characters, symbols, or special characters from the text data. It may also include converting all text to lowercase to ensure case-insensitive analysis.
- Normalization aims to standardize the text data by converting contractions to their full forms (e.g., "can't" to "cannot") and expanding abbreviations (e.g., "USA" to "United States of America"). This step helps in reducing lexical variations and improves the consistency of the data.[3]

16.2.2   TOKENIZATION AND STEMMING

- Tokenization is the process of dividing a text into smaller units called tokens, which can be individual words or even smaller units like n-grams (n-word sequences). Tokenization makes feature extraction and representation easier in subsequent steps.
- The process of reducing words to their base or root form by removing suffixes or prefixes is known as stemming. For example, stemming "running," "runs," and "run" yields the root word "run." This phase reduces the dimensionality of the data while increasing computational efficiency.

16.2.3   STOPWORD REMOVAL

- Stopwords are common words that appear frequently in the language (e.g., "the," "and," and "is") but rarely add significantly to the overall meaning of the text. Stopwords are removed to reduce noise and focus on more relevant words that provide crucial information.

16.2.4   FEATURE EXTRACTION METHODS FOR TEXT DATA

- **Bag-of-Words (BoW):** A popular text representation technique, BoW turns text into a numerical vector that represents the frequency of each word in the document. Each word is processed individually, and the resulting vector is known as a term frequency (TF) vector.
- **TF-IDF (Term Frequency-Inverse Document Frequency):** TF-IDF is a weighting technique that gives more weight to words that appear frequently

in a document but are uncommon throughout the corpus. It aids in highlighting key and distinguishing words in each manuscript.[5]

- Word embeddings are dense vector representations of words in a continuous vector space that capture semantic links between words. Word embeddings that have been pretrained, such as Word2Vec or GloVe, can be used to represent words in a more meaningful way.

16.2.5 HANDLING SPARSE DATA AND DIMENSIONALITY REDUCTION TECHNIQUES

- Because of the wide vocabulary, text data frequently yields sparse high-dimensional feature vectors. Dimensionality reduction techniques such as Singular Value Decomposition or Principal Component Analysis (PCA) can be used to minimize the feature space while keeping vital information to deal with this.[6]
- Furthermore, approaches such as feature selection or feature engineering can be used to focus on the most important traits while removing noisy or irrelevant ones.

Preprocessing and text representation help to turn raw text data into an organized and comprehensible manner, laying the groundwork for effective text mining. These transformed representations can then be fed into various machine-learning algorithms for tasks such as text classification, clustering, sentiment analysis, topic modeling, and more. Proper preprocessing and representation are essential for extracting accurate and useful insights from text data as well as increasing the overall performance of text mining models. Figure 16.2 depicts the activity diagram detailing the preprocessing procedures within the context of text mining.

16.3 SUPERVISED LEARNING FOR TEXT CLASSIFICATION

Supervised learning for text classification is a machine-learning approach where a model is trained on labeled text data to predict the category or class of new, unseen text instances.[5] It involves using a set of input features (representations of text data) and their corresponding labels (class labels) to train a classifier that can make predictions on new, unlabeled text instances. Text classification has numerous real-world applications, including spam detection, sentiment analysis, topic categorization, and document classification.

16.3.1 SUPERVISED LEARNING ALGORITHMS FOR TEXT CLASSIFICATION

1. Naive Bayes:
- Naive Bayes is a probabilistic classification technique that is based on the theorem of Bayes. Despite its simplicity, it has performed admirably in a variety of text classification tasks.

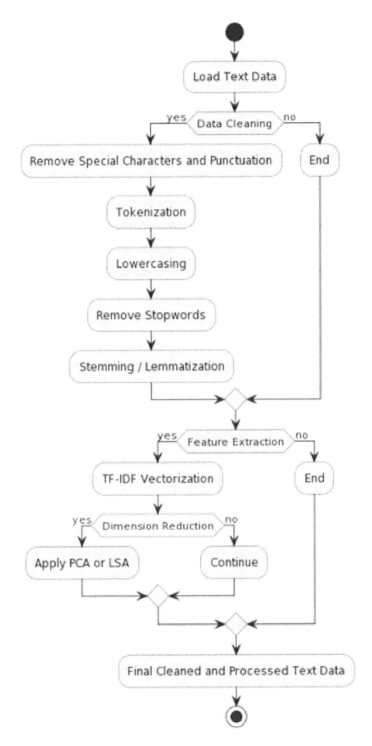

FIGURE 16.2 Preprocessing working.

- In the context of text categorization, Naive Bayes posits that the presence of one word in a document is unrelated to the presence of other words (thus the term "naive"). It computes the likelihood of a text belonging to a specific class based on the likelihood of individual words occurring in that class.
- Naive Bayes is a computationally efficient method that requires little training data. It is effective for high-dimensional feature spaces such as BoW representations.

2. Support Vector Machines (SVMs):

- SVMs are a strong and commonly used supervised learning technique for text classification. Its goal is to determine the ideal hyperplane in a high-dimensional space for separating data points of different classes.
- SVM attempts to discover the hyperplane in the feature space that optimizes the margin between data points of various classes in the context of text classification. It is useful for applications with complex decision boundaries and can efficiently handle high-dimensional feature vectors.
- SVM can handle noisy data and performs well with less training data. However, when dealing with very huge datasets, it may experience scaling challenges.

3. Decision Trees:

- Decision Trees are a non-parametric supervised learning approach that can be used for classification and regression applications. They partition the data recursively based on feature values to generate a tree-like structure that predicts the class labels of subsequent occurrences.
- Decision trees in text classification make binary judgments at each node based on the values of specific words or features, which results in the assignment of a class label at the tree's leaves.
- Decision Trees are easily interpretable and visualized, making them useful for understanding the decision-making process in text categorization problems. They are, nevertheless, prone to overfitting, particularly with deep trees and noisy data.

4. Neural Networks:

- Because of their ability to automatically learn complicated patterns from text input, neural networks, particularly deep learning models, have gained great interest in text categorization.
- For sequential data such as words or texts, RNNs and long short-term memory (LSTM) networks are appropriate. They are capable of capturing text's sequential dependencies, making them useful for sentiment analysis and language modeling.
- CNNs are frequently employed for text classification problems, particularly when dealing with fixed-length input like BoW representations. From text data, CNNs can learn local patterns and hierarchical representations.
- Transfer learning with pretrained language models such as BERT and GPT-3 has also demonstrated exceptional performance in text categorization tasks, exploiting knowledge obtained from large-scale pretraining.

Each supervised learning algorithm has its strengths and weaknesses when applied to text classification. The choice of algorithm depends on factors like the size of the dataset, the complexity of the task, the interpretability required, and the availability of computational resources. Proper evaluation and experimentation are crucial to selecting the most suitable algorithm for a specific text classification problem. Figure 16.3 presents the activity diagram delineating the operational flow of Supervised Learning for Text Classification within the domain of text mining.

16.3.2   FEATURE ENGINEERING FOR TEXT CLASSIFICATION TASKS

Text classification feature engineering is translating raw text data into meaningful and useful numerical representations (features) that may be utilized as input to machine-learning algorithms. By capturing essential information and patterns from text data, effective feature engineering plays a crucial role in increasing the performance of text classification models. Here are some examples of commonly used feature engineering techniques in text classification:

1. **Bag-of-Words (BoW):**
   - BoW is a common and simple text data representation approach. It entails generating a vocabulary of unique words (or tokens) found across the dataset. Each document is then represented numerically as a vector, with each entry representing the frequency of a certain term in the document.
   - BoW treats each word separately and disregards word order and context. While straightforward, it captures the incidence of various words in documents, making it appropriate for text categorization tasks such as sentiment analysis and spam detection.
2. **TF-IDF (Term Frequency-Inverse Document Frequency):**
   - The TF-IDF representation is a variant of the BoW representation that assigns a weight to each word in the document to indicate its relevance in the document relative to the overall dataset.
   - TF is a measure of the frequency of a term in a document, whereas Inverse Document Frequency (IDF) is a measure of the rarity of a word across all documents. The TF-IDF weight is the product of these two variables.
   - TF-IDF aids in the identification of words that are discriminative and informative for a given class because they are common in the document of interest but uncommon in other documents.
3. **Word Embeddings:**
   - Word embeddings are continuous vector space-dense vector representations of words. Word embeddings represent the semantic relationships between words, allowing algorithms to comprehend word similarity and context.
   - In text classification tasks, pretrained word embeddings such as Word2Vec, GloVe, and FastText are extensively employed. These embeddings are derived from big text corpora and can be applied to

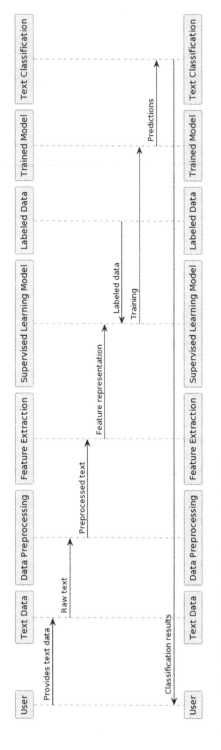

FIGURE 16.3 Supervised learning for text classification.

new text classification tasks to boost performance, particularly when training data is scarce.

4. Part-of-Speech (POS) Tagging:
- POS tagging entails marking each word in a document with the appropriate part of speech (e.g., noun, verb, adjective). POS tags can provide useful information about sentence grammaticality and can be employed as features in some text categorization tasks.

5. N-Grams:
- N-grams are contiguous sequences of N words taken from a single document. Using N-grams as features can assist capture local word order and context, giving the classifier extra information.
- Unigrams ($N = 1$) represent single words, but bigrams ($N = 2$) and trigrams ($N = 3$) represent two-word and three-word sequences, respectively.

6. Domain-Specific Features:
- Domain-specific traits can be important and informative in some text categorization tasks. In sentiment analysis of customer evaluations, for example, features such as the presence of emoticons, capitalization, or special characters may contain sentiment-related information.

7. Word Frequency and Document Length:
- As features, basic statistics such as word frequency and document length (the amount of words in a document) can be employed. These data may provide insight into the text's writing style or subject.

It is vital to note that the selection of feature engineering techniques is dependent on the individual properties of the text data as well as the classification task requirements. Feature engineering is an iterative process, and experimenting with various strategies might assist in identifying the most relevant features for a certain text classification task. Combining multiple feature engineering strategies can also result in increased model performance in complicated text classification tasks.

16.3.3 Case Studies and Real-World Examples of Text Classification Tasks

16.3.3.1 Case Study 1: Sentiment Analysis in Social Media

Objective: To perform sentiment analysis on social media data to understand the overall sentiment (positive, negative, or neutral) of tweets related to a specific product or brand.

Data: A large collection of tweets mentioning the product/brand, manually labeled as positive, negative, or neutral sentiment.

Approach:

1. **Data Preprocessing:** Clean the text data and remove URLs, special characters, and emojis. Tokenize the tweets and remove stopwords.
2. **Feature Engineering:** Convert the preprocessed tweets into numerical representations using TF-IDF or word embeddings.

3. **Model Selection:** Train numerous classifiers such as Naive Bayes, SVMs, and deep learning models such as LSTM or BERT.
4. **Model Evaluation:** To evaluate the performance of each model, use metrics such as accuracy, precision, recall, and F1 score.
5. **Prediction:** Deploy the best-performing model to predict sentiment for new tweets in real time.

Real-World Example: A company wants to gauge public sentiment about their latest product release. They use sentiment analysis to analyze thousands of tweets mentioning the product. The analysis reveals that overall sentiment is positive, but some negative feedback points to specific issues that need to be addressed for product improvement.

16.3.3.2 Case Study 2: Spam Detection in Emails

Objective: To build a classifier that can automatically identify spam emails and distinguish them from legitimate ones.

Data: A labeled dataset containing emails, marked as either spam or non-spam (ham).

Approach:

1. **Data Preprocessing:** Clean the emails, remove HTML tags, and normalize the text (e.g., convert to lowercase).
2. **Feature Engineering:** Convert the text into numerical representations using BoW or TF-IDF.
3. **Model Selection:** Train classifiers like Naive Bayes, SVMs, or Decision Trees.
4. **Model Evaluation:** Use metrics like accuracy, precision, recall, and F1 score to evaluate the model's performance on a separate test set.
5. **Prediction:** Deploy the best-performing model to automatically classify incoming emails as spam or ham.

Real-World Example: An email service provider wants to protect its users from spam emails. By employing a spam detection system using supervised learning, they can accurately filter spam emails and improve user experience and security.

16.4 UNSUPERVISED LEARNING FOR TEXT CLUSTERING

Unsupervised learning for text clustering is a machine-learning approach where the goal is to automatically group similar text documents into clusters without using any predefined class labels. Text clustering aims to discover hidden patterns and structures within the text data, allowing for effective organization and summarization of large document collections.[5]

Approach:

1. **Data Preprocessing:** Similar to supervised learning, the text data undergoes preprocessing steps like data cleaning, normalization, tokenization, stemming, and stopword removal.

2. **Text Representation:** The preprocessed text data is then converted into numerical representations using techniques like BoW, TF-IDF, or word embeddings. These representations capture the semantic meaning and context of words, making it possible to compute similarities between documents.

3. **Clustering Algorithms:** Various unsupervised clustering algorithms are used to group similar documents together. Some commonly used algorithms include K-means, Hierarchical Clustering, DBSCAN, and Mean Shift.

4. **Similarity Metrics:** To measure the similarity between documents, appropriate distance or similarity metrics like Cosine Similarity or Euclidean Distance are employed. These metrics help determine how close or dissimilar documents are in the feature space.

5. **Clustering Evaluation:** Unlike supervised learning, there are no predefined class labels for unsupervised text clustering. As a result, evaluation becomes more challenging. Internal clustering evaluation metrics, such as the Silhouette Score or the Davies–Bouldin Index, can be used to assess the quality of clustering results.

6. **Cluster Interpretation:** Once the clustering is performed, post-processing steps may be employed to interpret and label the clusters based on their content or characteristics. This step is important for understanding the topics or themes represented by each cluster.

Benefits:

1. Unsupervised text clustering is valuable in exploratory data analysis and knowledge discovery, especially when there is no prior knowledge of the document categories.

2. It helps in organizing large document collections, enabling more efficient information retrieval and content recommendation systems.

3. Unsupervised clustering can be used as a preprocessing step for supervised learning tasks, reducing the dimensionality and complexity of the text data.

Challenges:

1. Determining the optimal number of clusters (K) can be challenging, as there is no ground truth available for unsupervised text clustering tasks.

4. Text data can be high-dimensional and sparse, making it challenging to find meaningful clusters and handle noise.

5. The effectiveness of clustering heavily depends on the choice of text representation and clustering algorithm, which requires careful consideration.[5]

Unsupervised learning for text clustering is a valuable technique for discovering patterns and organizing large text corpora without the need for explicit class labels. Its applications span across various domains, including information retrieval, content analysis, and document organization. However, proper evaluation and interpretation of clusters are essential for deriving meaningful insights from unsupervised text clustering. Figure 16.4 delineates the operational mechanics underlying Unsupervised Learning for Text Clustering.

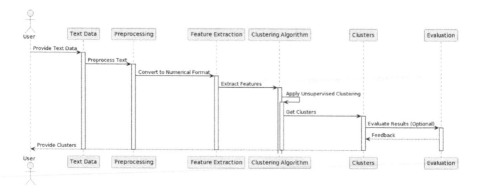

FIGURE 16.4 Unsupervised learning for text clustering.

16.4.1 Unsupervised Clustering Algorithms

1. K-means Clustering:
- K-means is a widely used partition-based clustering algorithm that aims to divide data points into K clusters.
- It starts by randomly initializing K cluster centroids in the feature space. Each data point is then assigned to the nearest centroid based on a distance metric (usually Euclidean distance).
- After the initial assignments, the centroids are updated to the mean of the data points within each cluster. The assignment and centroid update steps are repeated iteratively until convergence.
- K-means is simple, fast, and effective for spherical-shaped clusters. However, it requires specifying the number of clusters (K) beforehand, and its performance may degrade with non-linear or irregularly shaped clusters.

2. Hierarchical Clustering:
- Hierarchical clustering creates a hierarchy of clusters by iteratively merging or splitting clusters based on similarity.
- It can be performed in two ways: Agglomerative (bottom-up) and Divisive (top-down).
- Agglomerative starts with each data point as its own cluster and repeatedly merges the most similar clusters until a single cluster containing all data points is formed.
- Divisive starts with all data points in one cluster and repeatedly splits the least similar clusters until each data point is in its own cluster.
- Hierarchical clustering produces a dendrogram, which can be used to visualize the clustering hierarchy. The number of clusters is determined by cutting the dendrogram at an appropriate level.
- Hierarchical clustering is useful for understanding the hierarchical structure of data and is not sensitive to the number of clusters.

3. Density-Based Spatial Clustering of Applications with Noise (DBSCAN):
- DBSCAN is a density-based clustering algorithm that groups data points based on their density and identifies noise points as well.
- It defines two important parameters: Epsilon (ε) and MinPts. Epsilon determines the neighborhood radius around each data point, and MinPts sets the minimum number of points required to form a dense region (core point).
- A core point is a data point with at least MinPts neighbors within its ε-radius. Any data point within the ε-radius of a core point is considered part of the same cluster. Non-core points that are within the ε-radius of a core point are called border points and may belong to the same cluster or be considered noise.
- DBSCAN is robust to noise and can discover clusters of arbitrary shapes. It does not require specifying the number of clusters beforehand and is suitable for datasets with varying cluster densities.

Each of these unsupervised clustering algorithms has its strengths and weaknesses. The choice of algorithm depends on the specific characteristics of the data and the nature of the clusters to be discovered. Experimenting with different algorithms is essential to find the most suitable one for a particular clustering task.

16.4.2   FEATURE REPRESENTATION FOR CLUSTERING TASKS

Feature representation for clustering tasks involves transforming raw data into a suitable numerical format that captures the essential characteristics of the data for clustering.[6] Effective feature representation is crucial for achieving meaningful and accurate clustering results. Here are some common feature representation techniques for clustering tasks:

1. **Numeric Feature Representation:** For data with numerical attributes, no special preprocessing is required, and the features can be directly used as they are.
2. **One-Hot Encoding:** For categorical data, one-hot encoding is used to convert categorical variables into a binary representation. Each category is represented as a binary vector, where only one element is set to 1, indicating the presence of that category.
3. **Bag-of-Words (BoW):** BoW is a widely used representation for text data in clustering tasks. It converts text documents into numerical vectors representing the frequency of each word in the document. Each word is treated as a separate feature, and the resulting vector is called a term frequency vector.
4. **Term Frequency-Inverse Document Frequency (TF-IDF):** TF-IDF is an extension of BoW that assigns higher weights to words that are frequent in a document but rare across the entire corpus. It helps in highlighting important and discriminative words for each document.

5. **Word Embeddings:** Word embeddings are dense vector representations of words in a continuous vector space. They capture the semantic relationships between words, making them effective for text clustering tasks.

6. **Image Feature Extraction:** For image data, feature extraction techniques like Histogram of Oriented Gradients, Local Binary Patterns, or pretrained deep learning models (e.g., CNN features) can be used to obtain numerical representations of images.

7. **Vector Space Model (VSM):** VSM represents documents as vectors in a multi-dimensional space, where each dimension corresponds to a term in the document collection. The presence or absence of terms in each document determines the vector's value.

8. **Graph-Based Feature Representation:** For data with a graph structure (e.g., social networks), graph-based representations like node embeddings or graph kernels can be used to convert the graph data into numerical vectors suitable for clustering.

9. **Statistical Features:** Statistical measures like mean, standard deviation, or variance can be used to represent data points based on their attribute values.[5]

10. **Composite Features:** Combining multiple features or applying dimensionality reduction techniques like PCA or t-distributed Stochastic Neighbor Embedding (t-SNE) can be beneficial for capturing complex relationships and reducing the feature space's dimensionality.

The choice of feature representation depends on the nature of the data and the clustering task at hand. Proper feature engineering is essential for achieving accurate and meaningful clustering results and plays a critical role in the success of clustering algorithms.

16.4.3   Case Studies Illustrating Text Clustering Techniques

16.4.3.1   Case Study 1: News Article Clustering

Objective: Cluster a collection of news articles into distinct groups based on their topics and content.

Data: A dataset of news articles from various sources, such as newspapers, blogs, and online media. Each article contains the article text and its publication source.

Approach:

1. **Data Preprocessing:** Clean the text data by removing special characters, numbers, and stopwords. Tokenize the text into words and apply stemming or lemmatization to reduce words to their base form.

2. **Feature Representation:** Represent the preprocessed articles using TF-IDF or word embeddings to obtain numerical vectors for each article. TF-IDF captures the importance of words in each document relative to the entire corpus, while word embeddings represent words in a continuous vector space.

3. **Clustering Algorithm:** Apply K-means clustering algorithm to group similar articles together. Choose the optimal number of clusters (K) using techniques like the Elbow Method or Silhouette Score.
4. **Cluster Evaluation:** Evaluate the clustering results using internal evaluation metrics like Silhouette Score or external evaluation metrics like Adjusted Rand Index (ARI) if ground truth labels are available.
5. **Visualization:** Visualize the clustering results using dimensionality reduction techniques like t-SNE to plot the articles in a 2D space based on their numerical representations. Assign each article a color corresponding to its cluster label.

Real-World Application: This clustering technique can be used by news aggregator platforms to categorize and organize news articles into different topics, enabling users to access relevant news easily and efficiently.

16.4.3.2 Case Study 2: Customer Review Clustering

Objective: Group customer reviews of a product into distinct clusters based on the sentiment and topics expressed in the reviews.

Data: A dataset of customer reviews for a specific product, containing the review text and corresponding ratings (e.g., 1–5 stars).

Approach:

1. **Data Preprocessing:** Clean the review text by removing special characters, punctuation, and stopwords. Perform sentiment analysis to categorize reviews as positive, negative, or neutral based on their star ratings.
2. **Feature Representation:** Use TF-IDF or word embeddings to represent the preprocessed review text as numerical vectors. Additionally, consider adding sentiment scores as additional features.
3. **Clustering Algorithm:** Apply K-means or DBSCAN clustering algorithm to group reviews with similar sentiments and topics together. Experiment with different sentiment-based and content-based features.
4. **Cluster Evaluation:** Evaluate the clustering results using internal evaluation metrics like Silhouette Score or external evaluation metrics like ARI if ground truth sentiment labels are available.
5. **Interpretation:** Analyze the reviews within each cluster to understand the common sentiments and topics expressed by customers.

Real-World Application: Businesses can use this clustering technique to gain insights from customer feedback, identify common issues or strengths in their products, and make data-driven decisions for product improvements or marketing strategies.

These case studies demonstrate how text clustering techniques can be applied to real-world scenarios, such as organizing news articles into topics and understanding customer sentiments from reviews. Text clustering is a powerful tool for knowledge discovery, information retrieval, and customer insights in various industries.

16.5 SENTIMENT ANALYSIS AND OPINION MINING

16.5.1 SENTIMENT ANALYSIS AND ITS SIGNIFICANCE

Sentiment Analysis, also known as opinion mining, is an NLP technique that aims to identify and extract subjective information from text data, especially determining the sentiment or emotion expressed in the text. The goal of sentiment analysis is to classify the text as having positive, negative, neutral, or sometimes more nuanced sentiments like happiness, sadness, anger, etc.[1]

Approach:

1. **Data Preprocessing:** Clean the text data and remove irrelevant information, special characters, and punctuation. Tokenize the text into words and apply stemming or lemmatization to reduce words to their base form.
2. **Feature Representation:** Convert the preprocessed text into numerical representations using techniques like BoW, TF-IDF, or word embeddings. These representations capture the semantic meaning and context of words.
3. **Sentiment Classification:** Utilize supervised machine-learning algorithms, such as Naive Bayes, SVMs, or deep learning models like LSTM or BERT, to classify the sentiment of the text. These models are trained on labeled data with sentiment annotations.[3]
4. **Sentiment Analysis Output:** The output of sentiment analysis is the classification of the text into positive, negative, or neutral sentiments.

Applications:

1. **Business and Product Reviews:** Sentiment analysis is used to analyze customer reviews and feedback to understand the overall sentiment toward products or services.
2. **Social Media Monitoring:** Companies monitor social media platforms to gauge public sentiment toward their brand or marketing campaigns.
3. **Market Research:** Sentiment analysis helps businesses in market research to identify trends, customer preferences, and brand perceptions.
4. **Customer Support:** Sentiment analysis can be applied to customer support interactions to gauge customer satisfaction and detect potential issues.[5]

Significance:

1. **Customer Insights:** In business, sentiment analysis is crucial for understanding customer sentiment toward products, services, and brands. It helps companies gauge customer satisfaction, identify areas for improvement, and make data-driven decisions for marketing and product development.
2. **Brand Reputation Management:** Sentiment analysis aids in monitoring and managing brand reputation on social media and other platforms. Companies can address negative sentiment and respond to customer feedback promptly.

3. **Market Research:** Sentiment analysis is used in market research to analyze public opinions on products, competitors, and market trends. It provides valuable insights for businesses to develop competitive strategies.
4. **Social Media Analysis:** Sentiment analysis is extensively used in social media monitoring to understand public sentiment toward specific topics, events, or public figures. It helps in gauging public reactions and predicting trends.
5. **Customer Service and Support:** Sentiment analysis is employed in customer service and support interactions to assess customer satisfaction levels and identify potential issues or dissatisfied customers.
6. **Political Analysis:** In political contexts, sentiment analysis is used to analyze public sentiment toward political figures, policies, and events. It can provide insights into public opinion during election campaigns.
7. **Product Reviews:** Sentiment analysis assists in analyzing and summarizing product reviews and feedback to identify recurring themes and sentiments among customers.

Overall, sentiment analysis is a powerful tool for understanding human emotions and opinions from vast amounts of text data. Its significance extends across various domains, helping businesses, researchers, and organizations make informed decisions, enhance customer experiences, and improve overall communication strategies.[4] Illustrated in Figure 16.5 is the procedural representation of the operational workflow within the domain of sentiment analysis.

16.5.2 Supervised and Unsupervised Approaches to Sentiment Analysis

1. **Supervised Sentiment Analysis:** Supervised sentiment analysis is a machine-learning approach where the sentiment analysis model is trained on a labeled dataset that contains text samples along with their corresponding sentiment labels (positive, negative, neutral, etc.). The model learns from this labeled data to make predictions on new, unseen text data.
   - **Approach:**
     - **Data Preparation:** The labeled dataset is prepared with text samples and sentiment labels. Text data undergoes preprocessing, including cleaning, tokenization, and normalization.
     - **Feature Representation:** The preprocessed text is converted into numerical representations using techniques like BoW, TF-IDF, or word embeddings.[1]
     - **Model Training:** Supervised learning algorithms like Naive Bayes, SVMs, Logistic Regression, or deep learning models like LSTM or BERT are trained on the labeled data to learn the relationships between the textual features and sentiment labels.
     - **Model Evaluation:** The trained model is evaluated on a separate test dataset to measure its performance using metrics like accuracy, precision, recall, F1 score, etc.
     - **Prediction:** Once the model is trained and evaluated, it can be used to predict the sentiment of new, unseen text data.

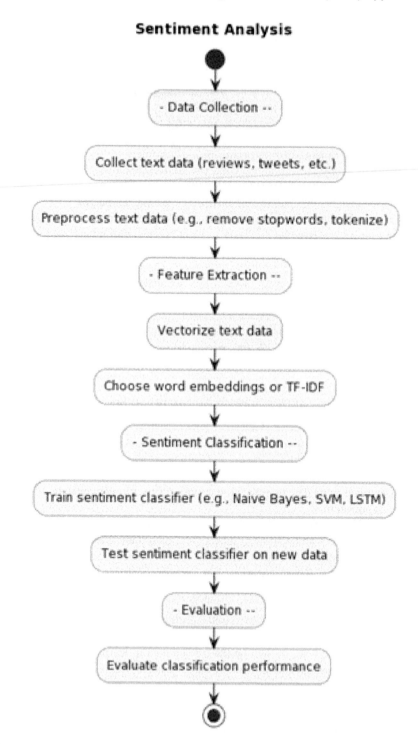

FIGURE 16.5   Sentiment analysis working.

- **Pros:**
  - Supervised learning provides accurate sentiment predictions when trained on sufficient and representative labeled data.
  - It can handle complex relationships between features and sentiment labels.
- **Cons:**
  - Requires a large amount of labeled data for training.
  - Performance may suffer if the training data is biased or does not fully represent the distribution of sentiments in real-world data.

2. **Unsupervised Sentiment Analysis:** Unsupervised sentiment analysis is an approach where the sentiment analysis model is not provided with labeled data during training. Instead, it aims to identify patterns and structures in the data without predefined sentiment labels

- **Approach:**
  - **Data Preparation:** Text data undergoes preprocessing, including cleaning, tokenization, and normalization.
  - **Feature Representation:** The preprocessed text is converted into numerical representations using techniques like BoW, TF-IDF, or word embeddings.
  - **Clustering:** Unsupervised clustering algorithms like K-means, Hierarchical Clustering, or DBSCAN are applied to group similar text samples together based on their numerical representations.
  - **Sentiment Assignment:** Sentiments are assigned to the clusters based on the predominant sentiment of the text samples within each cluster. For example, if most samples in a cluster are positive, that cluster is assigned a positive sentiment.
  - **Evaluation (Optional):** Since unsupervised sentiment analysis doesn't have labeled data for evaluation, the quality of the clusters can be assessed using internal clustering evaluation metrics.
- **Pros:**
  - Unsupervised approaches can be applied when labeled data is scarce or unavailable.
  - It can discover hidden patterns and structures in the data without relying on predefined sentiment labels.
- **Cons:**
  - The sentiment assignments may not always match human judgment or predefined sentiment labels.
  - It can be challenging to interpret and validate the accuracy of the results in the absence of labeled data.

Hybrid Approaches: Some sentiment analysis systems combine both supervised and unsupervised techniques. For example, an unsupervised approach might be used to cluster data into groups representing different sentiments, and then a smaller labeled dataset might be used to train a supervised model on each cluster to fine-tune sentiment predictions.

Overall, the choice between supervised and unsupervised approaches depends on the availability of labeled data, the nature of the sentiment analysis task, and the desired accuracy and interpretability of the results.

16.5.3 APPLICATIONS OF SENTIMENT ANALYSIS IN SOCIAL MEDIA

1. **Brand Monitoring:** Companies use sentiment analysis to monitor mentions of their brand on social media platforms. It helps them gauge public sentiment and identify potential issues or negative feedback that require prompt responses.
2. **Social Listening:** Sentiment analysis allows businesses to listen to what customers are saying about their products, services, or marketing campaigns. It provides insights into customer preferences and expectations.
3. **Reputation Management:** Brands use sentiment analysis to manage their online reputation. It helps in identifying and addressing negative sentiment and managing public perception.
4. **Campaign Evaluation:** Sentiment analysis is employed to evaluate the success of marketing campaigns or product launches. Positive sentiment indicates a well-received campaign, while negative sentiment indicates areas for improvement.
5. **Customer Support:** Sentiment analysis assists in customer support interactions on social media. It helps prioritize and address customer issues based on sentiment.
6. **Influencer Marketing:** Brands use sentiment analysis to assess the sentiment of influencer content and its impact on the brand's reputation.

Applications of Sentiment Analysis in Customer Feedback:

1. **Product and Service Improvements:** Sentiment analysis of customer feedback helps companies identify specific product features or service aspects that need improvement based on customer sentiments.
2. **Customer Satisfaction Measurement:** Sentiment analysis allows businesses to measure overall customer satisfaction by analyzing sentiments in feedback.[5]
3. **Competitor Analysis:** Sentiment analysis helps compare customer sentiments toward competitors' products and services, providing insights for competitive strategy.
4. **Market Research:** Sentiment analysis is used in market research to gather consumer opinions and preferences, helping businesses develop targeted marketing strategies.[5]
5. **Review Aggregation:** Sentiment analysis is used in review aggregators to classify reviews as positive, negative, or neutral, providing a summary of overall customer sentiments.
6. **Feedback Trend Analysis:** Sentiment analysis assists in analyzing trends in customer feedback over time, identifying changing sentiments or emerging issues.

Overall, sentiment analysis plays a significant role in understanding customer sentiments, preferences, and opinions. It provides businesses with valuable insights for making informed decisions, enhancing customer experiences, and improving products and services based on customer feedback.

16.6 NER AND ENTITY LINKING

16.6.1 Introduction to NER

NER is an NLP task that involves identifying and classifying named entities in a text into predefined categories such as person names, organization names, location names, date expressions, numerical quantities, and more.[1] Named entities are specific words or phrases that refer to unique entities in the real world, such as names of people, places, companies, products, and dates.[1]

Objective:
The main goal of NER is to automatically recognize and classify these named entities in a given text, extracting valuable information and structuring unstructured text data into a more structured format.

Approach:

1. **Data Preprocessing:** The text data is cleaned and tokenized into individual words or phrases.
2. **Linguistic Features:** NER systems often use linguistic features, such as POS tagging, to identify named entities. Certain POS patterns are indicative of named entities, like proper nouns.
3. **Machine-learning Models:** NER is often approached as a supervised learning problem, where machine-learning models are trained on annotated text data that includes the labeled named entities. Popular machine-learning algorithms like conditional random fields (CRFs), SVMs, or deep learning models like bidirectional long short-term memory (BiLSTM) networks are commonly used.[2]
4. **Named Entity Classification:** During training, the model learns to classify each word or phrase in the text into predefined categories, such as "Person," "Organization," "Location," etc.
5. **Named Entity Extraction:** Once the model is trained, it can be used to process new, unseen text data and identify and extract named entities present in the text.

Significance:
- NER has various practical applications across different domains:
  - **Information Extraction:** NER is used to extract valuable information from unstructured text, helping in knowledge discovery and information retrieval.
  - **Search Engines:** NER improves the accuracy of search engines by identifying and recognizing entities mentioned in search queries or web pages.

- **Question Answering:** NER aids in identifying relevant entities in the context of a question, enabling better responses in question-answering systems.
- **Chatbots and Virtual Assistants:** NER helps chatbots and virtual assistants understand user queries and provide more accurate and contextually relevant responses.
- **Document Categorization:** NER assists in categorizing documents based on the named entities mentioned, aiding in content organization.
- **Information Retrieval:** NER enhances the precision and recall of information retrieval systems by indexing and linking named entities.

Overall, NER is a fundamental NLP task that plays a crucial role in various downstream applications, improving the understanding and processing of text data by identifying and classifying specific entities of interest. Depicted in Figure 16.6 is the sequential process illustrating the operational flow of NER functioning.

16.6.2 NER TECHNIQUES: RULE-BASED AND MACHINE-LEARNING METHODS

1. **Rule-Based NER Techniques:** Rule-based NER techniques rely on predefined rules or patterns to identify and classify named entities in text data. These rules are usually created manually by domain experts or linguists based on linguistic patterns and characteristics of named entities.[1] Rule-based approaches are straightforward to implement and can be useful when dealing with specific types of entities or domains where labeled training data may be limited.
   - **Approach:**
     - **Rule Definition:** Linguists or domain experts define rules based on patterns, regular expressions, or syntactic structures that are indicative of named entities. For example, patterns like capitalization, specific POS tags, or word sequences can be used to identify person names, locations, or organizations.
     - **Tokenization:** The text data is tokenized into individual words or phrases.
     - **Rule Application:** The defined rules are applied to the tokenized text to identify and classify named entities based on the specified patterns.
     - **Entity Categorization:** The recognized named entities are categorized into predefined entity types, such as "Person," "Organization," "Location," etc.
   - **Pros:**
     - Rule-based NER is interpretable and allows experts to fine-tune the system easily.
     - It can work well in specific domains or with limited training data.

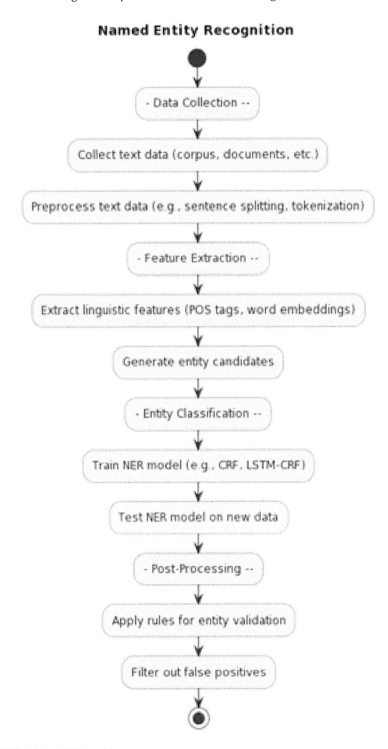

FIGURE 16.6 NER working.

- **Cons:**
    - Creating accurate and comprehensive rules can be labor intensive and time-consuming.
    - Rule-based approaches may struggle with handling complex or ambiguous cases.

2. **Machine-learning-Based NER Techniques:** Machine-learning-based NER techniques use supervised or unsupervised learning methods to automatically learn patterns and features from labeled training data. These methods have become more popular due to their ability to handle complex linguistic patterns and generalize well across different domains.

   - **Approach:**
       - **Data Preparation:** A labeled dataset is prepared, where the text data is annotated with entity labels (e.g., "Person," "Organization," "Location," etc.).
       - **Feature Extraction:** Features are extracted from the text data, such as word embeddings, POS tags, contextual information, etc., to represent the words in a numerical format suitable for machine-learning algorithms.
       - **Model Training:** Supervised machine-learning algorithms, like CRF, SVMs, or deep learning models like BiLSTM networks, are trained on the labeled data to learn the relationship between the features and entity labels.
       - **Model Evaluation:** The trained model is evaluated on a separate test dataset to measure its performance using metrics like precision, recall, F1 score, etc.
       - **Prediction:** Once the model is trained and evaluated, it can be used to predict named entities in new, unseen text data.
   - **Pros:**
       - Machine-learning-based NER can automatically learn complex patterns and generalize to different contexts and domains.
       - It can handle large amounts of data and adapt to new data.
   - **Cons:**
       - Requires a significant amount of labeled data for training.
       - Model complexity and training time may be higher compared to rule-based methods.

Hybrid Approaches:

In practice, hybrid approaches that combine both rule-based and machine-learning techniques are often used. Rule-based methods can be used for specific entity types or known patterns, while machine-learning models can be applied to handle more ambiguous cases or new entity types. Such hybrid approaches leverage the strengths of both techniques to improve NER performance.

In conclusion, NER is a crucial task in NLP, enabling the extraction of valuable information from text data. Both rule-based and machine-learning-based techniques have their advantages and applications, and the choice between them depends on the specific requirements and characteristics of the NER task at hand.

16.6.3   REAL-WORLD APPLICATIONS OF NER

1. **Information Extraction:** NER is widely used in information extraction tasks to identify and extract specific pieces of information from unstructured text. It helps in extracting names of people, organizations, locations, dates, and more, making it easier to organize and analyze textual data.
2. **Search Engines:** NER enhances search engine capabilities by recognizing and categorizing named entities in search queries and web documents. It improves search result relevance and provides more accurate answers to user queries.
3. **Social Media Monitoring:** NER is used in social media monitoring tools to identify and track mentions of specific entities, products, or brands. This enables businesses to gain insights into social media conversations and public sentiments.
4. **Customer Support:** NER assists in automating customer support interactions by identifying entities mentioned in customer queries, allowing for more personalized and efficient responses.
5. **Chatbots and Virtual Assistants:** NER is employed in chatbots and virtual assistants to understand and respond to user queries more accurately and contextually.
6. **Question–Answering Systems:** NER plays a vital role in question–answering systems by identifying entities relevant to user questions and providing targeted responses.
7. **Document Categorization:** NER helps categorize documents based on named entities mentioned in the text, enabling content organization and retrieval.
8. **Biomedical and Clinical Text Mining:** In the medical domain, NER is used to identify and extract biomedical entities, such as genes, proteins, diseases, and drugs, from research papers and clinical notes.

Real-World Applications of Entity Linking:

1. **Knowledge Base Population:** Entity linking is crucial for knowledge base population, where mentions of entities in unstructured text are linked to their corresponding entries in a structured knowledge base, such as Wikipedia or DBpedia.
2. **Cross-Document Coreference:** Entity linking is used to resolve cross-document coreference, where mentions of the same entity in different documents are linked together.
3. **Question Answering Systems:** In question answering systems, entity linking is employed to link named entities mentioned in the question to their corresponding knowledge base entries, which improves the accuracy of the system's responses.
4. **News Analysis and Event Tracking:** Entity linking aids in analyzing news articles and tracking events by linking mentions of entities to their

representations in a knowledge base. It helps in understanding the relationships between entities and events.

5. **Semantic Web and Linked Data:** Entity linking plays a vital role in the Semantic Web and Linked Data initiatives, where unstructured textual data is linked to structured data on the web, creating a network of interconnected information.

6. **Information Retrieval:** Entity linking helps in improving information retrieval systems by linking mentions of entities in documents to relevant knowledge base entries.

7. **Data Integration:** In data integration tasks, entity linking is used to integrate data from different sources by linking mentions of entities to a unified representation.

8. **Machine Reading Comprehension:** Entity linking is utilized in machine reading comprehension tasks to link entities in a passage to their corresponding knowledge base entries.

Overall, NER and Entity Linking are powerful NLP techniques with various real-world applications across diverse domains. They contribute to improving information retrieval, knowledge extraction, and understanding in the era of big data and unstructured text.

16.7   DEEP LEARNING FOR TEXT MINING

16.7.1   INTRODUCTION TO DEEP LEARNING FOR NLP

Deep Learning is a form of machine learning that employs multiple-layer neural networks to learn and represent complicated patterns in data. Deep learning has demonstrated exceptional effectiveness in a variety of text mining applications, including NLP, sentiment analysis, text classification, machine translation, text generation, and others.[2] Deep learning is powerful because it can automatically build hierarchical representations of text data, incorporating both local and global semantic links. In Figure 16.7, the operational mechanism of employing Deep Learning for the purpose of Text Mining is visually elucidated.[6]

Deep Learning Architectures for Text Mining:

1. **Recurrent Neural Networks (RNNs):** RNNs are widely used for sequential data processing, making them suitable for handling text sequences. They have a feedback mechanism that allows them to maintain a hidden state and consider the context from previous words while processing each word in a text. However, RNNs suffer from the vanishing gradient problem, limiting their ability to capture long-range dependencies in texts.

2. **Long Short-Term Memory (LSTM):** LSTMs are a type of RNN that addresses the vanishing gradient problem. They introduce memory cells that allow information to be stored and retrieved over long periods, making them better at handling long sequences and capturing long-term dependencies in text.[5]

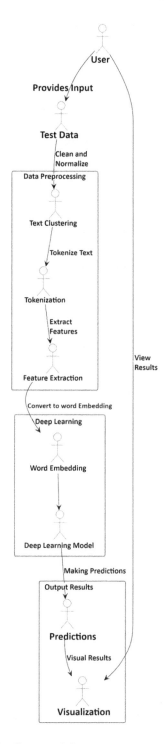

FIGURE 16.7   Deep learning for text mining.

3. **Gated Recurrent Units (GRUs):** GRUs are another variant of RNNs designed to address the vanishing gradient problem. They have fewer parameters than LSTMs and are computationally more efficient, making them popular choices for text-processing tasks.

4. **Convolutional Neural Networks (CNNs):** Originally developed for image processing, CNNs have been successfully applied to text mining tasks, particularly for text classification. They use convolutional layers to capture local patterns in text, such as n-grams, and pooling layers to aggregate information globally.

5. **Transformer-based Models:** Transformers have revolutionized NLP and text mining tasks. They use self-attention mechanisms to process entire sequences of words simultaneously, capturing long-range dependencies effectively. The Transformer architecture is the basis for state-of-the-art models like BERT, GPT-3, and RoBERT.

Benefits of Deep Learning for Text Mining:

1. **Automatic Feature Learning:** Deep learning models can automatically learn useful representations and features from raw text data, reducing the need for manual feature engineering.

2. **Semantic Understanding:** Deep learning models excel at capturing complex semantic relationships between words and sentences, enabling them to understand the context and meaning in texts.

3. **Transfer Learning:** Pretrained language models like BERT and GPT-3 can be fine-tuned on specific text mining tasks, leveraging their knowledge from a large corpus to improve performance on domain-specific data.

4. **Handling Sequence Data:** Deep learning models like RNNs and Transformers are well-suited for processing sequential data like text, where the order of words is essential.

Challenges:

1. **Data Requirements:** Deep learning models require large amounts of labeled data for training, which may be challenging to obtain for certain specialized domains.[2]

2. **Computational Resources:** Training deep learning models can be computationally intensive and may require significant computational resources and time.

3. **Interpretability:** Deep learning models are often complex and lack interpretability, making it difficult to understand the exact reasoning behind their predictions.

Despite these challenges, deep learning has demonstrated remarkable advancements in text mining and continues to be a driving force in NLP research and applications. With ongoing research and development, deep learning models are likely to play an increasingly vital role in understanding and processing text data for various real-world applications.

16.7.2 CASE STUDIES SHOWCASING THE EFFECTIVENESS OF DEEP LEARNING IN TEXT MINING TASKS

16.7.2.1 Case Study 1: Text Classification using CNN and LSTM

Objective: Classify news articles into predefined topics using deep learning models.

Data: A dataset of news articles with corresponding topic labels (e.g., Sports, Politics, Technology, etc.).

Approach:

1. **Data Preprocessing:** Clean the text data by removing stopwords and special characters, and perform tokenization.
2. **Word Embeddings:** Convert the preprocessed text into word embeddings using techniques like Word2Vec or GloVe, representing each word as a dense numerical vector.
3. **Model Architecture:** Utilize a combination of CNN and LSTM layers to capture both local and global features in the text data. The CNN layers identify local patterns (e.g., n-grams), while LSTM layers process the sequential information.
4. **Model Training:** Train the deep learning model on the labeled dataset using cross-entropy loss and backpropagation. Fine-tune the model on the training data to optimize the classification performance.
5. **Evaluation:** Evaluate the model on a separate test dataset using metrics like accuracy, precision, recall, and F1 score.

Results: The deep learning model achieves high accuracy in classifying news articles into their respective topics. The combination of CNN and LSTM allows the model to effectively capture relevant features and patterns in the text, leading to improved performance compared to traditional machine-learning methods.

16.7.2.2 Case Study 2: Sentiment Analysis with BERT

Objective: Perform sentiment analysis on customer reviews to determine the sentiment (positive, negative, or neutral) expressed in the text.

Data: A dataset of customer reviews with corresponding sentiment labels.

Approach:

1. **Data Preprocessing:** Clean the text data by removing noise, special characters, and stopwords.
2. **BERT Embeddings:** Use pretrained BERT (Bidirectional Encoder Representations from Transformers) to convert the text data into contextualized word embeddings.
3. **Fine-tuning BERT:** Fine-tune the pretrained BERT model on the sentiment analysis task using the labeled dataset. Update the model's weights to adapt to the specific sentiment classification task.
4. **Model Training:** Train the fine-tuned BERT model on the labeled dataset, using categorical cross-entropy loss and gradient descent optimization.
5. **Evaluation:** Evaluate the BERT-based sentiment analysis model on a separate test dataset using metrics like accuracy, precision, recall, and F1 score.

Results: The fine-tuned BERT model demonstrates superior performance compared to traditional sentiment analysis models. BERT's contextual embeddings capture nuances in the text, leading to more accurate sentiment predictions and better generalization across different domains.

Conclusion: These case studies demonstrate the effectiveness of deep learning in text-mining tasks. By leveraging deep learning models like CNN, LSTM, and BERT, text classification and sentiment analysis tasks can achieve higher accuracy and better generalization compared to traditional machine-learning methods. Deep learning has revolutionized text mining and NLP, allowing for a more sophisticated and context-aware understanding of textual data, enabling a wide range of applications in various domains.

16.8   CHALLENGES AND ETHICAL CONSIDERATIONS

16.8.1   CHALLENGES IN DEEP LEARNING FOR TEXT MINING

1. **Data Quality and Quantity:** Deep learning models require large amounts of labeled training data to achieve optimal performance. Obtaining high-quality labeled data can be challenging, especially for specialized domains where expert annotations are necessary.[2]
2. **Overfitting:** Deep learning models are prone to overfitting, where they memorize the training data and perform poorly on unseen data. Regularization techniques and data augmentation are used to address this issue.
3. **Interpretability:** Deep learning models are often considered black boxes, making it challenging to interpret their decisions and understand the reasoning behind their predictions. This lack of interpretability can be a significant concern in critical applications.
4. **Computation and Resources:** Training deep learning models, especially large-scale ones like Transformers, can be computationally intensive and require significant computational resources and time.
5. **Hyperparameter Tuning:** Deep learning models have many hyperparameters, and finding the optimal combination can be time-consuming and requires expertise.
6. **Domain Adaptation:** Deep learning models may not perform well when applied to different domains or when the distribution of the test data differs significantly from the training data.

16.8.2   ETHICAL CONSIDERATIONS IN DEEP LEARNING FOR TEXT MINING

1. **Bias and Fairness:** Deep learning models can inherit biases present in the training data, leading to biased predictions. This can perpetuate societal biases and lead to unfair treatment or discrimination.[1]
2. **Privacy:** Deep learning models trained on sensitive text data, such as personal conversations or medical records, can raise privacy concerns. Proper data anonymization and data access controls are essential to protect user privacy.

3. **Misinformation and Fake News:** Deep learning models can be used to generate fake text, leading to the spread of misinformation and fake news. Ethical considerations involve ensuring the responsible use of text generation capabilities and implementing fact-checking mechanisms.

4. **Regulatory Compliance:** Deep learning models used in text mining must adhere to legal and regulatory requirements regarding data privacy, security, and fair use.

5. **Data Ownership and Consent:** The use of text data for training deep learning models should comply with data ownership rights, and consent should be obtained from users whose data is used.

6. **Safety and Security:** In certain applications, like chatbots or virtual assistants, deep learning models should be designed to avoid harmful behavior or providing harmful information.[5]

7. **Transparency and Accountability:** Organizations using deep learning models in text mining should be transparent about their model's capabilities, limitations, and potential biases. They should also be accountable for the outcomes of their applications.

8. **Social Impact:** Deep learning models deployed in text mining can have significant societal impacts, both positive and negative. Ethical considerations should ensure that these impacts are carefully assessed and managed.

Addressing these challenges and ethical considerations requires a comprehensive and multidisciplinary approach, involving collaboration between data scientists, domain experts, ethicists, and policymakers. Responsible development and deployment of deep learning models for text mining are crucial to ensure the technology benefits society while minimizing potential risks and harms.

16.9 EMERGING TRENDS AND FUTURE DIRECTIONS IN MACHINE LEARNING FOR TEXT MINING

Machine learning for text mining has seen rapid advancements in recent years, driven by the growing availability of large text datasets, improved deep learning architectures, and innovative research.[1] Several emerging trends and future directions are shaping the field of text mining and its applications:

1. **Transfer Learning and Pretrained Models:** Transfer learning has become a game-changer in text mining. Pretrained language models like BERT, GPT-3, and RoBERTa have shown impressive results by learning rich contextual representations from vast amounts of data. Fine-tuning these models on domain-specific tasks has become a popular approach to leverage their capabilities for downstream applications.

2. **Multimodal Learning:** The integration of text with other modalities, such as images, audio, or videos, is gaining traction. Multimodal learning enables machines to understand and analyze the context of text in a more comprehensive manner, opening up new possibilities for tasks like visual question answering, speech recognition with text comprehension, and more.

3. **Explainable AI for Text Mining:** The interpretability of deep learning models is a significant concern. Advancements in explainable AI techniques aim to make deep learning models more interpretable, allowing users to understand the reasoning behind model predictions. This is particularly crucial in critical applications and compliance with regulatory requirements.

4. **Low-resource and Few-shot Learning:** Research is focusing on developing machine-learning models that can perform well with limited labeled data, known as low-resource learning. Few-shot learning techniques aim to train models with minimal labeled data, making them more adaptable to new tasks with limited samples.

5. **Domain Adaptation and Transfer Learning:** Improving model performance on target domains with limited labeled data is an active area of research. Techniques like domain adaptation and transfer learning aim to bridge the gap between different domains and leverage knowledge learned from one domain to benefit another.

6. **Bias Mitigation and Fairness:** Addressing bias in text mining is critical to ensure fair and unbiased decision-making. Researchers are working on techniques to mitigate bias and promote fairness in text-mining applications, particularly when making predictions that may impact individuals or groups.

7. **Multilingual and Cross-lingual Text Mining:** With the increasing globalization of information, there is a growing demand for text mining techniques that can handle multiple languages and cross-lingual data. Multilingual pre-trained models and cross-lingual transfer learning are becoming essential components of text mining pipelines.

8. **Continual Learning and Lifelong Learning:** Traditional machine-learning models often forget previously learned knowledge when trained on new data. Continual learning and lifelong learning aim to develop models that can learn from new data while retaining knowledge from previous tasks, enabling more efficient and adaptable systems.

9. **Real-time and Online Learning:** Text mining applications that require real-time processing, such as social media monitoring or chatbots, demand models that can learn and update incrementally. Online learning approaches are being explored to enable models to adapt to changing data streams.[2]

10. **Unsupervised and Self-supervised Learning:** Reducing the dependency on labeled data is an ongoing challenge. Unsupervised and self-supervised learning methods seek to leverage the abundance of unlabeled data to improve model performance, making text mining more scalable and accessible.

11. **Privacy-Preserving Techniques:** Protecting user privacy and sensitive information in text mining is gaining significant attention. Research is focusing on privacy-preserving techniques like differential privacy and federated learning to safeguard individual data while still enabling meaningful insights.

12. **Reinforcement Learning for Text Mining:** Reinforcement learning, which involves training models to interact with an environment and learn from feedback, is finding applications in text generation and dialogue systems. It holds promise for developing more natural and interactive text-based interfaces.

The future of machine learning for text mining is exciting, with continuous advancements unlocking new possibilities and applications. As the field progresses, ethical considerations, responsible AI development, and societal impacts will remain essential components of shaping the direction of text mining research and its transformative applications.[5]

16.10   CONCLUSION

In this chapter, we have explored the dynamic and transformative field of "Machine Learning Techniques for Effective Text Mining." Text mining, powered by machine learning and deep learning, has emerged as a powerful tool to extract valuable insights from unstructured text data, enabling us to make informed decisions and understand human language in novel ways.

We began by delving into the definition and scope of text mining, understanding its importance in processing vast amounts of textual data and extracting meaningful information from it. We discussed how text mining is employed in various real-world applications, including sentiment analysis, NER, text classification, clustering, and more.

Supervised learning algorithms, such as Naive Bayes, SVMs, Decision Trees, and Neural Networks, showcased their effectiveness in text classification tasks. We explored the process of preprocessing and text representation, laying the foundation for building accurate and robust text classification models.

The chapter then shifted its focus to unsupervised learning techniques, where algorithms like K-means, Hierarchical Clustering, and DBSCAN have been instrumental in discovering patterns and structures in unlabeled text data through text clustering.

Deep learning stole the spotlight as we delved into its application in text mining. RNNs, LSTM, and the revolutionary Transformers have redefined NLP and pushed the boundaries of text understanding and generation.

Real-world case studies illustrated the effectiveness of machine-learning techniques in solving practical text mining challenges, showcasing their significance in diverse domains, including social media monitoring, customer feedback analysis, sentiment analysis in news articles, and more.

However, we also acknowledged the challenges and ethical considerations in text mining. Data quality, interpretability, bias, and privacy emerged as key concerns that demand careful attention and responsible AI development.

As we look to the future, emerging trends in transfer learning, multimodal learning, and low-resource learning promise to shape the landscape of text mining, opening up new possibilities and applications. Ethical considerations, transparency, and accountability will remain paramount in driving the responsible advancement of text mining technologies.

In conclusion, the fusion of machine learning and text mining has paved the way for unprecedented opportunities in understanding and utilizing textual data. As this field continues to evolve, researchers, practitioners, and policymakers must collaborate to ensure the ethical and responsible development of text mining techniques, harnessing the potential of machine learning to empower us with insights and knowledge from the vast realm of human language. The journey of text mining is one of continuous exploration, discovery, and innovation, and its impact on society is set to grow in profound ways in the years to come.

REFERENCES

[1] Cohen, Aaron M., and William R. Hersh. "A survey of current work in biomedical text mining." *Briefings in Bioinformatics* 6, no. 1 (2005): 57–71.

[2] Doğan, Emre, K. Buket, and Ahmet Müngen. "Generation of original text with text mining and deep learning methods for Turkish and other languages." In: *2018 International Conference on Artificial Intelligence and Data Processing (IDAP)*, pp. 1–9. IEEE, 2018.

[3] Lewis, David D., Yiming Yang, Tony Russell-Rose, and Fan Li. "Rcv1: A new benchmark collection for text categorization research." *Journal of Machine Learning Research* 5, no. (2004): 361–397.

[4] Albert, Noel, and Matthew Thomson. "A synthesis of the consumer-brand relationship domain: using text mining to track research streams, describe their emotional associations, and identify future research priorities." *Journal of the Association for Consumer Research* 3, no. 2 (2018): 130–146.

[5] Jin, Gang. "Application optimization of NLP system under deep learning technology in text semantics and text classification." In: *2022 International Conference on Education, Network and Information Technology (ICENIT)*, pp. 279–283. IEEE, 2022.

[6] Zhao, Bei, and Wei Gao. "Machine learning based text classification technology." In: *2022 IEEE 2nd International Conference on Mobile Networks and Wireless Communications (ICMNWC)*, pp. 1–5. IEEE, 2022.

17 Emails Classification and Anomaly Detection using Natural Language Processing

Tanvi Mehta, Renu Kachhoria,
Swati Jaiswal, Sunil Kale, Rajeswari Kannan,
and Rupali Atul Mahajan

17.1 INTRODUCTION

The Enron Corporation, an American energy business with headquarters in Houston, Texas, and amongst the five largest accountancy and audit firms in the world, filed for bankruptcy as a result of the Enron controversy, which became public in 2001 [1]. Enron was noted as the worst audit failure at the time in addition to being the biggest bankruptcy reorganization in American history. The majority of its clients had left, and the business had eventually stopped functioning [2]. Despite suffering billion-dollar losses in pensions and asset prices, Enron's employees and stockholders only won little compensation through litigation.

Customer satisfaction (CS) assessment is now a key metric for assessing the success of businesses in the market [3]. Client satisfaction has become the top priority for all business kinds. Analyzing client reviews and comments for a product or service is one technique to gauge CS [4]. Domo claims that we produce more than 2.5 quintillion bytes of data every day, with this data generated from a variety of sources, including social media, emails, Amazon, YouTube, and Netflix.

The earliest method of business communication is said to be email. It is inevitable in a workflow scenario that involves both internal and external actors and is defined by both [5]. The email bodies inherently include the characteristics of the organizational process viewpoint. The organizational model, however, has not been fully taken into account in numerous publications that concentrated on email analysis for process model mining [6]. So, this research proposes ways like Anomaly Detection, Social Network Analysis, Email Classification, and Word Cloud, that are employed using Machine Learning, and Natural Language Processing to evaluate the information and assist toward corporate development.

Anomaly detection, also known as outlier detection, is a technique used in data mining to locate unusual things that happen or observations that stand out from the bulk of the data in a way that raises questions [7]. Generally, anomalous objects will point to some sort of issue, like financial fraud, a structural flaw, a health issue, or syntax errors in a text. For instance, sudden bursts of activity rather than infrequent items are frequently intriguing objects in the context of abuse and network intrusion detection [8]. Isolation Forest is used to create a model of typical behavior and identify unusual conduct before the public controversy.

Finding the communities inside a virtual community is crucial because it enables the identification of members who have common interests and behavior prediction [9]. Social network analysis is a method for analyzing social systems utilizing networks and graph theory [10]. By changing the visual representation of a network's nodes and edges to reflect certain properties of interest, these visualizations offer a method for qualitatively evaluating networks. Additionally, emails in the collection are categorized into documentation, transactions, attorney, etc. This is accomplished by first employing a bag of words, then SVM, Naive Bayes, and RNN approaches. Furthermore, a word cloud is created for visualization and comparative analysis is done.

A survey of the preceding scholarly papers is provided in Section 17.2. A comprehensive outline of the methods employed in the aforementioned investigations is provided in Section 17.3. An explanation of the approaches used is given in Section 17.4. Section 17.5 offers an in-depth description of how the suggested tasks are executed. In Section 17.6, the conclusions and observations of the research are in-depth analyzed. Section 17.7 addresses the outcome and prospective applications.

17.2   LITERATURE REVIEW

Hyenkyun Woo., in 2021 [11], introduced a matrix factorization technique that uses low dimensional estimates of the source data to detect abnormalities in a natural way. Block Coordinate Descent is the foundation of the iterative method of Text Outliers using Nonnegative Matrix Factorization. The term-document matrix is defined in blocks so that the function may be solved. They always changed one matrix unit to the best possible state using the most recent updates to the values of the other blocks. The method resulted in an accuracy of 93.40%.

Vipin Kumar et al., in 2017 [12], intended to offer a detailed and organized summary of the anomaly detection studies. They divided current approaches into many groups according to the fundamental philosophy behind each technique. They identified important presumptions for each category that the approaches rely on to distinguish between typical and abnormal behavior. These presumptions can be utilized as guides to determine if a particular approach is effective in a given area when applied to it.

Philip Branch et al., in 2020 [13], employed a triangle model with three vertices to represent the problem (large demography), methods/algorithms (outliers), and tools (big data software solutions), and described the situation of feature extraction in large features of data. Moreover, recent methodologies and applications necessary for the enhancement of outlier detection were examined along with the shortcomings of classic approaches and current tactics of high-dimensional data.

Nisheeth Srivastava et al., in 2022 [14], showed how knowledge of the linguistic contents of textual data enables the identification of word and subject occurrences that are statistically uncommon but contextually reasonable for the model being monitored, and thus, not abnormal. It was accomplished by bootstrapping a unique textual clustering technique for outlier identification that utilizes Linear discriminant analysis (LDA) on specific datasets to a frame of reference method that works on independent corpora of generic text connections (WordNet). The algorithm gave an accuracy of 88.64%.

Anuradha Pillai et al., in 2017 [15], reviewed several natural language and text mining methodologies to extract a social network from text data. These techniques include Automatic Summarization, Chunking, Named Entity Relation, Disambiguation, and Fact Extraction. Furthermore, they analyzed the challenges of implementation corresponding to every technique. They concluded that linguistics techniques will make searches more user-friendly, and mining text will tap into its intelligence.

Sotiris Kotsiantis et al., in 2015 [16], classified the text by utilizing many machine learning techniques. They primarily focused on the process of classifying the text which includes Text data, tokenization, Stemming, Representing Vectors, Feature Selection and Transformation, and using algorithms. By first examining the qualities of training corpora and then providing an approach for creating learning text semi-automatically, the authors attempted to provide a method for creating high-quality training corpora for better classification performance.

Kelly Wilkinson et al., in 2021 [17], investigated the patterns of text in the graphical form of a word cloud representing the knowledge of students. This approach was implemented to let the instructors evaluate if the students have grasped the concepts or made any mistakes. They analyzed that it can also be utilized to give academic feedback to students.

Sidra Abbas et al., in 2022 [18], categorized the text using deep learning techniques. They employed artificial neural network, long short-term memory (LSTM), and gated recurrent unit for classification. LSTM model outperformed with the highest accuracy of 92% on the Titanic textual data.

Tiantian Zhang et al., in 2021 [19], implemented an isolation-based technique called Isolation Forest Algorithm to detect the anomaly points. An elevated algorithm, Cluster-Based Isolation Forest based on this approach translates localized outliers before clustering into global outliers of nearby collections and then determines the outlier score for every cluster's data point. This research increased the accuracy by 6%.

17.3 TECHNIQUES

The proposed techniques for analyzing the emails of the Enron organization are briefly explained in this section.

17.3.1 ISOLATION FOREST

Employing a tree-like framework in accordance with traits selected arbitrarily, an isolation forest is applied to examine randomly subsampled data [20]. The fragments that crossed farther into the tree required more cuts to separate, thus making them less probable to be anomalies [21]. Similar to the last example, data that end up on shorter branches tend to be anomalies since the tree found it simpler to distinguish them from others.

$$S(x, n) = 2^{-\frac{E(h(x))}{c(n)}} \tag{17.1}$$

where $S(x, n)$ = score of an anomaly; $E(h(x))$ = observations' path length x; $c(n)$ = unsuccessful search path length that is average; n = count of nodes that are external.

17.3.2   SUPPORT VECTOR MACHINE (SVM)

SVM can be applied to address categorization challenges. In this supervised approach, data are separated using the hyperplane, which acts as the ideal selection boundary [22]. It identifies the extreme points, termed as support vectors, to help build the hyperplane. It also has a positive hyperplane that crosses a minimum of one of the closest positive indicators, as well as a negative hyperplane that traverses either of them or more of the nearby negative points [23]. The ideal hyperplane is the one where, as demonstrated, the margin – the space between the ideal hyperplane, and the ideal hyperplane is at its greatest.

17.3.3   NAÏVE BAYES (NB)

NB, a guided method, is used to solve classification problems and is built on the Bayes Theorem. It is mostly used to classify text, including large training datasets [24]. It assists in creating efficient and precise machine learning models and producing prompt forecasts.

17.3.4   RECURRENT NEURAL NETWORK (RNN)

A sort of neural network called an RNN uses the output of a previous stage as an input for the current stage [25]. Inputs and outputs in traditional neural networks are distinct from each other, but when it comes to predicting the subsequent word in a phrase, it is vital to remember the prior phrases. As a result, RNN was developed, and it employed a Hidden Layer to address this problem [26]. The Hidden state of RNNs, which saves specific information about a sequence, is its central and most significant feature.

17.3.5   NATURAL LANGUAGE TOOLKIT (NLTK)

One of the most popular platforms for creating Python applications that use human language data is called NLTK [27]. In addition to a selection of text-examining libraries for categorizing, encoding, rooting, labeling, parsing, and linguistic thinking for industrial-strength NLP libraries and an active discussion forum, it offers simple designs for accessing more than 50 corpus and semantic assets including WordNet.

17.3.6 GENSIM

Gensim is an unrestricted Python toolkit that aims to represent documents as semantic vectors as quickly and painlessly as possible for humans and computers [28]. Gensim uses unsupervised machine learning methods to analyze unstructured, uncooked digital messages.

17.3.7 BAG OF WORDS (BoW)

When text is being modeled using deep learning and machine learning techniques, BoW is a method of expressing text data [29]. This model counts the number of times each word appears to convert any text into fixed-length vectors. This approach is referred to as the vectorization process. By extracting text characteristics, this straightforward method is used to address issues with language modeling and document categorization [30]. It provides a great deal of customization options for certain text data.

17.4 PROPOSED FRAMEWORK

The usual implementation approach for email text analysis is outlined in this section. Figure 17.1 depicts an illustration of the research methodology. The procedure is briefly covered below:

17.4.1 EMAIL DATASET

The Enron email dataset consists of around 0.5 million emails between the employees and managers of the company. This data is needed to be cleaned and processed for feature extraction and selection.

17.4.2 TEXT AND VISUAL FEATURE EXTRACTION

For feature extraction various natural language processing techniques like Tokenization and Lemmatization are used. Bag of Words is employed on the text data to extract vital features.

17.4.3 FEATURE SELECTION

Features are selected on the basis of POS Tagging, stopwords removal, etc. The genism library of natural language processing is used for this purpose.

17.4.4 MODEL FORMATION

Several techniques are used for examining the data of emails, including anomaly detection, social network analysis, email classification, and word cloud formation.

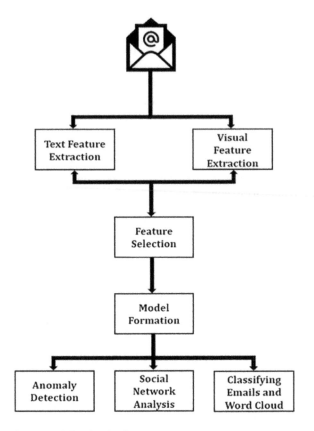

FIGURE 17.1 Framework for the pipeline.

17.5 PROPOSED METHODOLOGY

17.5.1 PROBLEM STATEMENT

One of the biggest business collapses in history was caused by the Enron scandal and collapse. Among the major energy firms in America before 2000 was Enron. After being exposed for fraud, it then plummeted into insolvency in less than a year. There are 150 former Enron workers, most of whom are top executives, and around 500,000 emails between them. Its value is increased by the fact that it is the only sizable public database of authentic emails. In reality, data scientists have been studying and researching with this dataset for years. This experimentation puts forward tasks like Anomaly Detection, Social Network Analysis, Email Classification, and Word Cloud generation that are to be performed on the dataset for visualization.

17.5.2 ANOMALY DETECTION

Finding patterns in the data that do not match the anticipated (normal) behavior is known as anomaly detection. Novelties, noise, outliers, exceptions, and deviations

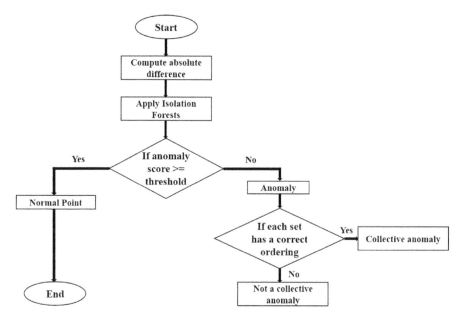

FIGURE 17.2   Algorithmic flow of isolation forest.

are other terms for anomalies. The algorithmic flow of the Isolation Forest technique is demonstrated in Figure 17.2.

17.5.2.1   Importing Libraries

Various libraries like numpy, pandas, matplotlib, seaborn, email, tqdm were imported at the initial stage.

17.5.2.2   Data Preprocessing and Creating Data Frame

This step involves all needed transforms to interpret the data and then use it for future tasks. Converting data to table format for running various queries and processes is required.

17.5.2.3   Adding Content Length as a Column

This is a crucial column for analysis since it shows how long each email is and will be highly useful for highlighting data points that deviate from the overall trends. Typically, emails that are not responses are substantially greater in size than those that are.

17.5.2.4   Adding a Column for Whether an Email Is a Reply or Not

Later, this column will serve as a field for finding anomalies. It also shows the number of brief exchanges occurring as a feature in the dataset, which will be shown later. The column also indicates that, as will be shown later, letters in this column tend to be shorter than usual.

17.5.2.5 Generating Time-Series Data

In order to achieve this, the data must be grouped by day and hour. After that, time series analysis and anomaly detection may be done using this data. For different fields, an aggregate like a mean or count is often taken, and the results are displayed as and when they are applied to all emails received during that specific hour.

The number of mails shoots up very fast in a very specific time frame which indicates anomalous behavior in that period of 2–3 days, as shown in Figure 17.3. Similar anomalous hours are also seen about a week after that. This can also be a strong indicator of fraudulent activities like the deletion of large amounts of records and other instructions being passed and expecting immediate reporting on the same.

Sharp anomalous surges in the number of emails to be preceded by surges in the length of emails thus it is also a very important indicator of fraudulent activity, as shown in Figure 17.4.

The number of replies in most conditions is very low or extremely high depending on the hour being considered, which can be viewed in Figure 17.5. These points of multiple replies on the same topic can be of key interest in some cases.

Figure 17.6, shows that in most cases anomalies are in one of the three dimensions and rarely in all of them together. Some points are slightly anomalous in terms of length and replies but do not deviate significantly.

17.5.2.6 Performing Anomaly Detection Using Isolation Forests:

Initially, IsolationForest library is imported from sklearn. It creates trees using data and arbitrary splits. Anomalies will be distinct from these random separations since they will be removed from the data.

17.5.2.7 Considering Data Points for Analysis

Using 0.1 as a threshold and few data points are considered, and anomalies are printed.

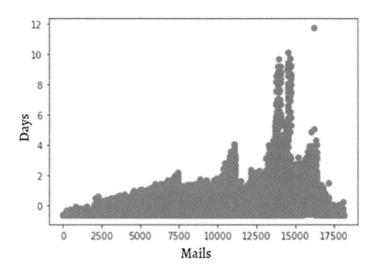

FIGURE 17.3 Drastic change within 2–3 days.

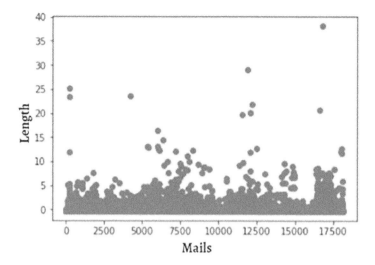

FIGURE 17.4 Sharp surges of emails.

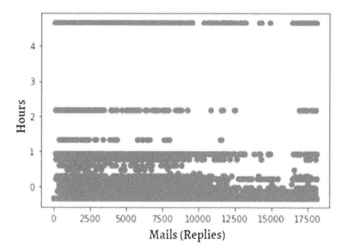

FIGURE 17.5 Conditions on an hourly basis.

17.5.2.8 Using Local Outlier Factor

First, LocalOutlierFactor library is Imported using the sklearn library. Novelty helps in detecting new features using k-nearest neighbors, and n-neighbors help in deciding the density for outliers. Data seems to have a very high density in two major regions, as shown in Figure 17.7. So, this technique doesn't seem to work very well, and thus Isolation forests will be used.

17.5.2.9 Creating a Count of Mail Sent by Every Source and Receiver

Most of the mails have been sent by the top 200 employees, as seen in Figure 17.8, and thus it would be more relevant to consider only their data in general so that external factors don't influence them significantly.

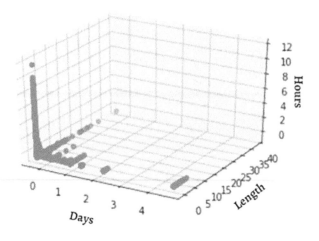

FIGURE 17.6   Anomalous behavior in a 3D graph.

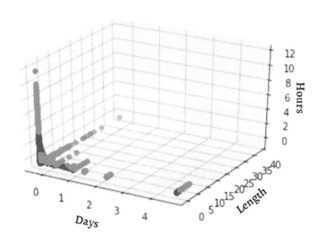

FIGURE 17.7   Anomalies depicted using local outlier factor.

Figure 17.9 shows that top the 500 recipients have actually received most of the emails in the organization.

17.5.2.10   Creating a Count of Every Pair of Source and Destination

Creating a new feature for every pair involved in a mail. This will help in identifying new novel communication patterns.

17.5.2.11   Finding Unique External Emails

Unique external senders and recipients have been noted as they are vents for the organizational information to escape.

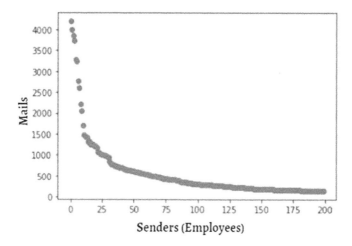

FIGURE 17.8 Senders.

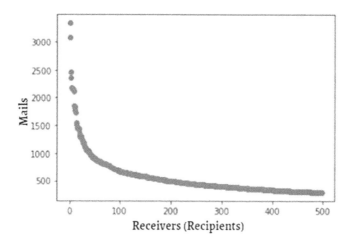

FIGURE 17.9 Receivers.

17.5.2.12 Creating Data and Anomaly Detection

Creating a numpy array that has all features to consider for final anomaly detection, This involves printing all columns being used as features and adding number of unique sources and several emails too per hour. Then, the final anomaly detection system using Isolation Forests was detected. When the number of emails is factored into the features; most features end up becoming white noise and thus are redundant. These features can then be removed. Hence, the anomalies are detected.

17.5.3 SOCIAL NETWORK ANALYSIS

Networked structures are described in terms of nodes and the ties, edges, or links connecting them. Social media networks, the dissemination of memes, the flow of information, friend and acquaintance networks, and commercial networks are a few examples of social structures that are frequently represented by social network analysis.

17.5.3.1   Importing Libraries

Various libraries like numpy, pandas, seaborn, matplotlib are imported that are used for data preprocessing and visualization.

17.5.3.2   Data Extraction

Data is imported into the Pandas Dataframe which is then used for further computations and analysis.

17.5.3.3   Functions to Extract Information from Mail

Libraries like tqdm are imported to extract the information. It returns the series with text sliced from a list split from each message. After this, the mails that are not in the proper structure are cleaned or removed.

17.5.3.4   Analysing the Social Network

To examine the social network libraries like network, and nxviz are imported.

The Arc plot can be visualized in Figure 17.10. It can be seen that the nodes or employees are at the bottom and the dominance of the one node is on the right side. Since the dataset contains about 5 lakhs of emails, the emails from the 150 Enron executives contained in the full dataset are considered.

The Circos plot is shown in Figure 17.11. It is clearer and easier to comprehend this plot. Finally, the social network is drawn as part of the result.

17.5.4   EMAIL CLASSIFICATION AND WORD CLOUD

Various techniques are used to classify emails based on different topics. Text preprocessing is done using NLP, and for classification, SVM, NB, and RNN models are employed.

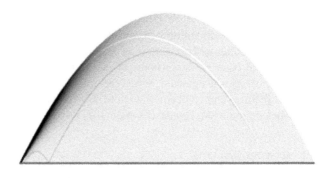

FIGURE 17.10   Arc plot.

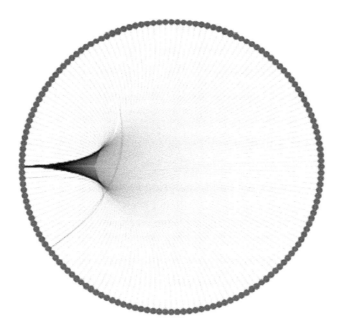

FIGURE 17.11 Circos plot.

17.5.4.1 Importing Libraries

Many libraries such as numpy, pandas, matplotlib, genism, spacy are imported for further preprocessing.

17.5.4.2 Tokenization

In this type of text preprocessing concept, first, the text is normalized, converted to lowercase, punctuations are removed, and finally split into words; these words are called tokenizers.

17.5.4.3 Stop Words Removal

In this step, the words that are used often across the corpus of documents or sentences are eliminated. These words are most likely to be "a, an, the, etc.".

17.5.4.4 Lemmatization and Stemming

Lemmatization and stemming often relate to carrying out procedures correctly using a lexicon and semantic evaluation of words with the goal of removing only affixation ends and returning the lemma, or dictionary form, of a word.

17.5.4.5 Sklearn Pipeline Using CountVectorizer() and TfidfTransformer()

The tokenize function is supplied as a parameter when using the CountVectorizer () to provide vocabulary and encode new documents with that vocabulary. The operator transfers a count vector to a standardized tf illustration. This word weighting technique is widely used in information retrieval and is very effective in document categorization.

17.5.4.6   Using Point-Wise Mutual Information (PMI) for Feature Selection

PMI is a statistical technique frequently used to model the relationship between words. The following definition of PMI exists between the terms "word1" and "word2":

$$\text{PMI (word1, word2)} = \log_2 \left[\frac{p(\text{word1 \& word2})}{p(\text{word1}) xp(\text{word2})} \right] \tag{17.2}$$

17.5.4.7   Developing Model and Analyzing Evaluation

The model is developed using SVM, NB, and RNN. Their performance is analyzed using several metrics like accuracy, precision, recall, and F1 score. The formulae are given as:

$$\text{Accuracy} = \frac{TP + TN}{TP + TN + FP + FN} \tag{17.3}$$

$$\text{Precision} = \frac{TP}{TP + FP} \tag{17.4}$$

$$\text{Recall} = \frac{TP}{TP + FN} \tag{17.5}$$

$$F1 \text{ Score} = \frac{2TP}{2TP + FP + FN} \tag{17.6}$$

17.5.4.8   Developing a Word Cloud

A text visualization approach called a "word cloud" or "tag cloud" is used to display tags or terms from web pages. These keywords are frequently single words that describe the content of the website from which the word cloud was derived. A Word Cloud is created by grouping these words collectively.

The font size and color of each word in this word cloud may be changed. A word's significance in relation to other words in the cluster is more accurately portrayed by a word's larger font size. Depending on the authors' concept, word clouds may be constructed in a variety of forms and sizes. The overall number of words is important when creating a Word Cloud. A Word Cloud with more words is not always better since it becomes congested and harder to read. A word cloud must always represent its intended usage appropriately and have semantic significance.

17.5.5   Pseudocode

```
function: ClassifyEmailText(t): (T, 1)
input:      t: string - the email text to be distinguished.
```

```
output:     T = {w₀, ..., wₙ} - an ontology's set of concepts
that may categorize the present email text.
                1: integer - the resemblance between the terms
on a scale.
        1       Ω = PreprocessEmailText(t) - generates a list
of words after textual preprocessing
        2       1 = ∞ - finest resemblance level.
        3       T = ∅
        4       for each wₖ Ɛ Ω do
        5           Θₖ = ComputeSimilerLevels(wₖ,0).
        6               for each <wj, 1ⱼ> Ɛ Θₖ
        7                   if 1ⱼ < 1 then
        8                               T = {wⱼ}.
        9                               1 = 1ⱼ.
        10                      else if 1ⱼ = 1 then
        11                              T = T U{wⱼ}.
        12                  end-if
        13              end-for each
        14      end-for each
        15      return<T, 1>.
```

17.6   EXPERIMENTAL RESULTS AND ANALYSIS

17.6.1   RESULTS OF ANOMALY DETECTION

In Figures 17.12–17.16, it can be seen that most of the outliers are now being detected and flagged. The number of flagged cases is about 550 hours out of 18,000 hours which can be analyzed as it is only about 3% of all the cases.

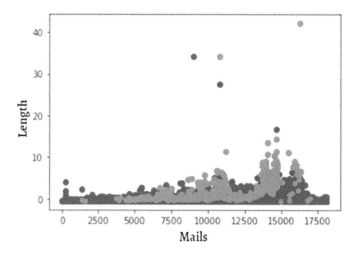

FIGURE 17.12   Content length.

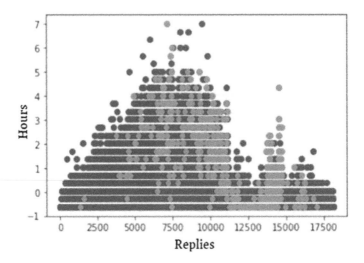

FIGURE 17.13 Reply.

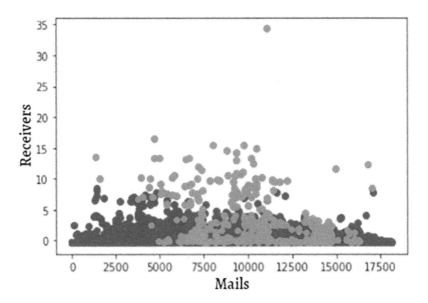

FIGURE 17.14 Outside receiver.

17.6.2 RESULTS OF SOCIAL NETWORK ANALYSIS

The social network shown in Figure 17.17 has been plotted with different "tension" on the spring layout to depict different options for visualizing this network.

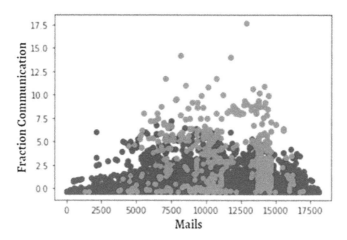

FIGURE 17.15   Fraction communication.

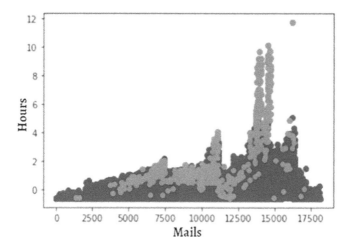

FIGURE 17.16   Number of emails.

17.6.3   RESULTS OF EMAILS CLASSIFICATION AND WORD CLOUD

Accuracy, recall, precision, and F1 score are three metrics utilized to express the output of different models. Table 17.1, Figures 17.18 and 17.19 present these outcomes with efficiency. It demonstrates that RNN achieves the highest accuracy possible of 97.8%.

The word clouds generated using NLP techniques are depicted in Figures 17.20 and 17.21.

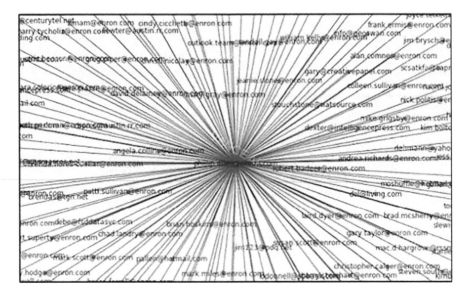

FIGURE 17.17   Social network.

TABLE 17.1
Evaluation Metrics

Models	Positive			Negative			Accuracy
	Precision	Recall	F1 Score	Precision	Recall	F1 Score	
NB	0.92	0.91	0.89	0.87	0.93	0.91	0.924
SVM	0.85	0.89	0.86	0.98	0.86	0.87	0.873
RNN	0.97	0.97	0.97	0.97	0.97	0.97	0.978

17.7 CONCLUSION

This research suggests different methods for analyzing the email dataset of Enron company. Techniques like Anomaly Detection, Social Network Analysis, Email Classification, and Word Cloud generation are used for examining the anomalies. Enhanced and futuristic technologies like natural language processing and machine learning are applied to investigate the mails and the social network formed. Algorithmic techniques like Isolation Forest, NB, SVM, and RNN are used to train suitable models. The RNN model was the most accurate, reaching 97.8%, based on the findings. An experiment has been conducted as part of this study to elevate the model's analytical outcomes. The goal is to investigate and perform more research on anomaly detection in line with fraud analysis in various sectors using the hybrid approach, wherein the dataset may be hosted in a cloud environment like AWS.

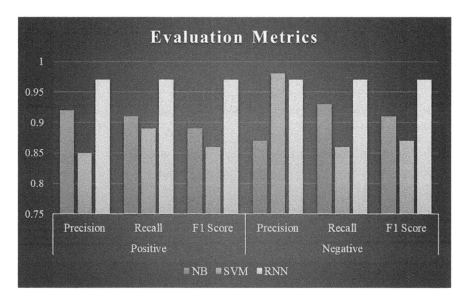

FIGURE 17.18 Evaluation metrics for models.

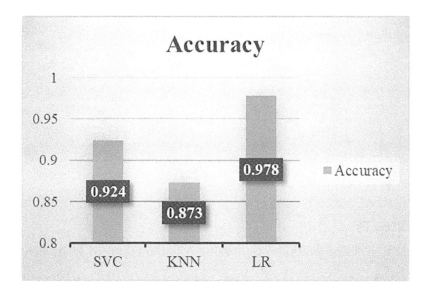

FIGURE 17.19 Accuracy of models.

As a consequence, all the traits and features are analyzed, tested, and the most accurate findings are obtained. As a result, this will significantly aid in both the growth and success of organizations as well as the advancement of business.

FIGURE 17.20 Word cloud with white background.

FIGURE 17.21 Word cloud with black background.

REFERENCES

1. N. Shashidhar et al. (2022). Topic modeling in the ENRON dataset. In: Hu B., Xia Y., Zhang Y., Zhang L.J. (eds) *Big Data-BigData 2022. BigData 2022. Lecture Notes in Computer Science*, vol. 13730, Springer, Cham. doi:10.1007/978-3-031-23501-6_4.
2. M. MacDonnell et al. (2022). Exploring social-emotional learning, school climate, and social network analysis. *Journal of Community Psychology*, 51(1), 84–102.
3. R. Benbenishty et al. (2017). A research synthesis of the associations between socioeconomic background, inequality, school climate, and academic achievement. *Review of Educational Research*, 87(2), 425–469.
4. T. Mehta et al. (2022). A comparative study on approaches for text quality prediction using machine learning and natural language processing. In: 2022 International Conference on Smart Generation Computing, Communication and Networking (SMART GENCON), Bangalore, India, 2022, pp. 1–5.

5. V. Sonakshi et al. (2023). An employee feedback model based on sentimental analysis and word clouds. In: Data Science and Intelligent Computing Techniques, SCRS, India, pp. 79–92.

6. N. El Gayar et al. (2019). Sentiment analysis using unlabeled email data. In: *2019 International Conference on Computational Intelligence and Knowledge Economy (ICCIKE)*, Dubai, United Arab Emirates, pp. 328–333. doi:10.1109/ICCIKE47802.2019.9004372.

7. T. Mehta et al. (2023). Sentiment analysis of political tweets for israel using machine learning. In: *Machine Learning and Big Data Analytics, ICMLBDA 2022, Proceedings in Mathematics and Statistics,* vol. 401, Springer, New York.

8. M. Kurdi (2022). Identifying and analyzing communities within a social network using automatic topic labelling: application to the enron dataset. In: *18th International Conference on Machine Learning and Data Mining*, New York, USA.

9. N. Thakur et al. (2020). Evaluating cohesion score with email clustering. In: *Proceedings of First International Conference on Computing, Communications, and Cyber-Security (IC4S 2019). Lecture Notes in Networks and Systems*, Punjab, India, vol. 121.

10. O. Elisha et al. (2022). MessageNet: message classification using natural language processing and meta-data. arXiv preprint arXiv:2301.01808.

11. C. Aggarwal et al. (2017). Outlier detection for text data. In: *Proceeding of SIAM International Conference on Data Mining*, Houston, Texas, USA.

12. A. Banerjee et al. (2009). Anomaly detection: A survey. *ACM Computing Surveys*, 41. doi:10.1145/1541880.1541882.

13. J. Jin *et al.* (2020). A comprehensive survey of anomaly detection techniques for high dimensional big data. Journal of Big Data, 7, 42.

14. J. Srivastava et al. (2012). Contextual anomaly detection in text data. *Algorithms*, 5, 469–489. doi:10.3390/a5040469.

15. D. Juneja et al. (2017). Extracting information from social network using Nlp. *The International Journal of Computational Intelligence Research*, 13, 621–630.

16. S. Kotsiantis et al. (2005). Text classification using machine learning techniques. *WSEAS Transactions on Computers*, 4, 966–974.

17. K. Wilkinson et al. (2014). Get your head into the clouds: using word clouds for analyzing qualitative assessment data. *TechTrends*, 58, 38–44. doi:10.1007/s11528-014-0750-9.

18. S. Abbas et al. (2022). An efficient approach for textual data classification using deep learning. *Frontiers in Computational Neuroscience*, 16, 992296. doi:10.3389/fncom.2022.992296.

19. R. Gao *et al.* (2019). Uniform mixture model in the case of regression. Journal of Physics: Conference Series, 1237, 052023.

20. R. S. Prasad (2019). Influence of language-specific features for author identification on Indian literature in Marathi. In: *Soft Computing and Signal Processing's of 2nd ICSCSP 2019.* Hyderabad, India.

21. R. Kachhoria et al. (2023). Lie group dee learning technique to identify the precision errors by map geometry functions in smart manufacturing. *The International Journal of Advanced Manufacturing Technology.* 10.1007/s00170-023-10834-2.

22. M. Lee et al. (2019). Use of social network analysis in the development, dissemination, implementation, and sustainability of health behavior interventions for adults: A systematic review. *Social Science & Medicine*, 220, 81–101.

23. S. Kale et al. (2018). Author identification on imbalanced class dataset of Indian literature in Marathi. *International Journal of Computer Sciences and Engineering.* vol. 6, pp. 542–547.

24. C. Haythornthwaite et al. (2018). Social network analysis: An approach and technique for the study of information exchange. *Library & Information Science Research*, 18(4), 323–342.

25. K. Rao et al. (2017). Text analysis for author identification using machine learning. *Journal of Emerging Technologies and Innovative Research.* 4(6), pp.138–141.
26. T. Mehta et al. (2022). YouTube Ad view sentiment analysis using deep learning and machine learning. *International Journal of Computer Applications* 184(11), 10–14.
27. S. D. Kale et al. (2017). A systematic review on author identification methods. *International Journal of Rough Sets and Data Analysis (IJRSDA).* 4(2), pp. 81–91.
28. K. Chang et al. (2011). Word cloud model for text categorization. *IEEE 11th International Conference on Data Mining*, Vancouver, BC, Canada, 2011, pp. 487–496.
29. S. D. Kale et al. (2018). Author identification using sequential minimal optimization with rule-based decision tree on Indian literature in Marathi. Procedia Computer Science. *Procedia Computer Science, Elsevier*, vol. 35, pp. 1086–1101.
30. F. Chang et al. (2019). Hot topic community discovery on cross social networks. *MDPI Future Internet*, 11(3), 60–76.

Index